THE ARDEN SHAKESPEARE
GENERAL EDITOR: RICHARD PROUDFOOT

MEASURE FOR MEASURE

THE ARDEN SHAKESPEARE

THE ARDEN EDITION OF THE
WORKS OF WILLIAM SHAKESPEARE

MEASURE FOR
MEASURE

Edited by
J. W. LEVER

ROUTLEDGE

LONDON and NEW YORK

The general editors of the Arden Shakespeare have been
W. J. Craig (1899–1906), R. H. Case (1909–44),
Una Ellis-Fermor (1946–58), Harold F. Brooks (1952–82),
Harold Jenkins (1958–82) and Brian Morris (1975–82)

Present general editor: Richard Proudfoot

This edition of *Measure for Measure*, by J. W. Lever,
first published in 1965 by
Methuen & Co. Ltd
Reprinted 1966

First published as a University Paperback in 1967
Reprinted eleven times
Reprinted 1987

Reprinted 1988
by Routledge
11 New Fetter Lane, London EC4P 4EE
29 West 35th Street, New York, NY 10001

Editorial matter 1965 Methuen & Co. Ltd

ISBN (hardback) 0 416 47530 2
ISBN (paperback) 415 02697 0

Printed and bound in Great Britain by
Richard Clay Ltd, Bungay, Suffolk

CONTENTS

PREFACE

I WAS first asked to prepare this edition by Una Ellis-Fermor as long ago as 1953. Like many others, I shall always be grateful for her stimulus and encouragement, and preserve warm memories of her lovable personality. Since that time I have become deeply indebted to the present general editors, Professor Harold Jenkins and Dr H. F. Brooks, for their unfailing and infinitely painstaking help. I wish to thank Professor Allardyce Nicoll for the facilities generously provided during the two years in which I worked at the Shakespeare Institute, Stratford-upon-Avon, as well as for his valuable personal advice. Professor G. K. Hunter and Professor Peter Ure have helped with various suggestions, and I have benefited by the interchange of ideas with other colleagues. I owe thanks to the Trustees of the Folger Shakespeare Library and the Huntington Library for fellowships held during the summer of 1958, to the staffs for their kind assistance, and to Dr James McManaway in person for encouraging me to set down my views on the date of *Measure for Measure* in an article for *Shakespeare Quarterly*. Finally, I am grateful to *Magyar Országos Levéltar* (State Archives), Budapest, for supplying me with the microfilm of a letter whose contents bear upon the plot of the play, and to Dr A. I. Doyle, of Durham University Library, for checking my transcription. The text of this letter is reproduced in Appendix I.

J. W. LEVER

The University, Durham.
October 1963

ABBREVIATIONS

The abbreviated titles of Shakespeare's works are those of C. T. Onions, *A Shakespeare Glossary*. Line numbers and quotations accord with W. J. Craig's Oxford Shakespeare. The usual abbreviations for stage directions (S.D.) and scene headings (S.H.) are employed.

F, F2, F3, and F4 signify the four seventeenth-century Folios. Collected editions subsequent to these are referred to by the names of their editors, except the 'Variorum' of 1821 (Var. 1821), and the Cambridge Shakespeare of W. G. Clark and Aldis Wright (Cam.). Editions of Johnson and Steevens, or Steevens and Reed, are indicated by 'Steevens' and the date of publication (e.g. Steevens '73).

Abbott	E. A. Abbott, *A Shakespeare Grammar* (1869). (References are to numbered sections.)
Baldwin	T. H. Baldwin, *William Shakespeare's Small Latine & Lesse Greeke*, 2 vols. (1944).
B.D.	*The Basilicon Doron of King James VI*, ed. James Craigie, 2 vols. (1944).
Beaumont and Fletcher	*The Works of Beaumont and Fletcher*, ed. A. R. Waller (1910).
Chapman	*The Plays of George Chapman*, ed. T. M. Parrott (1910, 1914).
Cinthio	Giraldi Cinthio, *Gli Hecatommithi* II, Década 8, Novella 5 (1565).
Dekker	*The Dramatic Works of Thomas Dekker*, ed. Fredson Bowers, 4 vols. (1953–61).
Douce	Francis Douce, *Illustrations of Shakespeare*, 2 vols. (1807).
E.L.H.	*English Literary History* (periodical).
Epitia	Giraldi Cinthio, *Epitia* (1583).
Halliwell Nb.	J. O. Halliwell-Phillipps, Notebooks to Shakespeare's Plays (Birthplace Library, Stratford-upon-Avon).
J.E.G.P.	*Journal of English and Germanic Philology* (periodical).
Jonson	*The Works of Benjamin Jonson*, ed. C. H. Herford and Percy and Evelyn Simpson, 11 vols. (1925–52).
Kyd	*The Works of Thomas Kyd*, ed. Frederick S. Boas (1901).
Lascelles	Mary Lascelles, *Shakespeare's 'Measure for Measure'* (1953).
Lyly	*The Complete Works of John Lyly*, ed. R. W. Bond, 3 vols. (1902).
M.L.N.	*Modern Langiage Notes* (periodical).
Marlowe	*The Works and Life of Christopher Marlowe*, general ed. R. H. Case, 6 vols. (1930–3).
Marston	*The Plays of John Marston*, ed. H. Harvey Wood, 3 vols. (1934–9).

ix

Middleton	*The Works of Thomas Middleton*, ed. A. H. Bullen, 8 vols. (1885–6).
Montaigne	*Essays*, trans. J. Florio (1603, reprinted 'Everyman', 3 vols. 1910).
M.S.R.	*Malone Society Reprints.*
N. & Q.	*Notes and Queries* (periodical).
Nashe	*The Works of Thomas Nashe*, ed. R. B. McKerrow, 5 vols. (1910; re-edited F. P. Wilson 1958).
Noble	R. Noble, *Shakespeare's Biblical Knowledge* (1935).
Onions	C. T. Onions, *A Shakespeare Glossary* (1911, revised 1946).
O.D. Eng. Prov.	*The Oxford Dictionary of English Proverbs*, ed. W. G. Smith and J. E. Heseltine (1935).
O.E.D.	*A New English Dictionary* ['*The Oxford Dictionary*'], ed. J. A. Murray, H. Bradley, W. A. Craigie, and C. T. Onions, 13 vols. (1888–1933).
P.M.L.A.	*Publications of the Modern Language Association* (periodical).
P.Q.	*Philological Quarterly* (periodical).
Prom.	George Whetstone, *The Right Excellent and Famous Historye of Promos and Cassandra*, 2 parts (1578).
R.E.S.	*Review of English Studies* (periodical).
Schmidt	Alexander Schmidt, *Shakespeare-Lexicon* (3rd ed. Sarrazin, 1902).
Sh. Apoc.	*The Shakespeare Apocrypha*, ed. C. F. Tucker Brooke (1908).
S.Q.	*Shakespeare Quarterly* (periodical).
S.S.	*Shakespeare Survey* (periodical).
Stud. Bibl.	*Studies in Bibliography* (periodical).
Sisson, *N.R.*	C. J. Sisson, *New Readings in Shakespeare*, 2 vols. (1956).
1, 2 *Siuqila*	Thomas Lupton, *Siuqila. Too good to be true* (1580); *The Second Part and Knitting up of the Boke entituled Too good to be true* (1581).
Thiselton	R. G. Thiselton, *Notes on 'Measure for Measure'* (1905).
Tilley	M. P. Tilley, *A Dictionary of Proverbs in England in the Sixteenth and Seventeenth Centuries* (1950).
T.L.S.	*The Times Literary Supplement* (periodical).
Webster	*The Works of John Webster*, ed. F. L. Lucas (1927; 1958).

Editions of 'Measure for Measure':

Hart	H. C. Hart, 'Arden' Shakespeare (1905).
N.C.S.	A. Quiller-Couch and J. Dover Wilson, The New Cambridge Shakespeare (1922).
Durham	W. H. Durham, The Yale Shakespeare (1926).
Ridley	M. R. Ridley, The New Temple Shakespeare (1935).
Bald	R. C. Bald, 'Pelican' Series (1956).
Winny	James Winny, Hutchinson Educational (1959).

INTRODUCTION

I. THE TEXT

Measure for Measure was first printed in the Folio of 1623, where it appears as the fourth play of the Comedies section, occupying the whole of quires F and G (pages 61–84). Textually, these four plays, *The Tempest*, *The Two Gentlemen of Verona*, *The Merry Wives of Windsor*, and *Measure for Measure*, make up a group. All are divided into acts and scenes. All, except *The Merry Wives of Windsor*, are supplied with a list of characters, appended on the last page of the play. Two, *The Tempest* and *Measure for Measure*, are also provided in the same place with a stated locale—'An vn-inhabited Island' and 'Vienna' respectively. The exceptions are more apparent than real, since on the last page of *The Merry Wives* there was insufficient space left for a list of characters, while the settings of this play and of *The Two Gentlemen of Verona* were self-evident from their titles. All four plays, moreover, show certain characteristics of spelling and punctuation which are not accounted for by the habits of the Folio compositors.

It is generally accepted that the copy for these plays, as well as for *The Winter's Tale*, was the work of Ralph Crane, a professional scrivener who was connected with the King's Men in the early 1620's.[1] Several transcripts prepared by Crane for private patrons are extant. Their characteristics are more marked in some manuscripts than others, and some spelling-forms were not uncommon in this period; but taken together they reveal a distinctive style. Typical of this was the hyphenation of adjectives or participles with the nouns they qualified, and of prefixes or adverbs with their verbs and verb-stems; the use of apostrophes to signify colloquial ellipses, inflections and 'Jonsonian elision' (where the vowels to be elided are written down); and a liberal use of brackets round phrases in apposition, exclamations, or appellatives. All these prac-

---

1. For accounts of Crane and his style, see F. P. Wilson, 'Ralph Crane, Scrivener to the King's Players', *Library*, ser. 4. VII (1926), 194–215 (the pioneer study), and W. W. Greg, 'Some Notes on Crane's Manuscript of *The Witch*', *Library*, XXII (1942), 208–22. Further information is to be found in the introductions to the Malone Society Reprints of Middleton's *The Witch* (1950) and Fletcher's *Demetrius and Enanthe* (1951).

tices of Crane have left their mark on the Folio text of *Measure for Measure*, where they appear sporadically as a kind of 'show-through' of the manuscript copy. The hyphenation occurs, for example, in *with-draw* (I. i. 81, F1), *run-by* (I. iv. 63, F2ᵛ), *all-building-Law* (II. iv. 94, F5), *palsied-Eld* (III. i. 36, F5ᵛ), *vnpre-par'd* (IV. iii. 66, G3ᵛ); the apostrophes in such formations as *'please, 'pray, this'* ('this is'), *ha'st, do's, I'am*; the brackets in *Now (pious Sir)* (I. iii. 16, F2), *But (oh) how much* (III. i. 190, F6ᵛ), etc. More important still as evidence of Crane's hand is the presence of a number of spellings which are rare or entirely absent from the Folio outside this group of plays, though consistently used in the identified transcripts. *Sirha* ('sirrah') appears three times in *Measure for Measure* (G2, G5, G6), and eight times in the four comedies, but only twice elsewhere in the Folio[1]; *misterie* ('mystery') five times on one page (G2ᵛ) but nowhere else; *ceizes* ('seizes') only on F3 (with *ceiz'd* in *Cymbeline*, II. ii. 7, zz6ᵛ); *midle* ('middle') only on G2. Crane's spelling of *-ness* as *-nes*, though widespread amongst his contemporaries, was unusual in the Folio: it occurs in this play in such words as *witnes, newnes, seednes*.

The use of a Crane transcript explains some, though not all, of the general features of *Measure for Measure*. It may account for the division into acts and scenes, and the remarkable bareness of the stage directions, a feature of the other plays of the group, with the exception of *The Tempest*.[2] It may also explain the consistency of the speech-prefixes, the list of characters, and the absence of oaths or references to the deity where such might have been expected (e.g. 'Heaven in my mouth', II. iv. 4). On the other hand, it was not usual for Crane to remove necessary directions which helped to make the action comprehensible to a reader. Some indications of the Duke's changes in and out of disguise, and directions for the sounding of the trumpets in IV. vi and V. i, might have been expected. There are, besides, a number of places in the text which show signs of 'doctoring' to expand colloquial abbreviations and correct the grammar at the expense of the metre. This treatment was not a habit of Crane's, but it has parallels in the Folio texts of *2 Henry IV* and *Othello*, which also resemble *Measure for Measure* in their division into acts and scenes, in their paucity of stage directions, and in the appearance of lists of characters. *2 Henry IV* is lightly purged of profanity, and *Othello* very thoroughly. The textual history of both these plays is very much in dispute, and at present can shed little light upon that of *Measure for Measure*. All one

---

1. At sigs. x4 and qq4ᵛ (*H8*, v. iv. 31, and *Lear*, I. iv. 128).

2. Frank Kermode, in his introduction to the 'Arden' edition of *The Tempest*, xi–xii, regards the elaborate stage directions as an imitation of the descriptions in masques.

can say is that, while it is clear that Crane's hand transcribed the entire play, some other influence may have been present.

C. Hinman, in his major bibliographical study of the Folio,[1] has distinguished the work of no less than four compositors, designated as A, B, C, and D, in *Measure for Measure*. Five of the play's twenty-four pages in Folio show the characteristic type-setting of Compositor B. These are sigs. F5^v, 6, G2^v, 3, and 3^v, covering the text of II. iv. 104 ('Then must your brother die') to III. i. 148, and IV. ii. 33 to IV. iv. 1. A sixth page, sig. G1^v (III. ii. 145–end of III) was, in Hinman's opinion, possibly set by B, but more probably by D. Of the remaining pages, sigs. F1, F3^v–4^v, G2, 5, 5^v, 6 (and possibly G4 and 6^v) are found to have been set by A, sig. F2^v by C, and sigs. F1^v, 2, 3, 5, 6^v, G1, 1^v (?), 4(?), 4^v, 6^v(?) by D.[2] There is evidence that Compositor A was a conscientious and accurate workman; but B is known to have been careless in following his copy, with a tendency to omit words or even lines, to improvise and misread, to confuse verse and prose, and to 'justify' by breaking long lines of verse into short ones. Of the relative skills of Compositors C and D nothing is known as yet.

The text thus reaches us after at least two stages of transmission: through the transcript of Crane, a careful but idiosyncratic copyist; and through the type-setting of four compositors, one at least with a reputation for unreliable workmanship. Inquiries into its origin must reckon, then, with these intervening factors. They must also take into account the conditions of Elizabethan staging if they are to avoid the common error of forgetting that Shakespeare's plays are primarily written for the theatre.

Most editors have commented on the widespread anomalies and corruptions they have found in *Measure for Measure*. These range over the details of time-scheme and plot, the presence of mute or near-mute characters, and the faulty condition of some verse and prose passages. In consequence, and supported by a theory of dating to be considered in the next section, J. Dover Wilson in the New Cambridge edition, pp. 97–113, set forth a complex theory of successive revisions. Shakespeare's play was said to have been drastically cut for the court performance on 26 December 1604, and then expanded after 1606 by an unidentified reviser who added

1. *The Printing and Proof-Reading of the First Shakespeare Folio*, 2 vols., 1963.
2. See Hinman, II. 380, 386. The portions of the text so distributed are: Compositor A: I. i, II. i. 148–II. iii. 29, IV. i. 1–IV. ii. 32, v. i. 154–515, IV. iv. 2–v. i. 38(?), v. i. 516–end of v(?); Compositor C: I. iv. 1–II. i. 17; Compositor D: I. ii, I. iii, II. i. 18–147, II. iii. 30–II. iv. 104 ('My body up to shame'), III. i. 149–III. ii. 144, III. ii. 145–end of III (?), IV. iv. 2–v. i. 38(?), v. i. 39–153, v. i. 516–end of v (?).

hundreds of lines of prose and verse couplets to the already revised text. The details of this theory have been judiciously examined and dismissed by Sir Edmund Chambers.[1] They depend upon subjective estimates of what is or is not good enough for Shakespeare to have written, supported by a belief in the presence of 'verse-fossils' —that is, metrical fragments embedded in passages of prose— which are taken as signs of adaptation by the 'prose reviser'. Verse rhythms, in fact, appear frequently in Shakespeare's prose (as do prosaic lines in his verse); nor is any writer constantly at the top of his own style. Such an elaborate theory of revision is no longer generally accepted; nevertheless, the view that *Measure for Measure* is a corrupt or mangled text still prevails, and has even been maintained, in modified form, by Chambers and the late Sir Walter Greg.[2] We shall have to consider what anomalies do exist and how far they give support to this estimate.

1. TREATMENT OF TIME

Elizabethan playwrights were little concerned with strict consistency of time, and Shakespeare was no exception. What mattered to him most was its dramatic significance for the audience. In *Measure for Measure*, as in *Othello*, a kind of 'double time' operates. Tension is all-important in the main plot, where everything turns upon the imminent execution of Claudio. In the comic scenes, however, the tension is deliberately relaxed, and time becomes vague and elastic. No one cares to ask how, within two hours of Angelo's proclamation, Pompey and Mistress Overdone have re-established themselves at a 'hot-house' in the city and already offended the respectability of Elbow's wife. Dramatically, Pompey's rambling evidence in II. i, due to 'last out a night in Russia', contrasts effectively with the urgency of Claudio's plight. Again in Act III, though it is only a day later according to the main time-scheme, Pompey is re-arrested, after 'double and treble admonition': here too the leisurely comic time-scheme provides emotional relief. 'Double time' is also operative in the matter of the Duke's activities. While events must be telescoped into a few days, the Duke's absence from Vienna must yet appear long enough to be of major

---

1. *William Shakespeare: A Survey of Facts and Problems* (1930), I. 233–4, 456–7.

2. 'Careless composition has perhaps been made worse by subsequent patching. . . Scribal peculiarities point to a manuscript by Crane . . . rather carelessly made from foul papers that had been a good deal altered' (W. W. Greg, *The Editorial Problem in Shakespeare* (1942), 146). A more optimistic view emerges from the surveys of Mary Lascelles, *Shakespeare's 'Measure for Measure'* (1953) and R. J. Shedd, *The 'Measure for Measure' of Shakespeare's 1604 Audience* (Doctoral dissertation, University of Michigan, 1953).

public concern. He is supposed to have travelled to Poland (I. iii. 14); some say he is with the Emperor of Russia; others think he is in Rome (III. ii. 85–6). After Angelo has received a number of mutually contradictory letters from him (IV. iv. I), he returns in state in Act V, with trumpets blowing and crowds assembled, as if from a long journey abroad. These anomalies are intentional, and serve an artistic purpose. In the main time-scheme, however, a much greater degree of consistency is to be expected. The attention of the audience is focused on a close sequence of events, and inconsistencies here may well upset the dramatic illusion.

The following discrepancies have been pointed out by critics:

(i) Failure to provide for Claudio's reprieve after Isabella's first visit to Angelo in II. ii. 'In II. iv comes the second Isabella–Angelo interview . . . [yet] we know that in accordance with the instructions to the Provost Claudio should already be dead.'[1]

(ii) Confusion as to the hour of Claudio's execution: fixed at nine in the morning (II. i. 34); arranged for four (IV. ii. 51); for eight (IV. ii. 62); and for four again, according to Angelo's special message (IV. ii. 119), with the head to be sent at five (line 121).

(iii) Inconsistency as between Angelo's final demand for Isabella's answer 'tomorrow' (II. iv. 166) and her statement to Claudio (III. i. 100), 'This night's the time', etc.

(iv) Confusion as between day and night in IV. iii. The Provost is seen carrying a head to Angelo for the appointed hour of 5 a.m. Isabel is greeted by the Duke with 'Good morning' (line 111) and by Lucio with 'Good even' (line 148).

Of these the first two are more apparent than real, and amount to little more than a lack of explicitness in the dialogue.

(i) While Angelo issues no definite countermand to his instructions in II. i, the Provost is present throughout Isabella's first interview and must know that Claudio has been granted an extra day's grace. This is indeed the sole dramatic justification for his continued presence, despite the urgent order he has received to attend to Juliet,

(ii) It was customary for an hour's interval to elapse between the time of execution and the official pronouncement of death; hence quite understandable that Angelo as judge should give orders for Claudio to be executed 'by nine', while the Provost in charge of the arrangements should speak of his death 'by eight'. Similarly, when the message arrives in IV. ii stating the hour of Claudio's death as 'four of the clock', the evidence—Claudio's head—is to be sent 'by five'. However, the audience has learned at the beginning of the scene that *two* men, Claudio and Barnardine, are to die that morn-

1. Ridley, p. xii.

ing. The Provost arranges for the block and axe to be ready at four, and again mentions Barnardine and Claudio: he informs Claudio that 'by eight' he must be 'made immortal', and immediately afterwards asks: 'Where's Barnardine?' (62–3). The inference is surely that the Provost has arranged for Barnardine to be executed at four, and for Claudio to die at eight. Angelo's message, therefore, not only frustrates the hope that a countermand has arrived: it heightens tension by advancing the time of Claudio's execution by four hours, and postponing Barnardine's until the afternoon.

Discrepancies (iii) and (iv) are more substantial, though they have attracted less notice from editors. Nothing is said by Angelo in II. iv about an assignation on the same night: Isabella has apparently been given another day to make up her mind. There is, dramatically, no need for Angelo's second 'tomorrow' in II. iv; tension is increased by the fact that subsequent action ignores it. Again, Lucio's 'Good even' in IV. iii is a very noticeable blunder after the Duke's 'Good morning' and the mention at the end of IV. ii that 'it is almost clear dawn'. While Angelo's unnecessary 'tomorrow' is easily explained as the slip of a writer too closely following his sources (see note to II. iv. 166), Lucio's confusion of day and night suggests a more puzzling anomaly.

Besides these, there are some minor inconsistencies. Mistress Overdone's announcement in I. ii. 62–3 that 'within these three days' Claudio will have his head chopped off is followed by Angelo's order on the same day for Claudio to die 'tomorrow' (II. i. 34). This may be taken as a further instance of 'double time'. Since Overdone's mention of three days there have been three intervening scenes, and the audience will hardly realize that it is supposed to be still the same day. There is Claudio's allusion to penalties which have not been applied for 'nineteen zodiacs' (I. ii. 157) and the Duke's talk of neglect for 'fourteen years' (I. iii. 21). The number may have been misread, or Shakespeare may have forgotten: in any case the information makes no difference to the action. And there is the Duke's request to the Provost in IV. ii. 159–60 for 'four days' respite' which conflicts with his promise to return to Vienna 'within these two days' (IV. ii. 197). 'Four days' is clearly wrong: here too, a number may have been wrongly read, or a negligent compositor (at this point, Compositor B) may have confused the words he was carrying in his head, making 'two days' respite: for the which' into 'four . . for . . .'.

Of all these discrepancies, actual or supposed, only Lucio's greeting in IV. iii amounts to more than the usual hesitations of an author *currente calamo* or the misreadings or oversights of scribe and compositor. It will be seen later than IV. iii presents further difficulties in the same portion of its text.

2. CHARACTERS

The appearance of certain shadowy or redundant characters has also been seen as evidence of corruption or large-scale revision. The most important of these is Juliet. She is on the stage three times (in I. ii, H. iii, and v. i) but speaks only in II. iii. In I. ii her entry is announced by Pompey and indicated in the stage directions; yet the dialogue that follows hardly suggests that she is at hand. In the last few minutes of the play she is brought on by the Provost, in company with Claudio and Barnardine, but again has nothing to say. Is she a late addition, or had she a larger speaking part in some earlier version?

Juliet is certainly not a Shakespearean afterthought. Her counterpart, Polina, appears likewise in three scenes of Whetstone's *Promos and Cassandra*, the main source-play, where she laments Andrugio's impending execution, mourns his supposed death, and is happily reunited with him at the end. Both characters serve to heighten the pathos, and add to the pleasure of the *dénouement*: but little would be gained by an enlargement of their parts. Nor is there any real anomaly about Juliet's mute appearance in I. ii. Until her situation has been fully explained by Claudio, it is more effective for her to be seen than heard.[1] At the end of the play, attention is completely centred on the Duke and his decisions: no more than the visible presence of Claudio, Juliet, the Provost, and Barnardine is required if the complex resolution of the plot is to be understood without distraction.

Other problematical characters are the Justice in II. i, who has nothing to do beyond speaking ten trivial words at the end of the scene; Varrius, who, though cordially addressed by the Duke in IV. v and listed straight after the Duke's name for the ceremonial entry of v. i, has no speaking part at all; and a redundant Friar.

Here too the exigencies of Elizabethan staging must be taken into account. After Angelo's impatient exit at II. i. 137, Escalus is left alone in charge of the court. When Elbow and the other comics have gone, it is time for the audience to be recalled to Claudio's plight. Escalus needs to speak to someone about the case; moreover, decorum requires that he be escorted off-stage. The obvious accessary for both purposes is the Provost, who could very well have been kept 'on' after the unexpected irruption of Elbow and his

1. See note to I. ii. 107.

prisoners at line 40. No exit for him is marked in F, and he is not given an answer to Angelo's commands at line 36 which would supply a cue for his departure. However, the Provost must enter at the beginning of the next scene, and stage practice would rarely permit an exit followed by an immediate re-entry. Possibly this difficulty was not foreseen until II. i was completed: if so, it would explain the hasty substitution of a 'Justice', as well as the rather awkward tacking on of his name by scribe or book-keeper to the scene heading.

Varrius may have owed his existence to much the same problem of staging. In IV. v, for the first time since Act I, the Duke appears out of disguise, no longer a humble friar but suitably attired as the head of the state. The business of the scene is unimportant: its real purpose is to prepare the audience for the Duke's ceremonial re-entry into Vienna. In his new splendour, however, he cannot make his exit alone, nor should a mere friar conduct him. Some gentleman of the court must appear to lead off the Duke-as-Duke, and also to escort him in through the city gates at the beginning of V. i before he is met by Escalus and Angelo. If Varrius was created for this purpose, the longest speech he need deliver would only be such a brief greeting as the 'Happy return be to your royal Grace' of Angelo and Escalus at V. i. 3. It is possible that some such phrase has dropped out of the text; any belief that a substantial cut has been made would seem unfounded. As for the dialogue of IV. v, with its suggestions of last-minute activity, the handing over of letters and the summoning of Flavius, Valencius, Rowland, and Crassus—all unknown figures—this provides, as Greg pointed out,[1] background for the visual presentation of the Duke in his proper person. The only function of these 'characters' will be to 'bring the trumpets to the gate' and sound a royal fanfare, and there is no reason for fuller detail. What does seem lacking is some advance notice to the audience that the Duke has friends such as Varrius and the others, and intends to meet them on his return. Information of this kind would have prevented the surprise given by a sudden mention of their names in IV. v and the tendency to suppose that the 'friends' will have a significant, perhaps mysterious part to play.

Finally there are the friars 'Thomas' and 'Peter', whose parts, as Johnson and others have noted, could well be merged in one. As a practical dramatist Shakespeare too must have known this; or if not, the book-keeper would surely have pointed it out. It may

1. *The Shakespeare First Folio* (1955), 355. There is another random collection of names in *All's Well*, IV. iii, which includes 'Sebastian', 'Jaques', 'Lodowick', and 'Corambus'.

fairly be assumed that only one friar was meant to appear.[1] Probably 'Frier Thomas' was tentatively written in the scene heading to I. iii (like 'Francisca a Nun' in I. iv), but the name, not having been used in the dialogue, may well have been forgotten by the time Act IV was written; so that when a friar's name was again called for, 'Peter' took its place.

3. TEXTUAL ANOMALIES

Three major instances of corruption in the text have been adduced as indications of revision.

(i) I. ii. 1–96

J. Dover Wilson regards this portion of the scene as falling into three sections: lines 1–55, the dialogue between Lucio and the Two Gentlemen, with its 'sorry fooling'; lines 56–74, in which Mistress Overdone announces that she has seen Claudio arrested, with the First Gentleman's comment that this is 'agreeing with the proclamation'; and lines 75–107, in which Pompey reports to Overdone that 'yonder man is carried to prison' and that according to the proclamation 'All houses in the suburbs of Vienna must be plucked down'.[2] Mistress Overdone expresses surprise at the news, despite having been, according to her own account, an eye-witness of Claudio's arrest. Wilson finds the style of lines 1–55 unworthy of Shakespeare, and regards the incompatibility of the second and third sections as further proof of revision. Stylistic evidence, a doubtful and subjective quantity, need not be considered here; but the anomaly of the second and third sections must be faced. Miss Lascelles is alone in finding them consistent, on the grounds that Pompey's 'yonder man' refers to someone other than Claudio, and that the First Gentleman's comment on the proclamation, made in the course of withdrawing, was not heard by Mistress Overdone.[3] But nothing is said in the play, before or after this dialogue, to suggest that anyone else has been arrested in like circumstances to Claudio's, and the audience—as Shakespeare must have known— would undoubtedly assume that Claudio was meant. Even accepting Miss Lascelles's assumption, Overdone's surprise would be unaccountable: if Claudio has been arrested, why not others, too? Yet the anomaly can at least be localized. For in fact the first and third sections, according to Wilson's analysis, are organic to the structure. Lucio's chatter may or may not be 'sorry fooling', but

1. The Duke's 'Moe reasons for this action / At our more leisure shall I render you' (I. iii. 48–9) anticipates a further meeting with this first friar.
2. *N.C.S.*, p. 99.   3. *Op. cit.*, 51–2.

it cannot be dismissed as irrelevant. Lucio is an important character: this dialogue serves to introduce him and the attitudes he
propounds, besides preparing for the entries of both Overdone and
Claudio. The third section, introducing Pompey with details of the
proclamation and his plans to evade it, is equally relevant as a preparation for the comic scenes of II. i and III. ii. The whole extent
of the anomaly is contained within lines 79–85, from Pompey's
'Yonder man is carried to prison' to his 'with maid by him'. Omit-
ting these lines, Pompey would answer Overdone's 'What's the
news with you?' with 'You have not heard of the proclamation,
have you?' and the whole passage would become structurally coherent; for Mistress Overdone's 'What proclamation, man?' need
not imply ignorance that a proclamation has been made, but only
curiosity as to its contents and their bearing upon her own way of
life. The suspicion that the anomalous lines were not meant to be
printed is strengthened by the abnormally crowded appearance of
sig. F1^v where the passage occurs, with its extremely compressed
spaces for stage directions and scene headings. It is clear that the
compositor found he had too much material for his page: a fact
which rather suggests that he was including some six or seven lines
which the caster-off had not taken into account.[1]

For the compositor to have made this mistake, lines 79–85 must
have appeared on his copy; and since the copy was a scribal transcript, it may be assumed (*i*) that the lines were also present, without clear excision marks, on the manuscript from which the scribe
worked; (*ii*) that they were marked in some way on the scribal
transcript after its completion. Perhaps, following *Promos and
Cassandra*, Shakespeare began his second scene with the entry first
of Mistress Overdone and then of her clown; realized, before introducing Claudio, that Lucio must make a preliminary appearance;
and turned back to recommence the scene on another page with the
dialogue between Lucio and his friends, and a new entry for Overdone, overlooking the fact that the matter of Claudio's arrest had
already been mentioned to her by Pompey in the passage that
would now follow.

(ii) IV. i. 60–5 (*The Duke's soliloquy*)

Five and a half lines of soliloquy are provided for the Duke in
this scene to cover the retirement of Isabella and Mariana and the
disclosure of the Duke's plan to outwit Angelo. Not only is the time

---

1. This crowding is pointed out, and part of the page (sig. F1^v) reproduced, in
C. Hinman's 'Cast-off Copy for the First Folio of Shakespeare', *S.Q.*, VI (1955),
259–73. There may be some significance in the change of speech-heading in this
passage from *Clow.* to *Clo.*

allowed insufficient, but the soliloquy itself, as Warburton first noted, has been taken from an earlier monologue of the Duke's, beginning at III. ii. 179. Miss Lascelles is surely right in thinking that the lines in IV. i originally preceded those standing in III. ii,[1] which end with a couplet. Evidently there has been some botching behind the present text.

Here too it may be assumed that IV. i is, in other respects, dramatically consistent and structurally sound. At this juncture in the play, Mariana must be introduced; the audience must also be made to know that she accepts the Duke's plan, without having to hear yet again the story of Angelo's requirements. Some manœuvring of exits, re-entrances, withdrawals, and returns is therefore necessary. Mariana is first introduced to the audience, through the Boy's song; she departs while Isabella informs the Duke of her arrangements for the meeting with Angelo; returns in order to withdraw with Isabella and hear her proposal; and comes forward with her again to receive the Duke's assurance that 'to bring you thus together 'tis no sin' (line 73). The awkwardness of this second withdrawal and return would be reduced were it presented as something less than a full stage exit and re-entry. Such simplification is in fact provided for in the dialogue. The Duke's 'Make haste, The vaporous night approaches', implies a speedy return, and Mariana's invitation for Isabella to 'walk aside' suggests merely a retirement from the front of the stage. Exit and entry directions appear in the Folio, but these may well be no more than scribal additions. Nothing is anomalous, therefore, except the length and content of the Duke's soliloquy. A soliloquy there must be at this point; one of roughly ten lines to leave time for the retirement and return; and one of suitable relevance to the occasion. Instead the text offers no more than six lines which have been taken from their proper place in III. ii and introduced here as a crude attempt to fill up a gap.

Such an operation is unlikely to have been performed in the printing-house, if only because the passage in III. ii (sig. G1v) and that in IV. ii (sig. G2) were set up by different compositors. Nor is it probable that Crane, as scribe, acted of his own initiative. The half-line 'And rack thee in their fancies', which completes the soliloquy in IV. i, is unsuitable as it stands for inclusion in a reconstructed ten-line speech at III. ii. 179, and must originally have been a full pentameter, foreshortened in transfer to make up a new line with the Duke's 'Welcome; how agreed?' Such transferring and re-shaping of a verse passage would seem well beyond the scope of

1. *Op. cit.*, 107.

a scribe's function. Nor would some hypothetical 'memorial reconstruction', whereby the lines were supplied by an actor whose memory tricked him into repeating part of a formerly delivered speech, explain the neat apportionment as between III. ii and IV. i, and the metrical adjustments. One can only conclude that the book-keeper or some other member of the company noticed that a necessary soliloquy was missing and patched up the empty place as best he could. Whether Shakespeare here showed an unusual degree of neglect, or whether he wrote a speech for the Duke which his colleagues or the censor found unacceptable, there is no way of knowing today. Whatever the reasons were, it is evident that six lines were taken from the Duke's soliloquy in III. ii—as many as could be spared without making a new gap; and since the replacement in IV. i was unavoidably brief, the actor taking the Duke's part must have been required to deliver these lines with exceptional slowness and deliberation.

(iii) IV. iii. 92–end of scene

In IV. iii, the Duke's preparations for the *dénouement* of Act V are set in motion. Letters are to be written and sent 'to Angelo'; Friar Peter is to be summoned to Mariana's house; the Provost, having delivered the head to Angelo, is required to 'make a swift return' that he may be taken into the Duke's confidence. The difficulties here have been summed up by Ridley as follows:

> he [the Duke] announces his intention of writing letters to Angelo for the Provost to bear. As the Provost returns while the Duke is still talking, and then departs in haste, the Duke has no opportunity of writing them. And in his remarks he says that he will desire an innominate 'him' to meet him a league from the city, whereas it is clear from IV. iv that Angelo was to meet him 'at the gates'. Either then 'to Angelo' [line 92] is wrong, or at some stage 'him' was clearly defined as someone else, possibly one of the friends of IV. v who are so sketchily alluded to.[1]

To this may be added further inconsistencies spread over the remainder of the scene. The Provost, though urged to return swiftly, does not come back. Isabella, provided with a token letter and a verbal message for Friar Peter, and dismissed by the Duke, stays on after Lucio's arrival, with no later exit marked for her in the stage directions or implied in the dialogue. Lucio enters at line 148 with an anomalous 'Good even', though it is understood (lines 45, 69, 111) to be morning. If we continue to scene v, we find the Duke

1. p. xiv. See also *N.C.S.*, 147 (note to IV. iii. 92).

meeting Friar Peter at an unspecified place, and informing him that 'The Provost knows our purpose and our plot'. Soon after, Varrius appears—a character who has not been prepared for and whose identity is likely to puzzle an audience. Lastly, at v. i. 137–8, Lucio repeats his anachronism in alluding to the events of iv. iii: 'But *yesternight*, my lord, she and that friar, / I saw them at the prison'.

All these anomalies point towards a hasty and rather careless rewriting of the end of iv. iii, substituting Lucio's entry for the return of the Provost. The change of time from morning to evening in this section implies that it was written on another occasion than the rest of the scene, and the awkward lingering of Isabella suggests that she was originally meant to depart before the intended arrival of the Provost (who knows that Claudio is not dead) but was retained for the substituted encounter with Lucio. It is clear that a choice had to be made between a 'Provost ending' and a 'Lucio ending'. If the Provost were to return and receive the Duke's intimation of 'such things / That want no ear but yours', Lucio could not be present: if, on the other hand, Lucio was brought on, there would be no point in the Provost's reappearance. Lucio had not been seen since Act iii; his abuse of the Duke and the fact of his having begotten a child, matters that would be dealt with at the close of the play, needed to be brought again before the attention of the audience. Unless, therefore, two separate encounters, one with Lucio and one with the Provost, were to be provided for, and the scene be considerably protracted, it was desirable that the latter encounter be scrapped. On this hypothesis the remark at iv. v. 2, 'The Provost knows our purpose and our plot', may be seen as a patch to indicate that the promised disclosure of the Duke's secrets had somehow taken place after all.

There remains the problem of the 'innominate "him"' in iv. iii. 96. If this be Angelo, there is a discrepancy between the allusion in this speech to a meeting at the 'consecrated fount' and the provision for Angelo and Escalus to meet the Duke at the city gates. But 'to Angelo' in iv. iii. 92 may, as both Wilson and Ridley have thought, be a mistake: the same phrase appears in the previous line and could have been wrongly repeated by either the scribe or the compositor. If so, who is to be invited to the consecrated fount? Friar Peter is already in the Duke's confidence, and will besides be called to meet him at Mariana's house (line 140). Varrius, however, is needed as an escort in iv. v and v. i, and for him, unlike Friar Peter, the fiction of the Duke's absence from Vienna and return should be kept up. A reference to Varrius here would make good dramatic sense in that it would prepare the audience for this character's appearance in iv. v—a scene which, on the unlocalized stage, might well be supposed to take place at the 'consecrated fount' mentioned in iv. iii. (See note to the scene heading of iv. v.)

From these considerations a new picture of the text emerges, justifying on the whole the optimism of Miss Lascelles and R. G. Shedd. Many supposed anomalies have vanished on closer scrutiny. Those remaining seem less serious and extensive than had once been supposed. All are compatible with the oversights, hesitations, and changes of plan normal to a writer in the course of composition. That these traces remain is in itself evidence that the text had its basis in Shakespeare's own papers. In the prompt-copy and actors' parts the anomalies would necessarily have been smoothed away; while had the copy been put together from the memory of the actors collectively, or of the prompter as an individual, they would not have come to mind at all. Revisions, abridgement, or expansion may, of course, have been carried out later, for a first or subsequent performance. Changes may well have been required for a private theatre or a performance at court, and many topical references (notably in I. ii) would soon have lost their point. But that is another matter. What the evidence suggests is that the copy for the Folio text was ultimately based on 'foul papers', or more precisely, on what Greg called a 'rough draft':

> By a rough draft is not to be understood a first sketch but a copy representing the play more or less as the author intended it to stand but not in itself clear or tidy enough to serve as a prompt book.[1]

When allowance is made for scribal transcription and setting up by printers, it will be found that the general character of the text supports this view.

4. STAGE DIRECTIONS

The bareness of the stage directions is a noticeable feature, and suggests some form of editing. On the other hand, directions for disguise or the sounding of trumpets, necessary in prompt-copy, would not normally have been removed by Crane, and it is more likely that they do not appear because they were not in the rough draft. Some of the entry directions, moreover, point to authorial origin. We find '*Enter Lucio and two other Gentlemen*' (I. ii); I. iii has '*Enter Duke and Frier Thomas*'; and I. iv, '*Enter Isabell and Francisca a*

---

1. *The Shakespeare First Folio*, 106.

Nun'. The names Thomas and Francisca do not appear in the dialogue; it would seem that Shakespeare wrote them at the head of
the scenes in case he should later decide to use them, while Crane
allowed them to stay (as the list of characters shows, he assumed
that Peter and Thomas were two friars rather than two names for
one friar). In contrast, only the generic term is used for Vincentio
(*Duke*), Pompey (*Clown*), and Mistress Overdone (*Bawd*). These
characters appear in more than one scene, and the standardization
was probably carried out in the course of transcription. Had it been
done by the book-keeper, one would be hard put to explain the survival of the name Vincentio in the list of characters: if, on the
other hand, it was effected by Crane, 'Vincentio' might have been
copied for his list from the original heading of i. i before it disappeared in transcription. The placing of '*Iustice*' after '*seruants*' in
ii. i could be due to its absence from the stage directions in the
draft and represent a last-minute addition taken from the speech-
prefixes. The direction at the head of v. i, '*Enter . . . at severall
doores*' is, as Greg noted,[1] consistent with Shakespeare's manner as
an experienced playwright; and it is equally characteristic that at
v. i. 276, where another 'several doors' entry is needed, this form
of direction should not be used. For internal entries, the directions
are where an author would place them—immediately before the
new character speaks or is addressed in the dialogue—and not
where they might appear in prompt-copy, a few lines ahead as
advance notice to the actors. The centring of directions—'*Lucio
within*',[2] etc.—is a feature of this play, and does not seem to have
been a practice of Crane's or of any Folio compositor. There should
also be an entry for Lucio after i. iv. 15, and a 'within' direction for
Isabella at iii. i. 44—instead of the premature entry which has been
inserted in its absence.

Except for the return of the servant at ii. ii. 17 (and he has only
gone to the door) all entries are marked. Although most editions
supply one for the Provost at the beginning of v. i, this is probably
due to a misunderstanding of Friar Peter's words at lines 251–2
(see note). There are, however, about twenty missing exits[3]: not
an unusually large number in rough drafts. Many are self-evident,

1. *The Editorial Problem in Shakespeare*, 35.
2. The term 'within' ('without' to an audience) would occur naturally to an
experienced writer for the theatre.
3. At i. i. 15 (Attendant); ii. i. 36 (Provost), 208 (Froth), 272 (Elbow); ii. ii. 2
(Servant), 22 (Servant), 162 (Isabella, Lucio, Provost); ii. iv. 19 (Servant);
iii. ii. 82 (Officers with Pompey), 200 (Officers with Mistress Overdone); iv. i. 9
(Boy); iv. ii. 68 (Claudio), 105 (Messenger); iv. iii. 64 (Abhorson and Pompey),
157 (?) (Isabella); iv. v. 10 (Friar); v. i. 128 (?) (Isabella), 252 (Attendant), 269
(Attendant), 467 (Provost), 536 (Exeunt omnes).

being implied in the dialogue or concerning figures with small or mute parts, and less care has been taken with the comic than with the serious characters. The omitted exit for Isabella in iv. iii has already been noted; there is also no indication of her exit after the order for her arrest at v. i. 124. The Duke's 'To prison with her' is strange, too, at this point, since he continues as if she were still present. It would seem that, in a scene full of complicated comings and goings, Shakespeare was uncertain at what point Isabella was to make her exit and in doubt whether he should send her to prison or merely withdraw her from the main stage—an action that would need no 'exit' direction.

Besides necessary exits, a number of unnecessary ones have been inserted by editors. In i. iv Francisca the nun surely does not leave the novice Isabella alone with Lucio: she will retire to the door until the interview is over, and the two women will then make a joint exit. Crane himself was probably responsible for the exit of Isabella and Mariana at iv. i. 59, where the dialogue indicates that only a brief withdrawal from the front stage was intended. Still more misleading is the provision by later editors of exits for the Duke and Provost at iii. i. 52 and for Claudio at iii. i. 172. In this scene the two older men must merely retire while Claudio and Isabella confer (if the Duke left the stage, he would not be able to 'hear them speak'). At line 151 the Duke comes forward again, leaving the Provost behind. Isabella is about to make an angry departure, but at the Duke's request she agrees to 'attend . . . a while' (lines 157–8). While she waits behind, Claudio is persuaded by the Duke to accept the idea of his imminent death. He withdraws at line 172 to ask his sister pardon; and as he does so, the Duke calls the Provost forward, leaving the way clear for a mimed reconciliation with Isabella.[1] Then, and only then, is it time for Claudio to make his exit in the custody of the Provost, just as he entered with him at the beginning of the scene. This neat piece of staging has been obscured by interpolated exits, leading critics into pointless speculation about Shakespeare's 'failure' to reconcile Isabella and Claudio. Another unnecessary exit has been provided for the Duke at line 270 of this scene, on the assumption that the entry of Elbow and Pompey brings a change of location, with an immediate re-entry of the Duke in an editorially created second scene. In terms of the Elizabethan stage, the action is continuous, and the Duke remains 'on' until the whole act ends.[2] Yet another example is the

1. Lascelles (90–1) has been the first to point out that the Folio stage directions permit a reconciliation of Isabel and Claudio in iii. i. One may disagree, however, with some details of her proposed staging.

2. To save difficulty in cross-reference with other editions, the traditional

insertion of a special exit for Lucio just before the end of the play. For Lucio to leave under guard at this point would fetch a premature laugh from the audience, and distract attention from the Duke's last speech. After this speech, when the procession in pairs has made its way out, it will be time for the officers to remove Lucio alone.

5. SPEECH-PREFIXES

Throughout the play, speech-prefixes are very consistent. Generic titles or their abbreviations—'Duke', 'Clown', 'Nun', and 'Bawd'—are used for Vincentio, Pompey, Francisca, and Overdone.[1] Such regularity points to scribal editing, as does the careful distinction of the supposed two friars 'Thomas' and 'Peter' as, respectively, '*Fri.*' and '*Peter*': having chosen the generic title in i. iii, Crane may have felt it necessary to fall back upon the proper name 'Peter' in iv. v. vi and v. i. Despite some complicated exchanges in dialogue, cases of erroneous speech-prefixes are rare. At iv. ii. 41–5, part of Abhorson's speech seems to have been wrongly assigned to Pompey. Again, in lines 98 and 99 of the same scene, '*Duke*' and '*Pro.*' (Provost) are mistakenly transposed and '*Pro.*' at iv. iii. 64 has slipped a line. All three passages were set up by Compositor B. Some editors have preferred to distribute the speech at i. ii. 12–16, giving only the query 'Why?' to the First Gentleman, and the rest to Lucio: this emendation, however, is not really necessary. The speech-prefix is omitted for the Provost as the reader of Angelo's letter (iv. ii. 118). But in this instance no doubt could arise.[2]

6. VERSE AND PROSE

Chambers has enumerated the chief kinds of errors made by compositors in setting up dramatic texts.[3] They range over omissions of lines, words, or letters, transpositions, faulty division of blank verse, the printing of verse as prose and prose as verse, and other forms of metrical corruption. 'Such results', he remarks, 'are

---

division of Act iii into two scenes has been retained in the line-numeration of the present text. There is no other advantage in preserving it.

1. Compositor B almost always used the speech-heading *Duke*; his collaborators varied this with *Duk*. For Isabella, B usually has *Isa.*, and the other compositors, again less consistently, *Isab*.

2. Thus in the Folio text of *All's Well*, iii. iv. 4, the 'Steward' prefix is omitted. In the Trinity autograph MS. of Middleton's *A Game At Chess*, the reader of the letter in iii. i is not indicated. 'The Letter' (as at *Meas.*, iv. ii. 118) is a customary heading in texts based on 'rough drafts'.

3. *William Shakespeare*, i. 179–84.

much like those which the loose memories of actors and reporters also yield.'[1] The difference between 'good', 'doubtful', and 'bad' texts is in this respect mainly one of degree. Where there is sustained corruption, or where there are marked areas of corruption, the suspicion that one is dealing with a 'reported' text may be well founded. Suspicions are least likely to arise in the case of a scribal transcript like *Measure for Measure*, and here in fact the discernible errors are neither very numerous nor very strange. One cannot be certain just how often they occur, since there is no parallel text for comparison; but fair inferences may be drawn from the difficulties editors have met with in the past. There are thirty-seven lines of recognizable prose printed as rough verse.[2] Some instances are due to line justification, where, instead of splitting a word or leaving a gap in a prose setting, a long line of prose has been arranged as two lines of verse. No passage of prose as verse occupies more than five lines in F, and all the comparatively longer runs were set by Compositor B. Besides the difficulty of distinguishing verse from prose in dramatic manuscripts of the time, Shakespeare's tendency to slip into rough pentameters when writing prose must be reckoned with, and this play shows a frequent alternation, with the Duke often speaking verse in a prose context. Less frequent still is the converse error of printing verse as prose. Not more than about a dozen lines can be clearly distinguished,[3] and the longest run of them, at iv. iv. 13–16, occurs after a passage of prose dialogue and immediately before a verse soliloquy correctly set up. The reasons for confusion are nearly always the same—unexpected variations from verse to prose or difficulty in arranging half-lines, as in the passage immediately after Isabella's entrance in iii. i.

The position is much the same as regards mislineation, which occurs about ten times.[4] Here too the dislocation does not continue for more than two or three lines at a stretch. The causes are varied: line-justification might, for instance, have led to a splitting of ii. ii. 114, while it is probable that Isabella's 'Merciful Heaven' was originally written as an exclamatory line to itself. Her 'Spare him, spare him' in line 84 was almost certainly so intended. Other instances occur at i. iv. 71–2 and v. i. 33–4. Short lines in passages of blank verse, as well as interlineations and the occasional practice of writing a half-line continuously with the full line before or after

1. *Ibid.*, 180.

2. At i. ii. 42–3; iii. ii. 27–8, 226–7, 249–50; iv. ii. 2–4, 100–4, 113–16, 168–73; iv. iii. 27–8, 30, 38–9, 163–4; v. i. 279–82.

3. ii. i. 137, 252–3; iii. i. 3–4, 44–5, 49; iv. iv. 13–16.

4. At i. ii. 131–3; ii. i. 21–2; ii. ii. 63–4, 114–15; ii. iv. 118; iv. i. 34–6; iv. iii. 86–7; v. i. 83–5, 256–8, 311–12.

it, were liable to confuse both scribe and compositor, and result in unfortunate attempts at stringing together pentameters. At II. i. 21–2, F reads:

> Guiltier then him they try; what's open made to Iustice,
> That Iustice ceizes; What knowes the Lawes

Here, it would seem, the lines were first composed without the words between the semi-colons, which look like an afterthought. Not only has an attempt to work them in led to a faulty division after the first 'justice' instead of after 'made', but also, it would appear, to an interpolated 'That'—perhaps introduced because of uneasiness at the iterated 'justice justice'. Again at IV. i. 34–6 F has:

> There haue I made my promise, vpon the
> Heauy midle of the night, to call vpon him.

Here, too, the phrase between commas appears to be a marginal addition, or interlineation, so badly distributed between the two lines that the metre is spoiled in both.

7. OMISSIONS AND TRANSPOSITIONS

A few omissions are to be suspected where breaks in the sense suggest that a line, two half-lines, or a pair of couplets has dropped out. Such lacunae occur at I. i. 8 in the Duke's first speech, and in the couplets of his monologue at the end of Act III. A phrase of greeting by Varrius in IV. v, acknowledged in the Duke's 'I thank thee Varrius' (line 11) seems to be missing; and other omissions may be guessed at. They are not peculiar to one compositor but tend to occur mainly in the outer sheets of the two quires F and G. Here and there, too, the absence of a syllable produces irregular lines with no compensating poetic or dramatic merit, as at II. iv. 81 and 171, III. i. 107, IV. i. 54, V. i. 94 and 239. Usually the omission of some simple monosyllabic word may be taken as their cause.[1]

There are also some transpositions, with an obvious example at III. i. 52[2] and possibly one in the placing of 'Well' at II. ii. 58.[3] It is clear that 'time' and 'place' have been transposed in III. i. 247–8, where the words may have appeared at about the same place in two consecutive lines. On the same page, 'bestowed her on her own lamentation, which she yet wears for his sake' (III. i. 228–9), might be a finer conceit if read as 'bestow'd on her her own' etc.

---

1. E.g. 'But marke me [well]' (II. iv. 81); 'Has he [such] affections in him' (III. i. 107); 'the matter: [pray] proceed' (V. i. 94).

2. F. 'Bring them to heare me speak'. Perhaps the mistake came from a spelling of ' 'em' for 'them' in the rough draft.

3. 'well, belieue this' for 'believe this well'.

Here may be another instance of officious alteration due to suspicion of the repeated 'her her'.

Textual faults due to omissions, transpositions, mislineations, and the like are usually not hard to distinguish from the metrical variants which are typical of Shakespeare's mature manner and the early Jacobean tendency towards a dramatic verse style based on stress units rather than number. While pentameters are the norm, shorter lines may serve to end a speech, or indicate a pause, gesture, or sign of hesitation. Hexameters appear occasionally for rhetorical or theatrical effect. Isabella's threat

Or with an out-stretcht throate Ile tell the world aloud
(II. iv. 152)

suits manner to matter. Her trailing line at I. iv. 5[1] 'covers' the interruption of Lucio's knock at the door, and the Duke's long line at v. i. 491[2] 'covers' Isabella's visible agitation at finding in the same moment her brother saved and herself offered the Duke's hand in marriage. More commonly, extra-metrical lines occur with a slack syllable, or six full feet, where there is a long caesura; especially if two speakers are sharing the line or one person is addressing two characters in turn. This adds much to the required effect of awkwardness and tension during Isabella's first interview with Angelo, and similarly at her meeting with Claudio. Interjections such as Angelo's repeated 'Well'[3] and Lucio's 'Aye' in II. ii *passim*; Angelo's 'Nay' (II. iv. 123), which Isabella retorts to him at line 127; or the Duke's sarcastic 'belike' (v. i. 129, 134) serve a similar dramatic purpose. They are in keeping with the general features of this style, and need not be considered as actors' interpolations.[4] Such features reflect the trend towards vigour and realism in the work of Shakespeare's middle period. They are not to be judged by the ten-syllable yardstick of eighteenth-century editors.

Taken in aggregate over the whole play, the various anomalies, oversights, and contaminations are not as numerous or important as has been supposed. There are some misplaced or superfluous words and a few lost ones. Some lines, half-lines, and a couplet have dropped out, a missing soliloquy of about ten lines has been clumsily patched up in IV. i, and about half a dozen lines due for excision in I. ii have remained. The end of IV. iii has been hurriedly

1. 'Vpon the Sisterstood, the Votarists of Saint *Clare*'. See the note to this line.
2. 'He is my brother too: But fitter time for that:'.
3. A trick of speech that also characterized Shylock (*Mer. V.*, I. iii).
4. See footnote to Angelo's 'ha?' (II. ii. 164), and cf. his 'o fie, fie, fie' (line 172) which is metrically regular and has its precedent in Whetstone.

and rather carelessly revised. These are not very serious flaws in a text that has sometimes been condemned as hopelessly corrupt. Behind some slapdash work in the printing house, and a number of scribal idiosyncrasies, stands Shakespeare's own rough draft, in reasonably good condition.

II. DATE

In the Revels Accounts a play called 'Mesur for Mesur' by 'Shaxberd' was listed as having been acted in the banqueting hall of Whitehall on St Stephen's Night (26 December) 1604.[1] This is the first record of a performance of *Measure for Measure*, but a number of allusions in the dialogue suggest that the play was composed and probably acted in the summer season of 1604.

> (i) *Lucio.* If the Duke, with the other dukes, come not to compo-
> sition with the King of Hungary, why then all the dukes
> fall upon the King.
> *1 Gent.* Heaven grant us its peace, but not the King of
> Hungary's! (I. ii. 1–5)

Dover Wilson saw here a reference to the 'disgraceful' peace signed between the Holy Roman Emperor and the Turks at Zsitva-Török on 11 November 1606, and inferred a large-scale revision of the play after that date.[2] But contemporary opinion and modern historians have found nothing disgraceful about this peace, which was generally considered honourable to Christendom.[3] It is more likely that the dialogue here turned upon King James's negotiations for a settlement with Spain, the issues being suitably veiled in view of the censor's objection to the discussion of current political affairs on the stage. Peace negotiations had proceeded tentatively since the autumn of 1603. On 20 May 1604 a conference opened at Hampton Court, attended by delegates from Spain and the Austrian Netherlands; a draft treaty was prepared in July; and on 19 August 1604 James ratified this by oath. Between May and August, therefore, the prospects of peace with Spain were of special public concern. The anxiety of Lucio's companions at the imminence of an end to the war reflected a mood prevalent amongst gentlemen of fortune who feared for their occupation as soldiers or

---

1. E. K. Chambers, *William Shakespeare* (1930), II. 331.   2. *N.C.S.*, 104–5.
3. 'The first signal success achieved by western Christendom against its arch-foe since Lepanto'; 'the first "peace with honour" concluded by a Habsburg Emperor with his arch-foe' (A. W. Ward, *The Cambridge Modern History*, IV. 8, 701). The peace of Zsitva-Török was greeted in Vienna with bonfires and joyous celebrations.

pirates.[1] Once the peace was signed, the topicality of the dialogue would have been superseded by events.

Albrecht's equation of 'the Duke' with James I, 'the King of Hungary' with the King of Spain, and 'the other dukes' with the United Netherlands, James's allies,[2] may be too explicit. Dramatic requirements would have been satisfied by any bandying about of titles and place-names suggested by the play's locale. Hungary, the setting of *Promos and Cassandra* and for many years the seat of war against the Turks, also supplied a familiar pun on 'hungry' soldiers, a 'hungry' peace, etc.[3] 'The other dukes' might suggest any continental potentates, and could well have hinted at the presence in London of envoys from the Austrian Archdukes, Albert and Isabel, who also held the titles of Dukes of Burgundy, Styria, and other provinces.[4]

(ii) *Mistress Overdone.* Thus, what with the war, what with the sweat, what with the gallows, and what with poverty, I am custom-shrunk.   (I. ii. 75–7)

Overdone's complaint links a number of factors operative in the winter of 1603–4: the continuance of the war with Spain; the plague in London; the treason trials and executions at Winchester in connection with the plots of Raleigh and others; the slackness of trade in the deserted capital.

(iii) *Pompey.* You have not heard of the proclamation, have you? . . . All houses in the suburbs of Vienna must be plucked down.   (I. ii. 85–9)

In *Promos and Cassandra* Lamia and Rosko are threatened with eviction by Promos' agents; but the allusion here is more specific, as well as more sweeping. A proclamation dated 16 September 1603[5] called for the pulling down of houses and rooms in the suburbs of London as a precaution against the spread of the plague by

1. 'This peace was more ioyfully accepted then the people made shew for, by reason the multitude of pretended gallants, banckrouts, and vnruly youths weare at this time setled in pyracie accompting whatsoeuer they got, good purchase' (Stow, *Annales* (1615), 845, col. 2).

2. Louis Albrecht, *Neue Untersuchungen zu Shakespeares Mass für Mass* (1914), 216 ff.

3. The pun occurs in Hall, Dekker, Jonson, and other writers of the time; see note to I. ii. 4–5. Chambers, *op. cit.*, I. 454, pointed out the celebrated instance in *2 Tamburlaine*, I. ii, II. i, ii, of a 'composition' entered into and treacherously broken by Sigismund of Hungary.

4. The peace treaty of 19 August 1604 was proclaimed between James I and 'the High and mighty Prince Philip the 3 . . . and Albert and Isabell, Archdukes of Austria, dukes of Burgundy, &c.' (Stow's *Annales*, ed. 1615, p. 845, col. 2)

5. See Steele, *Catalogue of Tudor and Stuart Proclamations* (1910), I, no. 969.

'dissolute and idle persons'. The measure, which was strictly enforced during the following months, bore heavily upon the numerous brothels and gaming houses which proliferated on the outskirts of the city.

(iv) *Pompey.* ... Master Starve-Lackey the rapier and dagger man
... Master Forthright the tilter ... and wild Half-can that
stabbed pots ... are now 'for the Lord's sake'.

(IV. iii. 14–20)

Brawling in the streets of London amongst soldiers and 'roaring boys', aggravated by feuds between Englishmen and Scots, was strictly prohibited and punished under the 'Statute of Stabbing' passed during the parliamentary session of 19 March–7 July 1604.

(v) *Duke.* I love the people,
But do not like to stage me to their eyes:
Though it do well, I do not relish well
Their loud applause and *Aves* vehement;
Nor do I think the man of safe discretion
That does affect it. (I. i. 67–72)

Angelo. Why does my blood thus muster to my heart,
Making both it unable for itself
And dispossessing all my other parts
Of necessary fitness?
So play the foolish throngs with one that swounds,
Come all to help him, and so stop the air
By which he should revive; and even so
The general subject to a well-wish'd king
Quit their own part, and in obsequious fondness
Crowd to his presence, where their untaught love
Must needs appear offence. (II. iv. 20–30)

These two passages, and especially the second, referring to 'a well-wish'd king' (though the ruler in the play was a Duke), have been taken since Malone's time as allusions to James I's dislike of popular acclaim, manifested during his progress through England in the spring of 1603.[1] There is, however, no evidence of any such dislike at that time: on the contrary, contemporary accounts stressed the king's pleasure at his enthusiastic welcome by the people.[2] With the spread of the plague soon after James's arrival in London, public ceremonies were cancelled, and it was not until the following year that any opportunity arose for direct contact with crowds. On 15 March 1604 the first royal progress through the capital took place; the crowds were well marshalled and no un-

1. See *Plays and Poems of William Shakespeare*, ed. Boswell (1821), II. 383–7.
2. See J. W. Lever, 'The Date of *Measure for Measure*', *S.Q.*, x (1959), 381–4.

seemly incidents occurred. But on or about the same day, the king and queen paid a would-be secret visit to the Exchange, intending to watch the merchants unobserved. The news of the visit leaked out and noisy throngs pressed so closely that the stair door had to be closed against them. The only report of the incident is contained in *The Time Triumphant*, a tract published under the name of Gilbert Dugdale in 1604.[1] According to the author, the king's displeasure was both vocal and vehement:

> And contrymen let me tell you this, if you hard what I heard as concerning that you would stake your feete to the Earth at such a time, ere you would run so regardles vp and downe . . . *this shewes his loue to you, but your open ignorance to him*, you will say perchance it is your loue, *will you in loue prease vppon your Soueraigne thereby to offend him, your Soueraigne perchance mistake your loue and punish it as an offence*, but heare me when hereafter [he] comes by you, doe as they doe in *Scotland* stand still, see all, and vse silence. . .[2]

In a dedicatory epistle Robert Armin, one of the leading members of Shakespeare's company, claimed to be the actual writer of the tract, basing his account upon the observations of Dugdale, his kinsman. It was in the main an eye-witness report of the progress through London on 15 March, in which Shakespeare and his fellow-actors participated; and it made especial mention of the promotion of their company to the title of the King's Players. There would seem to be a strong likelihood that *The Time Triumphant* was read by Shakespeare, and the italicized phrases in the passage quoted above bear a close verbal resemblance to Angelo's mention of 'a well-wish'd king', as well as of the crowd's 'untaught love' which 'Must needs appear offence'. Nor need it be assumed, with Wilson, that lines 26–30 of Angelo's soliloquy (from 'and even so' to 'offence') form a kind of postscript to the speech. Angelo's earlier conceit, of his blood mustering to his heart like 'the foolish throngs' that keep the air away from 'one that swounds', belongs to the same association of ideas. The king, as heart of the nation, is subjected to the same strain as the heart of the fainting bystander when the crowds press too closely, and both images are relevant to Angelo's condition at this point of the play.

The Time Triumphant was entered in Stationers' Register on 27 March 1604 and probably appeared soon after. Taking its

---

1. On this incident, and Armin's authorship of *The Time Triumphant*, see Lever, *loc. cit.*, 384–6. The tract and its significance were noted independently by David L. Stevenson in 'The Role of James I in Shakespeare's *Measure for Measure*', *E.L.H.*, xxvi (1959), 191–3.

2. Sig. B2. (This editor's italics, except '*Scotland*'.)

account of events at the Exchange as the occasion for Shakespeare's remarks in the above two speeches, a date of composition not earlier than March may be assumed for *Measure for Measure*.

Taking the various allusions together, there are good grounds for supposing that *Measure for Measure* was written between May and August 1604. The theatres, closed throughout 1603 on account of the plague, re-opened on 9 April 1604; and the play was probably performed for the first time in the summer months of that year.

III. SOURCES

The primary story of Claudio's offence, Angelo's infamous bargain and breach of pledge, and Isabel's appeal to the Duke has its direct antecedents in Giraldi Cinthio's *Hecatommithi* (1565), Part II, *Década 8, Novella 5*; Cinthio's posthumous drama *Epitia* (1583); George Whetstone's two-part play *The Right Excellent and Famous Historye of Promos and Cassandra* (1578); and Whetstone's story in his *Heptameron of Civil Discourses* (1582), republished as *Aurelia* (1592).[1] The relationship between these and Shakespeare's play has been closely considered in a number of source studies.[2] At the same time, various additional 'analogues' and 'possible influences' have been suggested. It becomes increasingly plain that in a work of such complex artistic integration as *Measure for Measure* no clear line can be drawn between distinct fictional sources and a wide, alluvial tract of literary and historical influences in which the play was orientated. Both aspects may be taken into account by considering the structure in terms of three traditional plot-components, known in a variety of forms and carrying with them, through modifications and accretions, a range of ethical and political significances. The first, concerning the actions of Angelo, Claudio, and Isabella, with

---

1. See Appendix I. Geoffrey Bullough, *Narrative and Dramatic Sources of Shakespeare*, II (1958) gives Cinthio's novella in translation, selections of *Epitia*, and Whetstone's *Promos and Cassandra*, pp. 420–513. Other editions of *Promos and Cassandra* are by J. S. Farmer (1910) and Collier and Hazlitt, *Shakespeare's Library* (1875), Part II, vol. 2. Whetstone's story is in Collier, *Shakespeare's Library* (1843), vol. 2; Collier and Hazlitt, Part I, vol. 3. It adds nothing to the material of his play, and need not be considered in this edition.

2. Notably, Louis Albrecht, *Neue Untersuchungen zu Shakespeares Mass für Mass* (1914); F. E. Budd, 'Materials for a Study of the Sources of *Measure for Measure*', *Revue de Littérature Comparée*, XI (1931), 711–36; Thomas C. Izard, *George Whetstone* (1942), 53–79; R. H. Ball, 'Cinthio's *Epitia* and *Measure for Measure*', *Elizabethan Studies . . . In Honor of George F. Reynolds* (1945), 132–46; Mary Lascelles, *Shakespeare's 'Measure for Measure'* (1953), 6–42; Kenneth Muir, *Shakespeare's Sources*, I (1957), 101–9; Geoffrey Bullough, *op. cit.*, II. 399–417. Madeleine Doran in *Endeavors of Art* (1954), 385–9, sums up the main features of Cinthio's and Whetstone's plots.

the accretion of the comic sub-plot, may be described as the story of the Corrupt Magistrate[1]; the second, relating to the role of the Duke and Lucio, as the legend of the Disguised Ruler; and the third, which concerns the part played by Mariana, as the tale of the Substituted Bedmate.

The Corrupt Magistrate

Angelo's abuse of authority has its countless precedents in the long history of human corruption, and similar tales of judicial infamy have doubtless been told since society began.[2] But the distinctive pattern of events in Shakespeare's play may be traced back to a particular case, described in anecdotes or given fuller literary treatment from not earlier than about the middle of the sixteenth century. What would seem to be the first extant account is in a private letter written from Vienna in 1547 by a Hungarian student named Joseph Macarius.[3] This alluded to the conduct of an unnamed Spanish count or captain near Milan in the time of Ferdinand of Gonzaga. Soon afterwards the events were dramatized by Claude Rouillet in his neo-Senecan verse tragedy *Philanira* (Latin, 1556; French, 1563). Numerous prose renderings of the story continued to appear in the sixteenth and seventeenth centuries, usually in popular collections of quasi-historical anecdotes, some repeating the date 1547, the ruler's name, the judge's nationality, and the location, others varying these details considerably.[4] Thomas Lup-

1. Miss Lascelles entitles this 'The Monstrous Ransom'. But the contemporary setting of the story seems to be one of its salient features, and it is perhaps better to choose a title less suggestive of pure folklore.

2. Bullough, ii. 418–19, prints an analogue from St Augustine's *De Sermone Domini In Monte*. The corrupt bargain here was not proposed by the magistrate.

3. The first notice of this letter appeared in *Századok* (periodical of the Hungarian Historical Society) for May 1893, and parallels to Whetstone's and Shakespeare's plots were noted in the June number. L. L. K. in 'The Plot of *Measure for Measure*', *N. & Q.* (1893), 83–4, describes it, giving a free translation from the Hungarian rendering in *Századok*. The original Latin text, from the Nádasdy archives of *Magyar Országos Levéltár*, is given in Appendix I.

4. Budd provides a complete list. Of versions published before 1604, *Tragica seu tristium historiarum libri ii* (1597), 107–8, translated by Thomas Beard in *The Theatre of Gods Judgements* (1597), 313–14, and Goulart, *Histoires admirables et memorables de nostre temps* (1603), i, fol. 221, give the date 1547, the location as Como, a Spanish captain as the corrupt magistrate, and Gonzaga Duke of Ferrara as the wise ruler. Belleforest in the added sixth book of *Histoires Tragiques* (1582), locates events at Turin, attributes the corruption to the captain of the garrison and the wise judgment to the Governor of Piedmont, prorex to Henri II. Estiene's villain in *Traité de la Conformité des merveilles anciennes avec les modernes* (1566), 210, was a Prevost de la Vouste (also in Goulart, fol. 224). Danett's account in *The Historie of Philip de Commines* (1596), 247–48, ascribes the villainy to Oliver le Dain in the time of Louis XI. Another anecdote in Beard, 313, tells

ton's account[1] was exceptional in that it mentioned no real names, places, or date, and was given as an example of the execution of justice in *Mauqsun*, a kind of Puritan utopia.

In essentials, this primary version of the story was as follows. A man lay in prison awaiting execution for a murder committed in hot blood. His wife appealed for mercy to the authority locally responsible for administering the law. In secret she was offered a corrupt bargain whereby, in return for surrendering herself to the desires of the magistrate (and, in some versions, providing him with a large bribe of money), she was promised that her husband would be freed. After she had reluctantly consented and performed her side of the bargain, the promise was broken by the magistrate and the husband was put to death. Overcoming her shame, the wife, now a widow, appealed for justice directly to the ruler of the land. The behaviour of the local authority was investigated and his guilt exposed. A twofold sentence was inflicted on the corrupt magistrate: first, he must restore the widow's lost honour by marrying her; secondly, he must be executed for his crime immediately after the marriage ceremony was over.

Much of the tale's popularity was due to its almost Solomonic merit as an object lesson in the workings of true justice. Through the ruler's dual sentence the corrupt magistrate suffered the same fate as his victim, and the wronged woman was at once rehabilitated and revenged, without being placed in the intolerable position of having to live with a second husband responsible for her first husband's death. The moral was plain, that he who refused mercy must receive inexorable justice. Besides these essentials, the various renderings of the story also showed some concern for character and motivation. According to Lipsius, the Prefect had been but newly appointed, and broke his pledge through fear that the husband might later seek revenge. Belleforest's Captain struggled against a lust that proved overpowering, and finally confessed to his misdeeds. Lupton's Judge declared that if the gentlewoman had not offered to do anything he required of her, his desire would not have been awakened. The wife's consent to the original bargain was also extenuated. Macarius had stated in his letter that she first consulted her relatives, who assured her that such action under duress was free from sin. Lipsius declared that she refused, but was

of how Otho I when in Italy sentenced a seducer to death, despite his previous voluntary marriage to the wronged woman. Albrecht notes that in 1547 Cinthio was living in Ferrara.

1. *The Second Part and Knitting up of the Boke entituled Too Good To Be True* (1581), sig. L4ʳ–O4ᵛ. Reprinted with some abbreviation in Bullough, 514–24. See Appendix I.

won over by her husband's entreaties. Estiene commented that she resolved to prefer her husband's life to her own honour. It is to be noted that in every version the wife's surrender in the given circumstances was regarded as blameless.

Shakespeare may well have known one or more of these accounts and taken hints from them for the treatment of his characters. His debt to Lupton's version was more specific. The lengthy dialogues between the Gentlewoman and the Judge contain several verbal parallels to Isabella's debates with Angelo in II. ii and II. iv. The Gentlewoman's plea and the Judge's replies, more developed than in any other rendering, follow broadly the same course. Lupton's time-scheme of three days is repeated,[1] and his one-day intervals between each interview and the assignation correspond with the iterated 'tomorrows' of the play, including the dramatically anomalous 'tomorrow' proposed by Angelo in II. iv. 166. The 'privie dore' through which the woman passed to her secret encounter with the Judge is a further detail paralleled in Angelo's instructions to Isabella as reported in IV. i. 32–3.[2]

Nevertheless, the main design in Shakespeare's plot followed the radically altered pattern given to the story by Cinthio, while incorporating Whetstone's elaborations. Cinthio's novella contained a number of details to be found in other renderings, such as the passionate nature of the original crime, the inexperience of the magistrate, and the beauty and eloquence of the heroine. His two drastic innovations were to make the heroine, Epitia, sister instead of wife to the condemned man, and to change the original offence from murder to the forcible seduction of a virgin. The effect was to soften the harsh outlines of the plot so that draconic justice might be averted and a happy ending supplied. The crime of the brother Vico was not such as to require a capital sentence, nor was the 'ingratitude' of the governor Iuriste towards Epitia personally so extreme as to merit death. While traditional sentiment could not tolerate the restoration of a wife's lost honour by a lasting marriage to the slayer of her first husband, it readily approved the marriage of a wronged maiden to her seducer. In general, the story took on a more romantic and humanistic cast. All the characters except the Emperor were young, Epitia not yet eighteen and Vico almost a

1. Cf. Overdone, 'within these three days his head to be chopped off' (I. ii. 57–8) and Lupton's 'hee muste be executed within these three or foure dayes . . . within these two or three dayes' (App. I, 196–7).

2. 'to morrowe at night . . . at such a priuie dore of my house I will receyue you my selfe. . . Then said she, "I will be here at your priuie dore to morrow at night" ' (App. I, 196, 198. Bullough, 520, notes the parallel.) On Angelo's 'garden house' see note to IV. i. 28–36.

boy. The law of Innsbruck under which Vico's offence was punishable by death was not one which Cinthio's readers were expected to approve, and Iuriste, a young courtier recently promoted to governor, showed his inexperience by attempting to enforce it. The end of the story was explicitly designed to show the courtesy, magnanimity, and justice of the Emperor Maximian. After her successful suit, Epitia regretted the imperial decision that her new husband must die. Not wishing to be thought cruel or revengeful, she made a second plea, this time for Iuriste's life to be spared; and Maximian as an exemplary ruler granted her request. Through the heroine's love and the emperor's virtue, mercy was combined with justice, and marriage instead of blood-retaliation made amends.

Both as writer and as moralist, Cinthio sought to modify the classical nemesis of tragedy in keeping with Christian ethics and humanistic standards. Five of his eight published dramas were *tragedie di lieto fin*, including *Epitia*, the reworking of his earlier novella. The play followed the convention of the unities, opening after Epitia had fulfilled her side to the bargain. Most of the action was reported, and commented on by the chorus; the conflicting claims of equity and law, love and justice, were debated at a high intellectual level. Iuriste, now enamoured of Epitia, was prepared to marry her and release her brother; but fearful of the strict Podestà, who insisted on the rigour of the law, he abruptly changed his mind and ordered Vico's execution. In the last act a new turn was given to events. After the appeal to the Emperor and the familiar two-fold sentence, Iuriste's sister Angela and Epitia's aunt Irene begged the heroine to intercede for her husband's life. Finally a Captain of Justice revealed that Vico had not really been executed. Pitying the youth, the Captain had substituted for his head that of a desperate criminal resembling Vico so closely in features as to appear the very man. Thus the flawed 'happy ending' of the novella was made perfect, and the play was concluded with marriage, general pardon, and praises of the virtuous Emperor.

Shakespeare's debt to the *Hecatommithi* for the plot of *Measure for Measure*, as of *Othello*, has long been recognized. Early editors unacquainted with Whetstone's works even exaggerated the resemblances, but there can be no doubt that it served as a direct source. The opening dialogue between the Emperor and Iuriste, conferring the governorship of the city upon a young courtier, '*più lieto dell'ufficio . . . che buon conoscitore di sé stesso*',[1] afforded material for the first scene of *Measure for Measure*. Epitia's exclamation on hear-

---

1. 'more glad of the office . . . than sound in the knowledge of himself' (App. I, 155).

ing Iuriste's infamous proposal, '*la vita di mio Fratello mi è molto cara, ma vie più caro miè l'honor mio*',[1] was echoed (with a significant change) in Isabel's 'More than our brother is our chastity'. Cinthio's humanist heroine, with her trained mind, her gift of eloquence, and her implied debt of gratitude to the father who had provided for her education, supplied the basis for Shakespeare's conception of Isabella. Of at least equal importance was the inspiring figure of Maximian, Holy Roman Emperor and pattern to all rulers, whose blending of justice and mercy gave universal overtones to the story. In this magnanimous ruler, this intellectual heroine, and in the striking remark of Vico that Epitia's virtues might endear her not only to Iuriste but even to 'the emperor of the world',[2] Shakespeare could have found hints for his unique conclusion in which the Duke and Isabella were matched.

Cinthio's drama, in contrast, has only fairly recently been seriously considered as a source. Through the careful investigations of Albrecht, Budd, and Ball, a number of detailed parallels (given in footnotes to the present text) have been traced between *Epitia* and the last two acts of *Measure for Measure*. The device of the substituted head, resembling Claudio's and not 'mangled' as in Whetstone, was seen to correspond with that in *Epitia*. The intercession of Mariana with Isabella was paralleled by Angela's plea to Epitia, and it is possible that, as Ball suggests, Cinthio's introduction of Angela as a secondary heroine led Shakespeare on to the device of the substituted mistress: 'The betrothed . . . becomes Mariana, the forsaken fiancée, by a kind of inversion of Cinthio's plot which transforms the deputy's sister. This shift makes necessary the employment of the substitution . . . probably borrowed from *All's Well That Ends Well*.'[3] An inverse 'shift' had in fact been performed by Cinthio in transforming his primary heroine from wife to sister of the original accused. Resemblances were also found between the dialogue of Angelo and Escalus in II. i and the discussion between Cinthio's Podestà and Secretary. Like Angelo, the Podestà argues that mercy towards the guilty causes suffering to the innocent; like Escalus, the Secretary wants the case of the individual offender to be duly weighed, and he lays stress (more markedly than does Escalus) on the young man's noble rank. As a whole, Cinthio's drama, with its neoclassical structure and formal characterization, bears little obvious resemblance to Shakespeare's; but the high

1. 'My brother's life is very dear to me, but dearer still is my honour' (App. I, 158).

2. ('*ti può far cara . . . allo Imperadore del Mondo*'), App. I, 159.

3. Ball, *loc. cit.*, 133–4.

intellectual tone of *Epitia*, its serious treatment of judicial issues, its example of a potential tragedy steered to a happy conclusion, place it on an artistic level nearer to that of Shakespeare's play than any other version of the story.

Much closer in structure to *Measure for Measure* was Whetstone's *Promos and Cassandra*; a play which, for all its crudities, belonged to the same dramatic tradition as Shakespeare's. *Promos and Cassandra* displayed the exuberance, variety, and social interests of Elizabethan comedy. Its scenes were peopled with a wide range of figures. Besides the traditional roles, with Corvinus king of Hungary as the ruler, Promos as the corrupt governor, and Cassandra and Andrugio as counterparts to Epitia and Vico, the sweetheart of the condemned young man was given a name and speaking part as Polina. A Gaoler was provided for Andrugio; other prisoners arrested by the order of Promos appeared, as well as officers, a hangman, and various minor characters. Whetstone also added a comic sub-plot drawn from low life, representing the vices of a big city through the persons of Lamia, a courtesan, Rosko, her servant, and their associates, who appeared as foils to the relatively innocent Andrugio. In its main plot *Promos and Cassandra* followed the outlines of Cinthio's novella, but provided for Andrugio's survival by the substitution of 'A dead mans head, that suffered th'other day'. The head was 'mangled' and unrecognizable, unlike the head in *Epitia*, which closely resembled Vico's: this may have been an adaptation from Cinthio's drama, or an independent invention. Andrugio's offence was modified from forcible seduction to a love-relationship with mutual consent in anticipation of marriage. Promos, appearing in the company of Phallax, a Vice-like evil counsellor, was made responsible for reviving an old law against immorality which had long fallen into neglect. A susceptible greybeard, he was romantically infatuated with Cassandra and not merely impelled by lust. Andrugio, saved by his kindly Gaoler, hid in the woods wearing the habit of a hermit; but in the last act he revealed his identity before the king Corvinus, appealing on his sister's behalf for Promos' life to be spared, since Promos was now married to and loved by Cassandra.

Shakespeare greatly simplified Whetstone's elaborate settings and removed many of his minor characters. The part of Phallax disappeared, and the inner conflicts of Angelo were presented entirely through the medium of soliloquy. Angelo himself appeared neither as Cinthio's weak-willed youth nor Whetstone's doting greybeard, but as a mature and complex personality. The offence of the brother was yet further mitigated to cohabitation after a legal but unconsecrated marriage, and Claudio's common-law wife Juliet, counterpart to Andrugio's sweetheart Polina, was represented as pregnant with a child who would be fatherless if Angelo's sentence were carried out. Whetstone's Shrieve was developed into Escalus and his Gaoler into the Provost, possibly with hints from the parts of the Secretary and the Captain of Justice in *Epitia*. Shakespeare also took over Whetstone's sub-plot, but rehandled it freely. He substituted Mistress Overdone for Lamia and Pompey for Rosko, individualizing these characters with his natural comic facility and adding Elbow and Froth, Abhorson and Barnardine, from his stock repertoire of low-life figures. The contrast between the fortunes of the comic sinners and of Claudio, already suggested by Whetstone, was strengthened by prefixing a mock-trial of Pompey and Froth to the first court scene between Angelo and Isabella. At the same time Whetstone's troop of fellow-prisoners was eliminated, leaving Claudio as the sole victim in danger of death. Andrugio's romantic wanderings in disguise, a distraction from the main dramatic issues, were not incorporated. His improbable appeal for the life of Promos found no equivalent in Shakespeare's play, and Claudio only appeared in the last act after the dénouement and the successful pleas of Mariana and Isabella.

If Mariana's role at the end of the play was influenced by Angela's in *Epitia*, there are signs that elsewhere Shakespeare had Whetstone's Polina in mind. Believing that Andrugio her lover was dead, Polina had promised to visit his tomb daily and weep there in her gown of shame.[1] This was recalled in the Duke's figurative description of Mariana, forsaken by Angelo, as left to 'her own lamentation, which she yet wears for his sake; and he, a marble to her tears, is washed with them' (III. i. 228–30). In IV. i. 13 Mariana's apology for the Boy's song, 'My mirth it much displeas'd, but pleas'd my woe', echoes Polina's 'In my woes I sing', which actually formed part of her sung lament.[2] Mariana's withdrawal to the moated grange, too, may have been suggested by Polina's account of Promos' decree 'that the mayde, which sind, should euer after lyue / In some religious house, to sorrowe her misdeede'.[3] Almost certainly both Cinthio's and Whetstone's characters helped to shape the new part of Mariana.

Besides these borrowings of character and situation, most of the

1. '*Andrugios* Tombe with dayly teares, *Polina* worship wyll. . . These shameful weedes . . . shall show I morne for my *Andrugio*' (1 *Prom.*, v. iii).

2. 'Amyd my bale, the lightning ioy, that pyning care doth bring, / With patience cheares my heauy hart, as in my woes I sing' (2 *Prom.*, I. i).

3. 2 *Prom.*, III. iii.

plot-sequence of Shakespeare's first two acts was based on that of the corresponding portion of Whetstone's play, and almost every departure from it was due to the new material supplied by the Duke and Lucio. This appears very clearly when the events of the two plays are listed side by side.

Promos and Cassandra (Part I)	*Measure for Measure*
I. i. Investiture of Promos as Governor.	I. i. Appointment of Angelo and Escalus as deputies.
ii. Lamia, then Rosko reporting Promos' decree, Andrugio's arrest, and the threat to their trade.	ii. (Lucio and Two Gentlemen.) Overdone, then Pompey with similar report. (Lucio and Claudio, with Juliet mutely present, discuss Claudio's plight.)
II. i. Cassandra laments Andrugio's plight.	iii. (The Duke's visit to the Friar.)
ii. Andrugio visited by Cassandra: he bids her appeal to Promos.	iv. Isabella visited by Lucio: he bids her appeal to Angelo.
iii. Promos orders the Shrieve to show severity.	II. i. Angelo argues for severity with Escalus. (Comic trial of Pompey and Froth.)
Cassandra's first interview with Promos.	ii. Isabella's first interview with Angelo.
Soliloquy of Promos.	Soliloquy of Angelo.
iv. Phallax and Officers at work.	iii. (Duke as Friar visits Juliet in prison.)
v. Phallax acts as Vice to Promos.	
vi. Hangman with procession of prisoners.	
III. i. Soliloquy of Promos.	iv. Soliloquy of Angelo.
Cassandra's second interview.	Isabella's second interview.
Soliloquy of Cassandra.	Soliloquy of Isabella.

In III. ii the appearances of Pompey and Overdone under arrest parallel the arrests of Lamia and Rosko in *I Promos and Cassandra*, III. vi. The preparations for the Duke's re-entry into Vienna in IV. iv, vi, with the orders for stands to be set up and trumpets sounded, are a simplified version of the provisions for Corvinus' arrival in Julio in Part II of Whetstone's play.

Besides the Duke's special function, the main effects of Shakespeare's structural changes were to heighten the contrast between the treatment of Claudio and that of the brothel characters, and to keep Claudio apart from Isabella through the first two acts by employing Lucio as a go-between. These alterations are in keeping with the play's distinctive form; here it is enough to note that, as in no previous version of the 'Corrupt Magistrate' story, the first half of *Measure for Measure* was built upon systematized contrasts. The most important innovation, however, was the presentation of Isabella as a novice of the strict order of St Clare. No facile 'romantic' solution, such as both Cinthio and Whetstone had relied on, was to be admitted. Even the natural affections of kinship, the chief motivation in these writers' renderings, were brought into conflict with the moral rectitude to which Isabella aspired. Accordingly, lust was set over against abstinence, brothel against convent, mercy against justice, nature against spirit, with the life of a young husband and father in the balance.

The Disguised Ruler

Like that of the Corrupt Magistrate, the story of the Disguised Ruler has affinities with world folklore, and tales concerning monarchs who went about in secret amongst their people, discovering abuses and righting wrongs, are widely diffused in place and time. In the sixteenth century, however, a certain quasi-historical legend exercised a more serious influence on political thought.[1] In the *Historia Augusta*, attributed to Lampridius, and in Guevara's *Décadas de las vidas de los x. Cesares* (1539),[2] the Roman emperor Alexander Severus was presented as a paragon of rulers. Determined to stamp out vice and corruption, he insisted on upright judges, appointed two Censors to investigate abuses in Rome, and dispatched emissaries through Italy to listen to the people's complaints. Furthermore, he made his own private inquiries and meted out stern justice to offenders. The example of Severus was eagerly seized on by English reformers demanding stricter measures against the lax morals of their own time, and in their tracts the emperor's cunning and sagacity were embroidered on in the manner of popular tradition. Sir Thomas Elyot in *The Image of Governaunce* (1541) declared that Severus

> vsed many tymes to disguise hym selfe in dyvers straunge facions, as sometyme in the habite of a scholer of philosophie . . . oftentimes like a marchaunt . . . And . . . woulde one day haunte one parte of the citee, an other day an other parte . . . to see the state

1. See Lascelles, 101; also, Mary Lascelles, 'Sir Thomas Elyot and the Legend of Alexander Severus', *R.E.S.*, n.s. II (1951), 305–18.
2. Translated by Hellowes in 1577 as *A Chronicle, conteyning the Lives of Tenne Emperoures*.

of the people, with the industrie or negligence of theym that were officers.[1]

Severus' devious methods and sensational exposures of wrong-doers were dwelt on; especially his handling of the case of one Geminus who was falsely accused by his tenants. After making a show of sympathy with their complaints and leading them on to propose savage punishments, Severus staged a spectacular trial in the theatre at Pompeii where the accusers of Geminus were sudden-ly confronted with counter-witnesses and shown up as malicious plotters. George Whetstone's *A Mirrour for Magistrates of Cyties* (1584) was even more explicit on the contemporary relevance of Severus' methods. In his prefatory Epistle he deplored the growth of vice in London, and the proliferation of brothels and gaming-houses. The laws, he declared, were no more than 'written threatninges'; even proclamations had no force against 'brainsick iades' who needed a sharp bit. There was need for 'visible Lightes in obscure Corners'[2]—informers who could discover the true state of affairs. Whetstone recapitulated the story of Severus' wander-ings about Rome in disguise, and drew a specific parallel with the English scene by comparing his two imperial Censors with Henry VII's agents Empson and Dudley.

In these accounts Shakespeare may have found the original model for a 'Duke of dark corners' who was intent on discovering the true state of affairs in his city; who appointed two deputies for this purpose; who himself remained secretly omnipresent; and who finally staged a well-timed exposure of corruption. To the rather static figure of Cinthio's Emperor Maximian would thus be added the more active, intrigue-loving traits of the Roman Severus. This conflation would help to explain how Vienna, the seat of the Holy Roman Emperor, came to be the city in need of correction, while the names of the Duke's personal friends as men-tioned in IV. v were taken from classical history, 'Varrius' in par-ticular being apparently a recollection of the Varius mentioned as the father of Severus.[3] Shakespeare's Duke, however, was no mere amalgam of the qualities of Maximian and Severus as presented by sixteenth-century writers. Some later developments of the Dis-guised Ruler legend, both in literature and in life, must be reckoned with for an understanding of his derivation and significance.

In the 1580s the reforming campaign against corruption and vice, with which the name of Severus had been associated, was con-

1. Ed. 1556, sig. M3[r-v]. 2. Sig. A3[v].
3. 'whose father had to name Varius, which was lineally descended from the noble house of Metellus the Romaine' (*The Image of Gouernaunce*, sig. B4). Varius is also mentioned as a cognomen of Heliogabalus, Severus' predecessor.

ducted largely by Puritan extremists. Writers like Stubbes and Thomas Lupton called for a theocratic commonwealth which would put an end to the laxity of a time when fines, or standing in a white sheet, were considered sufficient punishment for whoredom. Strict measures, including the death penalty, were urged against prostitution, adultery, incest, and fornication.[1] With these abuses were coupled stage plays and popular amusements. Such zeal evoked a reaction in literary circles; Nashe's *The Anatomie of Absurdities* (1590) derided Stubbes and others,[2] asking, in effect, for 'more lenity to lechery' and analogous human failings. Moreover, the Queen's government took alarm at the seditious trend of the reform agitation, and from 1592 onwards, political Puritanism was sternly suppressed. Authors in the last years of the century preferred to dissociate the useful legend of the Disguised Ruler from its context of radicalism and instead to incorporate it in light fiction or comedies with 'safe' political bearings. Barnabe Riche's *The Adventures of Brusanus Prince of Hungaria* (1592)[3] exemplified the new trend. The romance tells of how Leonarchus, king of Epirus, left court to travel through his domains in the disguise of a merchant. The people are bewildered by his disappearance—

> Some, immagininge him to bee privily murthered, some thinking him secretly vowed to some monastery or other religious house, some thinking so manye thinges that some knowes not well what to thinke, and yet . . . the good king cannot be hard of.'[4]

Gloriosus, a vain and boastful courtier, encounters the king but fails to penetrate his disguise and charges the supposed merchant with treasonable talk. There is a trial before Dorestus, the king's son, who discourses on the need for judges 'to holde small faultes excused, or but lightly to punish them', and 'to use justice with

---

1. Stubbes, *Anatomie of Abuses* (1583), 99 (ed. New Shakespeare Soc., 1877, Ser. vi, 3 and 4). Stubbes had little hope of such drastic measures being adopted, and went on to suggest branding as an alternative punishment.

2. 'pretending forsooth to anatomize abuses and stubbe vp sin by the rootes . . . Speaking . . . of whoredome, as though they had beene Eunuches from theyr cradle. . . These be they that publiquely pretend a more regenerate holines, beeing in their priuate Chambers the expresse imitation of Howliglasse' (Nashe, I. 19–23, *passim*). On the controversy between the Presbyterian Thomas Cartwright, who urged the Old Testament death penalty for adultery, and Archbishop Whitgift, who saw the 'ceremonial law' as 'utterly abolished' for Christians, see Donald McGinn, 'The Precise Angelo', *J. Q. Adams Memorial Studies*, Washington (1948), 129–39.

3. Reprinted in abbreviation by Bullough, 524–30. Bullough cautiously describes the story as an 'analogue', not a 'source'. To this editor its resemblances to Shakespeare's plot, especially to the Lucio element, seem more than incidental.

4. Chap. 7; Bullough 527.

mediocrity'.[1] Finally Leonarchus is recognized by his son, and the slanderous courtier is banished.

Rulers in disguise became popular figures on the stage, as in *Fair Em*, *A Knack to Know a Knave*, *George a Greene*, and Part I of *Sir John Oldcastle*.[2] Shakespeare's Henry V plays a similar part on the eve of the Battle of Agincourt. In Rowley's *When You See Me You Know Me*, Henry VIII wanders by night through the disreputable quarters of London, encountering constables and watchmen of much the same type as Dogberry, Verges, or Elbow. Such episodes provided light entertainment in an English setting; but with the advent of a new satirical trend in Jacobean drama, a more sophisticated approach came into fashion. Marston's *The Malcontent* and *Fawn*, and Middleton's *Phoenix*, presented fictitious Italian dukes who put off their conventional dignity with their robes of state and gave strident expression to the contemporary questioning of values.[3] There was bitter railing against the vices of court and country, but Puritan zeal was equally castigated and the disguised dukes showed none of the ruthless rectitude which had endeared Severus to radical reformers. The titular hero of *The Malcontent*, his personality split between the dual roles of the scurrilous Malevole and the noble Altofronto, finally emerges as the model Christian-Stoic ruler who disdains to take revenge on his enemies, embraces his true friends, and reaffirms his love for his wife.

Dissociated from reformist publicity, the legend of the Disguised Ruler had thus become a flexible literary device. It served for romance, for light comedy, for popular 'exposures' of low life and, in the early years of the new century, for a more critical, self-wounding expression of social malaise. In its most serious form it confirmed the central humanist concept of royal authority, according to which the true ruler set an example of wisdom, temperance, and magnanimity:

> Princes, that would their people should doe well,
> Must at themselves begin, as at the head;
> For men, by their example, patterne out
> Their imitations, and reguard of lawes:
> A vertuous *Court* a world to vertue drawes.[4]

1. Chap. 12; Bullough 528.

2. See V. O. Freeburg, *Disguise Plots in Elizabethan Drama* (1915), chap. 7; M. C. Bradbrook, 'Shakespeare and the Use of Disguise in Elizabethan Drama', *Essays In Criticism*, II (1952), 159–68.

3. On the relationship of these plays to *Measure for Measure*, see W. W. Lawrence, *Shakespeare's Problem Comedies* (1931), 215; O. J. Campbell, *Shakespeare's Satire* (1943), 127; and Lascelles, 26–7.

4. Ben Jonson, *Cynthia's Revels*, concluding lines.

These familiar notions, and the Disguised Ruler theme itself, acquired fresh topicality with the accession of James I. Described as 'a Living Library, and a walking Study',[1] James sought in his discourse and public utterances to present himself as a philosopher-king who shaped his actions according to the best models of Christian humanism. His *Basilicon Doron* was at once a text-book of political ethics and a statement of personal aims. In forthright, idiomatic style it referred to the author's own experiences as a ruler; to his difficulties, his mistakes, and the lessons he had learned, as well as to the moral principles on which he based his private life.

The view that Shakespeare's Duke was deliberately modelled on the personality of King James was first suggested by Chalmers, and argued at length by Albrecht, who treated *Basilicon Doron* as a direct source of *Measure for Measure*. Similar claims have been put forward more recently in an important article by David L. Stevenson, and supported by Ernest Schanzer in his study of the play.[2] These writers overlook the shaping factor of the Severus legend, but the case for some measure of identification is too strong to be discounted. Shakespeare and his company, honoured and patronized by the new king, could hardly have been impervious to the political atmosphere of the time or quite uninfluenced by the most widely discussed book of 1603. Two principles at least, as set forth in *Basilicon Doron*, are given prominence in *Measure for Measure*. One was the duty of rulers to display virtue in action:

> So to glister and shine before their people . . . that their persons as
> brighte lampes of godlines and vertue may . . . give light to all
> their steppes . . .
>
> it is not ynough that ye have and retaine (as prisoners) within
> your selfe never so many good qualities and vertues, except that
> ye imploy them, and set them on worke . . .[3]

To audiences of 1604 the Duke's initial advice to Angelo

> Heaven doth with us as we with torches do,
> Not light them for themselves; for if our virtues
> Did not go forth of us, 'twere all alike
> As if we had them not   (I. i. 32–5)

1. William Barlow, *The Summe and Substance of the Conference . . . at Hampton Court* (1604), 84. (Cited by Stevenson, *E.L.H.* XXVI (1959), 200.)

2. Edward Chalmers, *A Supplemental Apology for the Believers in the Shakespeare-Papers* (1799), 404–5; Albrecht, *op. cit., passim*; David L. Stevenson, *loc. cit.*, 188–208; Ernest Schanzer, *The Problem Plays of Shakespeare* (1963), 120–5.

3. *B.D.*, 27, 61 (1603 text). James's views were largely traditional; but the personal approach and the work's topicality suggest that it had a more direct influence than earlier writings.

and the opening lines of the Duke's soliloquy at the end of Act III must necessarily have recalled the king's precepts. Of equal importance was the principle of temperance, or the Aristotelean mean, as the chief of virtues:

> make . . . Temperance, Queene of all the rest within you. I meane . . . that wise moderation, that first commanding your selfe, shall as a Queene, command all the affections & passions of your minde . . . even in your most vertuous actions, make ever moderation to be the chief ruler. For although holinesse be the first and most requisite qualitie of a Christian, yet . . . moderate all your outwarde actions flowing there-fra. The like say I nowe of Iustice . . . otherwaies *summum ius*, is *summa iniuria*. . . For lawes are ordained as rules of vertuous and sociall living, and not to be snares to trap your good subiectes: and therefore the lawe must be interpreted according to the meaning, and not to the literall sense. . . And as I said of Iustice, so say I of Clemencie . . . *Nam in medio stat virtus*. (pp. 137–43)

There could hardly be a more apt comment on the attitudes of the Duke, Angelo, and Isabella in Shakespeare's play. Besides James's general principles, a number of his personal traits went to the making of the Duke. James admitted in *Basilicon Doron* that he had ruled too laxly at the beginning of his reign[1]: similarly the Duke, without precedent either in the fictional sources or any version of the Severus story, confessed ''twas my fault to give the people scope' (I. iii). Again, James I's over-sensitive reaction to calumny,[2] and his desire that the laws should be put into execution against 'unreverent speakers', are matched in the Duke's complaint against 'back-wounding calumny' and his exceptionally severe rebukes to Lucio in the last act. With inverse effect, Lucio's slanders about the Duke's sexual morals form a ridiculous contrast to the king's earnest warnings against the sin of fornication.[3]

James's actions as well as his opinions may also have had their influence on Shakespeare's conception of the Duke. As often, life approximated to current trends in literature, and a romantic streak in the king's temperament would seem to explain his attempts to play the part of a Severus. He could not walk the streets of London disguised as a merchant; but his would-be secret visit to the Exchange in March 1604, with the object of watching the merchants while remaining unobserved, was an adventure in much the

1. P. 31.
2. 'the malice of the children of envy' (*B.D.*, 13); also 32–3, 52–3, 72, 93, and elsewhere.
3. 'thought but a light & veniall sinne, by the most part of the world: yet . . . count euerie sinne . . . as God . . . accounteth of the same' (*B.D.* 123).

same spirit.[1] James also sought to imitate legendary rulers in exemplary acts of justice. A celebrated occasion was the trial at Newark
in April 1603, when the king in person sentenced a pickpocket to
death but amnestied all the prisoners in the tower, thus demon-
strating that justice should be combined with mercy.[2] Robert A.
Shedd has cited an even more striking example of the 'Severus
touch' at Winchester in the winter of 1603-4 in connexion with the
Raleigh conspiracy.[3] After a number of executions, James resolved
upon a striking and carefully timed display of mercy. On the very
morning fixed for the execution of a group of conspirators, a letter
with the royal countermand was secretly conveyed to the sheriff.
The prisoners were actually brought out to the scaffold, expecting
immediate death; taken back without explanation; and at last recalled to hear a speech on the heinousness of treason and the sur-
passing mercy of the monarch who had pardoned their lives. This
time the king's *coup de théâtre* was an unqualified success:

> There was no need to beg a *plaudite* of the audience, for it was
> given with such hues and cries that it went forth from the Castle
> into the town and there began afresh. . . And this experience was
> made of the difference of examples of justice and mercy, that . . .
> no man could cry loud enough, 'God save the King!'.[4]

To see the Duke in *Measure for Measure* as an exact replica of
James I would be to misunderstand both Shakespeare's dramatic
methods and the practice of the contemporary stage. But to suppose
that no parallel was to be drawn between the two characters, or
that, according to the familiar formula, 'any resemblance to any
living person was purely accidental', would seem to be just as un-
tenable.[5] In times when real life took on the properties of legend, it
was likely enough that the chief playwright of the King's Men
should find fresh relevance in the theme of the Disguised Ruler,
and that a vital link between the disparate personalities of Severus
and Maximian should be perceived in the character of the new
sovereign.

1. See above, pp. xxxiii–xxxv.

2. See *A Jacobean Journal*, ed. G. B. Harrison (1941), 15.

3. In 'The *Measure for Measure* of Shakespeare's 1604 Audience' (unpublished
dissertation, Univ. of Michigan 1953, typescript 172 ff.).

4. Lucy Aikin, *Memoirs of the Court of King James the First* (1822, 2 vols.), I. 174
(cited by Shedd).

5. Schanzer writes: 'I think . . . that it is an idealized image, made up of the
qualities in a ruler which James had particularly praised; and that it is yet
sufficiently particularized, and endowed with traits peculiar to the King, to
enable Shakespeare's audience and James himself to recognize the likeness' (*The
Problem Plays of Shakespeare* (1963), 123).

While the story of the Corrupt Magistrate became in *Measure for Measure* a study of conflicting persons and principles, that of the Disguised Ruler served to erect a norm as well as an active force reconciling opposites through moderation and virtue. Between the extremes of justice and mercy, holiness and vice, tyranny and licence, stood the Duke, 'a gentleman of all temperance', exemplifying what most of Shakespeare's contemporaries would regard as the model ruler of a Christian polity. As a foil to the Duke, Lucio may well have been suggested by Riche's slanderous courtier. At the same time Lucio bore a generic likeness to the garrulous, ebullient Parolles of *All's Well That Ends Well*, and suitably typified the 'pretended gallants, banckrouts and vnruly youths . . . at this time setled in pyracie'[1] who clamoured against the peace policy of the new king. In his dialogue with the Duke, Lucio provided a necessary dramatic counterpoint. Whereas Marston's Altofronto had to assume the fantastic personality of Malevole in order to rail effectively at the corruption of the times, Shakespeare projected some of his satire through a second character, whose scurrility balanced the apparent conformism of the Duke in his guise of friar. Finally, it is possible that Angelo derived his distinctive personality not only from the traditional 'corrupt magistrate', but also from those traits in James's Puritan adversaries which the king hit off by contraries in the conclusion to Book I of *Basilicon Doron*:

> Keepe God more sparingly in your mouth, but aboundantly in your hart[2]: be precise in effect, but sociall in shew: kythe more by your deedes then by your wordes the love of vertue & hatred of vice: and delight more to be godlie and verteous in deed, then to be thought and called so; . . . inwardly garnished with true Christian humilitie, not outwardly (with the proud Pharisee) glorying in your godlinesse: . . . And . . . ye shall eschew outwardly before the worlde, the suspition of filthie proud hypocrisie and deceitfull dissimulation.[3]

The Substituted Bedmate

In Cinthio's prose version of the Corrupt Magistrate story, the heroine's relationship to the condemned man had been changed from wife to sister; and in his *Epitia* the brother was saved from death by the ruse of the substituted head. The way was left open for a restoration of the heroine's honour by a true and lasting marriage to her seducer and a finale of general pardon and reconciliation. Whetstone's play and story only differed in minor details. Shakespeare, however, chose to complicate the plot by introducing a

1. John Stow, *op. cit.*, 845. See above, pp. xxxi–xxxii.
2. Cf. II. iv. 4–7.   3. *B.D.*, 20–1.

range of spiritual issues. Angelo and Isabella appeared as taut, highly principled personalities, whose complexity ruled out a 'natural' solution by union in marriage. A second substitution was called for, which would leave either party free for a more suitable match. Not only must another head be found for Claudio's, but another maidenhead for Isabella's.

In general terms, the substitution of one partner for the 'repair i' the dark' was a time-honoured device of folk-lore and romance, so familiar on the Elizabethan stage as to make source-investigation unnecessary.[1] Mariana's part in *Measure for Measure*, however, is closely analogous to Diana's in *All's Well That Ends Well*. Diana's claim that Bertram was her husband according to his vows and handfasting

> If you shall marry,
> You give away this hand, and that is mine;
> You give away heaven's vows, and those are mine; . . .
> For I by vow am so embodied yours
> That she which marries you must marry me
>
> *(All's Well*, v. iii. 170–2, 174–5)

is echoed by Mariana:

> This is the hand which, with a vow'd contract,
> Was fast belock'd in thine: this is the body
> That took away the match from Isabel . . .
> As there comes light from heaven, and words from breath, . . .
> I am affianc'd this man's wife, as strongly
> As words could make up vows.   (v. i. 208–10, 224, 226–7)

There is similar word-play on the verb 'to know':

> You give away myself, which is known mine, . . .
> He knows I am no maid, and he'll swear to't;
> I'll swear I am a maid, and he knows not.
>
> *(All's Well*, v. iii. 173, 295–6)
>
>   Angelo,
> Who thinks he knows that he ne'er knew my body,
> But knows, he thinks, that he knows Isabel's.   (v. i. 201–3)

In both plays the man seeks to repudiate the claim by discrediting the witness's character, Bertram declaring that Diana was 'a common gamester to the camp' (*All's W.*, v. iii. 190), Angelo that Mariana's reputation was 'disvalu'd / In levity' (v. i. 220–1). In both plays the ruler, presiding over the case, puts on a show of suspicion at the woman's seeming equivocations. Although in

1. See G. K. Hunter, *All's Well That Ends Well*, Arden edition (1958), Intro., xliv.

Measure for Measure the intrigue is more complex than in *All's Well*, it is clear that Shakespeare was re-working material from his own earlier play, the plot of which was in turn taken from Boccaccio.

This resort to a familiar device, already employed in *All's Well*, did not wholly overcome the difficulties presented by the new play. There was a significant difference between the 'real' situations of Diana and Mariana. The audience knew that Diana had remained a virgin, her testimony being only a theatrical complication before the discovery that Helena, Bertram's wife, had in fact been the substituted bedmate. The virgin Mariana, on the other hand, had actually been seduced by Angelo, with the full connivance of Isabella, another virgin, who wished to remain inviolate. Here, it has been thought, was an unpalatable fact suggesting that Shakespeare in solving one problem had only created another.[1] As a ruse for reclaiming a truant husband, the substitution in *All's Well* may offend present-day susceptibilities, but in its own age it served the purposes of comedy and involved no breach of the traditional moral code. Employed as in *Measure for Measure* to save one girl's honour at the expense of another's, it has seemed an equivocal solution to Isabella's dilemma.

More closely considered, Shakespeare's handling of the device shows a careful provision to meet such objections. Mariana is presented from the start as in a special relationship to Angelo whose legal and moral significance would have been well understood by contemporary audiences:

> She should this Angelo have married: was affianced to her oath, and the nuptial appointed. Between which time of the contract and limit of the solemnity, her brother Frederick was wracked at sea, having in that perished vessel the dowry of his sister.
>
> (III. i. 213 ff.)

While Mariana may fairly be described as Angelo's fiancée, her legal position is rather to be seen as a state of conditional matrimony. English common law recognized two forms of 'spousals'. *Sponsalia per verba de praesenti*, a declaration by both parties that each took the other at the present time as spouse, was legally binding

---

1. For an extreme reaction, see Quiller-Couch: 'She [Isabella] is all for saving her own soul . . . by turning, of a sudden, into a bare procuress . . . it looks as if this virgin "enskied and sainted" had saved herself by a trick which denudes her own chastity' (*N.C.S.*, xxx). More temperately, Virgil K. Whitaker remarks that 'no argument can make acceptable the device by which Mariana substitutes for Isabella', but explains it by 'the incongruity between the Christian framework of the characters and the folk materials of the plot' (*Shakespeare's Use of Learning*, (1953), 221).

irrespective of any change of circumstances, and, whether the union was later consecrated or not, amounted to full marriage. *Sponsalia per verba de futuro*, a sworn declaration of intention to marry in the future, was not thus absolutely binding. Failure of certain conditions to materialize, notably failure to furnish the agreed dowry, justified a unilateral breach. It was this second form of agreement to which Angelo and Mariana were committed by oath, and which Angelo, because of the lost dowry, sought to repudiate. In one circumstance, however, *de futuro* spousals became automatically converted into absolute marriage:

> if a man contract spousals conditionally with a Woman . . . and . . . in the meantime he have access to her, as to his wife, these doubtful spousals do thereby pass into Matrimony.[1]

Abandoned by her intended husband because of the unavoidable loss of her dowry at sea, Mariana had only one recourse in the eyes of the law: to bring about a cohabitation with Angelo which would, *ipso facto*, make her his wife. Modest and retiring by nature, Mariana was not the person to initiate this step. Both the authority of the Duke as friar and Isabella's encouragement were required. While Isabel's own dilemma was resolved by the substitution, Mariana's case had its own strong claim, and no hypocrisy was involved on the part of her helpers where 'the doubleness of the benefit defends the deceit from reproof'.

As for the Duke's handling of the problem, moral as well as legal justification was offered in the assurance to Mariana:

> He is your husband on a pre-contract:
> To bring you thus together 'tis no sin,
> Sith that the justice of your title to him
> Doth flourish the deceit.   (IV. i. 72–5)

1. Henry Swinburne, *A Treatise of Spousals* (1686), 219–20. Written about a century before it was published, this work expressed the accepted common-law view of the time, based on canon law before the rulings of the Council of Trent, which were not held to be valid in Protestant England. For a church view, cf. William Perkins, *Of Christian Oeconomie*, chap. 4: 'if the parties betrothed, doe lie together before the condition . . . be performed; then the contract [of marriage] for the time to come, is without further controversie, sure and certaine. For . . . it is always presupposed, that a mutuall consent, as touching Marriage, hath gone before' (*Works*, vol. III, 1617 ed., p. 673). Davis P. Harding, 'Elizabethan Betrothals and *Measure for Measure*', *J.E.G.P.* (1950), 129–58, misses the important distinction between the two kinds of 'spousals', as did Arthur Underhill in *Shakespeare's England* (1916), I. 407–8. The significance is fully brought out by E. Schanzer, 'The Marriage-Contracts in *Measure for Measure*', *S.S.* 13 (1960), 81–9. Schanzer notes here (p. 89, n. 21) that in strict law Angelo could have pleaded *error personae*, but that for 'stage law', the Duke's ruse would be quite adequate.

In the view of churchmen, any kind of sexual relationship before a fully consecrated marriage was, of course, sinful. But the Duke, as the audience knew, was not a friar but a monarch. By secular standards Mariana's plight fully condoned her deceiving of Angelo, just as the plight of Helena condoned the deception of Bertram. Here indeed was a case for moral equity, an extension into the realm of conscience of that 'mediocrity' which James I so strenuously advocated in temporal affairs. In so far as analogies would almost certainly be drawn between the fictitious Duke of Vienna and the actual king of England, the Duke's solution would imply the authority of the supreme head of the church, and as such would appear as a final ruling.

In terms of dramatic construction, Angelo's relationship with Mariana provided an enlightening comparison with that of Claudio and Juliet. In both cases the sin had been committed of cohabitation before a church marriage, but in circumstances which, by normal human standards, showed up Claudio as a better man than his judge. While Angelo had broken his matrimonial vows and abandoned his intended wife when her dowry was lost, Claudio had kept his pledge and married Juliet in law, postponing the consecration only until the dowry became available. It was dramatic justice that Angelo's hypocrisy should be exposed by putting him in a similar situation to that of the man he had condemned. It was also dramatic mercy that by the Substituted Bedmate device he was saved from the far graver offence he had planned, and sentenced finally by his ruler to the same 'penalty' as Claudio's: namely, marriage in the eyes of the church as well as the law.

IV. THE PLAY

1. FORM

Critics are always liable to mirror their own dispositions, and the temper of the age, in their assessments of Shakespeare. Nowhere is the tendency so marked as in discussions of certain plays written at about the turn of the sixteenth century, ostensibly comedies, yet charged with a weight of moral and social preoccupations, of explicit political theorizing and psychological probing, beyond the limits of what the comic form could easily support. *Measure for Measure* especially has called forth a remarkable diversity of opinions. Samuel Johnson, judging by the standards of classical comedy, found 'the light or comick part very natural and pleasing', but objected that the 'grave scenes' in general showed 'more labour than elegance'.[1] Coleridge, in contrast, viewed the whole play as

1. *The Plays of William Shakespeare* (1765), I. 382.

profoundly disturbing. The comic elements were 'disgusting', the serious ones 'horrible'; this was felt to be the most painful of Shakespeare's dramas.[1] In the view of the radical Hazlitt, however, *Measure for Measure* showed a pleasing rejection of conventional morality and a sympathy with human beings of every level and degree: it displayed Shakespeare as 'a moralist in the same sense in which nature is one'.[2] On the other hand, Ulrici saw the play as a heart-warming demonstration of traditional ethics; he discovered 'an inexhaustible stream of joy' in its Christian message, which declared: 'we are all sinners, children of wrath and in need of mercy'.[3] In the twentieth century new critical labels have been used for responses different in degree rather than kind from those of an earlier period. With *All's Well That Ends Well*, *Troilus and Cressida*, and sometimes *Hamlet*, *Measure for Measure* was placed in the category of 'problem plays'—a term suggested by the new drama of Ibsen and Shaw.[4] For some, the 'problem' was located in the author's subjective dilemmas. E. K. Chambers regarded this group of plays as 'utterances of a puzzled and disturbed spirit, full of questioning, sceptical of its own ideals'.[5] Dover Wilson took them as evincing Shakespeare's 'self-laceration, weariness, discord, cynicism and disgust'.[6] As against the autobiographical approach to Shakespeare's art, 'historical' criticism traced the 'problem' to the spiritual exhaustion of the Jacobean age, the 'dread of death and horror of life', the 'all-comprehending doubt', the 'dead disgust' which resulted in a touching of 'the lowest depths of Jacobean negation'.[7] From either viewpoint, the 'natural morality' which delighted Hazlitt now suggested a total scepticism and abandonment of values. But in the 1930's a reaction began to set in, perhaps not unrelated to the rediscovery of Anglicanism and royalism by a new generation of writers. The notion of Shakespeare's 'mythical

1. T. M. Raysor, *Coleridge's Shakespearean Criticism* (1930), I. 113–15.

2. *The Characters of Shakespear's Plays (Complete Works*, ed. Howe, IV. 347).

3. Ulrici, *Shakespeare's Dramatic Art* (1846), 310 ff. 'Although mere human virtue is absolutely good for nothing, we have only need to confess our weakness to find in the divine grace not only true virtue, but strength likewise for exercising it' (314).

4. The term 'problem play' seems to have been first applied by Boas, *Shakespeare's Predecessors*, in 1896, and 'unpleasant play' by E. K. Chambers in his edition of the play in 'The Red Letter Shakespeare', 1906. Cf. W. W. Lawrence, *Shakespeare's Problem Comedies* (1931), E. M. W. Tillyard, *Shakespeare's Problem Plays* (1951), Ernest Schanzer, *The Problem Plays of Shakespeare* (1963).

5. 'The Red Letter Shakespeare', Intro., 7.

6. *The Essential Shakespeare* (1943), 117. Analogous views on Shakespeare in his 'tragic period' are expressed by Walter Raleigh, *Shakespeare* (1907), 131.

7. Una Ellis-Fermor, *The Jacobean Drama* (1936), 259, 260.

sorrows' was sharply contested by C. J. Sisson,[1] who found no support for it in the ascertainable facts of the dramatist's life. As for the supposed pessimism of the Jacobeans, R. W. Chambers produced convincing evidence that the beginning of James I's reign was seen by contemporaries as one of the most hopeful moments of English history.[2] Neither of these scholar-critics found a trace of cynicism or world-weariness in *Measure for Measure*. The play was certified as 'sound to the core, and profoundly Christian in spirit'.[3] Only those alienated from traditional values, only the modern rationalist or half-believer, could doubt this, or misinterpret such crucial evidence as the Duke's homily on life or Isabella's refusal to yield her chastity to save her brother from death.[4] This appreciation differed from Ulrici's in that the broad Christian message of charity and forbearance had become a much tighter, more exclusive statement of doctrine. Its corollary appeared in new interpretations of the dramatic form. Outlined by G. Wilson Knight,[5] schematically developed by Roy W. Battenhouse and Nevill Coghill, a theory was evolved in which *Measure for Measure* became an allegory of the Divine Atonement.[6] The disguised Duke was taken to symbolize the Incarnate Lord; Lucio was seen as the eternal Adversary; Isabella represented the soul of man, elected to be the Bride of Christ. Coghill adduced the medieval conception of comedy as set forth by Dante in his letter to the Can Grande, according to which human life was to be regarded as an allegory with a cosmic 'happy

1. 'The Mythical Sorrows of Shakespeare', Annual Shakespeare Lecture of the British Academy, 1934 (1935).

2. 'The Jacobean Shakespeare and *Measure for Measure*', Annual Shakespeare Lecture of the British Academy, 1937 (1938); reprinted in *Man's Unconquerable Mind* (1939).

3. Sisson, *ibid.*, 17.

4. 'Let there be no mistake about this; Shakespeare sets up Isabella as a heroine, who represents something in womanhood which Shakespeare . . . reveres with all his heart. Nothing but a pseudo-romantic sentimentalism . . . could fail to understand the rightness of Isabella and the reality of her dilemma . . . sin, and deadly sin at that, is fundamental in Christian thought. . . In a word, it is Isabella's soul that is at stake' (Sisson, *ibid.*, 16–17).

5. *The Wheel of Fire* (1930), chap. IV.

6. Battenhouse, '*Measure for Measure* and Christian Doctrine of the Atonement', *P.M.L.A.*, LXI (1946), 1029–59; Coghill, 'Comic Form in *Measure for Measure*', *S.S.*, 8 (1955), 14–27. Coghill, in collaboration with Raymond Raikes, produced the play for the B.B.C. (Third Programme) on 27 March 1955. Lucio's description of Claudio's love for Juliet (I. iv. 39–44) was omitted, as well as any sign of his presence with Isabel in II. ii. A verbal reconciliation for Claudio and Isabella was introduced in Act v, which ended with pealing bells and a Magnificat. The broadcast was criticized by Frank Kermode in a radio talk, 'The Properties of Government', on 26 April 1955.

ending'. Such 'doctrinal' interpretations have in their turn been
questioned. Clifford Leech has thought it 'particularly strange for
Shakespeare's plays to be the embodiment of theses'.[1] Hazelton
Spencer has described his own reaction as being: 'If Shakespeare
intended to mirror the process of the Atonement, he had involun-
tarily produced a parody.'[2] Frank Kermode, while allowing that
'problem' elements were to be found in all the comedies, and also
'something of the Dantesque pattern' in their endings, pointed to
'the recalcitrance and the variety of flesh and blood . . . nowhere
more than in *Measure for Measure*', which refused to conform to the
pattern of allegory.[3]

These conflicting assessments may be taken to reflect changes in
literary taste and intellectual orientation; but they are also—and
more significantly—related to a distinctive quality of the play itself. Each interpretation has its limited validity; each amounts to an
abstraction from the composite whole. Critics who regard *Measure
for Measure* as an expression of doubt and negation pass lightly
over its intense and positive concern with 'the properties of
government', the scope of secular and divine justice, the workings
of grace, the universal polarities of love and death. Those who see
the play as a religious fable or divine allegory are often blind to the
complexities of the leading characters and the obstinate challenge
to doctrinal rigidity presented by common erring humanity in the
comic scenes. The Duke in dominating the action resorts to shifts
and strategems more in keeping with the expected behaviour of a
seventeenth-century ruler than of the Incarnate Lord. His in-
fallibility is taxed by his own admission of fault in giving the people
'scope'; his omniscience by the unforeseen arrival of Angelo's
messenger in IV. ii, with orders for the execution of Claudio; his
omnipotence by Barnardine's dogged refusal to die at any man's
bidding. He is easily ruffled by Lucio's absurd slanders, and the
laughter of the audience is not altogether on his side. Isabella,
moreover, seems a disconcerting choice for the 'Bride of Christ'.
She is crucially dependent on Lucio's prompting and moral support at her first encounter with Angelo: as Donald A. Stauffer
observed, 'If it were not for this unprincipled rake, the two idealists

1. 'The "Meaning" of *Measure for Measure*', *S.S.*, 3 (1950), 66. E. T. Sehrt's
Vergebung und Gnade bei Shakespeare (1952) also presents a 'Christian' and 'doctrinal' interpretation but finds no allegory.
2. *The Art and Life of William Shakespeare* (1940), 351.
3. In 'The Properties of Government'. For further discussion of these opinions
see J. C. Maxwell, '*Measure for Measure*, A Footnote to Recent Criticism', *Down-
side Review*, LXV (1947), 45–59, and Robert M. Smith, 'Interpretations of
Measure for Measure', *S.Q.*, 1 (1950), 208–18.

would have killed Claudio between them.'[1] She doubts whether there is a case for mercy towards sinners; falls easily into Angelo's trap of logic at their second meeting; and at the crisis of events in III. i breaks out into hysterical abuse of her mother and brother. If Lucio is Satan, the Eternal Adversary, his services to both Isabella and Claudio show him as oddly useful, if not indispensable, to the purposes of the Duke, whether this personage be considered human or divine.

It is futile to debate whether a chessboard should be considered black or white: not only is the board chequered, but it is in the nature of the game that this should be so. *Measure for Measure* is made up of contrasts and antinomies juxtaposed and resolved, and the process is incorporated in its dramatic form. The characters evince too many human inconsistencies, the themes too many contradictory aspects, for allegorical drama. At the same time the sententious choric utterances, the intricate plot-mechanism, the finale with its universal pardons and multiple marriage unions, have little in common with the spirit of the modern 'problem' play. But there is a third way of viewing *Measure for Measure* which is compatible with all these qualities, and which suggests a more specific and contemporaneous form than either category. More than a century ago Gervinus declared that the play's basic concern was with the idea of moderation as applied to all human relationships:

> It calls us universally from all extremes, even from that of the good, because in every extreme there lies an overstraining, which avenges itself with the contrary reaction.[2]

This was expressed in the principle of equity which the Duke as a secular ruler upheld in his choric statements and his often devious practice:

> that circumspect equity . . . which suffers neither mercy nor the severe letter of the law to rule without exception, which awards punishment not *measure for measure*, but *with* measure.[3]

Ernest Schanzer's recent study of the play develops this approach with much cogency.[4] Its relevance to *Measure for Measure*'s distinctive form appears when this play is seen against the general background of Shakespearean comedy, and especially when the probable influence of a new trend in dramatic theory is taken into account.

---

1. *Shakespeare's World of Images* (1949), 149.
2. *Shakespeare Commentaries*, trans. F. E. Bunnett (1875), 504.
3. *Ibid.*, 502.   4. Pp. 114–20.

In his romantic comedies, Shakespeare had dramatized a range of attitudes to love, expressed mainly through character-relationships and correlated through a series of marriage unions, in which balance and good sense tempered the excesses of sentiment and desire. Discords in the individual, and in society as a whole, were at the same time comprehended and harmonized. Thus not only the problems of lovers, but psychic tensions and social usurpations or abuses, found their resolution through the exercise of reason, often in the form of an adjudication by the representatives of authority—Duke Theseus, the Duke of Venice, Duke Orsino, or the King of France. The degree of tension, and with it the importance of the part played by authority, varied considerably from play to play. In the comedies written in the last years of Elizabeth's reign, *All's Well That Ends Well* and *Troilus and Cressida*, discords are highly accentuated, while the harmonizing force of reason 'proves weak or untrue'. In *All's Well*, parental and royal authority is feeble and mainly ineffective; the happy outcome turns largely on the ingenuity of the traditional plot. In *Troilus and Cressida* no supreme authority exists; age and wisdom can only warn, without stemming the inevitable tide of war and lechery. The imbalance of tension and resolution is reflected in the indeterminate form of these plays, in which elements of satire, romance and potential tragedy are intermingled without a full integration. *Measure for Measure*, though usually placed in the same group, is different in structure. Not only are the tensions and discords wrought up to an extreme pitch, threatening the dissolution of all human values, but a corresponding and extraordinary emphasis is laid upon the role of true authority, whose intervention alone supplies the equipoise needed to counter the forces of negation. The form here is a close blend of tragic and comic elements, so carefully patterned as to suggest a conscious experiment in the new medium of tragicomedy.

Limited precedents for this treatment were to be found in the dramas of Cinthio and Whetstone. *Epitia*, primarily concerned to show the reconciliation of justice and mercy, took the form of a *tragedia di lieto fin*. Through a sudden reversal in the last act, Epitia was diverted from revenge and the Emperor from the severity of the law. Providence took the place of Fortune, as the final chorus proclaimed:

> *Puo Fortuna aggirar le cose humane,*
> *Con la natia inconstanza,*
> *Ma una viva speranza*
> *C'habbia l'huom nel Signore,*

> *Che del tutto è fattore,*
> *Le forze sue fà vane,*
> *E lieto quei rimane,*
> *A cui pena apportava ella, e dolore.*[1] (v. vii)

On a less speculative plane, *Promos and Cassandra* also provided a happy ending to a potentially tragic story; but its medley of farce and sentiment, its incongruous romance episodes and type characters, belonged to the English tradition of 'mongrell tragicomedy' and had little in common with the neoclassical and humanist approach of *Epitia*. Whetstone's structure, with its wide social range and comic sub-plot, was indeed the more familiar and congenial to Shakespeare, who broadly patterned the first half of his play upon it; but neither *Epitia* nor *Promos and Cassandra* offered a truly satisfactory model. There were, however, stimulating suggestions available in the field of dramatic theory which could point the way to a form transcending the limitations of both Cinthio's play and Whetstone's.

Guarini's *Compendio della Poesia Tragicomica* (1601) set forth a closely reasoned defence of 'true' tragicomedy, as distinguished from tragedy twisted to a happy ending or the loose medley of English tradition. The form was defined as a close blend or fusion of seeming disparates; taking from tragedy 'its great characters, but not its great action; a likely story, but not a true one; . . . delight, not sadness; danger, not death'; and from comedy 'laughter that was not dissolute, modest attractions, a well-tied knot, a happy reversal, and, above all, the comic order of things'.[2] This avoidance of extremes was said to be morally justified in the conditions of the modern world. In ancient times tragedy had performed the homœopathic function of purging terror with terror and pity with pity. But in a Christian society, which believed in the redemption of sinners, such drastic purges were unnecessary and unwelcome. Equally obsolete was the ancient comic purge of dissoluteness as a cure for melancholy. Hence tragicomedy, which qualified extremes and promoted a balanced condition of mind,

1. 'Fortune, with her native inconstancy, may turn human affairs about; but a lively hope in the Lord, who is creator of all things, frustrates her powers, and he remains glad to whom Fortune has brought pain and sorrow'.

2. '*dall' una, prende le persone grande e non l'azione; la favola verisimile, ma non vera; . . . il diletto, non la mestizia; il pericolo, non la morte; dall' altra, il riso non dissoluto, le piacevolezze modeste, il nodo finto, il rivolgimento felice, e sopratutto l'ordine comico*' (Guarini, ed. Bari (1914), 231). Guarini's theories are discussed by M. Doran, *Endeavors of Art*, 203–8, and Cinthio's theory and practice by Marvin T. Herrick, *Tragicomedy* (1954), chap. 3. See also Allan H. Gilbert, 'Fortune in the Tragedies of Giraldo Cinthio', *P.Q.*, xx (1941), 224–33.

was held to be the best form of contemporary drama. It employed a 'mixed' style, 'mixed' action, and 'mixed' characters—'passing from side to side, it works amongst contraries, sweetly tempering their composition'.[1]

The *Compendio* was printed together with *Il Pastor Fido* in 1602. In the same year an English translation of the play appeared, with a prefatory sonnet by Samuel Daniel, in which he claimed acquaintance with Guarini. The new theory was widely influential, and the term tragicomedy, previously fallen into disrepute, soon took on new dignity. Whether or not Shakespeare had read Guarini's treatise, its ideas were in the air after 1602 and may well have prompted the design of *Measure for Measure*, with its blend of serious and comic, extreme peril and happy solution, mixed characters and 'well-tied knot'. Structurally the play was divided into almost mathematical halves. Through the first part there was a progressive mounting of tension between opposed characters and conflicting principles, with no more than the enigmatic hope of a solution offered by the continuing presence of the Duke on the scene of events. At the point of total impasse in III. i the motion was reversed by the Duke's direct intervention. Thenceforth in his part of moderator the Duke was tirelessly engaged in 'passing from side to side,' 'working amongst contraries', and shaping a new course for the drama. Accordingly the play ended with pardon instead of punishment, marriage instead of death, reconciliation of enemies, harmony, and 'above all, the comic order of things'.

This is not to suggest that Shakespeare's play was specifically written to Guarini's formula or that it merely reproduced his quasi-Aristotelean design for tragicomedy. The influence of the new theories may well account for the very coherent structural pattern of *Measure for Measure* as compared with *All's Well That Ends Well* or *Troilus and Cressida*; but what is most vital in the play stems from Shakespeare's own genius, with its roots in the Elizabethan tradition. Conflicts and dilemmas are explored with a terrible insight beyond Guarini's limited reach: the laughter remains unrepentantly 'dissolute', the 'attractions' of the comic scenes are elemental rather than 'modest'. It is in his explicit stress on the virtues of moderation as upheld by the Duke that Shakespeare comes nearest to the spirit of the *Compendio*. The significance of this stress is often lost sight of or misrepresented in our own age. For Jacobean audiences, and probably for Shakespeare himself as a thoughtful man of his time, the importance of the *via media* may have seemed para-

---

1. '*discorrendo nelle altre parti, andrà con le contrarie qualità dolcemente temperando la sua testura*' (249).

mount in real life and likewise in dramas concerned with contemporary issues. That good sense brought with it some inhibition of creative energy was a consequence that we shall have to consider later. But first we need to look more closely at the interrelations of theme and character within a formal design planned to express the underlying ethic.

2. THEMES

In the broadest sense of the phrase, *Measure for Measure* deserves to be considered a drama of ideas. While the formal classifications 'problem play', 'allegory', 'morality', or 'satire' are misleading, there can be no doubt that the play is profoundly concerned with major intellectual issues. The following sub-sections describe the treatment of the themes of Justice and Mercy, Grace and Nature, Creation and Death. The approach will have some regard for the prevailing attitudes of Shakespeare's time, in so far as they find dramatic expression. But at no point is it intended to view the concepts independently of the characters in whose minds and passions they live and through whom they attain their dramatic validity. In Shakespeare's art neither character nor theme was fully autonomous: essence was fused with existence and the idea made incorporate in the person. Hence in a final assessment it will not be the pattern of themes, nor the character-relationships as such, but the values established through human experience in thought and action by which the play must be judged.

Justice and Mercy

Thus said the Holy One: 'If I create the world with mercy, sin will abound: and if I create it with justice, how can the world exist? Therefore I create it with both mercy and justice, and may it thus endure.'

MIDRASH, *Bereshith Rabbah.*

For the Elizabethan age, the polarity of justice and mercy was not only a matter for theological speculation, but a crucial issue to society. The title *Measure for Measure* recalls a verse in the Sermon on the Mount which had become proverbial: 'With what measure ye mete, it shall be measured to you again.' Closely linked to it in context was the command: 'Judge not, that ye be not judged.' That divine justice would be meted out to all without regard to rank or station was as much accepted doctrine as the belief in divine redemption. However, the precept not to judge presented a hard case for all concerned with the workings of secular authority. Elizabeth M. Pope's important article, 'The Renaissance Background of *Measure for Measure*',[1] describes the approach of respons-

1. *S.S.*, 2 (1949), 66–82.

ible thinkers of the time. A clear distinction was drawn between private and public spheres of life. While for private persons 'Judge not' was absolutely binding, for rulers and magistrates in their public capacity some qualification had to be inferred. As human beings they were obliged, like all men, to show mercy and forgive trespasses. But in their office they were considered to function as deputies of God on earth, or as deputies of these deputies, themselves bearing the title of 'gods'[1] and exercising under God the divine right to judge and condemn. In the words of Bishop Bilson in his coronation sermon before King James I:

> Since then Princes can not be Gods by nature, being framed of the same mettall, and in the same moulde, that others are; It foloweth directly, they are gods by Office; Ruling, Iudging, and Punishing in Gods steede, & so deseruing Gods name here on earth.[2]

The 'demi-god authority', thus balanced between the opposites of justice and mercy, saw himself as faced with a more difficult task of maintaining ethical poise than private individuals with only their own unregenerate impulses to control.

In outlining the proper rules of conduct for magistrates, Renaissance theorists were agreed that the state must concern itself with public morality. But the detailed application of this concern was not easy to prescribe. The law of the land did not follow the Mosaic Code, even though some reformers thought that it should; nor were Old Testament penalties necessarily binding for Christians. In practice, guidance was found less in the divinely inspired precepts of justice and mercy than in the classical *via media* of equity grounded on reason. Cicero's *De Officiis* and Seneca's *De Clementia*, rather than the Pentateuch or the Gospels, were the decisive authorities invoked in Sir Thomas Elyot's *The Governour*, in James I's *Basilicon Doron* and in other influential works. Midway between the extremes of rigour, characteristic of tyrants, and what Elyot termed 'vain pity', found in weaklings, lay 'a temperaunce of the mynde . . . called in Latine *Clementia*, and . . . alway ioyned with

1. The term 'gods' for rulers and judges was taken from Psalm lxxxii. 6: 'I have said, ye are gods, and all the sons of the most high', and from Exodus xxii. 9 (Geneva version, for 'judges').

2. '*A Sermon preached at Westminster before the King and Queenes Maiesties at their Coronations . . . by the Lord Bishop of Winchester* (1603), sig. A6. Commenting on Battenhouse's opinion that the Duke symbolized Christ, Miss Pope remarks: 'Any Renaissance audience would have taken it for granted that the Duke did indeed "stand for" God, but only as any good ruler "stood for" Him; and if he behaved "like power divine", it was because that was the way a good ruler was expected to conduct himself' (p. 71).

reason'.[1] Hence the true ruler or judge was not the most holy or zealous of men, but he whose reason and moderation exalted him above mere pity and passion.

The issues are clearly presented in the first scene of *Measure for Measure*, where the Duke delegates authority by investing his deputies with both 'terror' and 'love', leaving equally at their discretion 'mortality and mercy in Vienna'. With the Duke's resumption of authority in the final scene the attributes of rule revert to his keeping. Between the two, the play explores the widest range of responses to these concepts on the part of governors and governed, and the acute tensions set up by them in the personalities of all concerned.

Like Whetstone, Shakespeare presented his main story in a social setting of much contemporary relevance. Vienna was shown as 'a city much like London', with its idle gallants and cynical underworld. In the absence of strict control the appetite for wars and lechery had grown beyond accustomed bounds. Not Puritans only, but all responsible citizens would agree that it was a ruler's duty to repress 'the unbrideld lusts of mans corruption. . . Adulteries, Incests, Rapes, Robberies . . . which would overflow each Kingdome and Country, if the Princes Sword did not take due Reuenge'.[2] There was need for policy to be switched from over-indulgent laxity to a new severity; and the Duke's desire to avoid a semblance of arbitrary tyranny by leaving the task to his deputies would be understood and approved under an absolute monarchy where no two-party system automatically shielded the throne. In this situation Claudio's offence becomes a test-case of the new régime. Superficially the whole affair seems characteristic of the general state of 'too much liberty'. Claudio is introduced as an acquaintance of Mistress Overdone and one of Lucio's circle. His arrest is linked by Pompey with the enforcement of the proclamation for pulling down houses of ill-fame, and the judicial proceedings are paralleled by those against Pompey and Froth. Yet in reality Claudio's case is of a very different order. His union with Juliet was 'upon a true contract . . . she is fast my wife': the two are bound by *de praesenti* spousals, recognized by English common law as a valid marriage, and there is full intention to proceed later to a sacramental union. Morally, indeed, Claudio's conduct remains a kind of fornication, and therefore sinful: nevertheless in the eyes of a Jacobean audience secular justice should certainly temper any

1. Sir Thomas Elyot, *The Boke named The Gouernour*, ed. Stephen Croft (1883), II. 80-1.

2. Bilson, *op. cit.*, sig. C5. Cf. v. I. 316-17: 'I have seen corruption boil and bubble / Till it o'errun the stew'.

local law calling for the death penalty. Not the most zealous of
contemporary reformers seriously urged such an extreme measure
against anyone in Claudio's circumstances,[1] and a wise magistrate
would normally have seen here an obvious case for leniency, with
the marriage duly consecrated and the sin left to heaven. Instead,
the offences of Claudio and Pompey are judged by wholly incom-
patible standards, with the result that a well-intentioned young
man on the point of becoming a father is sentenced to death, and a
hardened professional bawd is discharged scot-free.

Shakespeare's duplication of deputies, without precedent in
earlier versions, is usually taken as a simple means of contrasting
Angelo's behaviour with that of a 'good' magistrate. The play's
main concern is with the excesses of rigour, and in its latter part
Escalus is indeed no more than a virtuous foil to his colleague; but
a more subtle balance is aimed at in the first two acts, where
Angelo and Escalus demonstrate respectively the extremes of
severity and 'vain pity'. The brief discussion at the beginning of
II. i serves to outline their attitudes. Angelo insists that the law
should be enforced with exemplary terror lest it fall into contempt.
Escalus replies that in some circumstances—'Had time cohered
with place, or place with wishing'—any man, even Angelo himself, might err like Claudio. Unwittingly this looks ahead to Angelo's fall, and Angelo's retort, stating his readiness to bear Claudio's
penalty should he similarly offend, is full of proleptic irony. But at
this early stage of the play the audience is scarcely aware of such
implications. More immediately apparent is the fact that the two
deputies effectively criticize one another's attitude. Angelo's concern not to 'make a scarecrow of the law' is justified later in the
same scene by the handling of the parallel case of Pompey, for
which Escalus is responsible. While Angelo's view of the law as an
engine for punishing all proven offenders takes no account of the
individual case, Escalus's claim that temptation may excuse any
man takes no account of the necessity for laws against crime.

In the court scenes of II. i and II. ii, Escalus the 'merciful man'
and Angelo the 'strict deputy' demonstrate their concepts of
justice. Infinite patience and toleration are applied by Escalus to
the confused affairs of Pompey, Froth, and Elbow. As their testimonies unfold through a haze of 'misplacings' and irrelevancies,
time, place, and all ethical distinctions lose their contours. 'Justice'

---

1. Stubbes seems to have been exceptional amongst Puritan writers in bracket-
ing fornication with adultery, rape, and incest as meriting death, and he frankly
admitted that there was no likelihood of his view being accepted. Lupton thought
public disgrace a sufficient secular punishment.

represented by Elbow, and 'Iniquity' by Pompey, seem inter-changeable and equally meaningless. The sinful trade of bawd is said to be unlawful simply because 'the law will not allow it'. Lechery, Pompey affirms, will continue in Vienna until youth is unsexed or the city unpeopled. At the close of the inquiry, the 'notorious benefactors' are dismissed with a caution which Pompey declares he has every intention of ignoring. In sharpest contrast, Angelo would limit all judicial procedure to the determination and punishment of guilt. Claudio, having infringed the law, must die 'tomorrow'. No extenuating circumstances need be considered, and since 'a dismiss'd offence would after gall', no reprieve can be entertained. What is more sinister, the execution of Claudio is seen as the first step in a policy aimed at a total eradication of the sins of the flesh. In his answers to Isabel, Angelo virtually identifies his function with that of a divine nemesis. 'Future evils', he declares, 'Are now to have no successive degrees'. All the annals of fallen man will be brought to a close, and secular justice, at least in Vienna, will become one with the justice of God. In the apposition of these scenes, the comic relaxation of unprincipled tolerance is set against the tragic constraint of terror. For Escalus, justice dissolves in the amoralism of nature: for Angelo it is impaled on the absolutes of the spirit.

But the true focus of attention is on the situation of the subject in a state where authority is abused. Claudio's youthful impulsive-ness, untaught by experience, and his 'mind of honour', shaped by family tradition rather than self-knowledge, hardly fit him for an independent stand. In the two speeches under arrest (I. ii. 112–22 and 134–44) his reaction to his own plight oscillates between the extreme attitudes of the Duke's two deputies. The first speech shows a docile acquiescence in the sentence imposed. 'The demi-god authority' is seen as rightly giving effect to 'the words of heaven', exacting vengeance and dealing measure for measure like God himself. But in the second speech Claudio indicts the tyranny of 'the new deputy now for the Duke', complains at the revival of 'the drowsy and neglected act', and sees himself as punished 'only for a name'. Both the scope of the secular power, and the spiritual implications of sin and repentance, are beyond his comprehension. Even in Act III, after learning the full extent of Angelo's infamy, he draws the naïve inference that since the deputy, 'being so wise', would not damn himself, the sin of which both he and Angelo are guilty must either be no sin at all, or else the least of the 'deadly seven'. In a choice between the moral law and the discredited semblance of authority, Claudio takes his standards from the latter.

And when, in a further emotional somersault, he falls into a state of terror at the thought of divine retribution, it may be said that he identifies God's justice with Angelo's, an essentially pagan justice that offers no hope for repentance and extends no mercy to sinners.

Claudio's vacillations are such as might be expected from a youth who has not yet developed beyond conventional responses. Isabel is intellectually his superior; she has a better grasp of principles than he; but she is possessed by a craving for spiritual absolutes unrelated to the particular occasion. In effect, this kind of immaturity results in a lack of independent approach quite comparable with Claudio's, though this is less immediately apparent because of the active part which she is called upon to take. Her rational pleading, like her brother's emotional reflexes, corresponds to the divergent attitudes of the Duke's two deputies, and even the incandescent ardour which will destroy Angelo's integrity is rather the obverse than the corrective of that judge's abstract zeal. At no point in the crucial debate of II. ii does she set forth Claudio's special case, or urge the arguments for moderation which stem from his individual plight. Her plea begins with an endorsement in principle of Angelo's proceedings. Lechery is the sin she 'most abhors' and most desires shall 'meet the blow of justice'. All she requests is that the fault should be condemned, and not her brother. Every criminal's sister, mother, or child might ask this: it amounts to a call for irrational pity subjoined to a generalized sanction of retributive justice. Angelo's reply that judges must condemn not only faults, but those who commit them, is the inevitable answer. Isabella is about to give up the suit at this point with a meek commendation of the 'just but severe law'; but urged by Lucio to appeal in more impassioned terms, she makes a second attempt. Calling on Angelo to participate in her own 'remorse', she suggests that, had her brother and Angelo changed situations, Angelo would have 'slipp'd like him'. It is a repetition of Escalus' argument for universal tolerance: 'Had time coher'd with place, or place with wishing', any man might sin; accordingly, no man should be condemned. With this plea, too, rejected, Isabella is driven on from common humanitarian considerations to the vast cosmic theme of Christian mercy. All mankind has sinned and been redeemed; let Angelo think of this, and not presume to judge. Faced with the categorical precept of the Sermon on the Mount, Angelo can only reply by an evasion of responsibility: 'It is the law, not I, condemn your brother'. The inherent tension between the personal and the social ethic is here stretched to the limit. Jacobean opinion would support Angelo in claiming that the exercise of private mercy must not supersede the divinely delegated task of administering justice in a commonwealth. On the other hand, justice could only be done by human beings to human beings. Stung by Isabella's demand for precedents to the killing of Claudio, Angelo gives full scope to his arrogant identification of secular justice with divine. He declares his apocalyptic resolve to extirpate evil and evil-doers like vipers' eggs, that the whole brood might be destroyed for ever. Isabella's answer is to burst into a furious denunciation of all human authority. Welding image to image, epithet to epithet with white-hot intensity, she reduces man in office to a grotesque caricature. 'Man, proud man' becomes no more than an angry ape whose absurd pretensions make the angels weep.

In this terrible encounter of absolutes, distorting the human image to reptilean and simian proportions, Shakespeare's dramatic empathy functions so powerfully as to make it clear that his creative energy is deeply engaged. But neither the scene nor the characters in it can be isolated from the total effect of the play. The debate between Angelo and Isabella has been described as 'The Contention of Justice and Mercy', presenting the conflict between 'Old Law' and 'New'.[1] Such morality or interlude titles imply an abstraction from the human actuality, the individual's problem of 'being in the world', which is central to Shakespearean drama. For the outcome of the debate is not the overthrow of one absolute by another, but a breakdown of personal integrity and of the social order which this sustains. The reasons for the breakdown were implicit in the Renaissance view of authority. In a Christian commonwealth, justice and mercy were not contenders, but joint supporters of the throne. On the secular plane there was neither 'Old Law' nor 'New', but the law of the land, administered in the last resort by the sovereign, himself a human being elected to rule with reason and temperance by the grace of God. Isabella's demand for judges to practise God's mercy was, in the created world, the counterpart of Angelo's claim to practise divine justice; of both it might be said, "'Tis set down so in heaven, but not in earth.' If Angelo's zeal for the eradication of sin was potentially a threat to human survival, Isabella's scorn for authority struck at the bases of order on which human society rested.[2]

1. M. C. Bradbrook, 'Authority, Truth and Justice in *Measure for Measure*', *R.E.S.*, xvi (1941), 385.

2. The analogy often drawn between Isabel's appeal to Angelo, and Portia's to Shylock, breaks down in view of the fact that Shylock, unlike Angelo, was a private individual, and, as such, bound to show mercy. To this he was enjoined

As mediator between extremes stands the Duke, 'a gentleman of all temperance'. Without the externals of sovereignty, without sanctions to enforce his will, he must deal as a man with men. Nevertheless the Duke's relationships with the other characters provide the exemplary norm of the play. The first manifestation of this is in his interview with the pregnant Juliet in II. iii. His attitude towards her is neither indulgent nor severe. She is addressed as a sinning but repentant young mother-to-be; not wholly deserving the title of 'wife' given to her by Claudio, but certainly not the 'fornicatress' of Angelo's crude description. Her readiness to 'take the shame with joy', her humble admission of guilt, coupled with love for the man that wronged her, are seen as hopeful signs that through grace the sin will be commuted to blessing. Later, in his approach to Claudio, the same concern with the individual predicament is evinced. The homily on death at the beginning of Act III is a case apart, to be considered later: there indeed the Duke is no more than an impersonal choric figure. Far more characteristic is the guidance he gives to Claudio after the dialogue between sister and brother. Claudio's impulses have led him, in his ignorance of the nature of justice, to a spiritual and moral paralysis. The Duke lifts from his shoulders all concern with 'the properties of government' as exercised by Angelo. Since the corruption of authority lies beyond the subject's power to rectify, it is best for him to preserve faith in the integrity of his superiors, and to believe that Angelo's proposition was merely a ruse 'to practise his judgment with the disposition of natures'. Claudio is bidden as a private person to prepare calmly and humbly for the divine judgment, where his case need not be seen as desperate. Meanwhile, unknown to him, his sovereign will labour to prevent the abuse of secular rule.

In a very different category are the true sinners, Pompey and his mistress. Arrested again after Escalus' over-lenient discharge, Pompey is addressed by the Duke in plain, vigorous terms. There is no generalized denunciation of vice, but rather a use of concrete physical imagery to bring home to him the 'abominable and beastly' nature of the bawd's trade. No comic equivocation is allowed after the fashion of II. i: Pompey is directed to prison for 'correction and instruction'. In the case of Mistress Overdone, Escalus himself at this juncture has learned the futility of mere tolerance. He is no longer to be wheedled as a 'merciful man'. The

---

under the 'Old' Law just as Portia was under the 'New': 'Thou shalt not hate thy brother in thine heart . . . Thou shalt not avenge . . . but thou shalt love thy neighbour as thyself' (Leviticus, xix. 17, 18).

bawd's mistress, who has not benefited from 'double and treble admonition', is packed off to prison with 'no more words'. Significantly, neither Pompey nor Overdone is regarded as meriting death; and for Pompey an opportunity arises of changing his trade to one which, in Jacobean society at least, was deemed necessary to the commonwealth. Yet, though hanging was a 'lawful trade', only the execution of one character, the self-confessed murderer Barnardine, is ordered by the Duke; an order which is represented as an error on the Duke's part and is first suspended and later rescinded. No politic benefit from the substitution of one death for another is allowed to weigh against the fact that Barnardine, like Claudio, is a living soul who must be prepared for a higher judgment before that of earthly courts is put into effect.

The Duke's wisdom is most thoroughly displayed in the finale of the play. Like Severus at Pompeii, like James I at Newark, he sets an example of justice by presiding over the trial in person. Angelo is allowed to fall into his own trap; is led to face the extreme penalty he has sought to inflict on others; and finally is saved by the Duke's act of clemency. But more is achieved than a demonstration of 'the properties of government' by the sovereign. The deeper moral of the trial is seen in its effects on the consciences of those tried. Angelo's recognition that death is his just desert at last removes the irony of his declaration to Escalus:

> When I that censure him do so offend,
> Let mine own judgment pattern out my death,
> And nothing come in partial. (II. i. 29–31)

He has regained his lost integrity as a judge; a necessary condition before clemency can be exercised that is not 'vain pity'. But the Duke further contrives that Angelo's fate should appear to depend on Isabella's pleading. She too is placed in a position which calls for a profound readjustment of values. The 'natural' urge to seek revenge for her dead brother must be converted into a desire for mercy that will benefit the living Mariana. To that end the fact that Claudio survives is withheld until she has made her decision. But the substance of her plea for Angelo is even more significant. Isabella's call for absolute mercy in the presence of false authority had produced only negative effects: now, in the presence of true authority, she balances the ethical considerations of the private person with those which must weigh with rulers. Her bid to save Angelo's life is motivated by a Christian forgiveness of private wrongs; yet at the same time the form of pleading takes due account of the judicial approach to the specific case. Angelo, she declares, was sincere and uncorrupted 'Till he did look on me'. He had offended only in thought and not in deed, whereas her brother 'did the thing for which he died'. Such arguments, grounded in legalities rather than ethics, may embarrass those who see Isabella as a paragon of holiness; yet they must always be of paramount importance where secular justice presides. Her plea is surely not designed to instruct her ruler in Christian mercy. She is in fact learning, not teaching, a lesson in public and private demeanour towards wrongdoers. The decision to show judicial clemency has already been taken by the Duke, who has himself ensured that Angelo should not commit the offences he planned, and who now pardons the culprit without disturbing the foundations of justice.

The same temperate wisdom shapes the Duke's judgments on the minor characters. Barnardine's 'earthly faults' are pardoned because his is a special case: as 'a prisoner nine years old' he should long since have been either sentenced or set free. The Provost's evasion of Angelo's injunctions is commended, but not as an instance of impulsive insubordination. Unlike Whetstone's Gaoler, the Provost only disregards the deputy's orders when shown the hand and seal of the Duke, his sovereign; even so, he has committed a personal wrong which calls for the exercise of Christian forgiveness by Angelo. Lastly there is Lucio, whose offence is to have slandered a prince. Like the one thief hanged at Newark while the other criminals were freed, for a moment Lucio appears to be the solitary victim. But it is only for a moment: then the spirit of comedy joins forces with clemency to commute his hanging to marriage.

Grace and Nature

Glory and honour appertaineth to God onely. And there is nothing so repugnant unto reason, as for us to goe about to purchase any for our selves. For, being inwardly needie and defective, and our essence imperfect, and ever wanting amendment, we ought onely labour about that. We are all hollow and emptie, and it is not with breath and words we should fill our selves.

MONTAIGNE (tr. Florio), 'Of Glory', *Essaies*, II, ch. 16

While the political issues of *Measure for Measure* were latent in all earlier versions of the story, the inner motivations of the main characters show striking departures from the source material. Angelo's precisianist zeal, Pompey's rationale of bawdry, Isabella's aspiration to the cloistered life, Lucio's 'foppery of freedom', are without precedents. Nor are they to be accounted for wholly as aspects of a more subtle individualization. The explicitness of each attitude, and the pattern of appositions and contrasts which they form, are evidence of a thematic design which adds to the political plane a further psychological dimension. The opinions as such may be related to the prevailing intellectual climate, with its cross-winds of Puritan reform agitation, Catholic traditionalism, and the late Renaissance cult of amoral naturalism. But the consistency of the design, and the complexity of its workings through the personality of each character, suggest a more fundamental concern than the mere reflection of contemporary ideas. Underlying such topicalities may be seen a dramatic treatment of the ancient concepts of grace, nature, and virtue as actualized in the experiences of individuals.

Christianity taught that man as a spiritual being was endowed with the divine gift of grace, which he might store for his soul's salvation, exercise in his dealings with his fellow-men, or decline from through sin, at his own free will. At the same time, he was also a part of the natural world, moved by the same urges and endowed with the same functions as other creatures; and in this sphere too he had the choice of conserving, exercising, or abusing his innate powers. *Measure for Measure* steers clear of theological disputes as to the relative merits of grace and good works—'grace is grace', Lucio declares, 'despite of all controversy'—but it is plainly concerned with the broader humanist problem of co-ordinating the spiritual and natural forces of personality for the welfare of man upon earth.[1] Such is the purport of the Duke's first speech to Angelo, requiring him to labour in the commonwealth:

> Thyself and thy belongings
> Are not thine own so proper as to waste
> Thyself upon thy virtues, they on thee. (I. i. 29–31)

The special measure of grace bestowed upon rulers should not be directed inwards to the cultivation of their own sanctity; virtues must 'go forth'; otherwise, ' 'twere all alike As if we had them not'. The maxim of the lighted torch, a Renaissance commonplace derived from the parable of the candlestick in Luke viii, reinforces the argument with both secular and religious overtones.[2] The next sentence of the speech adds a second consideration, drawn from another stream of ideas. Nature also enjoins the exercise of func-

1. Raymond Southall, '*Measure for Measure* and the Protestant Ethic', *Essays in Criticism*, xi (1961), 10–33, sees Grace as the central issue of the play, and believes that Shakespeare was maintaining the 'medieval', 'integrated' view as against the separation of social from spiritual grace in Catholic–Protestant controversy of the time. 'The great synthesising, integrating genius of *Measure for Measure* needs ultimately to be viewed as . . . asserting the centrality of human values' (p. 20). Southall fails to recognize that this 'centrality' belonged to the main humanist tradition of the age.

2. See note to I. i. 32–6.

tion: she is a 'thrifty goddess' who lends to man by way of invest-
ment, requiring him to use as well as enjoy his physical gifts, that
the stock of natural wealth might be enhanced.[1] This concept,
derived from Aristotelean and Senecan sources, was familiar to
Renaissance ethics and appears as a powerful influence elsewhere
in Shakespeare's work. Applied analogically both to biological and
to social functions—to both senses of 'husbandry'—it was a necessary coefficient with the operation of grace.

Bridging by its dual connotations the spiritual and natural fields
of action, and mediating between them, was virtue. This signified
a beneficent use of natural function which merited the gift of grace
as a concomitant; correspondingly, it implied a 'going forth' of
grace which might comprehend the conscientious payment of
nature's debt. Such temperance of the soul is recommended in the
Duke's precepts at the beginning of the play, and demonstrated in
his practice at the close. Through the main action, however, the
properties of grace and nature are dissociated and juxtaposed.
'Strict restraint' and 'immoderate use', the distorted attitudes of
convent and brothel, of precisian and libertine, are presented as
jarring disparates inducing a process of psychic disruption. In the
absence of virtue as a moderator, sexual function turns into the
abuse of lechery, and celibacy becomes cold-blooded self-regard.
At the spiritual level, excessive zeal is corrupted to pride, and
cloistered holiness subordinates charity to chastity. Most alarming
of all, there are the sudden slips from level to level, landslides of the
soul which transform zealot into lecher and saint into sadist.

The polarization of values follows directly upon the Duke's supposed departure from Vienna. Lucio's dialogue with his companions in I. ii amounts to a parody of the Duke's doctrine of natural
virtue. The three gallants, who fear the King of Hungary's—or any
other ruler's—peace negotiations, look upon military adventures as
their proper calling, and like the 'sanctimonious pirate' of their
joke, deem all restraint 'a commandment . . . from their functions'.
Peace, and similar manifestations of grace, belong to heaven; on
earth all trades are justified. Such amoralism, as contemporary as
the speakers, receives implicit criticism in the gentlemen's admission that they are wicked villains, 'despite of all grace', and that the
physical counterpart to their social activities, lechery, has wasted
their health and hollowed their bones. The amoralism is nevertheless sustained by Pompey, who consistently champions his own
trade of bawd against all legal restraints on the grounds that it
ministers to a natural function. Usury, an analogous trade, is said

1. See note to I. i. 36–40.

to be 'allowed'; so then should bawdry.[1] Even when driven to become a 'lawful hangman', Pompey insists that his former occupation is as much a 'mystery' as hanging.

At the opposite extreme, Angelo's zeal would inhibit any irregular functioning of nature by the direst penalties. In his application of the laws he is responsible for the pendulum swing from 'too much liberty' to a death-dealing restraint. The repression is also inward; for this the audience is prepared in advance by other characters' references to him as 'a man of stricture and firm abstinence', 'most strait in virtue', who 'scarce confesses / That his blood flows'.[2] Like the contrasted attitudes to justice and mercy, precisianism and amoralism are dramatically offset. The comic exuberance of Lucio and Pompey qualifies and is qualified by Angelo's taut righteousness, while the Duke's comments in I. iii on 'needful bits and curbs', as well as on 'seemers', challenge the validity of both. Even after Angelo as a person has been thoroughly discredited, his principles continue to be subjected to Lucio's gibes. It is impossible to extirpate lechery quite, 'till eating and drinking be put down'; Angelo's rigour would even prohibit the sparrows, creatures of nature, from building in his house-eaves.[3] At the same time Lucio's viewpoint is reduced to absurdity by his scurrilous aspersions on the Duke's kindness and charity, and his inability to recognize genuine virtue in his superiors.

These contrasts serve to frame the psychological drama, but the focus of interest is on the inner tensions and interactions of the three leading characters, Claudio, Isabella, and Angelo. To consider these persons as projections or embodiments of abstract qualities—'sense', 'spirit', 'seeming', and the like—is to ignore the process whereby each character involves the others in a total psychic impasse. In the working out of this chain-reaction the inner complexities of all three, and their subtle affinities with one another, play a necessary part.

Claudio, for all his sensual disposition, has only a tenuous connection with the exponents of 'immoderate use'. His admission to Lucio that 'too much liberty' has led him to nominal lechery is quickly followed by a declaration that he regards Juliet, in all but 'outward order', as his wife. Natural desire is coupled with virtuous intention, and could, under proper guidance, easily pass into the deeper channels where it would merge with the operations of grace. Lacking such guidance, however, Claudio's impulses easily tend to lapse back into the conditioned responses of mere instinct.

---

1. See notes to III. ii. 6–8.   2. I. iii. 12, II. i. 9, I. iii. 51–2.
3. III. ii. 99, 169–70.

Isabel's disposition, with its aspirations to celibacy and sanctity, affords an obvious contrast to Claudio's. Equally important, however, are the latent correspondences between her situation and her brother's. These are finely brought out through Lucio's role as intermediary in I. ii and I. iv, where he serves as a catalyst of underlying motives. Claudio almost at once sets himself apart from the fellowship of the brothel. Isabella likewise reveals in her dialogue with Lucio the essential disparity between her outlook and that of the convent sisters. Her first words in the scene, where as a one-day novice she calls for 'more strict restraint' in an ancient and austere order, suggest immature enthusiasm. Lucio's bluff manner of imparting his news brings out very clearly how precarious is her poise as a would-be nun. She is rendered uncomfortable by his light gallantries and ready talk of earthly kinship and procreation—'fair sister', 'unhappy brother', 'He hath got his friend with child'. And she is equally disturbed by his apologetic reference to her as 'a thing enskied and sainted'. Most indicative of all is her marked change of manner following Lucio's description of Claudio's union with Juliet:

> Your brother and his lover have embraced,
> As those that feed grow full, as blossoming time . . .

Out of character, and the more impressive as a formulation of standards, Lucio's speech is in the direct line of Reformation doctrine stemming from the arguments of Erasmus against celibacy in the classic *locus* of the *Encomium Matrimonii*.[1] Isabel's reply, 'Someone with child by him? My cousin Juliet?' is not the response of a novice, but of a typically frank-spoken Renaissance maiden, a Rosalind or a Portia. For the rest of the scene her responses cease even to approximate to those of a spiritual sister of Saint Clare. They are such as might be expected of a very natural sister of Claudio and school-friend of Juliet, already 'adoptedly' her 'cousin'. In accord with this reversion to familiar habits of thought is her impulsive comment, 'O let him marry her!' when Lucio's news sinks in. Apprised now that Claudio's life depends on her successful intercession with Angelo, and urged to use 'grace' by her 'fair prayer', she doubts her spiritual power. But she agrees to see what she can do by a use of feminine influence, which, as Lucio points out, works so potently on men. As she leaves the convent, to which she will never return, her virtuous intentions, like her brother's, are clearly apparent; but her inexperience will make the operation of her virtue in the secular world as doubtful as that of his in the realm of spiritual decision.

1. See pp. lxxxiii–lxxxv *infra*.

Isabella's condition would probably be understood by a Protestant audience of Shakespeare's age in the terms used by the first translator of *Encomium Matrimonii*: she was one of those young neophytes who would 'professe & vowe perpetuall chastyte before or they suffyciently knowe themselues and the infirmite of theyr nature'.[1] What is more, her youth and ignorance, her confusion of principle and impulse, make Isabel's very virtue dangerous to others equally blind to the workings of their inner selves, and shape her as the perfect instrument of Angelo's undoing. Her appeal to him on their first encounter in II. ii is not quite that of saint to zealot, nor is it quite that of maid to man. Perhaps either approach would have failed in its purpose; but neither would have had the same catastrophic effect upon Angelo's psyche. Instead, her plea for spiritual charity towards Claudio is transparently motivated by strong natural affection. Ethical principles are argued with hot-blooded passion. The *ad hominem* call for Angelo to acknowledge his own 'natural guiltiness' is all too plainly *a femina* and inadvertently suggestive. For the deputy's taut rectitude her approach is insidious and at last irresistible. Isabella's 'sense' causes his own 'sense' to 'breed with it'. To his horror and perplexity, zeal slips its channel and turns into an uncontrollable rush of physical desire.

In the soliloquy which ends II. ii, Angelo oscillates feverishly between his visions of Isabella, seen at one moment as a wanton temptress, at another as the incarnation of sunlike virtue, and yet again as the *diable en femme* of early Christian hagiology.[2] Before their second encounter, he is aware of having fallen from grace. Prayer and thought are disjoined; 'the state', his social position, has grown 'sere and tedious'; personal dignity no longer matters; the one remaining reality is desire. 'Blood, thou art blood.' To satisfy the call of the blood, he will 'write good angel on the devil's horn' and overthrow virtue by its own arguments.[3] By this means Angelo becomes the reciprocal instrument of Isabella's own psychic breakdown. The situation where he confronts her with the traditional infamous proposition is superficially like that of earlier versions. In essence, however, both Angelo's approach and Isabel's response differ considerably. While threats, and even an appeal for 'love' will follow, Angelo's primary argument is on ethical grounds, and corresponds with Isabel's at their previous meeting. He rounds upon her with her own plea to exercise Christian charity. Compelled sins do not rank in the reckonings of heaven; even if they did, there might be 'a charity in sin' when incurred for a brother's sake;

1. *A ryght frutefull Epystle . . . in laude and prayse of matrymony* (1532), translated by R. Tavernour; Dedicatory Epistle, sig. Aii.

2. See note to II. ii. 179–81.   3. See note to II. iv. 16–17.

or at worst, 'equal poise of sin and charity'. After her first impetuous retort, 'I had rather give my body than my soul',—a comment as revealing as 'O, let him marry her' in I. iv—Isabella proceeds, oddly for one so used to 'play with reason and discourse', to argue at cross-purposes. Her puzzled replies may be set down to maidenly innocence, or, as Angelo suspects, to wilful evasion. More useful than the guessing of motives is a recognition that the discrete nature of the dialogue serves a special dramatic end. On the one side Angelo, in a state of sin, is required to put the case for charity; on the other Isabella, the heroine, must be saved from engaging in a controversy where intellectual honours could only go to her opponent. At the abstract level of a 'contention' or *débat*, Angelo's argument was in itself entirely valid. 'Compelled sins' were indeed 'no sins', by Christian doctrine, by common consent, and by the literary precedent of Andrugio's similar assurance to Cassandra.[1] Isabella's avoidance of a commitment looks ahead to an ultimate position quite unlike Cassandra's, while not extenuating Angelo's villainy. At the same time the explicit statement of the familiar maxim regarding 'compelled sins' prepares for a later assessment of how valid her position may be.

Isabella's dismay when she perceives Angelo's drift is as 'natural' as the responses of Cassandra, Epitia, and others. What makes her conduct unique is her inability to surmount this initial reaction. Twentieth-century critics have weighed her intransigence by their own scales of values. They have either praised her for her spiritual integrity or condemned her for her lack of 'feeling'. What would surely have been evident to an earlier age is the fact that her stance is occasioned by no true principle. If lay heroines in previous versions of the story were commended for setting aside the thought of shame in order to save a brother's or a husband's life, the novice of a spiritual order might also overcome the fear of disgrace in the world's eyes and manifest true grace by a sacrifice made in self-oblivious charity. Chastity was essentially a condition of the spirit; to see it in merely physical terms was to reduce the concept to a mere pagan scruple. Yet this is indeed what Isabel's attitude implies. She is in a situation parallel with Angelo's at their previous meeting. Ethical arguments again carry sexual overtones, this time of male aggression rather than feminine entreaty, and her response is as perplexed as his had been. Dramatically, sympathy for Isa-

---

1. 'Compelled sins no sins' was proverbial (Tilley S 475). Cf. Bodin, *La Demonomanie*, IV. 516-17: 'Car le peché n'est point peché, s'il n'est volontaire, comme dit S. Augustin . . . se peut bien accommoder ce que dit Seneque en la tragedie de Thyeste, quem peccasse poenitet, penè est innocens'. In I *Prom.*, III. iv, Andrugio declares, 'For in forst faultes is no intent of yll'.

bella is preserved at the human level on account of her helplessness and Angelo's crude threats; but the scene ends with a soliloquy which should leave no one in doubt as to Isabella's psychic confusion. Horror of physical violation has become identified with concern for chastity, and is taken to justify a refusal of Angelo's demands at all costs. Accordingly 'shame' not sin, 'honour' not charity, are seen now as the all-important considerations, and Claudio's duty to Isabella as superseding her duty to him.[1] Her brother is no longer to be thought of as a victim to be rescued but as a potential chivalrous protector; his moral lapse is condoned as due to 'prompture of the blood'—a defence as valid as Angelo's own 'Blood, thou art blood'—and his 'mind of honour' is praised because it alone can redeem his sister's body from 'abhorr'd pollution'. In this transvaluation of values, chastity is yoked not to charity but to 'honour'. Standards have slipped down from a spiritual plane to the level of a brittle social code where nobility is the true virtue and chastity is an aspect of physical self-regard.

The climax of the inner drama is reached when all three characters, like roped climbers, are overwhelmed in the psychological landslide. Isabella visits Claudio, bearing the 'comfort' of Angelo's proposition. Her sole concern now is to make her brother evince the 'mind of honour' which alone can save her from what she most dreads; and in her appeal to him all other considerations become abstract, figurative, and emotively simplified. Death, for which Claudio is told to prepare, is put to him in a semi-jocular conceit: he is to be appointed as Angelo's perpetual ambassador to heaven. Life, the alternative he must reject, is described as 'everlasting durance' in the world-wide prison of dishonour. Claudio, however, is gradually awakening from the state of resignation induced in him by the Duke's homily. Behind his sister's circumlocutions, which he excuses as due to her 'flowery tenderness', he perceives more and more clearly that he has been offered a direct choice between life and death; between the world of nature that he knows, and the unknown world of spirit for which he is still unprepared. With growing alarm at his requests to know the concrete details of Angelo's offer, Isabel inveighs against his cowardice and dwells at the same time upon the 'perpetual honour' which he can earn. Mechanically Claudio gives verbal assent. He is the son of 'a most

1. 'From now on, Isabella bases her words and her conduct not on religious doctrine, . . . but on the secular code of honour which rated a woman's chastity as the *conditio sine qua non* of her own honourable reputation and that of her whole family'. Alice Shalvi, 'The Concept of Honour in Shakespeare's Problem Plays' (unpublished dissertation, Univ. of Jerusalem, 1962), typescript p. 240.

noble father' and does not question the social code of his upbring-
ing. But now, in his extreme predicament, he no longer finds in
honour the supreme virtue that can fortify his soul against death.
Claudio's outburst, 'Ay, but to die, and go we know not where', is
not occasioned, as Isabella's taunts would suggest, by a coward's
fear of the pain of dying, the universal experience common to man
and 'the poor beetle that we tread upon'. It springs from the deeper
fear of an unresolved soul confronted with all the uncertainties of
the world to come. Desperate, and aware in desperation that his
sister could save him if she would, he invokes the natural bond of
kinship as Andrugio and Vico had done in their turn.

> Sweet sister, let me live.
> What sin you do to save a brother's life,
> Nature dispenses with the deed so far
> That it becomes a virtue.   (III. i. 132–5)

For Isabella, this is the second male solicitation in a short space
of time. Angelo's arguments for charity are now complemented by
Claudio's plea for kindness. Both men require her to exercise 'virtue', spiritual or natural: both would drive her over the brink into
insupportable shame. Her compulsive reaction is a half-coherent
hysterical diatribe in which her brother is transfigured into a sub-
human lecher impelled by the monstrous urges of the brothel. A
'beast', a 'faithless coward', the unnatural son of her honourable
father, he would incestuously ingender his own life out of his sister's
disgrace. To show mercy to him would be to act as his bawd: he
must 'die, perish'; she will pray 'ten thousand prayers' for his
death, no word to save him.

To this extremity Isabella's passion for spiritual absolutes, her
craving to be 'a thing enskied and sainted', have led her. At the
climax of the drama there is no blurring of the ethical issues.
Charity of spirit, natural kindness—'virtue' in its dual manifestation—are overlaid by an essentially pagan notion of chastity and
honour which, in the eyes of the reformed church, was more damnable than the sins of Mistress Overdone. Critics who ask us to forget
our modern liberalism and judge Isabella by the standards of an
'age of belief' should bear in mind Tyndale's opinion of Lucrece as
a martyr to pagan chastity:

> She sought her owne glory in her chastite and not gods. When
> she had lost her chastyte, then counted she her selfe most ab-
> hominable in the sight of al men, and for very payne and
> thought which she had, not y^t she hath displeased god but y^t she
> had lost here honour, slew her self. Loke how great her glory and
> reioycing therin, and moch despised she them that wer other-

wise, and pytied them not, which pryde god more abhorreth then the whordome of anye whor.[1]

A real-life Isabella, despising Claudio for his unwillingness to sacrifice himself for his sister's 'glory', would surely have received scant sympathy from Shakespeare's contemporaries. Yet in the world of the drama there is no call for her character to be either defended or condemned. *Measure for Measure* as a tragicomedy is concerned with error, not evil; with correction, not retribution. Shakespeare's unique turn to the Corrupt Magistrate story, inverting the heroine's traditional decision to sacrifice her chastity for her brother's life, presupposes the intervention at this point of a true arbiter of values. It is in the nature of the play that Isabella's personality, like the personalities of Claudio and of Angelo, should seem neither 'good' nor 'bad', but basically self-ignorant, with inner tensions stretched to the point of moral collapse before the process can be reversed and a new psychic integration achieved.[2]

True virtue, like true authority, rests in the Duke. Dramatic convention may set the action in a foreign city where the 'old religion' prevails; yet the ruler of Vienna combines spiritual with secular powers like a sovereign of the reformed church. His direction of the moral conduct of individuals, his exculpation of Isabel and Mariana, take their ethical validity from this fact. Thus the Duke's activities in his disguise as friar appear neither incongruous nor sacrilegious, as they might have done to a Catholic audience, but as a fitting manifestation of his dual role as the head of church and state. Similarly the use of dissimulation, and the professed right to apply 'craft against vice' in frustrating Angelo's designs, were justified both in theory and in the practice of the ruling monarch, when exercised in the interest of the subject. It is thus as an acknowledged exemplar of virtue that the Duke applies principle and practice to the near-tragic situation.

Intervention is withheld until the climax of Act III, with the exception of the brief interview with Juliet in II. iii. Here the Duke's aim was to elicit rather than instil virtue. Juliet is actually in no need of moral guidance. She 'carries sin' and 'bears shame', discovering the spiritual resources of penitence and patience, and a

1. William Tyndale, *The Obedyence of a Chrysten Man* (ed. 1561), fol. 39ʳ. Cf. T. Carew, *Certaine godly and necessarie Sermons* (1603): '*Lucretia* and certaine Heathen women killed themselues that they might not be defiled with Souldiers, not knowing that the bodye is not defyled, if the minde bee chaste' (sig. M3).

2. D. A. Traversi has written of Isabel and Angelo: 'Virtue, as each of them conceives it, is still a partial and abstract thing, still an imposition of the reason planted a little aridly upon a whole world of sentiments and reactions which remain outside it' (*Scrutiny*, XI (1942), 52).

natural joy arising from her condition as an expectant mother. Her love for Claudio is as great as her love for herself; her repentance is directed towards heaven out of charity not fear. In this state only the blessing 'Grace go with you' is required. Juliet is not so much a 'case' for the Duke as a pattern for her lover Claudio, whose penitence is deeply tinged with fear, and for Isabel, whose dread of shame has corrupted her virtue.

For Claudio and Isabella more drastic measures are needed. Claudio's spiritual fears must be allayed from within; but as a preliminary the external standards which have collapsed must be restored in his mind. The Duke therefore assures him that his disillusionment was itself illusory. Angelo as a wise magistrate had merely made an 'assay' of Isabella's virtue; and she, 'having the truth of honour in her', had properly returned a 'gracious denial'. Virtue, truth, honour, and grace are back in their familiar places; the world stands on its traditional moral foundations; and the responsibility falls squarely upon Claudio to resolve his spirit for what must inevitably and rightly befall. The young man replies at once that he will ask pardon of Isabella and welcome death. The resolution is approved, and an opportunity is provided for a silent reconciliation with his sister.[1]

Isabella's psychic problem is more complex, and the Duke's ministrations are prolonged to the end of the play. From him she now receives soothing praise—together with a much-needed affirmation of the true hierarchy of values. Grace, she is told, is the 'soul' of her 'complexion', which will keep the body of it ever fair. This is a far cry from Isabella's obsession with 'shame' and 'pollution'. The Duke adds that 'Virtue is bold, and goodness never fearful.' With virtue thus distinguished from mere fastidiousness, the plan is outlined. For Isabella it involves two errands to be undertaken in person, both of which will call for physical and moral courage. In terms of plot-mechanics, it may be noted, Isabella's participation was by no means necessary: a message to Angelo, and the Duke's own visit to Mariana, would have been enough to operate the substitution device. Instead, even at the cost of some awkward staging in IV. i, Isabella must go to Angelo in person, report back, and instruct Mariana on her part in the deception. In keeping with the tenor of the Duke's first speech to Angelo, Isabella is being re-educated in the function of virtue as an active force in the world.

In the last act the demonstration of justice becomes at the same time an 'assay of virtue'. Angelo is made to undergo a subtle re-enactment of the psychological drama in the first part of the play.

1. See p. xxvi *supra*.

Ironically, his situation finally corresponds to Claudio's; he is guilt-stricken and contrite, facing a seemingly irrevocable sentence of death. In this condition, however, he acknowledges the supremacy of the Duke's grace, rightly comparable with 'power divine', and declares death to be the only grace he himself deserves. Mariana, the victim of his 'unjust unkindness', has had her honour, as conventionally understood, restored by marriage to Angelo, and is promised his possessions after the execution to 'buy her a better husband'. All egotistic motives for clinging to the match have been removed: yet, in face of the full exposure of Angelo's villainy, Mariana both forgives him and intercedes for his life, desiring 'no other nor no better man'. Like Juliet, she has converted infatuation into a selfless love that is truly charitable and merits grace. Lastly, Isabella is put to a many-sided test. Kept in ignorance of Claudio's survival, she has been made to proclaim in IV. iii the very passions of grief and revenge experienced by Epitia and Cassandra in similar circumstances. Driven on by these, she submits in Act v to even worse conditions than Epitia and Cassandra had faced; exposing herself to public shame; proclaiming to the world that she had let her sisterly remorse confute her honour; having her testimony scornfully dismissed; even undergoing physical arrest and indignity. The evolution is completed by the transcendence of both grief and revenge. In the end, Mariana's virtue calls forth Isabella's, so that, despite the Duke's reminder of the code of family honour,[1] Isabella joins in the appeal for her enemy's life. The chain-reaction whereby in the first part of the play three characters drew each other down into psychic disintegration is completely reversed, so that Mariana, Isabel, and Angelo achieve a mutual rehabilitation.

Creation and Death

> The good gentyll woman your mother is departed . . . your syster for sorowe and desyre is entred in to a hous of barren nunnys . . . the hope of your stocke is turned onely vnto you.
>
> ERASMUS (tr. Taverner), *Encomium Matrimonii*[2]

Such, in Taverner's translation, was the declared occasion for Erasmus' *Encomium Matrimonii*, written in the form of an epistle advising a friend to marry. Whether by accident or design, Shakespeare chose a parallel situation in *Measure for Measure*. The parents of Isabel and Claudio are dead; upon the marriages of

---

1. v. i. 431–4.
2. *A ryght frutefull Epistle . . . in laude and prayse of matrymony* (1532), sig. Aiii. On the historical importance of *Encomium Matrimonii*, see Emile V. Telle, *Erasme de Rotterdam et le Septième Sacrement* (1954). The *Encomium* was also translated by Sir Thomas Wilson in his *Arte of Rhetorike* (1553).

brother and sister the continuity of their house depends; yet at the beginning of the play one is about to enter a convent and the other to die for begetting a child. Fundamental to all issues of political justice and private morality was the categorical necessity for human survival. Reformation thinkers regarded the precept 'Increase and multiply' as the first of the divine commandments, enjoined upon Adam after the Fall and repeated to Noah after the Flood.[1] It was qualified, not superseded, by the law of Moses and the gospel of Christ, which prescribed a code of sexual ethics. Sin was to be punished; earthly rulers were entrusted with the divine prerogatives of justice and mercy; but the primary injunction to breed might not be abrogated by any principle of morality or law.

That Shakespeare was influenced by these views can hardly be doubted. In the archetypal wooing of *Venus and Adonis* the goddess of love shows a clear cognizance of the Reformation outlook:

> Therefore despite of fruitless chastity,
> Love-lacking vestals and self-loving nuns,
> That on the earth would breed a scarcity
> And barren dearth of daughters and of sons,
> Be prodigal ...   (751 ff.)

Similarly in *A Midsummer Night's Dream*, Theseus counsels Hermia to avoid 'the livery of a nun' and choose marriage as the 'earthlier happy' condition. The first group of the Sonnets, in many ways indebted to Erasmus' arguments,[2] warns the Friend against celibacy in universal terms:

> If all were minded so, the times should cease,
> And three score year would make the world away.   (xi)

Claudio's union with Juliet, in contrast, is described by Lucio as one of the beneficent works of nature, as normal as the act of eating, the coming of spring, the cultivation of the soil:

> As those that feed grow full, as blossoming time
> That from the seedness the bare fallow brings
> To teeming foison, even so her plenteous womb
> Expresseth his full tilth and husbandry.   (i. iv. 41 ff.)

Lucio's attitude is implicitly endorsed in the Provost's description of Claudio as 'A young man / More fit to do another such offence / Than die for this' (ii. iii. 13–15)—an opinion not contested by the

---

1. See Taverner, sig. A6ʳ–7ʳ; William Harrington, *The Commendacion of Matrymony* (1528), sig. Aiiᵛ; Bullinger, *The Christen State of Matrimony*, trans. Miles Coverdale, ed. 1546, sig. A3ᵛ–4ᵛ.
2. See J. W. Lever, *The Elizabethan Love Sonnet* (1956), 190–6.

Duke. Death for procreation is considered a monstrous penalty by virtuous and disreputable characters alike. While Pompey sees Angelo's policy as a threat to destroy 'all the youth of the city' (II. i. 227–8), Isabella describes the deputy as one who 'Nips youth i' th' head and follies doth enew' (III. i. 90). Lucio's comment on Claudio's 'vice', that 'it is impossible to extirp it quite . . . till eating and drinking be put down' (III. ii. 98–9), complements his earlier image, 'As those that feed grow full', and also suggests in the word 'extirp' a design for the destruction of the human race. Angelo's rigour, which would virtually turn justice into genocide,[1] exemplifies what the author of *Basilicon Doron* termed 'extreame tyrannie delighting to destroy all mankinde'.[2]

The viewpoint of the strict deputy is most explicitly put in the following lines:

> It were as good
> To pardon him that hath from nature stolen
> A man already made, as to remit
> Their saucy sweetness that do coin heaven's image
> In stamps that are forbid.   (II. iv. 42–6)

Sinful procreation was thus seen by Angelo as tantamount to murder. While the latter was the theft of a life from nature, the former stole the divine image, the soul of man, from heaven. Such casuistry ignored both the part of spirit in the created world and the difference between human power and divine. Murder was not only a theft from nature but a violation of man's divinely appointed right to life. Procreation, however, stole from neither nature nor God. 'Heaven's image' could not be spuriously put into the world, since human souls, whether in nature or in heaven, remained always in the divine keeping. While unconsecrated begetting was indeed a sin, procreation as such was in no way analogous to murder, and temporal authority might not equate the making of life to its destruction.

On the polarity of creation and death, all the issues of *Measure for Measure* ultimately turn. Throughout the play the theme is tirelessly reiterated. Unlike Whetstone's Polina or the unnamed mistress in Cinthio, Juliet is about to bear a child. Lucio's drab, too, was 'with child by him'; even Mistress Elbow in Pompey's rambling story is 'with child' and 'great-bellied'. Against this, Claudio 'must die', Barnardine 'must die', Angelo is sentenced to death, and Lucio to whipping and hanging, before they are reprieved; Abhorson the hangman is a visible presence of death and Pompey changes his trade from bawd to hangman's assistant. Figuratively, gestation

---

1. See especially II. ii. 91–100.   2. *B.D.*, 87.

and birth are set against disease and death. The Duke's haste to depart from Vienna is 'of so quick condition'; the brothels of the city will 'stand for seed'; Claudio's delay in consecrating his marriage was 'for propagation of a dower'; Juliet 'carries' her sin and 'bears' her shame; Angelo's heart contains 'the strong and swelling evil of his conception', and he arranges his rendezvous with Isabella 'upon the heavy middle of the night'. As against this, Overdone complains of the war, the sweat and the gallows; Lucio and his companions have pilled scalps and hollow bones; Claudio finds that men die of too much liberty 'like rats that ravin down their proper bane'; Claudio is told 'at dead midnight' that at eight he must die; Ragozine is dead 'of a most cruel fever'.

Furthermore, the opposed concepts are fused in imagery and word-play. Isabella expresses her readiness to die in erotic terms:

> Th' impression of keen whips I'd wear as rubies,
> And strip myself to death as to a bed
> That longing have been sick for . . . (II. iv. 101–3)

So does Claudio, with recollections of his marriage night:

> I will encounter darkness as a bride
> And hug it in mine arms.   (III. i. 83–4)

In the idiom of the time, the word 'die' had itself a sexual connotation, and the iterative phrase 'must die' carried grimly ironical overtones as applied to Claudio's plight. The quibbles on 'head' by Lucio and Pompey give this word, too, an equivocal sense, so that the cutting off of heads also suggests the act of procreation.[1] A particularly wide range of meaning is evoked by the phrase 'made a man'. Isabella begs Angelo to think of man's creation, fall, and redemption, which will cause him to breathe mercy 'like man new made'. Angelo regards murder as the theft of 'a man already made'. Claudio is accused by his sister of wishing to be 'made a man' out of her 'vice'. Pompey's whores are 'Pygmalion's images newly made woman'. Claudio is told by the Provost: "'Tis now dead midnight, and by eight tomorrow / Thou must be made immortal'. Turning upon the hub of one phrase, death and life sweep in a great arc through the worlds of nature and spirit, time and eternity.

Man upon earth is the focus of dramatic conflict, but the perspective is infinite. Created in sin, yet subject to redemption, man is at once a mortal and immortal being. He is commanded to live and breed in the world; at the same time his life is a journey to immortality. As a creature he must accept the law of nature and 'take the shame with joy'; as the 'glassy essence' reflecting heaven

1. See I. ii. 161–3, IV. ii. 1–4, and footnotes.

he must prepare his soul for death. To reject the polarity, to be 'absolute for death' in contempt of nature, or insistent upon life in disregard for, or dread of, the afterlife, is to shrink from man's dual role and be 'unfit to live or die'. At the crisis of *Measure for Measure*, these are the alternatives facing Claudio. He is placed in a situation analogous to that of Everyman; yet, as is characteristic of Shakespearean drama, the traditional morality presentation undergoes a profound change.

Superficially the Duke's homily to Claudio, 'Be absolute for death', might seem to be a statement of 'doctrine' by Holy Church in the guise of a friar. Its catalogue of the vanities of life recalls the spiritual exercise of the *ars moriendi*.[1] Similarly Claudio's reflections on the after-life, 'Ay, but to die', suggest the *contemplatio mortis* which formed the second part of the exercise. Considered more closely, both speeches are subtle distortions, and the 'doctrine' is to be found in neither. The Duke's description of the human condition eliminates its spiritual aspect and is essentially materialist and pagan. By Christian teaching, man's breath, far from being 'servile to all the skyey influences', came to him from God. His nobility and valour, happiness and certainty, were not 'nurs'd by baseness', but were spiritual qualities permeating natural life. The self was no Lucretian amalgam of 'grains / That issue out of dust', but an immortal soul. Even on the natural plane, though riches, health, and friendship might prove illusory, offspring was to be seen as a consolation and blessing. Moreover, Claudio's reflections form an equally heretical counterpart. Lucretian in its concept of both soul and body resolved after death into the four elements, it adds to this the pagan superstition, derided by Lucretius, of the afterlife as a state of eternal affliction.[2] Reacting against the call to be 'absolute

1. See Sister Mary Catharine O'Connor, *The Art of Dying Well* (1942). The *Ars Moriendi* was printed by Caxton in 1490, and later by Pynson and de Worde. Amongst other works in the tradition were: Hoccleve, *Dialogue XXIII*; Sir Thomas More, *The Four Last Things*; Erasmus, *De Preparatione ad Mortem*; Miles Coverdale, *A Treatise on Death*; Thomas Lupset, *A Treatise of Dying Well*; Innocent III, *The Mirror of Mans Lyfe* (trans. H. K., 1576); Becon, *The Sicke Mannes Salve*; Christopher Sutton, *Disce Mori: Learne to Die*; Peter Luccensis, *A Dialogue of Dying Wel* (trans. R. Verstegan, 1604). The image of life on earth as a prison sentence appears in More; T. Carew, *Sermons*, sig. O8, sees death as worse than 'Bridewell and the Hospitall, where men are whipt at their comming in and at their going out onely'. Hoccleve's dialogue is between a sinful young man 'vnready hens to hye' and a religious disciple; Luccensis' dialogue, between a merchant and a hermit.

2. See L. C. Martin, 'Shakespeare, Lucretius and the Commonplaces', *R.E.S.*, xxi (1945), 174–82. According to Martin, Claudio 'reflects . . . the mental state of the man who, according to Lucretius, has failed to banish care because he cannot use himself to the thought of complete extinction'. Palingenius (trans.

for death' out of disgust for life, Claudio is 'absolute for life' through horror of the world to come.[1]

It would be a mistake to see in these complementary distortions an expression of ultimate cynicism or despair. Neither speech provides an objective standpoint for judging the events of the play. Our attention is centred, not on the validity of the Duke's homily or of Claudio's reflections, but on the personal crisis of Claudio and Isabella, which mounts in the sixty-two intervening lines and comes to its peak in Isabella's outburst. The dramatic purpose of the two generalizing passages is to set this crisis of individuals in a universal perspective. With the equally distorted concepts of justice and mercy, chastity and charity, as presented in II. ii and II. iv, their negations reinforce the tragic predicament of the major characters Angelo, Isabella, and Claudio. At this turning-point of the play, when all principles seem lost and the significance of authority, virtue, and life itself is called in question, the Duke intervenes.

Through the Duke's practical wisdom, the tragic knot is untied. Events are directed into a new course and the characters are made to rectify their erroneous values. For Claudio the two roads, to life on earth and to immortality, are again opened up. The true spiritual exercise to prepare him for death is, first, to ask his sister's pardon, and then, to go on his knees before God. Meanwhile, through the Duke's efforts, his survival in the world of nature is to be assured, that he may fulfil his function in life through consecrated marriage and offspring. For this to come about, however, it was necessary to meet Angelo's demands by substituting another man's

---

B. Googe in 1576 as *The Zodiake of Life*) imitates Lucretian allusions to punishment after death as well as his sceptical attribution of such fears to the lies of ancient poets. Cf. Lupset, *op. cit.*, sig. M8^{r–v}: 'as to the fayning poetes, y^t speake of . . . diuers sore turmentes for vngracious soules after this life, mooste parte of olde clerkes gaue no maner of credence . . . much doubtfulnes was in theyr belefe'. Claudio's speech, and its mention of 'lawless and incertain thought', is read in the context of classical belief by T. W. Baldwin, *S.Q.*, 1 (1950), 296: Claudio speaks 'in terms of neither Christian hell nor Roman Catholic purgatory, but of the classical triple purgation by air, water, and fire'. Baldwin derives this from Virgil, with additions from Cicero's *Tusculans*. If, however, Claudio expresses the Lucretian attitude as seen through sixteenth-century eyes, both his fears and the tinge of scepticism are to be viewed as essentially pagan because 'ungracious', i.e. lacking the Christian belief in grace, which can redeem the soul from a hell that is nevertheless actual and unfeigned.

1. Lupset condemned as 'shamfull cowardnes' the extreme fear of men who would 'suffre al wretchednes, al beggari al peyn . . . to abide a while in this light', but allowed 'a mean measur of feare in death, that may be rekened honest and iuste because nature maketh it necessarie' (sig. M5^{r–v}). Sutton similarly permitted 'a moderate fear', so long as it did not regard death as 'the utter ruin and overthrow of all our being' (80).

head for Claudio's. Adequate provision had been made for the device in the dramas of Cinthio and Whetstone; but Shakespeare gave it a new turn by introducing the episode of Barnardine, with its peculiar dramatic significance.

In the view of Raleigh, Charlton, and others, Barnardine was 'a mere detail of the machinery', who should have died but 'blustered his way into Shakespeare's sympathy'.[1] This rather sentimental explanation can hardly be sustained. Barnardine was in fact no part of the original machinery taken over from Whetstone. The substitution device in *Promos and Cassandra* had been the provision by Andrugio's Gaoler of 'A dead mans head, that suffered th' other day'.[2] For this, the Shakespearean equivalent was clearly not the head of Barnardine, but of Ragozine, the pirate who had conveniently died on the morning when a substitution was required. But if Shakespeare had at first intended a variation in the shape of Barnardine, and then, reluctant to kill his new creation, had fallen back on a close correspondence with Whetstone's device, some other reason must be sought than an emotional attachment to a character with a stage life of not more than a few minutes. Much trouble had been taken in iv. ii to point out the suitability of Barnardine as a substitute for Claudio. His execution had been specifically ordered by Angelo; 'advice' of a spiritual kind would be wasted upon him; he was a self-confessed criminal; and in the view of the Provost it was he, not Claudio, who deserved to die:

> Th' one has my pity; not a jot the other,
> Being a murderer, though he were my brother.
>
> (iv. ii. 59–60)

These lines deliberately invoke a parallel and contrast between Claudio, the brother who deserved pity, and Barnardine who, even were he a brother, would deserve none. By implication they also counter Angelo's argument that Claudio's offence was tantamount to murder. Everything said would suggest to an audience the justice of executing an obdurate old murderer in place of a young man whose only crime was to have begotten a child. Had the execution of Barnardine been simply announced in the next scene, no sense of strain or moral outrage would have been felt, and the point would have been made that murder was incomparably more heinous than procreation.

Nevertheless, Barnardine does survive, despite all the convincing reasons given in iv. ii for the substitution of his head for Claudio's.

1. Walter Raleigh, *Shakespeare* (1907), 148–9; cf. H. B. Charlton, *Shakespearean Comedy* (1938), 215–17.
2. *1 Prom.*, iv. v.

One can only suppose that his appearance and refusal to die in
IV. iii express a change of intention so compelling as to have made
the further recourse to Ragozine seem worth while.[1] What gave the
episode significance was neither Barnardine's wit nor his personality, but his insistence on not dying today 'for any man's persuasion'. His reason, that he wished to be better 'prepared', introduces
a further parallel to Claudio's case; but it is unconvincing after
what is known of his conduct in the prison. The basic need for
Barnardine's existence on the stage was surely that he might assert
the major truth, that no man's life was so worthless as to be sacrificed to another's convenience. For a vivid moment the Duke, elsewhere the paragon of rulers, is revealed in his fallibility and exposed to the laughter of comedy. Barnardine's appearance and
survival demonstrate that, at the level of the individual's right to
live, authority must accept its limits. Otherwise even the most
sagacious of Dukes will incur 'God's scorn for all men governing'.

Through the rest of the play the Duke's remedial function works
according to plan. Justice is suitably combined with mercy, and
the comic form ensures that in this joint operation no character will
suffer death. True virtue is evinced in Mariana and Isabel, as previously in Juliet and Claudio. As for Angelo and Lucio, the extreme
precisianist and the extreme libertine, comedy required that their
lives should be spared; but the essentially Shakespearean approach
which typifies the whole play governs the manner of their sparing.
'Pure' satire might well have condemned these two to a public
whipping, for good measure in the same cart. Instead, both men are
required to obey the 'Commandment of Adam', qualified by the
sacrament of marriage. Finally, marriage is adopted as the true
way of life by the Duke, who had previously thought himself
immune to 'the dribbling dart of love', and by Isabella, whose
intention had been to take vows of celibacy. Modern critics have
too often found bathos in this solution. It has been said that Isabella
gladly jettisoned her principles at the prospect of marrying a Duke;
of Shakespeare, that he readily sacrificed the serious issues of his
play for a conventional peal of wedding bells. Both the character
and her creator may be fairly exonerated. Isabella's vocation as a
nun had seemed doubtful from the very first scene where she
appeared, perhaps from the first lines she spoke. Through four
subsequent acts she had undergone a process of moral education

1. Mary Lascelles, who argues well against the views of Raleigh and Charlton
(pp. 109-13), is of the opinion that 'Barnardine was never intended to die in the
play'. If a parallel between the Duke's preparing of Claudio for death and his
efforts to save him is to be seen in this episode, we should also need to see a
penitent Barnardine in IV. iii, and a Duke in full control of the situation.

designed to reshape her character. Dowden's comments may be thought to show a clearer understanding of the traditional Protestant attitude than is displayed by some present-day writers:

> She [Isabella] has learned that in the world may be found a discipline more strict, more awful than the discipline of the convent; . . . that the world has need of her; her life is still a consecrated life; the vital energy of her heart can exert and augment itself through glad and faithful wifehood, and through noble station more fully than in seclusion.[1]

Beside this may be set the opinion of one of the founders of the English Reformation:

> Let other prayse yᵉ kynd of lyfe, whereby mankynd decayeth and in processe of tyme shoulde be vtterly destroyed, yet wyll I commend that manner of lyfe, which begetteth and bryngeth forth to vs excelent kinges, noble Princes, Pryncelyke Dukes . . .[2]

Whatever Shakespeare's religion may have been, the main body of his work from the early comedies to *The Tempest* suggests that in his view consecrated marriage signified not only the 'happy ending' to a play but the gateway to man's fulfilment of his primary function in the natural world. The proper finale for a tragicomedy was at the same time the fitting solution to the basic human predicament.

3. CONCLUSIONS

Measure for Measure stands out amongst the dramas of Shakespeare's middle years for its equal emphasis upon the forces of discord and harmony. The tense antagonisms of the play's first half are subsequently woven into as close a texture of issues reconciled. This dual process is implied in the title itself, with its two connotations of weight set against weight and of a mutual tempering of extremes.[3] Twentieth-century taste, in art as in life, welcomes the discordant and the extreme, but is insensitive to the virtues of the mean: understandably, most modern critics have been preoccupied with the tensions in the earlier part of the play, and have projected upon Shakespeare an unlikely degree of sanctity or cynicism. Their reactions might seem to bear out the description of *Measure for Measure* as a 'problem play' in terms of a recent definition:

1. Edmund Dowden, *Shakespere: A Critical Study of His Mind and Art* (1875), 84.
2. Bullinger, *The Christen State of Matrimony*; from Becon's Preface, sig. A3.
3. 'The title hits closer to the actual play if it is taken as a praising of the Aristotelean mean . . . the hope for man is that measured or temperate action may meet with a like response' (Stauffer, *Shakespeare's World of Images*, 156).

A play in which we find a concern with a moral problem which is central to it, presented in such a manner that we are unsure of our moral bearings, so that uncertain and divided responses to it in the minds of the audience are possible and even probable.[1]

But this is to lay undue stress on part of the structure, and one may fairly suppose that the response of Jacobean audiences to the play as a whole was less equivocal. The first years of James's reign were marked by a profounder questioning, but also by more explicit affirmations, than Elizabethan times; and the need to hold on firmly to a middle way in the church, the state, and in private life was repeatedly stressed by the king himself. In this climate of ideas the mixed form of tragicomedy, exploring the double process of conflict and conciliation, would prove morally and aesthetically satisfying.

Yet the pattern of ideas, though firm and subtle, is not to be equated with the play's full dramatic truth. *Measure for Measure* is intensely concerned with the nature of authority, the workings of the psyche, and the predicament of man faced with the universal facts of procreation and death: but it is in the nature of Shakespearean drama that all such issues are taken up into the greater mystery of the actual individual. The art is 'incarnational', to borrow Graham Hough's useful term; and the play's true greatness is felt wherever its concepts are, in Hough's phrase, 'completely absorbed in character and action and completely expressed by them'.[2] Isabella is too complex a personality to be thought of as the static embodiment of Holiness or Chastity. At the beginning she aspired to the life of the cloister, but in the end she finds her vocation in marriage to the Duke: the rationale of either way of life turns upon its relationship to the inner laws of her being. Angelo's precisianism is sincere at the outset; under stress he proves to be a 'seemer'; ultimately he repents and is forgiven. Clearly he is much more than a personification of Zeal or Hypocrisy, Puritanism or False Authority, though at times evincing all these traits.[3] Even

---

1. E. Schanzer, *The Problem Plays of Shakespeare*, 6.

2. *A Preface to 'The Faerie Queene'* (1962), 107.

3. Several writers have seen the play as a treatment of Puritanism. Mary Suddard, 'The Poet and The Puritan', *Contemporary Review* (December 1909), viewed *Measure for Measure* as 'the supreme study of Puritanism in its essence, detached from all external accidents'. Donald J. McGinn, 'The Precise Angelo', *J. Q. Adams Memorial Studies* (1948), 129–39, regarded it as a 'contrast between the vindictiveness of Angelo and the loving-kindness of Isabella, between the Old Law and the New, between Puritanism and the Old Faith'. For A. A. Smirnov, *Shakespeare: A Marxist Interpretation* (1936), the play was 'a defence of humanist morality in contrast to the hedonistic amoralism of the degenerate nobility and the narrow-minded bourgeois morality of the Puritans' (cited by

Pompey, 'a poor fellow that would live', is no mere generic bawd but a vividly conceived individual; he is made to change his trade, but he remains Pompey still. As with some Elizabethan mansion built from the stones of a ruined abbey, *Measure for Measure* abounds in instances of morality and interlude devices made to serve new ends. Trials, 'contentions', and statements of 'doctrine' are frequent; yet on each occasion a deliberate imbalance of presentation directs the attention to the characters rather than to the ideas as such. From the dramatic viewpoint, the significance of Pompey's trial is not the exposure of bawdry but the comic ebullience of the private individual undaunted by institutions. Isabel's first interview with Angelo is, in conceptual terms, a 'contention' between Mercy and Justice; its dramatic effect, however, is to strain to breaking-point the tensions in Angelo's psyche.[1] Similarly at their second encounter Angelo's arguments for Charity, unanswered but juxtaposed to Isabella's insistence on Chastity, prepare the way for Isabella's own breakdown. The Duke's perverse homily in contempt of life, matched by Claudio's equally perverse plea for survival at all costs, do not illustrate the respective attitudes of Holy Church and Everyman, but by their very distortions, by the lurid lights and elongated shadows they cast, provide a universal vista to Claudio's tragic impasse. The last act is entirely taken up with a protracted judicial inquiry; but since the true facts are already known, dramatic interest centres not in the substance of the pleas but in what they reveal of the characters who advance them.

The 'incarnation' of ideas, principles, beliefs, is not at all points consistent and complete. As often happens in the drama of the age, strict consistency may be dispensed with for the sake of total effect. A lyrical account of the love of Claudio and Juliet is delivered by Lucio at I. iv. 40, not because he is Lucio but because he is the only available speaker. The same is true of the homily to Claudio at the beginning of Act III: its pessimism is out of keeping with the Duke's

---

Shedd). Angelo has been widely regarded as the typical Puritan; significantly, opinions on Isabel have differed widely. For Mary Suddard, she represented 'Puritanism under its most favourable aspect'; for R. Southall, the Catholic view of Grace; and for Smirnov, 'humanist morality'.

1. Shakespeare's interest in contemporary psychology, especially in the theories of Thomas Wright, *The Passions of the Minde* (1601), may be inferred from his treatment of Angelo; notably in Angelo's opening soliloquy of II. iv, describing the disjunction of thought and prayer, and the effects of passion on the blood and heart. Claudio's remarks on the 'speechless dialect' of women that moves men, and Isabella's on the 'drawing' power of appetite and 'prompture of the blood' (I. ii. 172–4, II. iv. 174–6) may have been similarly inspired. See footnotes to these passages.

attitude to life, yet only the Duke in his part of Friar could preach it at this juncture. But the attitudes of the three major characters, Angelo, Isabel, and Claudio, are integral to their personalities. The result is to convey an impression of complete and real human beings whose truth, imaginatively conceived, transcends their time and setting. Angelo's taut will-power, belief in his own principles, capacity for anguished soul-searching, and final readiness to face the consequences of his deeds, are qualities one associates with the Puritan cast of mind; likewise his ignorance at the crucial point of 'the dark and hitherto unsuspected forces of his own nature'.[1] But they are qualities of the whole man, the individual, and not just the type, who might have identified himself with other doctrines at other times. Isabella's strongly-sexed ardour and impetuosity, combined with her intellectual craving for absolutes, might in one age have led her to a martyrdom like Antigone's, in another to the frustrated life of a Dorothea Brooke: in the world of Shakespeare's play, marriage to the Duke is her true destiny. Claudio, easily affectionate, easily guilt-stricken, dependent on others for his ethical standards, is the average man of his time, and all times; the test-case, then as now, of systems and creeds. Through these characters and their interactions the drama reveals itself as essentially a quest for self-knowledge on the part of individuals who are, in Ulrici's words, 'sinners, children of wrath, and in need of mercy'. Like Lear, all three have ever but slenderly known themselves. In the course of the play their self-ignorance is fully manifested, and they are subjected to a process of moral re-education which would seem to be, in the last analysis, the true purpose of the Duke's experiment.

Yet it is just in this process that the basic defects of the play appear. As the experimenter with human lives, the Duke belongs to quite another level of dramatic presentation than that on which the other characters act and suffer. The representative of true secular and spiritual authority, he typifies the most widely approved models of the age. Political theory, literary tradition, and the precepts of the ruling monarch cast him for the part of an earthly providence who is, if not divinely omniscient, at least sagacious beyond the limits of the subjects he rules. In consequence he stands secure against vicissitude to a degree not known by actual rulers. No threats of war, revolt, or intrigue disturb him or cloud his vision. The result is a sacrifice of full humanity. Some individual

1. W. H. Durham, 'What art thou, Angelo?', *Univ. of California Publications in English*, VIII (2) (1951), 169. Durham argues that Angelo's primary fault is not hypocrisy but lack of self-knowledge.

traits are allowed him; he is modest, retiring, and scholarly, capable of a certain wry humour, and even given to occasional petulance. But he undergoes no inner development of character and achieves no added self-knowledge. His encounter with Barnardine suggests that even a model ruler may be fallible, but it is too brief to transform his personality; nor do we learn anything of the Duke's inner response to this experience. The offer of marriage to Isabella implies a farewell to hopes of 'the life removed' and an assurance that active virtue is required of rulers as well as subjects; it is, however, a formal decision rather than a change of heart. Unlike Shakespeare's Henry VI, whose longing for retirement proceeds from his innermost nature, unlike Henry V, who searches his conscience before battle and woos his wife not as king but as man, the Duke of Vienna never stoops to inquire into himself. Since, moreover, he must preside over all characters and actions in the latter half of the play, the other main figures lose much of their independent volition. Not only do they tend to behave like animated puppets in furtherance of the Duke's designs; often their moral education, too, seems to proceed through conditioned reflexes rather than through genuine self-discovery. Isabella's consent to the substitution device is too easily granted; so is Mariana's co-operation. In the last act Isabella's public humiliation is, no doubt, a necessary psychological purge, but her response to this is not very different in tone from the simulated rhetoric in which, under the Duke's coaching, she had previously denounced Angelo. Only in the dénouement, when Angelo repents his sins and Isabel, in defiance of the Duke's warning, pleads for his pardon, do these characters regain some spontaneity. But not for long: the Duke's final verdict is received with silent and general acquiescence. Angelo, about to be pardoned, reveals 'a quickening in his eye', and as much may perhaps be allowed to Claudio. But not even the impetuous Isabella, told by the Duke to 'give me your hand and say you will be mine', offers any verbal reply.

Rather more freedom is allowed to the minor characters in the latter part of the play. Mistress Overdone protests vociferously against being imprisoned; Pompey, in spite of the Duke's reprimand, still offers 'proofs for sin'. But Overdone soon disappears from the action and Pompey is left to exercise his wit at the expense of no one more important than Abhorson and Barnardine. The Provost at first refuses to obey the supposed Friar in the matter of the substituted head: by this he gives proof, not of his independence, but of his reliability as a loyal officer: once shown the hand and seal of the Duke, he is happy to do his master's bidding. Unlike

Whetstone's Gaoler or Cinthio's Captain of Justice, Shakespeare's counterpart is allowed no real initiative. Lucio alone persists to the end in challenging authority, speaking up volubly in defence of lechery, slandering the Duke in the 'Friar's' presence and the 'Friar' in the Duke's, and complaining bitterly against the sentence pronounced upon him.

Lucio's part is extremely heterogeneous. Elements of the slanderous courtier of romance, and the typical Jacobean gallant and 'fantastic', go to his making. He is jester, butt, and intermediary, a cold-blooded lecher, and a kindly, sympathetic friend to both Isabella and Claudio. The exceptional prominence of his role as well as his composite character are best explained by his special dramatic function. In the first two acts he is the indispensable go-between, passing from Claudio to Isabella, from Overdone to the nun Francisca; drawing Isabella from her cloister, leading her to the presence of Angelo, and ensuring that she persists in her suit. In reality it is Lucio, not Escalus or Angelo, who serves here as the Duke's true deputy. Thereafter, his function becomes subsidiary to the Duke's. He supplies his ruler with a comic foil, and his slanders provide emotional relief from the over-exemplary virtues of the supposed Friar. At the same time his character undergoes a progressive denigration. Besides gloating over Pompey's arrest, he would seem also to have informed against Overdone, whose services he had gladly employed. His gibes are directed not only against Angelo, but against the Duke himself. Increasingly he comes to typify the 'slanderous tongues' which perturbed both the Duke of Vienna and King James. In the end he seems to be cast as the solitary scapegoat of the comedy, though at the last minute he too is ignominiously reprieved.

These anomalies and distortions are best understood as results of the special difficulties latent in the Duke's role. In earlier versions of the story the ruler had served as a *deus ex machina*, who appeared at the end and pronounced judgment; here he was conceived as a secular providence immanent in the world of the play. But this great expansion of the part brought with it a new problem. To have made the Duke an active figure in the first half, when the tragic knot was in the course of being tied, would have dissipated his aura of mystery and reduced the suspense by a too overt assurance that all was well. Shakespeare's solution, suggested perhaps by the split ducal personality of Marston's Malcontent, was to project not only an *alter ego* to his own Duke, in the character of the supposed Friar, but also a scoffing polarity, Lucio, who carried out the practical tasks of a dramatic providence in the first two acts and later served to cushion both Duke and 'Friar' against the restiveness of audiences exposed to a prolonged object-lesson in 'the disposition of natures'. It is likely enough that through Lucio's prattle the exigencies of entertainment were met and interest in the Duke's part sustained. In terms of 'theatre' the exemplary ruler survived; with the support of a lord of misrule.

Yet to understand motives is not wholly to forgive effects. In *Measure for Measure* the tragicomic solution was brought about through the direct, explicit, and continuous intervention of 'the demi-god authority'. The vast speculative themes were knit together, the complex characters guided towards the middle path of virtue, through the transcendent wisdom of a Jacobean paragon. But the price to be paid was a substitution of precept and example for inner development and spontaneity. The dramatic poetry of the first half of the play, with its free-ranging, esemplastic imagery and flexible speech-rhythms, gave way to sententious prose, stiff gnomic couplets, and a blank verse which, though generally dignified, was basically uninspired. The Duke's Apollonian intellect resolved all conflicts in society and stilled all tumults in the soul; but in the process the autonomy of the individual was lost, and with it his innate right to choose as between evil and good. At the same time the Duke himself, a prisoner of his own exemplary image, failed as an authentic human being and remained a stage device, midway between personality and type.

If, as some critics think, each literary work is to be judged as a self-sufficient entity, *Measure for Measure* might fairly be described as a 'flawed masterpiece'. But if we choose to see this play as one phase in an organic creative process, it will have for us a more positive meaning. The enigma of authority vested in flesh and blood, which Shakespeare failed to resolve in the character of his Duke, was not solely a problem of technique, but a challenge to his artist's integrity. It presented itself with mounting urgency in the plays written at the turn of the century, in *Julius Caesar*, *Hamlet*, and *Troilus and Cressida*. Ultimately the challenge sprang from the central Renaissance paradox of man, 'noble in reason', 'infinite in faculties', yet the 'quintessence of dust'. Tragicomedy on a realistic plane, which turned on the deeds of a wise earthly providence immune to the weakness of common men, seemed theoretically to provide an answer. In practice it supplied only an evasion. Shakespeare's later tragedies, in contrast, looked the issues full in the face. They required that rulers, like other men, should 'in the destructive element immerse'. The king must be a beggar that he might become truly royal: a beggar in fact, not a mendicant friar by way of disguise. He must forfeit his sanity, not merely put an antic disposition on. Only when all outward trappings of authority had vanished could the truth in man be separated from the falsehood, and his reality from his seeming. Tragedy taught the hard lesson that self-knowledge came, not from reason and moderation, but from madness and excess; that evil, though in the end it destroyed itself, was not overcome by good; and that the magnanimous monarch ruled only in a country of the imagination. If *Measure for Measure*, for all its probing of the issues, brought no genuine transcendence, it prepared the way for *King Lear* and *Antony and Cleopatra*. Only after the tragic exploration had been completed did Shakespeare return to the affirmations of tragicomedy, in the sublimated simplicities of pastoral romance, where time and the cycle of generations restored natural good.[1] In *The Tempest* the demi-god authority was resurrected; again a secular providence shaped the course of human affairs and took over the direction of the play. But Prospero, unlike the Duke of Vienna, had suffered a sea-change. He no longer ruled a geographical territory by hereditary right. His attachment to 'the life removed' had made him an exile on an uninhabited island; his ministers Ariel and Caliban—unlike the deputies Escalus and Angelo—were pure creatures of the imagination, projections of the antinomies in his own being and in external nature; and the evil which assailed his private world with the coming of mankind, though contained, was not eradicated. In spite of this, or rather because of it, *The Tempest* celebrated a visionary triumph:

> O rejoice
> Beyond a common joy, and set it down
> With gold on lasting pillars. In one voyage
> Did Claribel her husband find at Tunis,
> And Ferdinand, her brother, found a wife
> When he himself was lost; Prospero his dukedom
> In a poor isle; and all of us ourselves
> When no man was his own.   (v. i. 206–13)

Self-knowledge, the essential quest in *Measure for Measure*, was the crowning achievement of the last plays.

1. G. K. Hunter finds in the development from *All's Well* to *The Winter's Tale* a corresponding widening of poetic vision. 'We have noticed . . . the odd combination of attitudes in the [former] play . . . its realistic and satirical elements, its brooding concern with problems of nature and nurture, innocence and action, birth and death, and its Christian (or at least spiritual) colouring. We find the same elements in the last plays, but there so disposed as to convey, not stress, but the multimundity of life' (Introduction to the 'Arden' edition of *All's Well That Ends Well*, 1959, lv).

MEASURE FOR MEASURE

DRAMATIS PERSONÆ

VINCENTIO, *the Duke.*
ANGELO, *the Deputy.*
ESCALUS, *an ancient Lord.*
CLAUDIO, *a young Gentleman.*
LUCIO, *a Fantastic.*
Two other like Gentlemen.
PROVOST.
FRIAR THOMAS *or* FRIAR PETER.
[JUSTICE.]
ELBOW, *a simple Constable.*
FROTH, *a foolish Gentleman.*
POMPEY, *Servant to Mistress Overdone.*
ABHORSON, *an Executioner.*
BARNARDINE, *a dissolute prisoner.*
[VARRIUS, *a Gentleman, friend to the Duke.*]
ISABELLA, *sister to Claudio.*
MARIANA, *betrothed to Angelo.*
JULIET, *beloved of Claudio.*
FRANCISCA, *a Nun.*
MISTRESS OVERDONE, *a Bawd.*
[Lords in attendance, Officers, Servants, Citizens, and a Boy.]

THE SCENE: VIENNA [*and its environs*].

DRAMATIS PERSONÆ] The names of all the Actors. F (*after text of play*).
FRIAR ... PETER.] *This edn;* $\left.\begin{array}{c}Thomas.\\ Peter.\end{array}\right\}$ 2. *Friers.* F.
POMPEY ... OVERDONE.] *Dyce subst.; Clowne.* F.

(i) The textual significance of the list of characters in F, as well as of the names or parts of Vincentio, 'Thomas or Peter', Justice, Varrius, Juliet, and Francisca, is discussed in the Introduction, pp. xi–xii, xvii–xix, xxv. The names Thomas and Francisca do not appear in speech-prefixes or dialogue of I. iii and I. iv respectively, and this edition follows F in using the speech-prefixes 'Friar' and 'Nun'.

(ii) Kenneth Muir, *Shakespeare's Sources*, I, 108, fn. 3, suggests that Erasmus' *Funus* (*Colloquia*) may have been consulted for 'background information about friars and nuns'. Among the names to be found (with Latin case-endings) were 'Francisco', 'Barnardino', and 'Vincentio'. None of these was uncommon, but their collocation in Erasmus may be of relevance to Shakespeare's choice.

MEASURE FOR MEASURE

ACT I

SCENE I [*Within Vienna.*]

Enter DUKE, ESCALUS, *Lords [and Attendants.*]

Duke. Escalus.

Esc. My lord.

Duke. Of government the properties to unfold
    Would seem in me t'affect speech and discourse,
    Since I am put to know that your own science   5

ACT I

Scene I

Measure For Measure] *Measvre, For Measure. F.*   *Act I Scene I*] *Actus Primus, Scena Prima. F.*   *Within Vienna*] *this edn; not in F; A Palace. Pope; A Room in the Duke's Palace. Capell; The Council-chamber in the Duke's Palace. N.C.S.*   S.D. *Lords and Attendants*] *Capell; Lords. F.*   5. put] *F; but conj. Hart.*

Measure for Measure] a commonplace signifying (i) just retribution and reward, or the just exaction of revenge (Tilley M 801). Originating in Matth., vii. 2: 'With what measure ye mete, it shall be measured to you again'. Cf. *3H6*, II. vi. 55: 'Measure for measure must be answered'; *Tit.*, v. iii. 66. (ii) moderation or temperance as a virtue. 'He that forsakes measure, measure forsakes him' (Tilley M 803). See John L. Harrison, *S.Q.*, 5 (1954), 4, and Intro., p. lix.

S.H. *Vienna.*] Editors generally locate Scene i in the Duke's Palace or (*N.C.S.*) council chamber, during a session of state. Lascelles, p. 47, points out that this is inconsistent with the dialogue, suggesting haste and uncertainty: the Duke should enter 'dressed for travel', taking leave 'in privacy'.

Lords and Attendants] F merely has 'Lords'. In Renaissance courts, the nobles often served their monarch in person.

3. *Of government the properties*] 'the qualities essential to the office of ruling'.

4. *affect*] often used by Shakespeare in the modern sense of 'practise artificially'.

5. *put*] compelled. Cf. *Cym.*, II. iii. 110: 'You put me to forget a lady's manners'.

science] knowledge; cf. *All's W.*, v. iii. 103. Often associated with *conscience*, 'emphasising the distinction to be drawn between theoretical percep-

Exceeds, in that, the lists of all advice
My strength can give you. Then no more remains
But that, to your sufficiency, as your worth is able,
And let them work. The nature of our people,
Our city's institutions, and the terms   10
For common justice, y'are as pregnant in
As art and practice hath enriched any
That we remember. There is our commission,
From which we would not have you warp. Call hither,
I say, bid come before us Angelo.   [*Exit an Attendant.*]
What figure of us, think you, he will bear?   16

7. remains] *F;* remains; *Rowe.*   8. But that, to] *F;* Put that to *Rowe, conj. Hart;*
But that *Steevens;* But that. To *Sisson.*   sufficiency, as . . . able] *F;* sufficiency
[. . . / . . .] as . . . able *Cambridge;* sufficiency [you add / Due diligency] as . . . able
conj. Theobald; sufficiencies . . . abled *conj. Johnson.*   10. city's institutions]
Rowe; Cities Institutions F.   15. S.D.] *Capell; not in F.*

tion of a truth and moral conviction' (*O.E.D.* 1 b).

6. *lists*] limits, boundaries.

7. *strength*] intellectual powers. 'Sciences and Arts are not cast in a mold . . . what my strength cannot discover, I cease not to sound and try' (Montaigne, *Apology of Sebond*, II. 273).

8. *But . . . able*] The line is obscure as well as hypermetrical. Interpretation depends on whether 'that' is a pronoun or a conjunction. If pronoun, it must stand for 'strength', line 7: the 'sufficiency' (fitness, ability) of Escalus only needs the Duke's 'strength' (political power) for the two to 'work'. But 'strength' has quite a different sense in line 7 (see note); while the clause 'as . . . able' seems unrelated. Sisson puts a stop after 'that', creating a new sentence, 'To your sufficiency . . .', which is equally obscure. If 'that' is a conjunction, we may assume a hiatus between 'sufficiency' and 'as'. Emendations can only be guesswork. Perhaps Escalus is being urged to add to his sufficiency of 'science' the Duke's 'conscience' (cf. note to *science*, line 5), as his 'worth' is 'able' (as he is competent to do), 'and let them work'. This would foreshadow a major theme of the play.

10. *institutions*] political or social customs. A 16th-cent. innovation and only here in Shakespeare. The word is italicized in F.

10–11. *terms For common justice*] (i) the conditions for administering, or (ii) the technical terms of, the common law (*O.E.D.* 'term' 10; 13). More probably (i) was intended. Halliwell Nb. cites Stephens, *Satirical Essayes*, III (1615 edn), p. 39: 'he that scornes our common lawe in rage / Because the tearmes are ouer growne with age . . .'

11. *pregnant*] resourceful, well-versed.

12. *art*] theory.

13–14. *There . . . warp*] The metaphor of warping emphasizes the distinction between the man and the office he is to fill, as represented by the commission. Cf. *AYL.*, III. iii. 92 f.: 'this fellow will but join you together as they join wainscot; then one of you will prove a shrunk panel, and like green timber, warp, warp.' In *Prom.*, I. i, 'the Kinges Letters Patents' are read out to Promos from a parchment scroll 'with some great counterfeate zeale [=seal]'.

16. *What figure . . . bear?*] suggested perhaps by the ducal stamp on the seal of the commission, and introducing

For you must know, we have with special soul
Elected him our absence to supply;
Lent him our terror, drest him with our love,
And given his deputation all the organs   20
Of our own power. What think you of it?

Esc. If any in Vienna be of worth
   To undergo such ample grace and honour,
   It is Lord Angelo.

Enter ANGELO.

Duke.   Look where he comes.

Ang. Always obedient to your Grace's will,   25
   I come to know your pleasure.

Duke.   Angelo:
   There is a kind of character in thy life
   That to th'observer doth thy history
   Fully unfold. Thyself and thy belongings
   Are not thine own so proper as to waste   30
   Thyself upon thy virtues, they on thee.
   Heaven doth with us as we with torches do,

---

the iterative 'stamp' or 'coin' image for the first time.

17–18. *with special soul Elected him*] *soul*: all the powers of the mind, intuitive and rational (*O.E.D.* 5). *Elected*: chosen for a special function or position. Cf. Hamlet on Horatio: 'Since my dear soul was mistress of her choice / And could of men distinguish, her election / Hath seal'd thee for herself' (*Ham.*, III. ii. 68 f.). In Jonson, *The Case Is Altered*, I. vi. 30 f., another Angelo is addressed in comparable circumstances.

19. *Lent him our terror*] Cf. *Sir Thomas More*, 'for to the king god hath his offyc lent / of dread of Iustyce, power and Comaund' (*M.S.R.*, Addition II, lines 221–2). 'Terror' is a worthy attribute of royalty, as in *H8*, v. v. 48: 'Peace, plenty, love, truth, terror'. Cf. I. iii. 26.

drest . . . love] 'adorned him with the outward signs of our love'. Cf. *1H4*, III. ii. 51.

20. *deputation*] appointment to act as deputy.

23. *undergo*] sustain, endure (cf. line 16).

27–9. *character . . . unfold*] 'character' was primarily an engraving or inscription, hence fig. for appearance or behaviour. Cf. Webster, *Appius and Virginia*, I. ii. 7–8: 'You give me (noble Lord) that character / Which I cood never yet read in my selfe'. The observer, says the Duke, can infer Angelo's history from his present behaviour.

29–31. *Thyself . . . on thee*] 'Neither your personality nor your virtuous attributes are so far your private property that either can be wasted in cultivating the other'. *belongings*: 'qualities pertaining to'. (*O.E.D.* I cites this as the only use of the word as substantive before the 19th cent.)

32–6. *Heaven . . . issues*] Kenneth Muir, *Shakespeare's Sources*, I. 8, cites Whiter on the biblical inspiration of this passage, combining (i) the parable

Not light them for themselves; for if our virtues
Did not go forth of us, 'twere all alike
As if we had them not. Spirits are not finely touch'd   35
But to fine issues; nor nature never lends
The smallest scruple of her excellence
But, like a thrifty goddess, she determines
Herself the glory of a creditor,
Both thanks and use. But I do bend my speech   40
To one that can my part in him advértise:
Hold therefore, Angelo.
In our remove, be thou at full ourself.

42.] S.D. *Giving him his commission. Hanmer.*

---

of the candlestick (Luke, viii. 16 etc.), (ii) the story of the woman with the issue of blood (*ibid.*, 43–6), where 'issue', 'touched', and 'virtue that went out' (or 'is gone out') appear. But (i) the parable had become a secular commonplace (Tilley C 39). Lyly's version in *Campaspe*, *Prol. at Court*, 17, 'these torches, which giuing light to others, consume themselues', is closer than Luke to the Duke's words. Shakespeare twice used the figure to signify the duty of procreation (*Ven.*, 755 f., with 'lamp'; *Sonn.*, I. 6, with 'light's flame', and 'waste' in line 12). P. Ure notes Chapman's 6th Sestiad of *Hero and Leander*, 60 ff., where the torch image has both social and sexual connotations: 'Sweet Torch, true Glasse of our societie; / What man does good, but he consumes thereby? . . . without love . . . maids are but Torches wanting light'. Here its social aspect predominates: cf. T. Carew, *Sermons* (1603), sig. P 7v: 'It is reported of a king that had painted in his armes a candlestick with a candle burning, and this posie written. *In seruing other I waste my selfe*'. (ii) 'go forth', 'touch'd', and 'issues' all have a non-biblical significance. 'Go forth', with 'virtues', relates to the 'torches' figure of the previous sentence. 'Touched' and 'issues', with 'fine' (=refined) suggest the 'touch' placed on gold coins of standard fineness before they were

passed into circulation (*O.E.D. v.* 8). Cf. Angelo's reply, lines 48–50, and the Duke, III. ii. 264–5.

36–40. *nor nature . . . thanks and use*] Nature's action here corresponds with Heaven's, line 32; together they show a blending of Christian ethics and Stoic philosophy. The implied coin image in lines 35–6 may have suggested Nature as creditor, who 'determines' (ordains) thanks and 'use' (usury). Cf. Seneca, *De Beneficiis* (tr. Golding, 1578, p. 93): 'Then are we indetted to the Sonne, and the Moone, . . . for their benefites. . . Among the greatest woorkes of nature, there is nothing wherein nature more gloryeth [than man]'. Death as the repayment of nature's loan, and the conceit of nature as a usurer, are Senecan ideas taken up in the Renaissance by Palingenius, Montaigne (II. 491), Spenser, *Faerie Queene*, II. xi. 45, and Shakespeare, *Sonn.*, IV, VI, and IX, where Nature lends life for man to 'invest' in progeny. *scruple*: small measure used by goldsmiths.

41. *my part in him advertise*] 'make my function (*part*) generally known through his own example'. In line 43 the Duke plays on 'part' in contrast to 'at full'.

42.] Perhaps the commission is tendered to Angelo here; but the Duke may only be requiring Angelo to 'hold on' to his reputation.

　　　Mortality and mercy in Vienna
　　　Live in thy tongue, and heart. Old Escalus,　　　45
　　　Though first in question, is thy secondary.
　　　Take thy commission.
Ang.　　　　　　　　Now, good my lord,
　　　Let there be some more test made of my metal,
　　　Before so noble and so great a figure
　　　Be stamp'd upon it.
Duke.　　　　　　　No more evasion.　　　50
　　　We have with a leaven'd and prepared choice
　　　Proceeded to you; therefore take your honours.
　　　Our haste from hence is of so quick condition
　　　That it prefers itself, and leaves unquestion'd
　　　Matters of needful value. We shall write to you,　　　55
　　　As time and our concernings shall importune,
　　　How it goes with us; and do look to know
　　　What doth befall you here. So, fare you well.
　　　To th'hopeful execution do I leave you
　　　Of your commissions.
Ang.　　　　　　　　Yet give leave, my lord,　　　60
　　　That we may bring you something on the way.
Duke.　My haste may not admit it;
　　　Nor need you, on mine honour, have to do

---

44. Mortality] *F;* Morality *Pope.*　　　48. metal] *F* (mettle), *Rowe.*

44–5. *Mortality . . . heart*] 'I delegate
to thy tongue the power of pronoun-
cing sentence of death, and to thy heart
the privilege of exercising mercy'
(Douce).

46. *in question*] under consideration.

secondary] 'an officer next vnto the
chiefe Officer' (Cowell's *Interpret-
er*).

48–50.] Angelo's reply takes up the
coin imagery of lines 35–6. He asks
whether his quality, like the fineness of
gold, has been sufficiently tested to
receive the royal stamp in the form of
the appointment to be the Duke's deputy. *metal*: F's 'mettle' was an alternative spelling, interchangeable with
'metal', which here draws attention to

the primary figure in Angelo's speech.

50. *evasion*] evasive argument, excuse (*O.E.D.* 3b).

51. *leaven'd*] from the operation of
yeast: tempered.

53. *so quick condition*] probably with
play on 'quick' as pregnant. Cf. IV. ii.
108. *condition*: quality.

54. *prefers itself*] sets itself before
other concerns.

unquestion'd] unconsidered; cf. 'question', line 46.

56. *concernings*] 'matters that concern (us)'.

importune] urge (*O.E.D.* 2). This
intransitive use appears only here in
Shakespeare.

61.] 'that we may escort you part of
the way'.

With any scruple. Your scope is as mine own,
So to enforce or qualify the laws   65
As to your soul seems good. Give me your hand;
I'll privily away. I love the people,
But do not like to stage me to their eyes:
Though it do well, I do not relish well
Their loud applause and *Aves* vehement;   70
Nor do I think the man of safe discretion
That does affect it. Once more, fare you well.

Ang. The heavens give safety to your purposes!
Esc. Lead forth and bring you back in happiness!
Duke. I thank you; fare you well.   *Exit.*   75
Esc. I shall desire you, sir, to give me leave
To have free speech with you; and it concerns me
To look into the bottom of my place.
A power I have, but of what strength and nature
I am not yet instructed.   80
Ang. 'Tis so with me. Let us withdraw together,
And we may soon our satisfaction have
Touching that point.
Esc.   I'll wait upon your honour. *Exeunt.*

75. S.D.] *F2; Exit. F (after 74).*

64. *scruple*] doubt, hesitation.

66. *to your soul*] Cf. 'soul', line 17.

67–72. *I'll privily . . . affect it.*] These remarks suggest an obvious parallel with James I's attitude to crowds and publicity as noted during the spring of 1604. Cf. II. iv. 24–30 and Intro., p. xxxiii. *stage*: 'put on the stage'. Shakespeare twice uses this figure (*Ant.*, III. xi. 30; v. ii. 216), each time in a context of distaste. Steevens quotes from Queen Elizabeth's speech to Parliament in 1586: 'We princes, I tel you, are set on stages, in the sight and viewe

of all the world'. James I reiterated the figure in *Basilicon Doron*, Epistle to the Reader, p. 12. *Aves*: from the Roman *Ave Caesar*, as a salute to royalty. For Elizabethan writers it often suggested crowd enthusiasms. Cf. Webster, *Appius and Virginia*, v. ii. 6–7: 'one rear'd on a popular suffrage, / Whose station's built on Avees and Applause'.

77. *free*] frank.

78.] 'to investigate my position fully'.

79. *power*] authority to act.

SCENE II [*The same. A public place.*]

Enter Lucio *and two other Gentlemen.*

Lucio. If the Duke, with the other dukes, come not to composition with the King of Hungary, why then all the dukes fall upon the King.

1 Gent. Heaven grant us its peace, but not the King of Hungary's!   5

2 Gent. Amen.

Lucio. Thou conclud'st like the sanctimonious pirate, that went to sea with the Ten Commandments, but scrap'd one out of the table.

2 Gent. 'Thou shalt not steal'?   10

Lucio. Ay, that he raz'd.

1 Gent. Why, 'twas a commandment to command the captain and all the rest from their functions: they put forth to steal. There's not a soldier of us all that, in the thanksgiving before meat, do relish the petition   15 well that prays for peace.

Scene II

Scene II] *Scena Seccnda. F.*   The same. A public place.] *this edn; not in F; The Street.*
Rowe.   12. Why,] *Pope;* Why? *F.*

1–3. *If . . . King.*] On this speech as a date reference, see Intro., pp. xxxi f. Lucio assumes that the Duke is absent on a political mission which may decide the question of peace or war. *composition*: agreement for a political settlement.

4–5.] On the topical significance, see Intro., p. xxxii. Echoing the litany, 'grant us thy peace'. 'The King of Hungary's peace' quibbles on 'hungry peace', a topical pun when English volunteers in Hungary were serving against the Turks. Down-at-heels ex-soldiers were sometimes nicknamed 'Hungarians'. Cf. *Wiv.*, I. iii. 21.

7–9. *sanctimonious pirate . . . table*] The pirate took the Ten Commandments, traditionally pictured on the 'tables' of stone, as his figurehead. The joke seems to be echoed in Middleton's *Your Five Gallants*, III. v: 'he will not

miss you one tittle in the nine commandments'. 'There's ten of 'em'. 'I fear he skips o'er one, Thou shalt not steal'. Piracy was widespread during the war with Spain, though strictly forbidden since James I's accession. *sanctimonious*: pious. An early instance of the word with an ironical connotation (*O.E.D.* 2).

11. *raz'd*] erased.

12–13. *to command . . . from their functions*] *function*: 'action proper to a person as belonging to a particular class' (*O.E.D.* 4). So Falstaff justifies highway robbery: ''tis no sin for a man to labour in his vocation' (*1H4*, I. ii. 116–17). A medieval commonplace which becomes the cynic's corollary to the Duke's injunction that virtues should 'go forth'.

15–16. *thanksgiving . . . peace.*] '"God save our Queen and Realm, and send

2 Gent. I never heard any soldier dislike it.

Lucio. I believe thee; for I think thou never wast where
    grace was said.

2 Gent. No? A dozen times at least.   20

1 Gent. What, in metre?

Lucio. In any proportion, or in any language.

1 Gent. I think, or in any religion.

Lucio. Ay, why not? Grace is grace, despite of all contro-
    versy; as for example, thou thyself art a wicked vil- 25
    lain, despite of all grace.

1 Gent. Well, there went but a pair of shears between us.

Lucio. I grant: as there may between the lists and the
    velvet. Thou art the list.

1 Gent. And thou the velvet; thou art good velvet; thou'rt 30
    a three-piled piece, I warrant thee: I had as lief be a
    list of an English kersey, as be piled, as thou art

---

22. *Lucio*] F (*Luc.*); *2 Gent. conj. Ritson (Var. 1821).*

us peace in Christ" was a common
grace before meat' (Durham). On the
soldier's attitude, cf. Montaigne: 'No
Physitian delighteth in the health of
his owne friend, . . . nor no Souldier is
pleased with the peace of his Citie' (1.
104).

18. *I believe thee; for I think thou*]
addressed to the 1 and 2 Gent.
respectively.

18–19. *never wast . . . said*] 'Ime sure
they say none at some Ordenaries . . .
they are either drunke, or haue such
mind a dice, they neuer remembert'
(John Day, *The Ile of Guls* (1606), sig.
B4ᵛ).

22–3. *proportion . . . language . . . religion*] Ritson thought that Lucio's
speech should have been given to
2 Gent. It is hard to be sure in the rapid
cross-patter, and Lucio's words may
have been sarcastically intended.
'Language' and 'religion' probably
hint at Latin graces and hence Roman
Catholic practice, as a dig at the religion of 2 Gent.

24–6. *Grace is grace . . . grace*] Based
on Romans, xi. 6 (Geneva): 'If it bee
of grace, then is it not nowe of workes:

for then grace is no more grace'
(Noble). Lucio evades a major theological dispute between Catholics and
Reformers, while playing on grace as
(i) thanksgiving, (ii) propriety, (iii)
divine mercy manifested towards
sinners.

27. *there went but a pair of shears between us*] proverbial (Tilley P 36). Cut
from the same cloth; of the same
nature.

28–9. *between the lists and the velvet*]
Lucio retorts that the 'shears' have cut
between the selvage, or border, and
the fine velvet which betokens a
gentleman.

31. *three-piled*] with a pile, or long
nap, of treble thickness.

31–3. *I had . . . velvet*] 'I would rather
be the selvage of plain cloth than expensive velvet with all its nap fallen
out; rather a plain, healthy Englishman than a fine gentleman with
French disease'. The 'velvet' joke
also appears in *All's W.*, IV. v.
100–5.

32. *Englisn kersey*] plain cloth, originally made in Kersey, Suffolk, and
exported since the 13th cent.; hence

pilled, for a French velvet. Do I speak feelingly now?

Lucio. I think thou dost: and indeed, with most painful
feeling of thy speech. I will, out of thine own confes-   35
sion, learn to begin thy health; but whilst I live,
forget to drink after thee.

1 Gent. I think I have done myself wrong, have I not?

2 Gent. Yes, that thou hast; whether thou art tainted or
free.   40

Enter Mistress OVERDONE.

Lucio. Behold, behold, where Madam Mitigation comes!
I have purchased as many diseases under her roof as
come to—

2 Gent. To what, I pray?

Lucio. Judge.   45

2 Gent. To three thousand dolours a year.

1 Gent. Ay, and more.

Lucio. A French crown more.

1 Gent. Thou art always figuring diseases in me; but thou
art full of error; I am sound.   50

Lucio. Nay, not, as one would say, healthy: but so sound

---

33. pilled] F (pil'd), *this edn.*   40. S.D.] *Dyce (so throughout play); Enter Bawde. F,
Theobald (at 53); Bawd, coming at a distance. Hanmer.*   41. *Lucio*] F (*Luc.*); *1 Gent.* /
Johnson.   41–3.] *as Johnson;* Behold . . . comes. / . . . Roofe, / . . . to / F.   46.
dolours] *F;* dollars *Rowe 3.*

---

representing the plain Englishman.
Cf. *LLL.*, v. ii. 414.

33. *pilled*] deprived of hair: a frequent effect of the mercury treatment
then given for venereal disease.
Steevens notes that the joke turned on
the similar sound of the words 'pilled'
and 'piled'. Frequently, as in F, the
spelling was the same.

feelingly] to the purpose (*O.E.D.*
2); which Lucio wilfully misinter-
prets in the next line as 'with feeling'
(*O.E.D.* 4).

36. *begin thy health*] begin drinking
'to thy health'. A new idiom.

37. *forget to drink after thee*] i.e. not
from his cup. 'Another upon the Gib-
bet calling for drinke, and the hangman drinking first, said, hee would not

drinke after him, for feare hee should
take the pox of him' (Montaigne, I.
270 (Hart, *N. & Q.*, 1908)).

41. *Madam Mitigation*] because her
trade mitigates desire.

46. *dolours*] punning on 'dollars',
Germ. *Thaler*, also applied to Spanish
'pieces of eight'. Shakespeare repeats
the pun in *Tp.*, II. i. 18–19; *Lr.*, II.
iv. 54.

48. *French crown*] another familiar
coin pun on the effects of the 'French
disease'. The French crown circu-
lated widely, having the value of
about 7s.

51–2. *sound . . . hollow*] 'sound' here
as resounding; cf. 'sound as a bell'.
'The Neapolitan bone-ache' was a
contemporary term for venereal dis-

as things that are hollow; thy bones are hollow;
impiety has made a feast of thee.

1 Gent. How now, which of your hips has the most profound sciatica?   55

Mis. O. Well, well! There's one yonder arrested and
carried to prison, was worth five thousand of you all.

2 Gent. Who's that, I prithee?

Mis. O. Marry sir, that's Claudio; Signior Claudio.

1 Gent. Claudio to prison? 'Tis not so.   60

Mis. O. Nay, but I know 'tis so. I saw him arrested: saw
him carried away: and which is more, within these
three days his head to be chopped off.

Lucio. But, after all this fooling, I would not have it so.
Art thou sure of this?   65

Mis. O. I am too sure of it: and it is for getting Madam
Julietta with child.

Lucio. Believe me, this may be: he promised to meet me
two hours since, and he was ever precise in promise-
keeping.   70

2 Gent. Besides, you know, it draws something near to the
speech we had to such a purpose.

1 Gent. But most of all agreeing with the proclamation.

Lucio. Away! Let's go learn the truth of it.

                              Exeunt [Lucio and Gentlemen].

Mis. O. Thus, what with the war, what with the sweat,   75
what with the gallows, and what with poverty, I am
custom-shrunk.

Enter POMPEY.

54.] S.D. (*to the Bawd*) *Capell.*   63. head] *F;* head is *Rowe;* head's *Capell.*
74. S.D.] *Capell; Exit. F; Exeunt. F2.*   77. S.D.] *Dyce (so throughout play);*
Enter Clowne. F (*after 78*).

ease. Middleton, *The Blacke Booke*
(1604) refers to 'monsieur Drybone,
the Frenchman' (VIII. 23).

54–5.] On the strength of this question, many editors have placed Mistress Overdone's entry here; some
have prefixed to 1 Gent.'s speech the
direction '*to her*'. While sciatica was
associated with bawds in Latin
comedy, the remark here is surely a
reply to Lucio's taunt.

71–3.] Nothing has been said before
about either speech or proclamation,
but *1 Prom.*, I. i, opens with the reading
of the Letters Patents, followed by the
speech of Promos threatening to
'scoorge the wights, good Lawes that
disobay'.

75–7.] All these circumstances
would have topical relevance in the
earlier part of 1604. See Intro., p.
xxxii.

How now? What's the news with you?

Pom. Yonder man is carried to prison.

Mis. O. Well! What has he done?   80

Pom. A woman.

Mis. O. But what's his offence?

Pom. Groping for trouts, in a peculiar river.

Mis. O. What? Is there a maid with child by him?

Pom. No: but there's a woman with maid by him. You   85
have not heard of the proclamation, have you?

Mis. O. What proclamation, man?

Pom. All houses in the suburbs of Vienna must be plucked
down.

Mis. O. And what shall become of those in the city?   90

Pom. They shall stand for seed: they had gone down too,
but that a wise burgher put in for them.

Mis. O. But shall all our houses of resort in the suburbs be
pulled down?

Pom. To the ground, mistress.   95

Mis. O. Why, here's a change indeed in the commonwealth! What shall become of me?

80. Well!] *this edn;* Well: *F.*

78.] So in *1 Prom.*, I. iii, the courtesan Lamia, on the entrance of her
man, exclaims: '*Rosko*, what newes,
that in such hast you come blowing?'

79. *Yonder man*] presumably Claudio: see Intro., pp. xix–xx.

80. *done*] Pompey interprets this
obscenely. Cf. II. i. 115 ff.

83. *Groping for trouts, in a peculiar
river*] generally, practising a confidence trick, but also used in a bawdy
sense for seduction, as in *Wint.*, I. ii.
194 f.: 'she has been sluiced in's absence,/And his pond fish'd by his next
neighbour'. *peculiar*: own (*O.E.D.* 1);
'yonder man's' own river, i.e. his own
wife; implicitly contrasting the 'offence' to that of Mistress Overdone's
customers. Cf. *Oth.*, IV. i. 68–70.

85. *with maid*] 'maid with child'
being strictly anomalous, Pompey
substitutes 'woman with maid' (i.e.
young of certain fish, *O.E.D.* 7).
Developed from the image of line 83.

88–9. *All houses . . . plucked down*] In
1 Prom., I. iii, Rosko says to Lamia:
'you must shut vp your shops, and
leaue your occupying'. Pompey's talk
of demolitions may have been suggested by the proclamation of 16 September 1603, intended as a precaution
against plague, but directed chiefly
against the brothel quarters of the
suburbs (Intro., pp. xxxii–xxxiii).

91. *stand for seed*] as of corn left to
ripen; but Pompey's remarks are, as
usual, equivocal.

92. *a wise burgher . . . them*] (i)
He interceded for them: so Rosko
mentions one Phallax who will protect Lamia despite the closing of her
house (*1 Prom.*, I. iii). (ii) He made
a bid to acquire them. Both senses may
well be present.

96–7. *a change . . . commonwealth*]
a phrase recalling the language of
the Elizabethan reform tracts. See
Intro., pp. xlv–xlvi.

Pom. Come: fear not you: good counsellors lack no
     clients: though you change your place, you need
     not change your trade: I'll be your tapster still;   100
     courage, there will be pity taken on you; you that
     have worn your eyes almost out in the service, you
     will be considered.
Mis. O. What's to do here, Thomas tapster? Let's with-
     draw!   105
Pom. Here comes Signior Claudio, led by the Provost to
     prison: and there's Madam Juliet.   *Exeunt.*

     Enter PROVOST [*and*] *Officers* [*with*] CLAUDIO *and* JULIET;
          LUCIO *and* [*the*] *two Gentlemen.*

Cla. Fellow, why dost thou show me thus to th'world?
     Bear me to prison, where I am committed.
Pro. I do it not in evil disposition,   110
     But from Lord Angelo by special charge.
Cla. Thus can the demi-god, Authority,
     Make us pay down for our offence by weight.
     The words of heaven; on whom it will, it will;

---

104. Thomas tapster] *Capell (subst.)*, *Munro; Thomas* Tapster *F; Thomas Tapster
F2 (subst.).   107. S.D. *Juliet*] *F; om. Hudson.   Lucio . . . Gentlemen.*] *F (Lucio, &
2 Gent.)* | *F; Lucio and the two Gentlemen following. Capell; Lucio following. Alexander;
Re-enter Lucio and two Gentlemen. Dyce (after 115).*   113–14. by weight. | *The
words*] *Warburton (after Davenant);* by waight | The words *F;* By weight; | I' th'
words *Hanmer;* by weight. | The sword *Staunton, conj. Steevens '73;* by weight |
The bonds *Sisson;* by weight | [ ] The words *conj. Johnson.*

---

102. *worn . . . service*] a sly allusion
to 'Blind Cupid', traditionally the
sign in front of brothels. Cf. *Lr*, IV.
vi. 141–2; *Ado*, I. i. 264. Prostitution
is 'the service', as if it were a public
service maintained for the good of the
state. Cf. III. ii. 116.

104. *Thomas tapster*] in F, only
'Thomas' is printed in the italics employed for proper names, and probably
goes with 'tapster' as a generic nick-
name: in the 19th cent. it was similarly applied to footmen and waiters
(*O.E.D.* 2).

107. S.D. *Enter . . . Juliet*] See Intro.,
p. xvii. A procession across the stage
seems intended, which is halted by the

Provost so that Claudio may be 'shown
to the world'. Juliet would thus be on-
stage, but far enough away to have no
part in the dialogue.

112. *the demi-god, Authority*] No sar-
casm need be inferred. 'Demi-god' (a
person raised to near-divine rank)
follows the Elizabethan commonplace
based on Exodus, xxii. 9 (Geneva) and
Psalm lxxxii. 6, that rulers and judges
had the attributes of gods. Cf. Henry
Smith, *The Magistrates Scripture* (*Sermons*, 1591, p. 702): 'the prince is like
a great Image of God, the Magistrates
are like little Images of God'. See
Intro., p. lxiv.

114–15.] Cf. Romans, ix. 15 (Gene-

On whom it will not, so; yet still 'tis just.   115

Lucio. Why, how now, Claudio? Whence comes this
    restraint?

Cla. From too much liberty, my Lucio. Liberty,
    As surfeit, is the father of much fast;
    So every scope by the immoderate use
    Turns to restraint. Our natures do pursue,   120
    Like rats that ravin down their proper bane,
    A thirsty evil; and when we drink, we die.

Lucio. If I could speak so wisely under an arrest, I would
    send for certain of my creditors; and yet, to say
    the truth, I had as lief have the foppery of free-   125
    dom as the morality of imprisonment.—What's thy
    offence, Claudio?

Cla. What but to speak of would offend again.

Lucio. What, is't murder?

Cla.   No.

Lucio.   Lechery?

---

117. liberty, my Lucio. Liberty, / As surfeit,] *this edn;* liberty, (my *Lucio*) Liberty /
As surfet F; Liberty, my Lucio, Liberty; / As surfeit *Rowe.*   126. morality]
Rowe (after Davenant); mortality F.

---

va): 'I will have mercie on him, to whom I will shewe mercie', also verse 18 (Noble, also citing *Oth.*, II. iii. 107–8).

117–18. *Liberty, As surfeit,*] Editors place a long stop after 'Liberty', making it only an iteration of the previous 'liberty'. This eliminates the play on 'fast' as antithesis to both 'surfeit' and 'liberty'.

120–2. *Our natures ... die*] The 'thirsty evil' is not lechery but liberty, which encourages desire, whose gratification incurs the 'restraint' of prison. L. C. Knights (*Scrutiny*, x. (1942) 226–7) found a confusion between the dual process of rat poisoning (arsenic inducing thirst and water causing death) and the single process of lechery incurring punishment. But the confusion springs only from editorial punctuation in line 117. Claudio's attitude recalls Palingenius, *Zodiake* (tr. Googe, 1565), p. 73: 'How many men have beene destroide by to much liberty? /

How many men in safety liue with bridles dost thou see?' *Like rats:* ratsbane and lechery were nevertheless associated in early Jacobean satire. Cf. Middleton, *Blacke Booke* (VIII. 6): 'the ratsbane of a harlot'.

123–4. *I would ... creditors*] with the implication that they would have *him* arrested too.

125–6. *foppery ... morality*] a clear antithesis; foppery = foolishness (*O.E.D.* 1); morality = moral instruction (*O.E.D.* 3). Lucio prefers the foolish or flippant talk of freedom to the moralizing of people under arrest. F 'mortality' has never been convincingly defended. Cf. Webster, *White Devil*, v. i. 177, where the 1612 Quarto has 'mortality', emended to 'morality' in all edd.

128.] Cf. *Per.*, IV. vi. 75 ff.: 'What trade, sir?' 'Why, I cannot name't but I shall offend'.

129. *Lechery? Call it so*] Cf. *1 Prom.*,

Cla.   Call it so.

Pro. Away, sir; you must go.   130

Cla. One word, good friend: Lucio, a word with you.

Lucio. A hundred—if they'll do you any good.
    Is lechery so look'd after?

Cla. Thus stands it with me: upon a true contract
    I got possession of Julietta's bed.   135
    You know the lady; she is fast my wife,
    Save that we do the denunciation lack
    Of outward order. This we came not to
    Only for propagation of a dower
    Remaining in the coffer of her friends,   140
    From whom we thought it meet to hide our love
    Till time had made them for us. But it chances
    The stealth of our most mutual entertainment
    With character too gross is writ on Juliet.

Lucio. With child, perhaps?

Cla.   Unhappily, even so.   145
    And the new deputy now for the Duke—
    Whether it be the fault and glimpse of newness,

131–3.] *as Johnson;* One . . . friend: / . . . you. / . . . hundred: / . . . after? *F; as prose, Pope.*   139. propagation] *F* (propogation); procuration *Collier 2;* preservation *White;* prorogation *Sisson, conj. Malone;* propugnation *conj. Staunton;* propriation *conj. N.C.S.*   147. fault] *F;* flash *conj. Johnson;* foil *conj. T. White (Camb.).*

II. i: 'The lecher fyerd with lust, is punished no more / Then he which fel through force of loue, whose mariage salues his sore'.

133. *look'd after*] 'kept watch upon' (Onions). A rare usage, this being the first recorded instance (*O.E.D. v.* 12 g).

134–8. *Thus stands it . . . order*] The common law contract of *sponsalia de praesenti*, a mutual recognition as husband and wife in the presence of witnesses, was still valid in England, though the church required a religious ceremony. See Intro., pp. liii f. *upon*: in consequence of. *fast*: bound; perhaps alluding also to 'handfasting' in the traditional *sponsalia* (*O.E.D. a.* 4b). *denunciation*: public announcement, especially of banns before matrimony.

139. *propagation*] breeding; used for a figurative gestation, i.e. actualizing of what was potential, and suggested here by the idea of the dowry having to be 'born' out of the coffer (not, as *O.E.D.* 3, 'increase'). F's 'propogation' was a not uncommon spelling variant.

139–42. *a dower . . . us*] If the girl was an orphan, her relatives were normally trustees of the dowry. *friends*: kinsmen, near relations. *made them for us*: put them on our side.

143. *our most mutual entertainment*] stressing the element of consent. For 'entertainment' cf. *Per.*, IV. ii. 60.

144. *character too gross*] too obvious signs of pregnancy. Cf. 'character' in I. i. 27.

147. *fault and glimpse*] probably a

Of whether that the body public be
A horse whereon the governor doth ride,
Who, newly in the seat, that it may know   150
He can command, lets it straight feel the spur;
Whether the tyranny be in his place,
Or in his eminence that fills it up,
I stagger in—but this new governor
Awakes me all the enrolled penalties   155
Which have, like unscour'd armour, hung by th' wall
So long, that nineteen zodiacs have gone round,
And none of them been worn; and for a name
Now puts the drowsy and neglected act
Freshly on me: 'tis surely for a name.   160

Lucio. I warrant it is: and thy head stands so tickle on
          thy shoulders, that a milkmaid, if she be in love,
          may sigh it off. Send after the Duke, and appeal to
          him.

Cla. I have done so, but he's not to be found.   165
       I prithee, Lucio, do me this kind service:
       This day my sister should the cloister enter,
       And there receive her approbation.

---

157. nineteen] *F;* fourteen *conj. Whalley (Camb.).*

---

hendiadys, i.e. faulty glimpse ('flash
or momentary shining', *O.E.D. sb.*
1).

152-3. *in his place,* / *Or in his eminence*] 'in the nature of his official position, or in his own self-importance'.
Cf. Marston, *Histriomastix,* IV (III. 280):
'the proud pild Eminence / Of this
same gilded Madam'.

154. *stagger*] 'waver, hesitate (to
say)'.

156. *like unscour'd armour*] a familiar
figure for disuse or neglect. Cf. *Edward
III,* I. ii. 29-31 (*Sh. Apoc.*).

157. *nineteen zodiacs*] The course of
the zodiac is completed in a year. But
in I. iii. 21, the Duke speaks of fourteen
years. The discrepancy may be due to
a confusing of the figures 4 and 9; or
Shakespeare may simply have forgotten what he wrote.

158. *worn*] The subject is 'penalties',

line 155, continuing the armour
simile.

for a name] for his fame, reputation.

159. *drowsy*] Cf. the figure of the
sleeping lion, I. i. 63-4.

161-3. *and thy head . . . sigh it off*]
'There seems to be no point in con-
necting Claudio's head with the milkmaid' (*N.C.S.*). The connection turns
on the equivocal 'head'. Cf. *Rom.,* I. i.
27 f.: 'I will cut off their heads . . . the
heads of the maids, or their maiden-
heads'. 'It' covers both meanings: 'if
the milkmaid's "head" were as tickle
(i.e. unstable) as yours she would sigh
it off'. See also *2H6,* IV. vii. 126 f.:
'The proudest peer . . . shall not wear
a head on his shoulders, . . . not a maid
. . . but she shall pay to me her maidenhead'. Cf. IV. ii. 1-4 *infra.*

168. *approbation*] novitiate. Cf. 'probation', V. i. 75.

Acquaint her with the danger of my state:
Implore her, in my voice, that she make friends   170
To the strict deputy: bid herself assay him.
I have great hope in that. For in her youth
There is a prone and speechless dialect
Such as move men; beside, she hath prosperous art
When she will play with reason and discourse,   175
And well she can persuade.

Lucio. I pray she may: as well for the encouragement of
the like, which else would stand under grievous
imposition, as for the enjoying of thy life, who I
would be sorry should be thus foolishly lost at a   180
game of tick-tack.—I'll to her.

Cla. I thank you, good friend Lucio.

Lucio. Within two hours.

Cla. Come, officer, away.   *Exeunt.*

173. prone] *F;* grace *Sisson;* power *conj. Johnson;* prompt *conj. Johnson, conj.
N.C.S.*   174. move] *F;* moves *Rowe.*

172–6. *For . . . persuade.*] There is an
undercurrent of irony in the equivocal words 'prone', 'move', and
'play', all capable of suggesting
sexual provocation. The overt drift,
however, is an application of psychology to the art of rhetoric. Cf. T.
Wright, *The Passions of the Minde,*
(1601) (1630 edn, p. 29): 'superiours
may learn to coniecture the affections of their subiectes mindes, by a
silent speech pronounced in their very
countenances. And this point especially may be obserued in women'.
prone: often 'eager' or 'apt'; but
Claudio means here the abject posture
of submission or helplessness (*O.E.D.*
4). Halliwell Nb. cites Southwell, *Saint
Peters Complaint* (1602), p. 33: 'Prone

looke, crost armes, bent knee, and contrite hart'. *dialect*: manner of speaking.
move: perhaps 'moves', but the plural
may be due to the influence of the two
precedent adjectives.

174–5. *beside, . . . discourse*] So Cinthio
described Epitia: '*La quale . . . haueua
vna dolcissima maniera di fauellare*'.

178. *the like*] The meaning would be
plainer if 'the' were read as 'thy',
which balances 'thy life', line 179.
Lucio is concerned for himself as well
as for Claudio.

179. *imposition*] accusation.

181. *tick-tack*] 'An old variety of
backgammon, played on a board with
holes along the edge, in which pegs
were placed for scoring' (*O.E.D.*).
With an equivocation.

SCENE III [*A Friar's Cell.*]

Enter DUKE *and Friar* THOMAS.

Duke. No. Holy father, throw away that thought;
　　Believe not that the dribbling dart of love
　　Can pierce a complete bosom. Why I desire thee
　　To give me secret harbour hath a purpose
　　More grave and wrinkled than the aims and ends　　5
　　Of burning youth.
Friar.　　　　　　　May your Grace speak of it?
Duke. My holy sir, none better knows than you
　　How I have ever lov'd the life remov'd,
　　And held in idle price to haunt assemblies,
　　Where youth, and cost, witless bravery keeps.　　10
　　I have deliver'd to Lord Angelo—
　　A man of stricture and firm abstinence—
　　My absolute power and place here in Vienna,
　　And he supposes me travell'd to Poland;
　　For so I have strew'd it in the common ear,　　15
　　And so it is receiv'd. Now, pious sir,
　　You will demand of me, why I do this.

Scene III

Scene III] Rowe; *Scena Quarta.* F.　　*A Friar's Cell*] N.C.S.; *A Monastery.* Rowe;
A Cell Capell.　　1. No.] *Sisson;* No: F; No; *Rowe;* No, *Capell.*　　10. witless] F;
and witlesse F2; a witless *N.C.S.,* conj. *Nicholson* (N. & Q. *1885*); with witless
conj. Camb.　　12. stricture] F; strict ure *Warburton.*

S.D.] *Thomas:* the name does not occur in the dialogue or the speech-prefixes of F, which give *Fri.* (Friar). See Intro., pp. xviii–xix.

1. *No*] The Duke is denying an off-stage suggestion that he has come to arrange a lover's rendezvous.

2. *dribbling dart*] N.C.S. cites *Shakespeare's England,* II. 381: 'an arrow falling feebly and thus unable to pierce a corslet'. Cf. 'a dribbed shot' (Sidney, *Astrophel and Stella,* III. 1).

3. *complete*] fully equipped, hence perfect. The association is with full armour, as in *Ham.,* I. iv. 52. With accent on first syllable.

10.] *witless bravery*: most editors insert 'and' or 'a' before 'witless'. The momentary pause may allow for a brief gesture of contempt, followed by strong stress on 'witless'. *cost:* costly display. *bravery:* ostentation. *keeps:* the quasi-singular form was a common Elizabethan usage (Abbott §333).

12. *stricture*] O.E.D. sb². and Onions gloss as 'strictness'; if so, a unique instance. But the common and more likely meaning was 'restriction' (O.E.D. sb.¹ 2). The word here alludes to Angelo's self-repression rather than to his strictness towards others.

15. *strew'd*] scattered, spread. Cf. 'broadcast'.

Friar. Gladly, my lord.

Duke. We have strict statutes and most biting laws,
    The needful bits and curbs to headstrong jades,   20
    Which for this fourteen years we have let slip;
    Even like an o'er-grown lion in a cave
    That goes not out to prey. Now, as fond fathers,
    Having bound up the threatening twigs of birch,
    Only to stick it in their children's sight   25
    For terror, not to use, in time the rod
    Becomes more mock'd than fear'd: so our decrees,
    Dead to infliction, to themselves are dead,
    And Liberty plucks Justice by the nose,

---

20. jades] *this edn;* weedes *F;* steeds *Theobald;* wills *N.C.S., conj. Walker (Dyce);* deeds *conj. Perring (Camb.).*   21. fourteen] *F;* nineteen *Theobald.*   slip] *F;* sleep *Theobald.*   26–7. rod / Becomes more] *Pope;* rod / More *F;* rod's / More *Singer 2;* rod / [ ] more *conj. N.C.S.*

19. *strict statutes and most biting laws*] 'strict' retains the Latin sense of 'drawn tight'; hence the figure of bits and curbs, line 20. Cf. *2H6*, IV. vii. 18–19: 'we are like to have biting statutes'.

20. *jades*] 'weedes' (F), though a common figure, creates a pointlessly mixed metaphor. 'jades' (wilful, spoilt horses) could have been misread in Shakespeare's handwriting as this word. Cf. Marlowe, *2 Tamburlaine*, IV. iii. 12: 'The headstrong jades . . . / That King Aegeus fed with human flesh, / And made so wanton'; also *R2*, III. iii. 179, and II. i. 252 *infra.* The application of the figure here, followed by 'twigs' and 'rod', lines 24, 26, may be indebted to Whetstone, *A Mirour for Magestrates of Cyties* (1584), sig. A4ᵛ–5: 'In times past, a Proclamation would keepe men in awe: and nowe, an Example of Iustice, scarse, makes in the wicked to chaunge countenance: but althouge, a Braynsicke Iade, wyll ronne with a Snaffle, a sharpe Bitte wyll bridle him . . . scourge him with the paine, and hee will crie, *Peccavi*'. See Intro., p. xlv.

21. *fourteen*] Cf. 'nineteen', I. ii. 157 and note.

slip] 'withdraw the head from the collar' (*O.E.D. v.¹* 17). Cf. *R3*, IV. iv. 112–13. The emendation 'sleep' results from editorial confusion between the 'o'ergrown lion' (line 22) and the sleeping lion of I. iv. 64.

22. *like an o'er-grown lion in a cave*] originally Horace, *Epist.*, I. i. 73–5, through Camerarius, *Fabellae Aesopicae*, a favourite schoolbook (Baldwin, I, 622 f.). An old lion, pretending to be sick, invited the other animals to visit him in his cave, thus saving himself the trouble of going out to catch his prey. Cf. I. iv. 63–4 and note.

23. *fond*] foolish.

25. *it*] the 'birch', now bound up.

26. *For terror, not to use*] so in Cinthio: '*ella credea, che tale fosse stata constituita la legge più per porre terrore*', etc. Cf. 'terror', I. i. 19.

26–7. *the rod . . . fear'd*] On the political application of the 'rod', cf. Lupton, *I Siuqila* (1580), p. 9: 'surely laws were as good vnmade as vnkept . . . to what end is a rod, if the childe be not beaten therewyth when it doeth offend?'

28.] 'if they are not executed, they are as good as dead'.

The baby beats the nurse, and quite athwart   30
Goes all decorum.

Friar.   It rested in your Grace
To unloose this tied-up justice when you pleas'd;
And it in you more dreadful would have seem'd
Than in Lord Angelo.

Duke.   I do fear, too dreadful.
Sith 'twas my fault to give the people scope,   35
'Twould be my tyranny to strike and gall them
For what I bid them do: for we bid this be done,
When evil deeds have their permissive pass,
And not the punishment. Therefore indeed, my father,
I have on Angelo impos'd the office;   40
Who may in th'ambush of my name strike home,
And yet my nature never in the fight
To do in slander. And to behold his sway,
I will, as 'twere a brother of your order,
Visit both prince and people. Therefore, I prithee,   45
Supply me with the habit, and instruct me
How I may formally in person bear
Like a true friar. Moe reasons for this action

---

42. in the fight] *F;* in the sight *Hanmer;* in the light *conj. Dyce;* win the fight *conj. Staunton.*   43. To do in] *F;* To do me *Halliwell;* So do in *Theobald;* To do it *Hanmer, Rann;* To die in *conj. Staunton.*   47. in] *F;* my *Pope.*   bear] *F;* bear me *Capell.*

30. *The baby beats the nurse*] Steevens referred to 'an ancient print, entitled "The World is turn'd Upside Down", where an infant is thus employed'. Cf. Nashe, Introduction to *Menaphon* (III. 315): 'it is no maruaile if euery Alehouse vaunt the table of the world turned vpside downe, since the child beateth his father, and the Asse whippeth his Master' (Hart, *N. & Q.*, 1908, p. 63).

35. *scope*] as in I. ii. 119.

36. *strike and gall*] combines the two previous figures of the rod and the 'bits and curbs'.

37. *we bid . . . done*] Cf. Seneca, *Troades*, 291: 'Qui non vetat peccare cum possit, iubet'.

41–2. *my name . . . my nature*] ducal authority as contrasted with the Duke in person.

43. *To do in slander*] to put in a discreditable position? 'Do': put or place (*O.E.D.* I. 1b), 'slander': ill repute (*O.E.D. sb.* 3). The phrase is hard to parallel, but emendations of 'sight' for 'fight' 'die' for 'do', etc. hardly improve the sense.

45. *prince*] the person with sovereign authority, irrespective of his title.

46. *habit*] attire of a friar.

47. *formally*] 'in outward appearance'.

bear] used intransitively as to 'carry oneself', 'behave'. Cf. *H5*, III. vii. 50; *Troil.*, II. iii. 252.

At our more leisure shall I render you;
Only this one: Lord Angelo is precise;   50
Stands at a guard with Envy; scarce confesses
That his blood flows; or that his appetite
Is more to bread than stone. Hence shall we see
If power change purpose, what our seemers be.   *Exeunt.*

SCENE IV [*A Nunnery.*]

Enter ISABELLA *and* FRANCISCA *a Nun.*

Isab. And have you nuns no farther privileges?
Nun. Are not these large enough?
Isab. Yes, truly; I speak not as desiring more,
But rather wishing a more strict restraint
Upon the sisters stood, the votarists of Saint Clare.   5

---

53. see] *F*; see, *Rowe.*   54. S.D.] *F2*; *Exèit. F.*

Scene IV

Scene IV] *Rowe*; *Scena Quinta. F.*   *A Nunnery*] *Rowe*; *The outer courtyard of a Nun-nery. N.C.S.*   S.D. *Francisca a Nun.*] *F*; *Francisca. Rowe.*   5. sisters stood, the]
this edn; Sisterstood, the *F*; Sisterhood, the *F2*; sister *Pope*; sisterhood, *Dyce 2.*

50. *precise*] strict in morals; puritanical.

51. *at a guard*] in a swordsman's posture of defence.

Envy] malice; here personified.

52. *That his blood flows*] Cf. I. iv. 57–8: 'whose blood / Is very snow-broth'.

53. *more to bread than stone*] a rather vague recollection of Matth., vii. 9 (Noble). Here 'possessed of natural desires' seems to be the meaning.

53–4. *Hence . . . seemers be*] Thiselton pointed out the fatuousness of Rowe's commas after 'see' and 'purpose', followed by later editors. Each half of line 54 contains an accusative noun clause, the object of 'see', the second marking the antithesis of seeming and being. Satire II in Marston's *The Metamorphosis of Pygmalions Image* (1589), directed against 'Precisians', was en-

titled *Quedam sunt, et non videntur.*

Scene IV

S.D. *Francisca*] The name does not occur in the dialogue. Speech-prefixes in F give *Nun.* See Intro., pp. xxiv f.

5. *Upon the sisters stood*] 'Sisterstood' in F ('sisterhood' in F2, and nearly all editions) is probably due to an auditory telescoping of final and initial 's'. A converse error appears in Marlowe, *1 Tamb.*, II. iii. 26, 'actions stop his speech', generally emended to 'actions top', etc.

Saint Clare] the founder of a famous order of white-habited nuns, known as the Poor Clares, at Assisi in 1212. Muir, *Shakespeare's Sources*, 108, n. 3, suggests that this detail is from Erasmus' *Funus*, in a passage also containing the names Bernardinus and Vincentius.

Lucio. [*within.*] Hoa! Peace be in this place!
Isab.   Who's that which calls?
Nun. It is a man's voice! Gentle Isabella,
  Turn you the key, and know his business of him;
  You may, I may not; you are yet unsworn:
  When you have vow'd, you must not speak with men 10
  But in the presence of the prioress;
  Then, if you speak, you must not show your face;
  Or if you show your face, you must not speak.
  He calls again: I pray you, answer him.   [*Retires.*]
Isab. Peace and prosperity! Who is 't that calls? 15

Enter LUCIO.

Lucio. Hail virgin, if you be—as those cheek-roses
  Proclaim you are no less—can you so stead me
  As bring me to the sight of Isabella,
  A novice of this place, and the fair sister
  To her unhappy brother Claudio?   20
Isab. Why 'her unhappy brother'? Let me ask,
  The rather for I now must make you know
  I am that Isabella, and his sister.
Lucio. Gentle and fair. Your brother kindly greets you.
  Not to be weary with you, he's in prison. 25
Isab. Woe me! For what?
Lucio. For that which, if myself might be his judge,
  He should receive his punishment in thanks:
  He hath got his friend with child.
Isab. Sir, make me not your story.
Lucio.   'Tis true. 30
  I would not, though 'tis my familiar sin,

---

6. S.D.] *Lucio within. F (centred S.D.).* 14. S.D.] *this edn; Exit Franc. Rowe; not in F.* 15. S.D.] *Rowe; not in F.* 17. stead] *Rowe;* steed *F.* 30. make me not] *F;* mock me not:— *Malone.* story] *F;* scorn *Dyce (after Davenant)*; sport *Singer 2.* 30–1. 'Tis true. / I] *as Capell* (Nay, 'tis true: / I); 'Tis true; I *F.*

9. *you are yet unsworn*] a point of importance in connection with the ending of the play.

14.] There is no need to provide Francisca with an exit here. She may stay, provided she does not speak (line 13), and she should not leave

Isabella alone with Lucio. See p. xxvi.

17. *stead*] 'be of service to'.

28.] 'I would give him only thanks instead of punishment'.

30. *make me not your story*] Onions and *O.E.D.* 5e gloss 'story' as 'theme for mirth', 'dupe'.

With maids to seem the lapwing, and to jest
Tongue far from heart, play with all virgins so.
I hold you as a thing enskied and sainted
By your renouncement, an immortal spirit,   35
And to be talk'd with in sincerity,
As with a saint.

Isab. You do blaspheme the good, in mocking me.

Lucio. Do not believe it. Fewness and truth; 'tis thus:
Your brother and his lover have embrac'd;   40
As those that feed grow full, as blossoming time
That from the seedness the bare fallow brings
To teeming foison, even so her plenteous womb
Expresseth his full tilth and husbandry.

Isab. Someone with child by him? My cousin Juliet?   45

Lucio. Is she your cousin?

Isab. Adoptedly, as schoolmaids change their names
By vain though apt affection.

Lucio.   She it is.

Isab. O, let him marry her!

Lucio.   This is the point.
The Duke is very strangely gone from hence;   50
Bore many gentlemen—myself being one—
In hand, and hope of action: but we do learn,

---

50. is] *F*; who is *Keightley*.   52. hand, and hope] *F*; hand, in hope *Keightley*;
hand and hope *Hart*; hand with hope *conj. Johnson*.

---

32. *to seem the lapwing*] The lapwing
cried when far from his nest, to deceive
birds of prey: hence proverbial for in-
sincerity (Tilley L 68).

34. *enskied*] placed in heaven: a
Shakespearean coinage.

38. *the good . . . me*] 'the good' is in
contrast, not in apposition, to 'me'.

39. *Fewness and truth*] 'truth is told in
few words'.

40. *lover*] frequently for a woman
(*O.E.D.* 2).

41–4.] Contrast Lucio's account
with Claudio's, I. ii. 117 ff. The
imagery of increase is typically Shakespearean. *seedness*: the state of being
sown. A provincialism, but Hart cites
two instances from Holland's Pliny

(1601). *foison*: plentiful harvest. Cf.
the marriage blessing in *Temp.*, IV. i.
110: 'Earth's increase, foison plenty'.
tilth: tillage: cf. *Sonn.*, III. 6: 'the tillage
of thy husbandry'. The commonplace
derives from Erasmus, translated in
Wilson's *Art of Rhetorike*: 'what punishment is he woorthie to suffer, that re-
fuseth to Plowe that lande which beyng
Tilled, yeldeth children' (ed. 1584,
p. 54). See Intro., p. lxxxiv.

51–2. *Bore . . . In hand, and hope of
action*] deceived ('Bore in hand') with
the hope of military service. Probably
of topical significance during the peace
talks with Spain (Intro., p. xxxi).
'Hand and hope' is a zeugma: 'in
hand, and in hope'.

By those that know the very nerves of state,
His giving out were of an infinite distance
From his true-meant design. Upon his place,   55
And with full line of his authority,
Governs Lord Angelo; a man whose blood
Is very snow-broth; one who never feels
The wanton stings and motions of the sense;
But doth rebate and blunt his natural edge   60
With profits of the mind, study and fast.
He, to give fear to use and liberty,
Which have for long run by the hideous law
As mice by lions, hath pick'd out an act
Under whose heavy sense your brother's life   65
Falls into forfeit: he arrests him on it,
And follows close the rigour of the statute
To make him an example. All hope is gone,
Unless you have the grace by your fair prayer
To soften Angelo. And that's my pith of business   70
'Twixt you and your poor brother.

Isab.   Doth he so,
  Seek his life?

---

54. giving out were] *F* (giuing-out, were)*;* giving out was *Collier 1;* givings out were *Rowe.*   61. fast.] *F2;* fast *F.*   70–1. pith of business / Twixt] *F;* pith / Of business betwixt *Hanmer.*   71–4. you . . . execution] *as Ridley;* you, . . . brother. / . . . so, / . . . life? / . . . already, / . . . warrant / . . . execution. / *F;* you, . . . brother. / . . . him / . . . hath / . . . execution. / *Hanmer, Camb.*

53. *nerves of state*] sinews, so fig. for the chief motivations of policy. Cf. *Troil.*, I. iii. 54–5: 'Agamemnon, . . . nerve and bone of Greece'.

56. *with full line*] with full scope. Cf. *2H4*, IV. iv. 39: 'Give him line and scope' (Hart).

58. *snow-broth*] melted snow. Still used in northern dialects. Cf. Marston, *Dutch Curtezan*, II. i: 'That I should love a strumpet I a man of Snowe!' (II. 83).

59.] *stings*: urges to desire. Cf. *Oth.*, I. iii. 335 f.: 'our raging motions, our carnal stings'. *motions of the sense*: the usual term in Elizabethan psychology for impulses or desires of a physical origin as communicated to the mind through the soul. Thomas Wright quotes St Augustine: '*Motus animae* . . .

alii affectiones, alii affectus, alii expressas passiones vocaverunt' (1630 edn, p. 7).

60. *rebate*] make dull.

edge] keenness of desire. Cf. *Ham.*, III. ii. 264.

63–4. *run by . . . As mice from lions*] from Aesop's fable of the sleeping lion (cf. I. iii. 22–3) through Camerarius (Baldwin, I. 618–19). But Aesop's moral was forbearance and gratitude: the lion saved the mouse and was in turn rescued by him.

65. *heavy sense*] grievous construction.

70. *my pith of business*] 'the essence of my business'.

71–2. *Doth . . . life?*] usually arranged as one line. The F division into half-lines is not only better for the

Lucio.   Has censur'd him already;
　　And, as I hear, the Provost hath a warrant
　　For's execution.
Isab. Alas, what poor ability's in me   75
　　To do him good!
Lucio.   Assay the power you have.
Isab. My power? Alas, I doubt.
Lucio.   Our doubts are traitors,
　　And makes us lose the good we oft might win
　　By fearing to attempt. Go to Lord Angelo,
　　And let him learn to know, when maidens sue,   80
　　Men give like gods; but when they weep and kneel,
　　All their petitions are as freely theirs
　　As they themselves would owe them.
Isab. I'll see what I can do.
Lucio.   But speedily.
Isab. I will about it straight;   85
　　No longer staying but to give the Mother
　　Notice of my affair. I humbly thank you.
　　Commend me to my brother: soon at night
　　I'll send him certain word of my success.
Lucio. I take my leave of you.
Isab.   Good sir, adieu.   90
                         Exeunt [*severally*].

75–7. Alas, . . . traitors] *as Hanmer;* Alas: . . . poore / . . . good. / . . . haue. / . . .
doubt. / . . . traitors / *F.*   78. makes] *F;* make *Rowe 3;* made *Johnson.*   82.
freely] *F;* truly *F2.*   90. S.D.] *this edn; Exeunt. F.*

metre: it also suggests Isabella's hesitation at putting her fear into words.
　72. *censur'd*] 'passed sentence upon'.
Cf. ii. i. 29.
　78. *makes*] quasi-singular verb to
plural subject (Abbott §333).
　81. *Men give like gods*] 'and what can
men doe to shewe themselues more
like Gods vpon the earth than in be-

stowing of this blessing to giue pardon
and life?' (B. Riche, *The Fruites of
Long Experience* (1604), p. 49).
　83. *owe*] own.
　86. *the Mother*] the head of the nun-
nery.
　88. *soon at night*] in the early part of
the night, i.e. evening. A common
idiom.

ACT II

SCENE I [*A Courtroom.*]

Enter ANGELO, ESCALUS *and Servants,* [*a*] *Justice.*

Ang. We must not make a scarecrow of the law,
    Setting it up to fear the birds of prey,
    And let it keep one shape till custom make it
    Their perch, and not their terror.

Esc.   Ay, but yet
    Let us be keen, and rather cut a little,   5
    Than fall, and bruise to death. Alas, this gentleman,
    Whom I would save, had a most noble father.
    Let but your honour know—
    Whom I believe to be most strait in virtue—
    That in the working of your own affections,   10
    Had time coher'd with place, or place with wishing,

ACT II

Scene 1

Act II Scene I] *Actus Secundus. Scœna Prima. F.*   *A Courtroom.*] *this edn; The Palace.*
Rowe; A Hall in Angelo's House. Capell; A Court of Justice. N.C.S.   S.D.] *F; Enter*
Angelo, Escalus, and a Justice; Provost, Officers and Others, attending. Capell.   8–9.]
as F; Let . . . believe | . . . virtue | Steevens '73; Let . . . (whom . . . believe | . . .
virtue) and consider | Capell.

A Courtroom] The scene is usually located in Angelo's house, but the dialogue suggests a session in court.

    S.D. *Justice*] See Intro., pp. xvii–xviii. 'Justice' could be any judicial officer, not necessarily a judge (*O.E.D.* 9b).

    2. *fear*] frighten.

    4. *terror*] Cf. I. i. 19, I. iii. 26.

    6. *fall*] 'let fall', as of felling a tree. Cf. *AYL.*, III. v. 5. The antitheses are not very clearly marked, and 'fall' is possibly a misreading of the adjective

'fell' = cruel or terrible, in contrast to 'keen', meaning (i) perceptive, (ii) sharp. The general sense is: 'Let us use the law as a pruning knife, not as an axe'.

    7. *had a most noble father*] Cinthio twice alludes to the father of Epitia and her brother, with the implication that he is dead. Nothing is said of his 'noble' character, to which Shakespeare reverts in III. i. 85–6 and 140.

    10. *affections*] physical desires.

Or that the resolute acting of your blood
Could have attain'd th'effect of your own purpose,
Whether you had not sometime in your life
Err'd in this point, which now you censure him,   15
And pull'd the law upon you.

Ang. 'Tis one thing to be tempted, Escalus,
Another thing to fall. I not deny
The jury passing on the prisoner's life
May in the sworn twelve have a thief, or two,   20
Guiltier than him they try. What's open made to justice,
That justice seizes. What knows the laws
That thieves do pass on thieves? 'Tis very pregnant,
The jewel that we find, we stoop and take 't,
Because we see it; but what we do not see,   25
We tread upon, and never think of it.
You may not so extenuate his offence
For I have had such faults; but rather tell me,
When I that censure him do so offend,
Let mine own judgement pattern out my death,   30
And nothing come in partial. Sir, he must die.

Enter PROVOST.

12. your] *Rowe (after Davenant);* our *F.*   22. What knows . . . laws] *F;* What
know . . . laws *Rowe 3;* what knows . . . law *Dyce 2;* who knows . . . laws *N.C.S.*
31. S.D.] *F; Collier (after 32); Provost coming forward | Hudson, N.C.S. (after 32.)*

12. *acting of your blood*] 'execution of
your sensual desires'. Alexander keeps
F 'our', which however jars with the
rhetorically iterated 'your' throughout
this speech.

15. *which now you censure him*] 'for
which you now pass sentence on him'.
Ellipsis with relative; cf. Abbott §394.

18. *I not deny*] a common construction (Abbott §305).

19. *passing on*] passing sentence on.
Cf. *Lr,* III. vii. 24: 'we may not pass
upon his life'.

19–21. *The jury . . . try*] 'The great
thieves hang the little ones' was proverbial, from the French (Tilley T
119). Cf. II. ii. 176–7.

21–22. *What's . . . seizes*] See Intro.,
p. xxix. It is unlikely that Shakespeare
wrote the lines in this form, which is

wordy and unmetrical. 'That' seems
to be a sophistication, and a more
probable arrangement would be
'What's open made / To justice, justice
seizes'.

22. *What knows the laws*] 'What cognizance can the laws take of the fact
that thieves are sentencing thieves?'
Cf. *Lr.,* IV. vi. 158 f.; 'handy-dandy,
which is the justice, which is the thief?'
Plural subject with quasi-singular
verb (Abbott §333).

23. *pregnant*] clear, obvious.

28. *For*] 'Because'.

29. *censure*] as in line 15.

30. *pattern out*] be a precedent for.
Cf. III. ii. 256.

31. *and nothing come in partial*] 'and
let no argument be introduced in my
favour'. Angelo argues (i) that though

Esc. Be it as your wisdom will.
Ang.   Where is the Provost?
Pro. Here, if it like your honour.
Ang.   See that Claudio
    Be executed by nine tomorrow morning;
    Bring him his confessor, let him be prepar'd,   35
    For that's the utmost of his pilgrimage.   *[Exit Provost.]*
Esc. Well, heaven forgive him; and forgive us all.
    Some rise by sin, and some by virtue fall.
    Some run from brakes of ice and answer none,
    And some condemned for a fault alone.   40

Enter ELBOW *[and] Officers [with]* FROTH *[and]* POMPEY.

Elbow. Come, bring them away. If these be good people
    in a commonweal, that do nothing but use their
    abuses in common houses, I know no law. Bring
    them away.

36. S.D.] *Rowe; not in F.*   38. Some . . . fall.] *Some . . . fall : F.*   39. from brakes of ice] *F* (Ice)*; through brakes of Vice *Rowe;* from brakes of vice *Steevens '78;* from breaks of ice *Collier 2, conj. Steevens (withdrawn); from brakes, off ice *conj. Knight.*   40. a fault] *F;* one fault *Sisson.*   alone] *F;* atone *conj. Ridley.* 40. S.D.] *Dyce; Enter Elbow, Froth, Clowne, Officers. F.*

tempted, he did not fall; (ii) that, even if he has had such 'faults', these mean nothing to the law unless they are an 'offence'—i.e. known to have been committed. The speech is full of dramatic irony.

    34. *by nine tomorrow morning*] At IV. ii. 62 the Provost tells Claudio: 'by eight tomorrow / Thou must be made immortal'. An hour would elapse before the prisoner was judicially considered dead. See Intro., p. xv.

    36. *his pilgrimage*] a biblical commonplace. Cf. Gen. xlvii. 9: 'the days of the years of my pilgrimage are an hundred and thirty years'.

    38.] a 'sententia' marked by italic printing in F. Cf. II. iv. 184.

    39. *brakes of ice*] The meaning is obscure if 'brakes' = thicket (*O.E.D. sb.*²). Interpretations of 'brake' as an engine of torture (Steevens), and as a cage (*N.C.S.*), are strained. Alexander, Sisson, and Bald accept Collier's

'breaks', Sisson citing *Troil.*, III. iii. 216, 'The fool slides o'er the ice that you should break' (*N.R.*, I. 79). But Rowe's emendation 'vice' for 'ice' with 'brake' as thicket, has been defended by James Winny (*T.L.S.*, 18 April 1958), who cites *H8*, I. ii. 75–6: 'the rough brake / That virtue must go through'. The F reading may possibly be understood as a reference to punishment in hell or purgatory, with 'brakes' as constrictions: cf. 'thrilling region of thick-ribbed ice' in Claudio's speech, III. i. 122. The meaning would then be 'hell pains'.

    40. *a fault alone*] with the stress on 'fault' as distinguished from 'offence' (cf. lines 28–9).

    41. *away*] 'this way'. Used often with 'come', as in 'Come away, death' (*Tw.N.*, II. iv. 51).

    42. *commonweal*] Cf. I. ii. 96.

    43. *common houses*] a euphemism for brothels; cf. the word 'commoner'

Ang. How now sir, what's your name? And what's the   45
matter?

Elbow. If it please your honour, I am the poor Duke's
constable, and my name is Elbow. I do lean upon
justice, sir, and do bring in here before your good
honour two notorious benefactors.   50

Ang. Benefactors? Well, what benefactors are they? Are
they not malefactors?

Elbow. If it please your honour, I know not well what
they are. But precise villains they are, that I am sure
of, and void of all profanation in the world, that good   55
Christians ought to have.

Esc. [*to Angelo*] This comes off well: here's a wise officer.

Ang. Go to. What quality are they of? Elbow is your
name? Why dost thou not speak, Elbow?

Pom. He cannot, sir: he's out at elbow.   60

Ang. What are you, sir?

Elbow. He, sir? A tapster, sir; parcel bawd; one that
serves a bad woman; whose house, sir, was, as they
say, plucked down in the suburbs; and now she professes a hot-house; which I think is a very ill house   65
too.

59.] *as Pope 2;* Why ... *Elbow? (as verse) F.*

prostitute) and Jonson's Doll Common.

47–8. *poor Duke's constable*] '"Duke's
constable" may be regarded as one
term or title' (Hart); but a transposition from 'Duke's poor constable' is
characteristic of Elbow. Cf. Dogberry
in *Ado*, III. v. 22: 'we are the poor
duke's officers'.

50–2. *benefactors . . . malefactors*]
Dogberry too confuses the two words.
Cf. *Ado*, IV. ii. 4–5.

54–6. *precise villains . . . have*] Cf.
I. iii. 50. Elbow's 'misplacings' form
an ironic commentary on Angelo's
principles.

58. *quality*] occupation, business, or
rank.

59. *Why . . . Elbow?*] The separate
lineation in F suggests a pause for
Elbow to answer.

60. *out at elbow*] without the wit to
reply. 'Your banquerout inuention
cleane out at the elbowes' (Nashe, III.
356).

61. *What*] what occupation or manner of person. A frequent Elizabethan
usage. Cf. IV. ii. 126 (Abbott §254).

62. *parcel*] partly, part-time. Jonson
has 'parcel broker', 'parcel poet', etc.

63–4. *as they say, plucked down*] Cf. I.
ii. 88–9.

64–5. *professes*] jocularly suggesting
the 'professed houses' of monks and
nuns, 'to profess' being to take the
vows of an order.

65. *hot-house*] literally a bath-house;
but these were notoriously blinds for
houses of ill-fame; hence the word
'stews'. Hart cites Jonson's Epigram
VII: 'Where lately harbour'd many a
famous whore, / A purging bill, now

Esc. How know you that?

Elbow. My wife, sir, whom I detest before heaven and
    your honour—

Esc. How? Thy wife?   70

Elbow. Ay, sir: whom I thank heaven is an honest wo-
    man—

Esc. Dost thou detest her therefore?

Elbow. I say, sir, I will detest myself also, as well as she,
    that this house, if it be not a bawd's house, it is pity of   75
    her life, for it is a naughty house.

Esc. How dost thou know that, constable?

Elbow. Marry, sir, by my wife, who, if she had been a
    woman cardinally given, might have been accused
    in fornication, adultery, and all uncleanliness there.   80

Esc. By the woman's means?

Elbow. Ay, sir, by Mistress Overdone's means; but as she
    spit in his face, so she defied him.

Pom. Sir, if it please your honour, this is not so.

Elbow. Prove it before these varlets here, thou honour-   85
    able man, prove it.

Esc. [*to Angelo*] Do you hear how he misplaces?

Pom. Sir, she came in great with child; and longing,
    saving your honours' reverence, for stewed prunes;

---

68. wife, sir,] *Rowe;* wife Sir? *F.*   89, 99, 107. prunes] *F* (prewyns).

---

fix'd vpon the dore, / Tells you it is a
hot-house: So it ma', / And still be a
whore-house. Th' are *Synonima*.' Elbow's remark is a mere gag: what
Mistress Overdone actually 'professed'
was a tavern.

68. *detest*] he means 'protest'. So
Mistress Quickly: 'I detest, an honest
maid as ever broke bread' (*Wiv.*, I. iv.
156–7) (Steevens).

76. *naughty*] wicked; also with an
innuendo, as in *MND*, IV. ii. 15.

79. *cardinally*] for 'carnally'.

82. *by Mistress Overdone's means*] i.e.
by her go-between or pimp. (*O.E.D.*
'mean' *sb.*² 9b: cf. Chaucer, *Troilus*,
III. 205, 'swych a mene / As maken
wommen vnto men to commen'. The
plural form was also used.)

85–6. *these varlets . . . thou honourable
man*] The epithets are transposed.
'Honourable man' had been made a
catch-phrase by Shakespeare himself
in *Julius Caesar*.

87. *misplaces*] puts words in the
wrong place. This intransitive use
seems to be Shakespeare's own (*O.E.D.
v.* 1c).

88–112.] The humour in Pompey's
rambling story depends mainly on its
run of equivocal words and phrases—
'stewed prunes', 'but two', 'stood',
'dish', 'pin', 'point', 'cracking the
stones', and perhaps others.

89. *stewed prunes*] the staple dish
offered in bawdy-houses, perhaps originally to evade the regulations
governing the licensed stews in South-

sir, we had but two in the house, which at that very   90
distant time stood as it were in a fruit-dish, a dish of
some three pence, your honours have seen such
dishes, they are not china dishes, but very good
dishes,—

Esc. Go to, go to: no matter for the dish, sir.   95

Pom. No indeed, sir, not of a pin: you are therein in the
right: but to the point. As I say, this Mistress Elbow
being, as I say, with child, and being great-bellied,
and longing, as I said, for prunes; and having but
two in the dish, as I said, Master Froth here, this very 100
man, having eaten the rest, as I said, and, as I say,
paying for them very honestly; for, as you know,
Master Froth, I could not give you three pence
again—

Froth. No, indeed.   105

Pom. Very well: you being then, if you be remembered,
cracking the stones of the foresaid prunes—

Froth. Ay, so I did indeed.

Pom. Why, very well: I telling you then, if you be remembered, that such a one and such a one were past 110
cure of the thing you wot of, unless they kept very
good diet, as I told you—

Froth. All this is true.

Pom. Why, very well then—

Esc. Come, you are a tedious fool. To the purpose: what 115

---

91. distant] *F;* instant *F2.*   99–100. but two] *F;* no more *F2.*

---

wark before 1546, which forbade the
sale of 'bread, ale, flesh, wood, coale, or
any victuals' (Stow, *Survey*, ed. Kings-
ford, II. 54). Hence, with a play on
'stewed', applied to the inmates. Cf.
1H4, III. iii. 127; Dekker, *Seven Deadly
Sins of London* (Percy Reprints, 4, p.
32): 'a house, where they set stewed
Prunes befor you'.

  90–1. *that very distant time*] F2 emended to 'instant' ('at that very time'),
which is clearly what Pompey means.
The case for 'distant' is that it provides
another example of 'misplacing'; but
would an audience catch this? A contracted MS. spelling of 'instant' as

'istant' might well have prompted
'correction' to 'distant'.

  93. *china dishes*] a new and expensive
import; but Pompey is again being
equivocal. 'China' provides innuen-
does in Wycherley's *Country Wife*, IV.
iii. Cf. John Braine, *Room At The Top*,
ch. 22: 'what in our private language
we describe as a fine piece of china'.

  111. *the thing you wot of*] Cf. I. ii. 42 ff.

  115. *a tedious fool*] Pompey is designated 'Clown' throughout the play.

  115–21. *what was done . . . by your
honour's leave*] further quibbles in the
manner of I. ii. 80 ff. *Come me to*: 'Proceed to' with 'me' as 'ethical dative'.

was done to Elbow's wife that he hath cause to complain of? Come me to what was done to her.

Pom. Sir, your honour cannot come to that yet.

Esc. No, sir, nor I mean it not.

Pom. Sir, but you shall come to it, by your honour's　120
leave. And I beseech you, look into Master Froth
here, sir; a man of fourscore pound a year; whose
father died at Hallowmas—was't not at Hallowmas, Master Froth?

Froth. All-hallond Eve.　125

Pom. Why, very well: I hope here be truths. He, sir,
sitting, as I say, in a lower chair, sir—'twas in the
Bunch of Grapes, where indeed you have a delight
to sit, have you not?

Froth. I have so, because it is an open room, and good for　130
winter.

Pom. Why, very well then: I hope here be truths.

Ang. This will last out a night in Russia
When nights are longest there. I'll take my leave,
And leave you to the hearing of the cause;　135
Hoping you'll find good cause to whip them all.

Esc. I think no less: good morrow to your lordship.

Exit [Angelo].

---

137. I . . . lordship.] *as prose, F.*　　　S.D.] *Warburton; Exit. F (after 136).*

121. *look into*] consider.

122. *a man of fourscore pound a year*] a
modest income, allowing little scope
for vice or extravagance. Cf. Marston,
Fawn, II: 'ist fower score a yeare thinkst
thou maintaines my geldings . . .
high play, and excellent company?'
(II, 164).

125. *All-hallond Eve*] Hallowe'en:
31 October.

127. *lower chair*] 'lower' meant reward, recompense (*O.E.D. sb.*); 'lower
chair' might signify 'best chair', 'chair
of honour'. Steevens mentions having
seen 'what was called a low chair,
designed for the ease of sick people'.
By then 'lower' was probably confused with the adjective 'low'.

127–8. *the Bunch of Grapes*] Names
were commonly given to the various

rooms in a tavern; e.g. the Half-moon
and Pomegranate (*1H4*, II. iv. 30, 42).

130–1. *an open room, and good for
winter.*] 'open' = public, as in 'open
court'. In winter a fire would burn
there all day, whereas in the private
rooms, which Froth could not afford,
fires would only be lit to order. Cf.
The London Prodigal, I. ii. 110 ff. (*Sh.
Apoc.*).

133. *a night in Russia*] Cf. *Err.*, III. ii.
101, on 'a Poland winter'; Webster,
Duchess of Malfi, IV. i. 115 ff., on 'a
Russian winter'.

134–6.] Angelo does not show neglect of duty or marked severity. Scene
ii, with no lapse of time indicated, has
him 'hearing of a cause' when the
Provost arrives; and whipping was a
normal punishment for bawds.

Now, sir, come on. What was done to Elbow's wife,
once more?

Pom. Once, sir? There was nothing done to her once.　140

Elbow. I beseech you, sir, ask him what this man did to
my wife.

Pom. I beseech your honour, ask me.

Esc. Well, sir, what did this gentleman to her?

Pom. I beseech you, sir, look in this gentleman's face.　145
Good Master Froth, look upon his honour; 'tis for a
good purpose.—Doth your honour mark his face?

Esc. Ay, sir, very well.

Pom. Nay, I beseech you, mark it well.

Esc. Well, I do so.　150

Pom. Doth your honour see any harm in his face?

Esc. Why, no.

Pom. I'll be supposed upon a book, his face is the worst
thing about him.—Good, then: if his face be the
worst thing about him, how could Master Froth do　155
the constable's wife any harm? I would know that
of your honour.

Esc. He's in the right, constable; what say you to it?

Elbow. First, and it like you, the house is a respected
house; next, this is a respected fellow; and his mis-　160
tress is a respected woman.

Pom. By this hand, sir, his wife is a more respected person than any of us all.

Elbow. Varlet, thou liest! Thou liest, wicked varlet!
The time is yet to come that she was ever respected　165
with man, woman, or child.

Pom. Sir, she was respected with him, before he married
with her.

Esc. Which is the wiser here, Justice or Iniquity? Is this
true?　170

138–57.] The whole dialogue turns
on the equivocal 'done'.

153. *supposed upon a book*] i.e. 'de-
posed'. 'I will take my oath on a bible'.

153–4. *his face is the worst thing about
him*] This sounds proverbial. Cf.
Escalus on Pompey, lines 214–15.

159. *and*] 'if'. The usual spelling of

the time, now too often rendered as
'an'.

respected] for 'suspected'. Dogberry
uses a converse 'misplacing' in *Ado*,
IV. ii. 79–80: 'Dost thou not suspect
my place? Dost thou not suspect my
years?'

169. *Justice or Iniquity*] morality play

Elbow. O thou caitiff! O thou varlet! O thou wicked
     Hannibal! I respected with her, before I was mar-
     ried to her? If ever I was respected with her, or she
     with me, let not your worship think me the poor
     Duke's officer. Prove this, thou wicked Hannibal,   175
     or I'll have mine action of battery on thee.
Esc. If he took you a box o' th' ear, you might have your
     action of slander too.
Elbow. Marry, I thank your good worship for it. What
     is't your worship's pleasure I shall do with this   180
     wicked caitiff?
Esc. Truly, officer, because he hath some offences in him
     that thou wouldst discover if thou couldst, let him
     continue in his courses till thou know'st what they
     are.   185
Elbow. Marry, I thank your worship for it.—Thou seest,
     thou wicked varlet now, what's come upon thee.
     Thou art to continue now, thou varlet, thou art to
     continue.
Esc. Where were you born, friend?   190
Froth. Here in Vienna, sir.
Esc. Are you of fourscore pounds a year?
Froth. Yes, and 't please you, sir.
Esc. So. [*to Pompey*] What trade are you of, sir?
Pom. A tapster, a poor widow's tapster.   195
Esc. Your mistress' name?
Pom. Mistress Overdone.
Esc. Hath she had any more than one husband?

---

personifications, as Johnson pointed
out. Hart mentions the contest between 'Judge' and 'Iniquity' in *Nice
Wanton* (1560). Jonson has 'Iniquity,
the Vice' in *The Devil Is An Ass*;
Shakespeare has 'the formal Vice,
Iniquity' (*R3*, III. i. 82); and Falstaff is
'that reverend vice, that grey iniquity'
(*1H4*, II. iv. 505–6). It is unlikely that
'Justice' refers to the Justice who is
silent almost until the end of the
scene: Pompey's adversary is Elbow
in this parody of the traditional situation.

172. *Hannibal*] for cannibal. Cf. 'Oh
wicked Caniball' (*Duchess of Malfi*, II.
ii. 47). The confusion seems to have
been widespread: Baldwin (II. 326)
cites a theme set for refutation in
Aphthonius' school primer: *Annibalis
exercitum humanas carnes edisse*.

174–5. *the poor Duke's officer*] Cf.
lines 47–8.

177. *took you*] 'struck you'.

181. *caitiff*] wretch.

182. *offences*] offences against the
law. Cf. line 27.

193. *and*] as in 159.

Pom. Nine, sir; Overdone by the last.

Esc. Nine!—Come hither to me, Master Froth. Master   200
Froth, I would not have you acquainted with tap-
sters; they will draw you, Master Froth, and you
will hang them. Get you gone, and let me hear no
more of you.

Froth. I thank your worship. For mine own part, I never   205
come into any room in a tap-house, but I am drawn
in.

Esc. Well: no more of it, Master Froth: farewell. [*Exit Froth.*]
Come you hither to me, Master tapster. What's
your name, Master tapster?   210

Pom. Pompey.

Esc. What else?

Pom. Bum, sir.

Esc. Troth, and your bum is the greatest thing about
you; so that, in the beastliest sense, you are Pompey   215
the Great. Pompey, you are partly a bawd, Pompey, howsoever you colour it in being a tapster, are
you not? Come, tell me true, it shall be the better
for you.

Pom. Truly, sir, I am a poor fellow that would live.   220

Esc. How would you live, Pompey? By being a bawd?
What do you think of the trade, Pompey? Is it a
lawful trade?

Pom. If the law would allow it, sir.

Esc. But the law will not allow it, Pompey; nor it shall   225
not be allowed in Vienna.

208. S.D.] *Rowe; not in F.*

202–3. *draw . . . hang*] with a play upon 'drawing', i.e. execution by dis-embowelling, the accompaniment to hanging in cases of high treason. 'Froth' is of course 'drawn' by the tapster.

213. *Bum*] The word should have two meanings if Escalus' remark in the next line is to 'come across'. It may have signified roguish or sham: cf. Lodge, *Wits Miserie*, F4ᵛ: 'vp starts cousenage with a bum dagger. . .

This fellow is excellent at a Bum card'.

214–15. *your bum . . . you*] a common expression (Tilley P 73), deriving from the fashion of wearing padded trunk-hose (which Pompey may have affected).

215–16. *in the beastliest sense . . . Great*] great in the crudest sense.

217. *colour*] disguise.

220.] Cf. Boult in *Per.*, IV. vi. 185 ff.: 'What would you have me do? Go to the wars, would you?'

Pom. Does your worship mean to geld and splay all the
   youth of the city?

Esc. No, Pompey.

Pom. Truly sir, in my poor opinion, they will to't then.   230
   If your worship will take order for the drabs and the
   knaves, you need not to fear the bawds.

Esc. There is pretty orders beginning, I can tell you. It is
   but heading and hanging.

Pom. If you head and hang all that offend that way but   235
   for ten year together, you'll be glad to give out a
   commission for more heads: if this law hold in
   Vienna ten year, I'll rent the fairest house in it
   after three pence a bay. If you live to see this come
   to pass, say Pompey told you so.   240

Esc. Thank you, good Pompey; and, in requital of your
   prophecy, hark you: I advise you, let me not find
   you before me again upon any complaint whatsoever; no, not for dwelling where you do. If I do,
   Pompey, I shall beat you to your tent, and prove a   245
   shrewd Caesar to you: in plain dealing, Pompey,
   I shall have you whipped. So for this time, Pompey,
   fare you well.

Pom. I thank your worship for your good counsel;

---

227. splay] *F;* spay *Steevens.*   233. There is] *F;* There are *F2.*   236.
year] *F;* years *Rowe.*   238. year] *F;* yeares *F2.*   239. bay] *F;* day
Rowe 3.

227. *geld and splay*] for castration of
males and females. Like the 'sanctimonious pirate' in I. ii. 7, Pompey sees
the order as 'a commandment to command them from their functions'.

231. *take order for*] make arrangements for; so in II. ii. 25.

231-2. *the drabs and the knaves*]
'drab': a cheap harlot; 'knave': a
rascally boy. Cf. *2H6*, II. i. 155: 'follow
the knave and take this drab away'
(Schmidt).

234. *heading*] beheading. Hanging
was the death penalty for common
felons, beheading for gentlemen.

239. *bay*] 'the space lying under one

gable, or included between two party-
walls' (*O.E.D. sb.*[3] 2).

240. *say Pompey told you so*] Cf.
Lucio's 'say that I said so' (III. ii. 178);
All's W., IV. iii. 257: 'And say a soldier,
Dian, told thee this'. A catch-phrase of
the time (Tilley S 111).

245-6. *I shall . . . a shrewd Caesar*]
Thiselton cites North's Plutarch:
'Then Pompey . . . being affrayde and
amazed with the slaughter sent from
above . . . retyred into his tent, speaking never a word' (Life of Caesar,
Tudor Transl., v. 48. See also Life of
Pompey, IV. 283). Cf. III. ii. 42-3.
shrewd: 'severe'.

> [*aside*] but I shall follow it as the flesh and fortune   250
> shall better determine.
>   Whip me? No, no, let carman whip his jade;
>   The valiant heart's not whipt out of his trade.   *Exit.*

Esc. Come hither to me, Master Elbow: come hither,
     Master constable. How long have you been in this   255
     place of constable?

Elbow. Seven year and a half, sir.

Esc. I thought, by the readiness in the office, you had
     continued in it some time.—You say seven years
     together?   260

Elbow. And a half, sir.

Esc. Alas, it hath been great pains to you: they do you
     wrong to put you so oft upon't. Are there not men
     in your ward sufficient to serve it?

Elbow. Faith, sir, few of any wit in such matters. As they   265
     are chosen, they are glad to choose me for them; I
     do it for some piece of money, and go through with
     all.

Esc. Look you bring me in the names of some six or
     seven, the most sufficient of your parish.   270

Elbow. To your worship's house, sir?

Esc. To my house. Fare you well. [*Exit Elbow.*] What's
     o'clock, think you?

Justice. Eleven, sir.

Esc. I pray you home to dinner with me.   275

Justice. I humbly thank you.

---

250. S.D.] *Johnson; not in F.*   252–3.] *as Rowe; prose, F.*   258. by the] *F;*
by your *Pope.*   272. S.D.] *Johnson; Rowe (at* think you *273); not in F.*   275.
home] *F;* goe home *F2.*

250. S.D.] The 'aside' is spoken while Pompey is retiring from the courtroom. At a safe distance, he turns and declaims his couplet to the audience.

250–1. *as the flesh . . . determine*] 'according to what human nature and fortune will decide—a better decision than yours'.

252. *jade*] Cf. I. iii. 20.

253. *The valiant heart's . . . trade*] Pompey's attitude was not uncommon in Jacobean drama. Cf. Middleton,

Michaelmas Term, IV. ii: 'To be bawd! Do not all trades live by their ware, and yet called honest livers?' So in Marston's *Dutch Curtezan*, I. i: 'everie man must follow his trade, and everie woman her occupation' (II. 73–4).

258. *the readiness*] the facility of performance. *the*: perhaps 'yʳ' misread.

264. *sufficient*] Cf. 'sufficiency', I. i. 8.

265. *few of any wit*] 'You might be a constable for your wit' was proverbial banter (*O.D. Eng. Prov.*, p. 605).

Esc. It grieves me for the death of Claudio,
    But there's no remedy.
Justice. Lord Angelo is severe.
Esc.   It is but needful.
    Mercy is not itself, that oft looks so;   280
    Pardon is still the nurse of second woe.
    But yet, poor Claudio! There is no remedy.
    Come, sir.   *Exeunt.*

SCENE II [*An ante-room to the same.*]

Enter PROVOST [*and a*] *Servant.*

Servant. He's hearing of a cause: he will come straight;
    I'll tell him of you.
Prov.   Pray you, do. [*Exit Servant.*] I'll know
    His pleasure, may be he will relent. Alas,
    He hath but as offended in a dream;
    All sects, all ages smack of this vice, and he   5
    To die for't!

Enter ANGELO.

Ang.   Now, what's the matter, Provost?

282. There is] *F;* There's *Pope.*

Scene II

Scene II] *Scena Secunda. F.*   *An ante-room to the same.*] *this edn; Angelo's House
Johnson; A Room in the same. Capell; The same. N.C.S.*   S.D.] *Rowe; Enter Prouost,
Seruant. F.*   2. Pray you, do] *Theobald;* 'Pray you doe *F;* Pray you do *F2.*
S.D.] *Capell; not in F.*   6. for't!] *F2;* for't? *F.*

280.] 'Seeming mercy is often not merciful in the long run'.

281. *Pardon . . . second woe*] a commonplace (Tilley P 50). Escalus expresses the same attitude as Angelo at II. ii. 101–5.

Scene II

4. *as offended in a dream*] 'offended as one might in a dream': the offence has to do with concepts, not with actuality.

5. *sects*] probably ranks or classes

(*O.E.D.* 1), rather than religious or political movements.

ages] either periods of history, or of a person's life.

smack of] taste of; hence, partake of.

6, 9, 12, 14.] These lines, divided between Angelo and the Provost, are metrically irregular but dramatically effective, suggesting Angelo's brusqueness and the Provost's embarrassment. They contribute to the impression of strain at the beginning of the scene.

Prov. Is it your will Claudio shall die tomorrow?

Ang. Did I not tell thee yea? Hadst thou not order?
　　Why dost thou ask again?

Prov.　　　　　　　　　　　Lest I might be too rash.
　　Under your good correction, I have seen　　　　10
　　When, after execution, judgement hath
　　Repented o'er his doom.

Ang.　　　　　　　　　Go to; let that be mine;
　　Do you your office, or give up your place,
　　And you shall well be spar'd.

Prov.　　　　　　　　　I crave your honour's pardon.
　　What shall be done, sir, with the groaning Juliet?　　15
　　She's very near her hour.

Ang.　　　　　　　　　Dispose of her
　　To some more fitter place; and that with speed.

[Enter Servant.]

Servant. Here is the sister of the man condemn'd,
　　Desires access to you.

Ang.　　　　　　　　　Hath he a sister?

Prov. Ay, my good lord, a very virtuous maid;　　　　20
　　And to be shortly of a sisterhood,
　　If not already.

Ang.　　　　　　Well, let her be admitted.　*[Exit Servant.]*
　　See you the fornicatress be remov'd;
　　Let her have needful, but not lavish means;
　　There shall be order for't.

Enter LUCIO *and* ISABELLA.

Prov.　　　　　　　　　Save your honour!　*[Going.]*
Ang. Stay a little while.

17. S.D.] *Capell; not in* F.　　22. S.D.] *Theobald; not in* F.　　25. Save] *John-son;* 'Saue F; God save *Camb.*　　S.D. *Going.*] *Alexander; not in* F; *Offering to retire. Var. 1821.*

12. *doom*] sentence.
mine] 'my affair'.
15. *groaning*] in labour.
23. *fornicatress*] The offence, to Angelo's mind, is fornication, not, as in Cinthio, rape.
24. *means*] conditions of living

in imprisonment.
25. *Save*] for 'God save', and printed with an apostrophe here and elsewhere in F (cf. F abbreviations 'Pray, 2; 'Please, 28).
26. *Stay a little while*] The Provost is kept back to witness the interview.

[*To Isabella*]   Y'are welcome: what's your will? 26
Isab. I am a woeful suitor to your honour;
    Please but your honour hear me.
Ang.   Well: what's your suit?
Isab. There is a vice that most I do abhor,
    And most desire should meet the blow of justice; 30
    For which I would not plead, but that I must;
    For which I must not plead, but that I am
    At war 'twixt will and will not.
Ang.   Well: the matter?
Isab. I have a brother is condemn'd to die;
    I do beseech you, let it be his fault, 35
    And not my brother.
Prov. [*aside*]   Heaven give thee moving graces!
Ang. Condemn the fault, and not the actor of it?
    Why, every fault's condemn'd ere it be done:
    Mine were the very cipher of a function
    To fine the faults, whose fine stands in record, 40
    And let go by the actor.
Isab.   O just but severe law!
    I had a brother, then: heaven keep your honour. [*Going.*]
Lucio. [*to Isab.*] Give't not o'er so.—To him again,
    entreat him,

---

28. Please] *Pope 2;* 'Please *F.*   40. fine the] *F;* find the *Theobald 2.*   42. S.D.]
Steevens '85; not in F.

---

27. *a woeful suitor*] The appeal of the
Gentlewoman to the Judge in *2 Siuqila,* sig. N^v, has the marginal comment: 'A lamentable suter'. In *1
Prom.,* II. iii, Cassandra's appeal
begins: 'Behold the wofull Syster
here'.

31–33. *For which . . . will not*] Cf.
2 Siuqila, sig. N: 'whose cause I come
not to defend, but for whom I come to
craue mercy'. Cinthio's Epitia at once
pleads mitigating circumstances for
her brother in his youth, inexperience,
and the goading of love. Whetstone's
Cassandra argues similarly.

33. *Well: the matter?*] 'I pray you,
sayde the Iudge, tell me your matter
and cause as briefly and plainely as
you can' (*2 Siuqila,* sig. N).

35–6. *let it be his fault, And not my
brother*] 'let the fault be condemned
and not the man'. Isabella is adapting
to her own purpose the familiar maxim
'Hate not the person but the vice'
(Tilley P 238). Cf. *1 Siuqila,* page 45:
'your king respects (i.e. regards) not
the offender, but the offence'.

37–41. *Condemn . . . actor*] substantially: 'The law condemns all faults in
advance; merely to repeat the condemnation and ignore the wrongdoer
would be to give up my function as a
judge'. *To fine the faults, whose fine stands
in record:* the faults have their punishment ('fine'), by being recorded as
faults; his task as a judge is not to
punish ('fine') them again, but to deal
with the wrong-doer.

Kneel down before him, hang upon his gown;
You are too cold. If you should need a pin,   45
You could not with more tame a tongue desire it.
To him, I say.

Isab. Must he needs die?

Ang.   Maiden, no remedy.

Isab. Yes: I do think that you might pardon him,
And neither heaven nor man grieve at the mercy.   50

Ang. I will not do't.

Isab.   But can you if you would?

Ang. Look what I will not, that I cannot do.

Isab. But might you do't, and do the world no wrong,
If so your heart were touch'd with that remorse
As mine is to him?

Ang.   He's sentenc'd, 'tis too late.   55

Lucio. [*to Isab.*] You are too cold.

Isab. Too late? Why, no. I that do speak a word
May call it again.—Well, believe this:
No ceremony that to great ones longs,
Not the king's crown, nor the deputed sword,   60
The marshal's truncheon, nor the judge's robe,
Become them with one half so good a grace
As mercy does.

---

58. again] *F;* back again *F2;* in again *N.C.S.*   Well,] *F;* Well *Theobald 2.*
59. longs] *F;* belongs *Rowe 3;* 'longs *Theobald 2.*   63–6. As . . . stern.] *as Capell;*
As . . . as he, / . . . like you / . . . sterne. *F;* As . . . as you, / . . . like him; / . . .
stern. *Johnson.*

47, 56, 111, 130, 133, 149.] Lucio's various interjections are for the most part extra-metrical, since they impinge upon, and are not taken up into, the main dialogue.

51–2.] In *2 Siuqila*, sig. N^v, the Judge says: 'Gentlewoman cease your sute, for it lieth not in my handes to helpe you: but if I coulde I would not'.

53. *the world*] society.

54. *remorse*] compassion.

58. *again*] emended on metrical grounds to 'back again', or 'in again', by all editors except Sisson, *N.R.*, i. 79, who comments: 'there is a marked and dramatic pause in the middle of the line, and no irregularity is

felt in the speaking of the passage'.

Well,] perhaps in answer to some gesture of refusal which occupies the missing 'foot': or there may be a transposition from 'Believe this well'.

59. *longs*] a variant of the verb 'belongs', not a contraction.

60. *the deputed sword*] the sword of justice committed to mayors or governors in token of their office. In *1 Prom.*, i. i, the Mayor invests Promos with it.

61. *truncheon*] baton; symbol of military command.

62. *Become . . . grace*] Isabella plays on 'grace', as seemliness and as a divine attribute, much as Lucio does in i. ii. 24 ff.

If he had been as you, and you as he,
You would have slipp'd like him, but he like you   65
Would not have been so stern.

Ang.   Pray you be gone.

Isab. I would to heaven I had your potency,
And you were Isabel! Should it then be thus?
No; I would tell what 'twere to be a judge,
And what a prisoner.

Lucio. [*to Isab.*]   Ay, touch him: there's the vein. 70

Ang. Your brother is a forfeit of the law,
And you but waste your words.

Isab.   Alas, alas!
Why, all the souls that were, were forfeit once,
And He that might the vantage best have took
Found out the remedy. How would you be   75
If He, which is the top of judgement, should
But judge you as you are? O, think on that,
And mercy then will breathe within your lips,
Like man new made.

Ang.   Be you content, fair maid;
It is the law, not I, condemn your brother;   80
Were he my kinsman, brother, or my son,
It should be thus with him. He must die tomorrow.

Isab. Tomorrow? O, that's sudden.

---

80. condemn] *F;* condemns *Rowe.*   83–4. sudden. / Spare] *as F;* sudden: Spare
Pope.

---

67. *potency*] power to act.

69. *tell*] know.

70. *there's the vein*] 'that is the right approach'. Perhaps fig. from the action of the physician seeking the vein for blood-letting. 'Vein' also signifies a style in writing or speech.

75–7. *How . . . are?*] 'Judge not, that ye be not judged' (Matth., vii. 1). See Intro., p. lxiii.

76. *top*] the most perfect example or type.

78–9. *And mercy then . . . new made.*] Redemption is a second creation of man in God's image. As Adam was given a soul when the Creator breathed life into his nostrils, so the new Adam is redeemed from the first Adam's sin by the breath of divine mercy in Christ, which moves on his lips when he speaks mercifully to his fellow men. Juridically, such imitation of Christ yokes the central Christian tenet to the concept of judges as gods (see note to I. ii. 112), as in the maxim 'It is in their mercy that kings come closest to gods' (Tilley M 898). So in Portia's speech, *Mer.V.,* IV. i. 196–7.

80. *the law, not I, condemn*] The form of the verb may be 1st person by attraction of the pronoun 'I', or plural by influence of the precedent noun and pronoun (cf. I. ii. 174).

Spare him, spare him!
He's not prepar'd for death. Even for our kitchens   85
We kill the fowl of season: shall we serve heaven
With less respect than we do minister
To our gross selves? Good, good my lord, bethink you:
Who is it that hath died for this offence?
There's many have committed it.

Lucio. [*to Isab.*]   Ay, well said.   90
Ang. The law hath not been dead, though it hath slept:
Those many had not dar'd to do that evil
If the first that did th'edict infringe
Had answer'd for his deed. Now 'tis awake,
Takes note of what is done, and like a prophet   95
Looks in a glass that shows what future evils,
Either new, or by remissness new conceiv'd,
And so in progress to be hatch'd and born,
Are now to have no successive degrees,
But ere they live, to end.

93. the first] *F;* the first man *Pope;* the first one *Collier 2;* he, the first *Capell,*
conj. *Tyndall;* but the first *White;* that the first *Dyce 2 (after Walker);* the first
he conj. *Spedding (Camb.).*   97. Either new] *Dyce;* Either now *F;* Or new
Pope; Either now born *Keightley;* Eggs now conj. *N.C.S.*   100. ere] *Hanmer;*
here *F;* where *Malone.*

84. *Spare him, spare him!*] printed as a
separate line in F; cf. I. iv. 72.

85-8. *Even . . . selves*] Cf. *Cæs.,* II. i.
173: 'Let's carve him as a dish fit for
the gods'.

86. *of season*] that is in season.

91.] Cf. I. ii. 159, I. iv. 63-4. White
cited a maxim attributed to Coke:
*Dormiunt aliquando leges, moriuntur
nunquam.*

96. *a glass*] a prospective or magic
glass for divination. Hart notes the
account of this method in Scot's *Dis-
coverie of Witchcraft.* References are
frequent, e.g. Chapman, *Gentleman
Usher,* IV. iii. 62-3; Jonson, *Alchemist,*
I. i. 44, 97. This is the glass borne by
the Eighth King in *Macbeth,* IV. i.

97-100. *Either . . . end*] a recurrent
image-cluster where prophecy and
hatching are associated. Cf. *Cæs.,* II. i.
32 f.: 'think him as a serpent's egg /
Which, hatch'd, would as his kind

grow mischievous, / And kill him in
the shell', with 'exhalations in the air'
presently mentioned; *Mac.,* II. iii.
63 ff.: 'prophesying with accents
terrible / Of dire combustion and con-
fus'd events / New hatch'd to th' woeful time'; also *Ant.,* I. ii. 138 f., and
Cym., V. v. 60, where the imagery
becomes diffuse.

97. *Either new*] 'new' and 'new conceiv'd' are well balanced, whereas F
'now' leads to an awkward repetition
in line 99. The *N.C.S.* conjecture
'Eggs' for 'Either' is not far-fetched in
this context, but makes poor sense in
apposition to 'conceived', and is already implicit in the imagery. 'Either'
may be a sophistication for 'Or'.

100. *ere*] Alexander keeps F 'here',
which blurs the sense; but 'ere', well
advocated by *N.C.S.,* could easily be
misheard or (spelt 'yere') misread as
'here'.

Isab.   Yet show some pity.   100
Ang. I show it most of all when I show justice;
    For then I pity those I do not know,
    Which a dismiss'd offence would after gall,
    And do him right that, answering one foul wrong,
    Lives not to act another. Be satisfied;   105
    Your brother dies tomorrow; be content.
Isab. So you must be the first that gives this sentence,
    And he, that suffers. O, it is excellent
    To have a giant's strength, but it is tyrannous
    To use it like a giant.   110
Lucio. [*to Isab.*] That's well said.
Isab.   Could great men thunder
    As Jove himself does, Jove would ne'er be quiet,
    For every pelting petty officer
    Would use his heaven for thunder; nothing but thunder.
    Merciful Heaven,   115
    Thou rather with thy sharp and sulphurous bolt
    Splits the unwedgeable and gnarled oak,

---

112. ne'er] *F2;* neuer *F.*   114.] *as Capell;* Would . . . thunder. / Nothing *F.*

108–110. *O, it is . . . giant*] The revolt
of the giants against Jove was a familiar myth, especially as told in Ovid,
Metamorphoses, I. Because they had the
divine attribute of strength, without
divine wisdom or forbearance, their
actions were tyrannous, a travesty
rather than an imitation of God. '*Plus
posse et nolle, nobile*', and cf. *Sonn.,* XCIV:
'They that have power to hurt, and
will do none'. 'it is' in line 108 seems to
be a sophistication of ''tis', and in 109
unnecessary.

111–14. *Could great men . . . but
thunder*] developed from Ovid, '*si
quoties peccant homines sua fulmina mittat /
Iuppiter, exiguo tempore inermis erat*'
(*Tristia,* II. 33–4). In a Christian context, '*inermis erat*' drops out and the
irony is turned against the great who,
in travestying divine justice, reveal
themselves as petty officials. *pelting:*
paltry. *officer:* official.

115–18. *Merciful . . . soft myrtle*] The
contrast of the stout oak or cedar
struck by thunder while the pliant
shrub survived was a commonplace for
divine or royal justice and mercy. No
particular shrub became a type.
'Myrtle' appears again (with 'petty') in
Ant., III. x. 8 ff., for the obscure Euph-
ronius contrasted to the fallen Antony.

117. *Splits the unwedgeable and gnarled
oak*] Cf. Marston, *Metamorph. of Pygmalion's Image and Satires* (1598), sig.
E5ᵛ: 'Why thus it is, when Mimick
Apes will striue / With Iron wedge the
trunkes of Oakes to riue.' With the ape
image, already latent in the 'petty
officer's' mimicry of Jove, Marston's
figure reinforces the satire against
great men and suggests the word 'unwedgeable'. Cf. Marston, *Antonio's
Revenge,* IV. iii (I, 115). *Splits:* 2nd person sing. (Abbott §340), cf. 'exists',
III. i. 20. *gnarled:* a unique variant if
not a misprint of 'knarled' or 'knurled';
it entered the language only in the
19th cent., perhaps under the influence
of this passage.

Than the soft myrtle. But man, proud man,
Dress'd in a little brief authority,
Most ignorant of what he's most assur'd—   120
His glassy essence—like an angry ape
Plays such fantastic tricks before high heaven
As makes the angels weep; who, with our spleens,
Would all themselves laugh mortal.
Lucio. [*to Isab.*] O, to him, to him, wench! He will relent; 125

123. makes] *F; make Johnson.*

119. *Dress'd in a little brief authority*]
Erasmus' adage: '*Magistratus virum
indicat*', proverbial as 'Authority
shows what a man is' (Tilley A 402).
Dress'd: a favourite Shakespearean
image; cf. *Mer.V.*, I. i. 91–2, *1H4*, III. ii.
51, etc. Here the description of a man
in office (with 'little brief' recalling
'pelting petty') suggests an ape in his
short coat and implies the analogous
proverb, 'The higher an ape goes, the
more he shows his tail' (*O.D. Eng.
Prov.*, p. 443), interpreted in T.
Carew's *Sermons* (1603), sig. P7: 'one
compares an euill officer to an Ape on
the top of a house highly pearched'.
120–1. *Most ignorant . . . essence*]
'most ignorant of his own spiritual
entity, though religion should make
him most certain of it'.—'*Nosce teipsum*'.
His glassy essence: see J. V. Cunningham, *E.L.H.*, XIX (1952), p. 266:
'Man's essence is his intellectual soul,
which is an image of God, and hence is
glassy for it mirrors God'. For 'glassy'
in this sense (not in *O.E.D.*), he compares *Ham.*, IV. vii. 168, *1H6*, v. iii. 62.
Cunningham adds: '"Brittleness",
"clarity", and "pellucidness" . . . are
. . . beside the point'. But it would be
quite Shakespearean for all these
secondary meanings to be co-present
without impairing the primary one.
Cf. Montaigne's *Apology of Sebond*,
which refers to man's 'ignorance of
divine essence' (II. 297).
121–3. *like an angry ape . . . weep*] The
ape image, latent in all the previous
figures of mimicry, vanity, and ignorance, is here explicit. Dekker fre-

quently associates 'apes' with 'fantastic
tricks': cf. *Old Fortunatus*, II. ii. 25, 210–
13, and *Seven Deadly Sins of London*
(Percy Reprints, 4, p. 43): 'Man is
Gods Ape, and an Ape is *Zani* to a
man, doing ouer those trickes . . .
which hee sees done before him'. For
'angry ape' cf. Middleton, *Micro-
Cynicon* (1599), VIII. 127: 'like an
ape in spiteful rage'. These attributes
of the ape blend with a simile from
Palingenius, 'And as the Ape that
counterfets, vs doth to laughter moue/
So we likewise doe cause and moue the
Saintes to laugh aboue.' (Googe,
Zodiake, sig. D7ᵛ). From 'giant' to
'great man'—to 'petty officer'—to
'angry ape': such is the degeneration
of those who travesty divine justice
while ignorant that their souls, reflecting God's nature, urge them to imitate
divine wisdom and mercy. *makes*:
singular verb to plural subject
(Abbott §333).
123–4. *who . . . mortal*] *spleens*: traditionally the seat of laughter. *laugh
mortal*: laugh themselves either to
death, or into the condition of mortals;
ultimately the meanings are much the
same. Palingenius' saints laugh; but
Shakespeare's angels weep. Theobald
noted Grotius' commentary on Luke,
xv. 10: '*Ob peccatum flentes angelos
inducunt Hebraeorum magistri*' (perhaps alluding to the Talmudic story
that God rebuked his angels for rejoicing at the drowning of the Egyp-
tians, telling them that they should
rather weep at the destruction of his
creatures).

He's coming: I perceive 't.

Prov. [*aside*]   Pray heaven she win him.

Isab. We cannot weigh our brother with ourself.
Great men may jest with saints: 'tis wit in them,
But in the less, foul profanation.

Lucio. [*to Isab.*] Thou'rt i' th' right, girl; more o' that.   130

Isab. That in the captain's but a choleric word,
Which in the soldier is flat blasphemy.

Lucio. [*to Isab.*] Art avis'd o' that? More on 't.

Ang. Why do you put these sayings upon me?

Isab. Because authority, though it err like others,   135
Hath yet a kind of medicine in itself
That skins the vice o' th' top. Go to your bosom,
Knock there, and ask your heart what it doth know
That's like my brother's fault. If it confess
A natural guiltiness, such as is his,   140
Let it not sound a thought upon your tongue
Against my brother's life.

Ang. [*aside*]   She speaks, and 'tis such sense
That my sense breeds with it.—Fare you well.   [*Going.*]

Isab. Gentle my lord, turn back.

---

127. ourself] *F*; yourself *Theobald.*   133. avis'd] *F*; advis'd *F3.*   142. She . . . 'tis such sense] *as F*; She . . . 'tis / Such sense *Steevens.*

126. *coming*] yielding.

127.] 'We cannot judge our fellow-man by the standards we use for ourselves'. Cf. v. i. 114. Isabella is speaking of human behaviour in general.

128. *jest*] trifle. Cf. *R2*, i. iii. 95.

131–2.] This might be proverbial, as is implied by 'sayings', line 134.

133. *Art avis'd o' that?*] 'Have you learnt that?' (Hart).

134. *put . . . upon me*] 'make these sayings applicable to me'.

135–7. *Because . . . top*] 'Because the holders of authority, although they have faults like other men, find in it a kind of palliative which covers over their vices without healing them'. *skins*: grows a new skin over. Cf. *Ham.*, iii. iv. 147.

138–41. *your heart . . . your tongue*] a recurrent antithesis.

142–3. *such sense That my sense breeds* *with it*] W. Empson, in *The Structure of Complex Words* (1952), 274, discusses the meanings of 'sense' here. He distinguishes (i) common sense or rationality; (ii) sensuality (emphasized by the sexual connotation of 'breeds'); the stimulus to (ii) also deriving from (i). 'To Angelo the combination of meanings . . . can only appear as a hideous accident. . . Yet the real irony, apart from the verbal accident, is that her coldness, even her rationality, is what has excited him'. The two meanings of 'sense' are similarly paralleled in *Sonn.*, xxxv. 9. But the main meaning of 'such sense' here is surely 'such import'. Isabella has directed Angelo's attention to his own 'natural guiltiness' and increased his desire by making him conscious of it. *breeds*: anticipating the imagery of lines 166–8.

Ang. I will bethink me. Come again tomorrow. [*Going.*] 145
Isab. Hark, how I'll bribe you: good my lord, turn back.
Ang. How! Bribe me?
Isab. Ay, with such gifts that heaven shall share with you.
Lucio. [*to Isab.*] You had marr'd all else.
Isab. Not with fond sickles of the tested gold,   150
　　　Or stones, whose rate are either rich or poor
　　　As fancy values them: but with true prayers,
　　　That shall be up at heaven and enter there
　　　Ere sunrise: prayers from preserved souls,
　　　From fasting maids, whose minds are dedicate   155
　　　To nothing temporal.
Ang.   Well: come to me tomorrow.
Lucio. [*to Isab.*] Go to: 'tis well; away.
Isab. Heaven keep your honour safe.
Ang. [*aside*]   Amen.

150. sickles] *F;* shekles *Pope* (*sc. shekels*); sicles *Camb.*   151. rate are] *F;* rate
is *Hanmer;* rates are *Johnson.*   158–9. Amen. / For I am] *as F;* Amen: for
I / Am *Steevens.*

145.] 'It is important to remember that the Provost is present, and that these words amount to a postponement of Claudio's execution which Angelo had originally resolved should take place "by nine tomorrow morning"' (Thiselton). See Intro., p. xv. In Cinthio, Epitia is merely told that the execution will be postponed. In *1 Prom.*, II. iii, Cassandra is told to return 'tomorrow'. So *2 Siuqila*, sig. N2.

146. *Hark, how I'll bribe you*] perhaps a recollection of the Judge's demand for six thousand crowns in *Siuqila*; but cf. *John*, II. i. 171–2: 'Ay, with these crystal beads [i.e. tears] heaven shall be brib'd / To do him justice and revenge on you'.

150. *fond*] foolishly esteemed: transferred epithet from the character of those who esteem them.

sickles] Hebrew 'shekel', through the late Latin form '*siclus*', but not necessarily a biblical influence: cf. T. Lodge, *Catharos* (1591), sig. C: 'here in *Athens* the father hath suffred his

sonne to bee hanged for forty sickles'.

tested gold] pure gold, tested by the touchstone.

151–2. *Or stones . . . them*] Cf. *Sonn.*, XCVI. 5–6, and *Cym.*, I. iv. 88. *whose rate are*: all editors except Alexander emend to 'rates' or 'is' to improve the grammar, but the F form is quite Shakespearean. Cf. I. ii. 174, II. ii. 80.

152–4. *but . . . sunrise*] a submerged lark-image, recurrent in Shakespeare. Cf. *Sonn.*, XXIX. 11–12: 'Like to the lark at break of day arising/From sullen earth, sings hymns at heaven's gate'; and for other analogies, see J. W. Lever, *Shakes. Survey*, 6 (1953), p. 82.

154. *preserved*] 'kept safe from harm' (*O.E.D.* 1). She is offering Angelo the prayers of her fellow-votarists.

156. *Well . . . tomorrow*] The awkward response is in keeping with the end of the interview, with Isabella speaking to Angelo, Angelo communing with himself, and Lucio pressing Isabella to leave.

158. *Heaven . . . Amen*] with a play on 'your honour' as a title and as an

> For I am that way going to temptation,
> Where prayer's cross'd.

Isab.   At what hour tomorrow   160
> Shall I attend your lordship?

Ang.   At any time 'fore noon.

Isab. Save your honour.   [*Exeunt all but Angelo.*]

Ang.   From thee: even from thy virtue!
> What's this? What's this? Is this her fault, or mine?
> The tempter, or the tempted, who sins most, ha?
> Not she; nor doth she tempt; but it is I   165
> That, lying by the violet in the sun,

---

160. prayer's cross'd] *this edn;* prayers crosse *F.*   162. Save] *Rowe;* 'Saue *F;* God save *Hudson, conj. Walker.*   S.D.] *Alexander; not in F; Exeunt F2; Exeunt Lucio and Isabella | Rowe; Exeunt Provost, Lucio and Isabella. Capell.*   164–5. most, ha? | Not] *as F* (most? ha?); most? | Not *Pope;* most?/Ha!/Not *Camb.;* most? | Ha! Not *N.C.S.*

---

attribute of Angelo's he is in danger of losing.

160. *Where prayer's cross'd*] Since there is only one prayer, that of Isabella, 'prayers' (F) seems to be a contraction, not a plural, with 'crosse' as a common *e–d* error. Cf. *Mer.V.*, III. i. 22 f.: 'Let me say "amen" betimes, lest the devil cross my prayer'. 'Cross' in this sense was only used transitively (*O.E.D. v.* 14).

162 ff.] Angelo's soliloquy is based on that of Promos after his first interview with Cassandra (*1 Prom.*, II. iii). Cf. lines 169–70 with Whetstone's 'I do protest...'; line 172, 'O fie, fie, fie', with 'fie *Promos* fie'; lines 183–6, 'Never . . . quite', with 'Though she . . . gaze'.

162. *From thee . . . virtue!*] repeats the play on 'safe' in line 158.

164. *ha?*] equivalent to our 'eh?' (*O.E.D.* 2). This little word has been persecuted by editors. Pope excluded it on metrical grounds, Capell made it a loud expletive, and the Cambridge editors gave it a line to itself. Steevens rejected it as a vulgar actor's gag ('this tragedy—Ha!'), Hart wished to 'throw it out', and *N.C.S.* displaced it to begin line 165. As an Elizabethan half-query, half-grunt, 'ha?' is un-obtrusive and metrically harmless.

166–8. *lying by the violet . . . season*] 'as the carrion grows putrid by those beams which increase the fragrance of the violet' (Johnson). A virtuous man, says Angelo, would have his virtue preserved or fortified by the radiant influence of Isabella; instead, this rouses his carnal desires. The sun typifies chaste influences ('sun-like chastity'); the violet, true virtues (cf. Ophelia's 'they withered all when my father died', *Ham.*, IV. v. 183–4). *virtuous season*: (i) the season when the sun's rays give the plants their strength to grow; cf. Chaucer's 'of which vertu engendred is the flour' (Prologue to *Cant. Tales*, line 4); (ii) the preservative for meats, etc. The meanings reinforce one another; instead of the flower growing, the corpse putrefies, 'breeding' the maggots of 'sense' (line 143). Analogous imagery appears in *Edward III*, II. i. 438–9 (Sh. Apoc.) and *Ham.*, II. ii. 183. Cf. Stubbes, *Anatomy of Abuses* (Shakes. Soc., 1877), pp. 79–80: 'no more is their fowlenes to be ascribed to the stelliferous beames of ye glistering Sun, then ye stench of a dead carcasse may be said to come of ye sun, and not rather of it own corruption'.

Do as the carrion does, not as the flower,
Corrupt with virtuous season. Can it be
That modesty may more betray our sense
Than woman's lightness? Having waste ground enough,
Shall we desire to raze the sanctuary   171
And pitch our evils there? O fie, fie, fie!
What dost thou, or what art thou, Angelo?
Dost thou desire her foully for those things
That make her good? O, let her brother live!   175
Thieves for their robbery have authority,
When judges steal themselves. What, do I love her,
That I desire to hear her speak again?
And feast upon her eyes? What is't I dream on?
O cunning enemy, that, to catch a saint,   180
With saints dost bait thy hook! Most dangerous
Is that temptation that doth goad us on
To sin in loving virtue. Never could the strumpet

170–2. *Having waste ground . . . there?*]
'Since there are places where putrefy-
ing matter can be deposited, why do I
want to ruin the temple and erect a
privy on its site?' The previous 'carrion
in the sun' image would suggest 'waste
ground', i.e. prostitution, as the fit
dumping-place for lust. *evils*: privies, a
lost word. Cf. *H8*, II. i. 67: 'Nor build
their evils on the graves of great men'.
Malone's illustration has been over-
looked, perhaps because the author
and date were not given. It is from Sir
John Birkenhead, *Two Centuries of
Pauls Churchyard* (1653 ed.), p. 61:
'29. Whither since the House of Com-
mons was locked up, the Speakers
Chaire hath not been a Close-stoole?
30. Whether it be not seasonable to
stop the Nose of my Evill?' On sanc-
tuaries defiled, see also Marston,
Malcontent, II. v and *Sophonisba*, IV. i,
based on Lucan's *Pharsalia* (I. 173; II.
48).

173.] Another variant of 'Know
thyself'; cf. line 120.

176–7. *Thieves . . . themselves*]
Angelo's comment, II. i. 22–3, is

now ironically turned upon himself.

179–81. *What is't I dream on . . . hook!*]
Cf. *Ham.*, I. v. 53–4, II. ii. 636–7.
Patristic writings and iconography
describe the devil as tempting saints in
the likeness of another saint or a virtuous woman. Authority was derived
from 2 Cor., xi. 14: 'Satan himself is
transformed into an angel of light'.
Lavater, *Of Ghostes and Spirites* (ed.
Wilson and Yardley, p. 163), adds: 'no
lesse may he take the shape of a Pro-
phete, an Apostle, Evangeliste, By-
shoppe, and Martyr'. Le Loyer, *Des
Spectres* (1586), lib. ii. 291, mentions
St Ambrose's dream of temptation in
which St Paul appeared with Sts Ger-
vase and Protase. St Jerome and other
hermits dreamt of the devil in the likeness of a virtuous woman (Migne,
Patrologia Latina, XXII. 398). See the
representation of '*Le Diable en Femme*'
in Didron's *Christian Iconography* (tr.
Millington), II. 129, where the devil is
a woman with arms outstretched in
supplication. Angelo imagines himself
as an anchorite tempted in a dream by
Satan disguised as a virgin saint.

With all her double vigour, art and nature,
Once stir my temper: but this virtuous maid   185
Subdues me quite. Ever till now
When men were fond, I smil'd, and wonder'd how. *Exit.*

SCENE III [*A Prison.*]

Enter [severally] DUKE [*disguised as a Friar*]
and PROVOST.

Duke. Hail to you, Provost—so I think you are.
Prov. I am the Provost. What's your will, good Friar?
Duke. Bound by my charity, and my bless'd order,
  I come to visit the afflicted spirits
  Here in the prison. Do me the common right   5
  To let me see them, and to make me know
  The nature of their crimes, that I may minister
  To them accordingly.
Prov. I would do more than that, if more were needful—

Enter JULIET.

Look, here comes one: a gentlewoman of mine,   10
Who, falling in the flaws of her own youth,

Scene III

Scene III] Scena Tertia. F.   A Prison.] Rowe; A Room in a Prison. Capell; A walled courtyard before a prison N.C.S.   S.D.] Staunton; Enter Duke and Prouost. F. 11. flaws] F (flawes); flames Warburton (after Davenant).

184. *art and nature*] the artifice of the courtesan combined with the natural appeal of sex.

185. *stir my temper*] disturb my mental balance; cf. *Lr.*, i. v. 52: 'Keep me in temper; I would not be mad'.

187. *fond*] infatuated (*O.E.D.* 2).

Scene III

1. *so I think you are*] added to support his disguise. The Duke-as-Duke would recognize his own Provost.

3. *charity*] Christian duty of love.

4-5. *I come . . . prison*] recalling I Peter, iii. 19: 'also he went and preached unto the spirits in prison' (Hart). The words lend the 'Friar' moral authority for this visiting of prisoners. *spirits*: persons.

5. *the common right*] i.e. of all clerics.

6. *make me know*] 'cause me to know'.

9. *needful*—] no punctuation mark in F, signifying, as often, a break in exposition.

11. *flaws*] (*O.E.D. sb.*[2], 'a sudden burst or squall of wind'). Cf. *Ham.*, i. iii. 41-2: 'And in the morn and liquid dew of youth / Contagious blastments are most imminent', and for the blister association, *Temp.*, i. ii. 323-4: 'a

Hath blister'd her report. She is with child,
And he that got it, sentenc'd: a young man
More fit to do another such offence,
Than die for this.   15
Duke. When must he die?
Prov.   As I do think, tomorrow.
   [*to Juliet.*] I have provided for you; stay a while,
And you shall be conducted.
Duke. Repent you, fair one, of the sin you carry?
Juliet. I do; and bear the same most patiently.   20
Duke. I'll teach you how you shall arraign your conscience
   And try your penitence, if it be sound,
   Or hollowly put on.
Juliet.   I'll gladly learn.
Duke. Love you the man that wrong'd you?
Juliet. Yes, as I love the woman that wrong'd him.   25
Duke. So then it seems your most offenceful act
   Was mutually committed?
Juliet.   Mutually.
Duke. Then was your sin of heavier kind than his.
Juliet. I do confess it, and repent it, father.
Duke. 'Tis meet so, daughter; but lest you do repent,   30
   As that the sin hath brought you to this shame,
   Which sorrow is always toward ourselves, not heaven,
   Showing we would not spare heaven as we love it,

---

17. S.D.] *Theobald; not in* F.   33. spare] F; seek *Pope;* serve *Collier 2;* share
conj. Collier 2.

---

south-west blow on ye, And blister you
all o'er'. But 'flames' (the emendation
of Warburton and others) is equally
Shakespearean; cf. *Ham.,* III. iv. 84–5:
'To flaming youth let virtue be as wax,
And melt in her own fire'; *AYL.,* I. ii.
47–8: 'when Nature hath made a fair
creature, may she not by Fortune fall
into the fire?'; *All's W.,* v. iii. 6–8.
N.C.S., explaining 'flaws' as 'flakes',
'sparks of fire' (*O.E.D. sb.*[1] 1), tries to
straddle both meanings.

12. *blister'd her report*] Whores were
traditionally branded on the forehead.
Cf. *Ham.,* III. iv. 42–4. *report*: reputation.

13–15. *a young man . . . for this*] The
Provost parallels Lucio's sentiments in
I. iv. 27–9.

17. S.D.] This remark must be
directed to Juliet: the Provost has
made no provision for the Duke as
Friar, whereas arrangements for Juliet
follow Angelo's instructions (II. ii.
23–5).

19. *the sin you carry*] i.e. her unborn
child.

21. *arraign*] interrogate, examine.

25.] i.e. as she loves herself.

31. *As that*] in that, because. So in
lines 33–5.

33. *spare*] refrain from distressing.

But as we stand in fear—
Juliet. I do repent me as it is an evil,   35
        And take the shame with joy.
Duke.   There rest.
        Your partner, as I hear, must die tomorrow,
        And I am going with instruction to him.
        Grace go with you: *Benedicite!*   *Exit.*
Juliet. Must die to-morrow! O injurious love,   40
        That respites me a life, whose very comfort
        Is still a dying horror!
Prov.   'Tis pity of him.   *Exeunt.*

SCENE IV [*The Ante-room.*]

Enter ANGELO.

Ang. When I would pray and think, I think and pray
        To several subjects: Heaven hath my empty words,

39. Grace . . . *Benedicite!*] *as F; Juliet.* Grace go with you! *Duke.* Benedicite!
Dyce (after Ritson).   S.D.] *F; He enters the prison N.C.S.*   40. love] *F;* law
Hanmer.

Scene IV

Scene IV] *Scena Quarta. F.*   *The Ante-room.*] *this edn; The Palace. Rowe; A Room
in Angelo's House. Capell.*

Repentance, says the Duke, may arise
from the selfish sorrow at being
shamed, not from the thought of the
sorrow sin causes in heaven.

36. *There rest*] 'Continue of that
opinion'.

38. *instruction*] moral or religious
precepts; such as the Duke will
deliver to Claudio in Act III.

40. *O injurious love*] Hanmer's 'law'
for 'love' has found much support, the
oxymoron 'injurious law' being very
effective. But Johnson defends F: 'Her
execution was respited on account of
her pregnancy, the effects of her love.
. . . Is not all this very natural?' Juliet is
not alluding to abstract love, but to its
physical effects: cf. 'the sin you carry',
line 19 *supra.*

Scene IV

1–30.] Promos too delivers a long
soliloquy before the second entry of
Cassandra (*I Prom.*, III. i), but presents
himself as the conventional romantic
lover rather than the fallen 'saint'.

2. *To several subjects*] His thoughts
and prayers take different directions;
praying for one thing while thinking
of another.

2–4. *Heaven . . . Isabel*] Cf. Claudius:
'My words fly up, my thoughts remain
below: / Words without thoughts
never to heaven go' (*Ham.*, III. iii. 97–
8). *invention*: fancy, rather than will or
understanding. 'Its office is . . . to
quicken and rayse the Minde . . .
whereby it is possessed with such a
strong delight in its proper object, as

Whilst my invention, hearing not my tongue,
Anchors on Isabel: Heaven in my mouth,
As if I did but only chew his name,   5
And in my heart the strong and swelling evil
Of my conception. The state whereon I studied
Is, like a good thing being often read,
Grown sere and tedious; yea, my gravity,
Wherein—let no man hear me—I take pride,   10
Could I with boot change for an idle plume
Which the air beats for vain. O place, O form,
How often dost thou with thy case, thy habit,
Wrench awe from fools, and tie the wiser souls
To thy false seeming! Blood, thou art blood.   15

9. sere] *Hudson;* feard *F;* sear'd *Rowe 1, Hanmer;* frayed *Sisson.*   12. vain]
F (vaine); vane *Rann.*   15. art blood] *F;* art but blood *Pope;* still art blood
Malone.

makes the motions thereof towards it,
to be restlesse and impatient' (E. Reynolds, *A treatise of the Passions and Faculties of the Soule of Man* (ed. 1647), p. 19).
Anchors on Isabel: cf. *Cym.,* v. v. 394,
'Posthumus anchors upon Imogen';
Ant., i. v. 33; *Sonn.,* cxxxvii. 6. The
roving 'invention' fastens itself upon
the 'subject' of attraction.

4–5. *Heaven in my mouth . . . his name*]
Cf. *Basilicon Doron,* p. 51: 'Keepe God
more sparingly in your mouth, but
aboundantly in your harte' (after
Matth., xv. 8). 'Heaven' is clearly a
substitution for 'God' (Intro., p. xii).
There is also the suggestion of a sacrilegious communion.

6–7. *And in my heart . . . conception*]
literally so, according to contemporary
psychology. Cf. T. Wright, *The Passions of the Mind:* 'First then, to our
imagination commeth by sense or
memorie, some obiect to be knowne
. . . presently the purer spirites, flocke
from the brayne, by certaine secret
channels to the heart, [which] draweth
other humours to helpe him' (1630 ed.,
p. 45). Cf. lines 20–30 *infra.*

9. *sere and tedious*] Rowe's 'sear'd' for
F 'feard' appears only in his first edition of 1709 and may have been a mis-

print. Hanmer's firm emendation,
though not allowing for an additional
d for *e* error, makes the phrase intelligible. Cf. Wright: 'if the inferior
appetite or passions obey and con-
curre with the will, . . . oftentimes they
take away the molestations and tedi-
ousnesse that occurre in the practise of
good woorks. For example, often in
prayer men feele arridity, . . . yet if . . .
our harts and flesh reioyce in God,
then paine is turned into pleasure'
(p. 16).

11. *boot*] advantage.

12. *for vain*] for vanity: *O.E.D.*7, as
sb., not as 'in vain', 5b; with a quibble
on 'vane' = weathercock (*N.C.S.*).
'The air beats the plume like a vane
for its vanity'. Cf. *LLL.,* iv. i. 97–8:
'What plume of feathers is he. . . What
vane? what weathercock?'

13. *case, . . . habit*] 'outer appearance,
. . . dress': contrasting with the 'idle
plume' above, and continuing the
dress imagery of being and seeming.
'case'= garments (*O.E.D. sb.*2 4b). Cf.
ii. ii. 61.

15. *thy false seeming*] a recurrent idea:
cf. i. iii. 54; line 149 *infra;* and iii. ii. 38.
Blood, thou art blood] in ironic contrast to i. iv. 57–8.

Let's write good angel on the devil's horn—
'Tis not the devil's crest.   [*Knock.*]
                    How now! Who's there?

Enter Servant.

Serv. One Isabel, a sister, desires access to you.
Ang. Teach her the way. [*Exit Servant.*] O heavens,
     Why does my blood thus muster to my heart,   20
     Making both it unable for itself
     And dispossessing all my other parts
     Of necessary fitness?
     So play the foolish throngs with one that swounds,
     Come all to help him, and so stop the air   25
     By which he should revive; and even so

---

17. 'Tis not] *F;* Is't not *Hanmer;* 'Tis yet *conj. Johnson, Steevens.*   S.D. *Knock.*]
this edn.   Enter Servant.] *F* (*after* there?); *Theobald* (*after* crest.); *Capell* (*after*
horn, *16*).   19. S.D.] *Capell; not in F;* (*Solus*) *Johnson.*

16–17. *Let's write . . . crest*] a much-
disputed and emended passage. *write*:
designate (*O.E.D.* 8); cf. 'write oneself
man', to call oneself a man. *the devil's
horn*: the part unmistakably revealing
the devil's identity. Cf. Didron, II. 130:
'The Devil, wishing to tempt St.
Juliana, . . . transformed himself into
an angel. . . Still horns projected from
his forehead'. '*Tis*: i.e. the style 'good
angel'. *crest*: the cognizance over the
shield of a coat of arms; fig. for the
special characteristic of a person.
Angelo will reveal the diabolical side
of his nature, 'the devil's horn', while
designating it with his own name
'angel', though this is not his real title.
Cf. II. ii. 180 ff.: the roles are now
reversed.
     S.D. *Knock*] Angelo's abrupt 'How
now! Who's there?' is usually transposed after the direction 'Enter Servant'. It is surely in frightened response to a knock, which follows
straight after mention of the devil. For
Angelo, Isabella is indeed 'the devil in
woman's form'.
     19. *Teach*] show, inform. But
Angelo also plays on 'access' in a phy-

sical sense, and speaks as much to himself as to the Servant.
     20. *Why . . . heart*] Cf. lines 6–7. 'What
causeth their motions to the heart;
they themselves, as it were, flie vnto
the heart? . . . I answere, that . . . the
partes from whence these humours
come, use their expulsiue vertue, sending the spirites choler, or blood, to
serue the heart in such necessitie'
(Wright, p. 36). *muster*: assemble; as of
crowds gathering or of troops called up
for training.
     24–6. *So play . . . revive*] Cf. Wright:
'for what reason, in fear and anger become men so pale and wanne, but that
the blood runneth to the heart, to
succour it?' (pp. 33–4).
     26–30. *and even so . . . offence*] not only
a general reference to King James's
dislike of crowds, but probably alluding to the King's visit to the Exchange.
See Intro., p. xxxiv. *the general subject*:
the common people. Cf. *Ham.*, II. ii.
597: 'cleave the general ear'. 'Subject': collective noun for subjects. Cf.
III. ii. 133. *Quit their own part*: abandon
their own functions; 'part' also as
member of the body (cf. line 22), and,

The general subject to a well-wish'd king
Quit their own part, and in obsequious fondness
Crowd to his presence, where their untaught love
Must needs appear offence.

Enter ISABELLA.

How now, fair maid?   30
Isab. I am come to know your pleasure.
Ang. [*aside*] That you might know it, would much better
    please me,
Than to demand what 'tis.—Your brother cannot live.
Isab. Even so. Heaven keep your honour.
Ang. Yet may he live a while; and, it may be,   35
As long as you or I; yet he must die.
Isab. Under your sentence?
Ang. Yea.
Isab. When, I beseech you? That in his reprieve,
Longer or shorter, he may be so fitted   40
That his soul sicken not.
Ang. Ha? Fie, these filthy vices! It were as good
To pardon him that hath from nature stolen

---

27. general subject] *F;* general subjects *F4;* general, subject *Steevens* '78.
30. S.D.] *Johnson; Enter Isabella.* F (*after* Maid).   34. honour.] *F;* honour.
[S.D.] *going | Rowe;* honour. [S.D.] *retiring | Malone.*

---

by analogy, the body politic. The continuity of thought and imagery rebuts Wilson's view (*N.C.S.*) that lines 26–30 were additions tacked on for a special performance. *obsequious fondness*: loyalty of an affectionate but foolish kind. *untaught*: Onions glosses 'uncultured, unmannerly'; but more probably 'uninformed' (cf. 'teach', line 19).

    30. *How now, fair maid?*] Iuriste addresses Epitia as *bella Giovane,* and Promos greets Cassandra as 'Faire Dame' (*1 Prom.,* III. ii).

    31–3. *I am . . . what 'tis*] Angelo plays on 'pleasure' in a sexual connotation.

    39. *in his reprieve*] during the time of his reprieve.

    40. *fitted*] supplied with what is suitable; Isabella has in mind such spiri-

tual guidance as the Duke gives to Claudio in III. i.

    42. *Ha?*] as in II. ii. 164.

    42–6. *as good . . . forbid*] 'one might as well pardon a murderer, who has taken life, as a fornicator, who has sinfully brought life into being'. *remit*: pardon. *saucy sweetness*: lascivious pleasure. *coin heaven's image In stamps that are forbid*: a recurrent image. Unlawful procreation of man, who bears God's image, is analogous to misusing the King's stamp on a coin. Malone (and Muir recently, *S.S.,* 6 (1953), 46) cites *Edward III,* II. i. 255 ff. (*Sh. Apoc.*): 'He that doth clip or counterfeit your stamp / Shall die, my Lord; and will your sacred selfe / Comit high treason against the King of heauen / To stamp his Image in forbidden mettel'.

A man already made, as to remit
Their saucy sweetness that do coin heaven's image   45
In stamps that are forbid. 'Tis all as easy
Falsely to take away a life true made,
As to put mettle in restrained means
To make a false one.

Isab. 'Tis set down so in heaven, but not in earth.   50

Ang. Say you so? Then I shall pose you quickly.
Which had you rather, that the most just law
Now took your brother's life; or, to redeem him,
Give up your body to such sweet uncleanness
As she that he hath stain'd?

Isab.   Sir, believe this: 55
I had rather give my body than my soul.

Ang. I talk not of your soul: our compell'd sins
Stand more for number than for accompt.

Isab.   How say you?

Ang. Nay, I'll not warrant that: for I can speak
Against the thing I say. Answer to this: 60
I—now the voice of the recorded law—
Pronounce a sentence on your brother's life:
Might there not be a charity in sin
To save this brother's life?

Isab.   Please you to do 't,

---

48. mettle] *F;* metal *Theobald.*   means] *F* (meanes); mints *N.C.S., conj.*
Steevens.   53. or] *Rowe (after Davenant);* and *F.*   58. for accompt] *F;* accompt
Rowe 3.   61. I—now...law—] *F* (I (now...Law)); If now...law *conj. N.C.S.*

---

48. *mettle*] Cf. 'metal', i. i. 48.
restrained] prohibited.

means] 'instruments' (*O.E.D.* 'mean'
*sb.*² 9). Steevens's conjecture 'mints'
is supported by Wilson (*N.C.S.*) and
Ridley. But 'means' implies both
minting and procreation through the
instrumentality of a woman, thus
answering to the two senses of 'mettle-
metal'.

51. *pose*] non-plus with a question
(*O.E.D. v.*² 2).

57–8. *our compell'd sins . . . accompt*]
Hart cites *1 Prom.*, III. iv: '*Iustice* wyll
say, thou dost no cryme commit: / For
in forst faultes is no intent of yll'. This

is spoken by Andrugio, in urging his
sister to submit to Promos. 'Compelled
sins are no sins' was a Christian commonplace (Tilley S 475). *more for number than for accompt*: formally recorded,
but not reckoned in the spiritual
'account'.

59. *warrant that*] endorse the above
commonplace. Angelo is withdrawing
for the moment a suggestion too crude-
ly phrased, and sheltering behind his
judicial privilege to test a witness.

61.] Angelo stresses that he is merely
voicing the law already recorded, not
making that law.

64. *Please*] 'if it please'.

I'll take it as a peril to my soul;   65
It is no sin at all, but charity.
Ang. Pleas'd you to do't, at peril of your soul,
Were equal poise of sin and charity.
Isab. That I do beg his life, if it be sin,
Heaven let me bear it; you granting of my suit,   70
If that be sin, I'll make it my morn prayer
To have it added to the faults of mine,
And nothing of your answer.
Ang.   Nay, but hear me;
Your sense pursues not mine: either you are ignorant,
Or seem so, crafty; and that's not good.   75
Isab. Let me be ignorant, and in nothing good,
But graciously to know I am no better.
Ang. Thus wisdom wishes to appear most bright
When it doth tax itself: as these black masks
Proclaim an enciel'd beauty ten times louder   80

---

73. your answer] *F;* yours answer *conj. Johnson.*   75. so, crafty] *Collier;* so
crafty *F;* so, craftily *Rowe (after Davenant).*   that's] *F;* that is *Collier.*   76. me
be] *F2;* be *F.*   80. enciel'd] *this edn;* en-shield *F;* enshield' *Capell;* enshield
White; enshielded *Kittredge;* enshell'd *Keightley, conj. Tyrwhitt (Steevens '78).*

66. *It is no sin*] Isabella takes Angelo's 'sin' to be an unwillingness to put
the law into effect.
67. *Pleas'd*] 'did it please' (a past
conditional to which 'Were', line 68, is
the apodosis).
68. *Were . . . charity*] 'Sin and charity
would weigh equally in the moral
assessment of your act'.
69. *if it be sin*] When Angelo refers
the decision back to her, Isabella
again assumes that 'sin' means leniency; this time, in her own moral
attitude.
71. *morn prayer*] Cf. II. ii. 152–4.
73. *nothing of your answer*] 'no part of
the charge you must answer' (in the
legal sense).
74. *Your sense pursues not mine*] 'sense'
is used here as in II. ii. 142.
75. *crafty*] quasi-adverbial: cf.
'crafty-sick', *2H4*, Ind. 37.
77. *graciously*] through divine grace.

79. *tax*] reprove. Isabella's claim to
be ignorant, says Angelo, is mock-
modest, intended to emphasize her
wisdom.
these black masks] taken by Tyrwhitt,
Steevens, and others as a direct allusion to the 'masks' worn by the ladies
in the audience. But 'these' might
merely indicate something in vogue,
as in our vulgarism 'these here'. Shakespeare would not wish to distract
attention from the stage at this critical
point. 'Masks' here are probably veils:
cf. *Gent.*, IV. iv. 160: 'her sun-expelling
mask'. *N.C.S.* (pp. 101–2) sees a covert
reference to the forthcoming performance of Jonson's *Masque of Blackness*
on 5 January 1605. But, as noted in
the 1950 edition, masks were not
worn by the participants on that occasion.
80. *enciel'd*] F 'enshield', emended
variously to 'enshielded', 'enshell'd'

Than beauty could, display'd. But mark me;
To be received plain, I'll speak more gross.
Your brother is to die.

Isab. So.

Ang. And his offence is so, as it appears,   85
Accountant to the law upon that pain.

Isab. True.

Ang. Admit no other way to save his life—
As I subscribe not that, nor any other,
But in the loss of question—that you, his sister,   90
Finding yourself desir'd of such a person
Whose credit with the judge, or own great place,
Could fetch your brother from the manacles
Of the all-binding law; and that there were
No earthly mean to save him, but that either   95
You must lay down the treasures of your body

---

90. loss] *F* (losse); loose *Kittredge, conj. Singer;* toss *conj. Johnson.*   94. all-binding law] *Johnson;* all-building-Law *F;* all-holding law *Rowe;* all-bridling law *Praz* (*T.L.S. 13 Feb. 1937*).

(taken by *N.C.S.* to support the alleged reference to Jonson's masque). The verb 'ceil' or 'ciel' (commonly spelt with initial s) meant to shade as with a canopy or screen. *O.E.D.* 2 cites its figurative use in Sylvester's *Du Bartas* (1598), and Wither (1615): 'A Bower . . . Seil'd so close with boughes'. The 'en-' prefix was a Shakespearean formation; cf. 'enskied', I. iv. 34.

82. *gross*] obviously.

85. *so*] such.

86.] 'liable to the law under that penalty (of death)'.

90.] Onions glosses: 'provided there is no dispute' ('loss': default; 'question': subject for enquiry). The meaning is more probably 'provided nothing more can be said for the defence'. Thiselton points out the law-Latin tag '*cadit quaestio*', the case falls'.

92. *place*] rank, station.

93. *fetch*] get back.

94. *all-binding law*] Johnson remarked: 'Mr. Theobald has *binding* in

one of his copies'. If so, it is now lost, but the emendation is generally accepted, though Durham supports F, with the dubious gloss 'upon which all is founded'. Thiselton suggested 'beild-ing' (=protecting), Praz (anticipated in *N. & Q.* 1907) 'bridling'. But the same reading of 'build' where 'bind' is evidently meant occurs in Webster's *Duchess of Malfi*, I. i. 562: 'How can the Church build faster?' J. R. Brown, *Stud. Bibl.*, VI (1954), 117–40, has shown that this text (like *Measure for Measure*) is probably based on a Crane transcript.

95. *mean*] means. Sing. and pl. were interchangeable, 'mean' being the earlier form. Cf. note to II. i. 82.

96. *the treasures of your body*] her virginity. Cf. *Ham.*, I. iii. 31: 'your chaste treasure open'; *Cym.*, II. ii. 41–2. The idea of a heavy bribe may be latent; cf. *2 Siuqila*: 'I buy my husbandes life with such a price, that all the treasure on the earth is not able againe to redeeme' (sig. N3ᵛ).

  To this suppos'd, or else to let him suffer:
  What would you do?
Isab. As much for my poor brother as myself;
  That is, were I under the terms of death,   100
  Th'impression of keen whips I'd wear as rubies,
  And strip myself to death as to a bed
  That longing have been sick for, ere I'd yield
  My body up to shame.
Ang.   Then must your brother die.
Isab. And 'twere the cheaper way.   105
  Better it were a brother died at once,
  Than that a sister, by redeeming him,
  Should die for ever.
Ang. Were you not then as cruel as the sentence
  That you have slander'd so?   110
Isab. Ignomy in ransom and free pardon
  Are of two houses: lawful mercy
  Is nothing kin to foul redemption.

---

103. longing have] *F;* longing I've *Rowe;* longing I have *Capell;* longing had *Knight;* longing, have *Neilson;* longings have *N.C.S.;* long I have *Sisson.* 111. Ignomy] *F;* Ignominy *F2.* 112–13. mercy / Is . . . kin] *F;* mercy sure / Is . . . kin *Pope;* mercy is / Nothing akin *Steevens '93.*

97. *To this suppos'd*] to this hypothetical person.

100. *under the terms*] under sentence.

101–4.] suggested by Cassandra's words to Andrugio, *1 Prom.,* III. iv: 'I rather chose, / With torments sharpe, my selfe he first should kyll'. 'At the beginning of this quotation Death is a beadle whipping a harlot; Isabella thinks of stripping herself for punishment, but the image takes on a sexual meaning' (Kenneth Muir, *London Magazine,* Dec. 1954, p. 106). Death and sexuality are similarly associated by Antony: 'I will be / A bridegroom in my death, and run into't / As to a lover's bed' (*Ant.,* IV. xii. 99–101). Cf. Claudio, III. i. 82–4. The image is more obviously suited to an Antony or Claudio than to the chaste Isabella: but its occurrence here is psychologically revealing. *longing have been*]: Lettsom's 'long I had been' (Dyce),

adopted substantially by Sisson, and other editors' attempts to improve the syntax, are unnecessary. Cf. I. ii. 174 and other instances of sing. subject with pl. verb.

105. *cheaper way*] 'better bargain'. Onions has 'costing little labour or effort' as a new, Shakespearean connotation. This is not Isabella's meaning, which looks forward to lines 106–8.

108. *die for ever*] the eternal death of the spirit.

110. *slander'd so*] accused of being cruel. 'So' is for 'thus', not as intensive.

111. *Ignomy*] a contracted form of 'ignominy' up to the early 19th cent.

ransom] release at a price, in contrast to 'free' pardon: from the same Latin root as 'redemption', line 113. Cf. *1 Prom.,* III. ii: 'In doubtfull warre, one prisoner still, doth set another free'.

112. *houses*] families; hence 'kin', line 113.

Ang. You seem'd of late to make the law a tyrant,
        And rather prov'd the sliding of your brother   115
        A merriment than a vice.
Isab. O pardon me, my lord; it oft falls out
        To have what we would have, we speak not what
            we mean.
        I something do excuse the thing I hate
        For his advantage that I dearly love.   120
Ang. We are all frail.
Isab.   Else let my brother die,
        If not a feodary but only he
        Owe and succeed thy weakness.
Ang.   Nay, women are frail too.
Isab. Ay, as the glasses where they view themselves,
        Which are as easy broke as they make forms.   125
        Women?—Help, heaven! Men their creation mar
        In profiting by them. Nay, call us ten times frail;

---

118. To . . . mean] *as Pope;* To . . . would haue, / . . . meane *F.*   122. feodary]
F2; fedarie *F;* foedary *Halliwell.*   123. thy] *F;* by *Rowe;* to *Capell;* this *Collier,*
conj. Malone (Var. 1821).

114–16.] *N.C.S.* finds no 'utterance of Isabella's, either in this scene or in II. ii, which would justify Angelo's accusation or her self-excuse', and so infers a cut after line 41. But this is surely Angelo's construction of 'tyrannous' in II. ii. 109 and of the plea that the fault, not the brother, be condemned (line 35).

117–20.] Isabella, manœuvred into a contradiction between her attitude to Claudio's chastity and to her own, and still supposing that Angelo is using a lawyer's wiles, retracts her plea of II. ii.

118.] The exceptionally long line (divided into two in F) may be due to a sophistication of the idiomatic contractions 'I' have', 'we'd'.

119. *something*] somewhat, to some extent.

121. *We are all frail*] proverbial (Tilley F 363), from Ecclesiasticus, viii. 5: 'remember that wee are fraile euery one' (Noble). 'Frail' means susceptible, rather than physically weak.

122–3. *If not . . . weakness*] a much-disputed passage. 'Feodary' ('Fedarie' F) combines two meanings: (i) confederate, accomplice (cf. *Cym.,* III. ii. 21, F 'Foedarie') from Lat. *foedus;* (ii) feudatory, i.e. hereditary tenant, from Lat. *feodarius.* The sense is thus: 'If my brother has no associates in this weakness you refer to, and no man else will in the way of nature inherit it, then let him die'.

123. *Nay, women are frail too*] Angelo widens the trap laid in line 121.

124–5.] 'A woman and a glass are ever in danger' (Tilley W 646), with the traditional association of glass and virginity (cf. *Per.,* IV. vi. 156). *forms:* likenesses; with a play on the physical 'form' of a person, made by breaking the 'glass' of the mother's virginity.

126–7. *Men . . . them*] The mirror now suggests, like 'glassy essence' in II. ii. 121, the soul reflecting the divine image. Men mar their creation in God's likeness by taking advantage of women.

For we are soft as our complexions are,
And credulous to false prints.

Ang.   I think it well;
And from this testimony of your own sex—   130
Since I suppose we are made to be no stronger
Than faults may shake our frames—let me be bold.
I do arrest your words. Be that you are,
That is, a woman; if you be more, you're none.
If you be one—as you are well express'd   135
By all external warrants—show it now,
By putting on the destin'd livery.

Isab. I have no tongue but one; gentle my lord,
Let me entreat you speak the former language.

Ang. Plainly conceive, I love you.   140

Isab. My brother did love Juliet,
And you tell me that he shall die for 't.

Ang. He shall not, Isabel, if you give me love.

Isab. I know your virtue hath a licence in 't,
Which seems a little fouler than it is,   145
To pluck on others.

Ang.   Believe me, on mine honour,
My words express my purpose.

Isab. Ha? Little honour, to be much believ'd,

141–2. My ... for 't] *as F;* My ... me / ... for it *Steevens '93.*   142. for 't] *F;* for it *Rowe 3.*

129. *credulous to false prints*] The general sense is that women are of a soft metal which easily takes false impressions. 'Prints' for any impress, especially the stamp on a coin, is fig. for conception, as in lines 45–6 *supra,* and is thus a variant on the recurrent coin image; cf. *Wint.,* v. i. 124 f.: 'Your mother was most true to wedlock, prince; / For she did print your royal father off, / Conceiving you'. The previous mirror imagery of 'forms' has suggested that of 'prints'. 'credulous': readily accepting.

130. *testimony*] a trisyllable, 'testim'ny'.

133. *arrest*] lay hold upon; so here, 'take you at your word'. Cf. *LLL.,* ii. i. 159.

135. *express'd*] revealed, manifested.

136. *warrants*] tokens.

137. *the destin'd livery*] 'the uniform of her kind, the frailty which is the natural destiny of women' (H. Jenkins).

144. *licence*] leave, 'liberty', rather than licentiousness (Steevens).

145–6. *Which seems ... others*] Isabella still clings to the notion that this is a lawyer's trap: if she agrees that fornication must be punished, she accepts Claudio's sentence; if she pleads for leniency in such matters, she can hardly refuse Angelo's proposal. Having abandoned (lines 117–20) the appeal based on Christian charity, she is entirely vulnerable.

And most pernicious purpose! Seeming, seeming!
I will proclaim thee, Angelo, look for't.   150
Sign me a present pardon for my brother,
Or with an outstretch'd throat I'll tell the world aloud
What man thou art.

Ang.   Who will believe thee, Isabel?
My unsoil'd name, th'austereness of my life,
My vouch against you, and my place i'th'state   155
Will so your accusation overweigh,
That you shall stifle in your own report,
And smell of calumny. I have begun,
And now I give my sensual race the rein:
Fit thy consent to my sharp appetite;   160
Lay by all nicety and prolixious blushes
That banish what they sue for. Redeem thy brother
By yielding up thy body to my will;
Or else he must not only die the death,
But thy unkindness shall his death draw out   165
To ling'ring sufferance. Answer me tomorrow,

152-3. Or . . . aloud / . . . art] *as F;* Or . . . world / Aloud . . . art *Rowe 3.*
world aloud] *F;* world *Hudson, conj. Dyce 2;* world [S.D.] *aloud. | conj. Gould
(Dyce 2).*

149. *Seeming, seeming!*] False appearance personified, as in *Ado,* IV. i. 56,
and in the allegorical figure *Faux-
semblant.*

150. *proclaim*] denounce (*O.E.D.*
2b).

151. *present*] immediate.

152. *outstretch'd*] opened wide
(*O.E.D.* 'stretch', *v.* 21b). Cf. Nashe,
Lenten Stuff (III. 175, 9–10): 'the most
outstretched ayry straine of elocution'
(Hart).

aloud] the word is hypermetrical;
consequently the line has been much
doctored. Isabella is suiting her voice
to her words, and needs an extra
long line for the purpose. See Intro.,
p. xxx.

155. *vouch*] formal attestation.

157-8. *stifle . . . calumny*] Steevens:
'A metaphor from a lamp or candle
extinguished in its own grease'. It is
more likely to be a play on 'report' as

(i) narration, (ii) reputation, as in
II. iii. 12.

159. *race*] combines the meanings
'natural disposition' (*O.E.D. sb.²* 7) as
in *Temp.,* I. ii. 358, and (fig.) 'stud of
horses' (*O.E.D.* 3b). Cf. I. iii. 20–1.

161. *nicety*] reserve, shyness.

prolixious] time-wasting (from 'prolix').

162. *That banish what they sue for*]
'That drive away the compunction for
which they plead'; i.e. forms of
modesty that provoke desire.

163. *will*] lust.

164. *die the death*] a biblical phrase
for judicial sentence of death. Also
used in *MND.,* I. i. 65.

165. *unkindness*] 'unnatural behaviour': whether towards Claudio or
Angelo himself.

166. *sufferance*] suffering. This threat
is not found in the sources.

Answer me tomorrow] Cinthio's

Or, by the affection that now guides me most,
I'll prove a tyrant to him. As for you,
Say what you can: my false o'erweighs your true.   *Exit.*
Isab. To whom should I complain? Did I tell this,   170
Who would believe me? O perilous mouths,
That bear in them one and the self-same tongue
Either of condemnation or approof,
Bidding the law make curtsey to their will,
Hooking both right and wrong to th'appetite,   175
To follow as it draws! I'll to my brother.
Though he hath fall'n by prompture of the blood,
Yet hath he in him such a mind of honour,
That had he twenty heads to tender down
On twenty bloody blocks, he'd yield them up   180
Before his sister should her body stoop
To such abhorr'd pollution.
Then, Isabel live chaste, and brother, die:

---

171. perilous] *F;* most perilous *Theobald;* these perilous *Keightley, conj. Seymour.*

Iuriste says: '*ne aspetterò per tutto domane la risposta*'. Whetstone has: 'I wyll two daies hope styll of thy consent' (*1 Prom.,* III. ii); and Lupton's Judge in *2 Siuqila:* 'within these two or three dayes' (sig. N3ᵛ). On this unnecessary 'tomorrow' (contrast III. i. 100), see Intro., p. xv.

168. *I'll prove a tyrant*] 'one who exhibits cruelty of almost any kind. . . Quite often he [Shakespeare] is thinking more of the familiar blustering tyrant of the old plays than of the despots of history'. A. G. Newcomer, note to *Ado,* I. i. 176, *Parallel Passage Edition,* line 170 (Stanford, 1929). Cf. III. ii. 189.

169. *my false o'erweighs your true*] Cf. 'overweigh', line 156 *supra.* The word rings changes on the 'measure' theme; and the phrase as paradox also suggests the lightness of false coin. (Cf. IV. ii. 28–9).

170–86.] Compare with this Cassandra's lament at the end of *1 Prom.,* III. ii, declaring that her beauty, instead of her virtue, has 'wrought regard'. Shakespeare stresses Isa-

bella's fear that she will not be believed, indicating why, unlike Cassandra, she does not intend to seek help from the ruler, and thus making all depend upon the Duke's initiative.

171–3. *O perilous . . . approof*] an acknowledgement that she has been trapped by Angelo's alternating condemnation and approval of Claudio's act. The recurrent mouth and tongue imagery for 'seeming' once more. '*these* perilous mouths' would improve line 171, which is short of a syllable. *approof:* sanction.

174–6. *Bidding . . . draws!*] Subjecting the law to their lust, and with it the discernment of right and wrong. Compare Wright: 'the sensitiue appetite being rooted in the same soule with the Wil, if it be drawne, or flieth from any object, consequently the other must follow; euen so, the obiect that haleth the sensitiue appetite, draweth withall, the Will' (p. 58).

177. *prompture*] prompting; a Shakespearean formation which Hart compares with 'stricture', I. iii. 12, 'expressure', *Tw.N.,* II. iii. 174, etc.

More than our brother is our chastity.
I'll tell him yet of Angelo's request,   185
And fit his mind to death, for his soul's rest.   *Exit.*

184. More . . . chastity.] *Rowe 3;* "More . . . Chastitie. *F;* "More . . . chastity." *N.C.S.*

184. *More . . . chastity*] printed in F with inverted commas at the opening of the phrase only, to mark a 'sententia'. Cf. II. i. 38. Isabella's affirmation derives from Cinthio: '*la vita di mio Fratello mi è molto cara, ma vie più caro mi è l'honor mio*'. Whetstone's Cassandra says: 'Honor farre dearer is then life' (*1 Prom.*, III. ii), but as a general maxim without direct reference to her brother. Note the change from 'honour' to 'chastity'.

186. *And . . . rest*] Cf. lines 40–1.

ACT III

SCENE I [*The Prison.*]

Enter DUKE [*disguised*] *and* PROVOST [*with*] CLAUDIO.

Duke. So then you hope of pardon from Lord Angelo?
Cla. The miserable have no other medicine
    But only hope:
    I have hope to live, and am prepar'd to die.
Duke. Be absolute for death: either death or life   5
    Shall thereby be the sweeter. Reason thus with life:
    If I do lose thee, I do lose a thing

ACT III

Scene I

Act III Scene I] *Actus Tertius. Scena Prima. F.*   *The Prison.*] *Rowe; A Room in the Prison. Capell; The courtyard before the Prison. N.C.S.*   S.D.] *this edn; Enter Duke Claudio, and Prouost. F; Enter Duke and Claudio; Provost at a distance, attending Capell; Enter Duke as a Friar, Claudio, and Provost. Collier.*   3–4. But . . . hope: / . . . die] *as Capell; prose in F;* But . . . am / . . . die *Hanmer.*

2–3.] Cf. Lyly, *Endimion*, III. ii. 11–12: 'there is no sweeter musicke to the miserable then despayre'; a sentiment which Claudio reverses.

5–41. *Be absolute . . . all even*] The Duke's speech has no single source, and there is no analogy to it in earlier versions of the story. A discourse on death, sometimes in dialogue form, belongs to the Renaissance genre of 'consolation' literature, inspired partly by Stoic, partly by Christian attitudes. See Intro., p. lxxxvii. The imagery is drawn from many sources or unconscious recollections, some traceable to particular authors, some commonplaces, and all re-shaped to a single purpose—the 'contempt' of death through a contempt of life. For the

rhetorical structure of the Duke's speech, see Baldwin, II, pp. 84–6, who points out that the argument is built up on Ciceronian principles, with *propositio* lines 5–6, *ratio* 6–8, *rationis confirmatio* 8–41, and *conclusio* provided in Claudio's answer, lines 42–3.

5. *absolute*] 'positive', 'free from all doubt'.

either . . . or] in the sense 'both of the two', not as alternatives. 'or . . . or' would be more Shakespearean.

7–8. *If . . . keep*] Noble cites John, xii. 25; but the resemblance is indirect and there is no mention here of 'life eternal'. Cf. Webster, *Duchess of Malfi*, IV. ii. 188: 'Of what is't fooles make such vaine keeping?'

That none but fools would keep. A breath thou art,
Servile to all the skyey influences
That dost this habitation where thou keep'st　　　10
Hourly afflict. Merely, thou art Death's fool;
For him thou labour'st by thy flight to shun,
And yet run'st toward him still. Thou art not noble;
For all th'accommodations that thou bear'st
Are nurs'd by baseness. Thou'rt by no means valiant;　15
For thou dost fear the soft and tender fork
Of a poor worm. Thy best of rest is sleep;
And that thou oft provok'st, yet grossly fear'st
Thy death, which is no more. Thou art not thyself;

9. Servile . . . influences] *F;* (Servile . . . influences) *Rann.*　　10. dost] *F;* do *Hanmer.*

9. *Servile*] subject.

skyey influences] influences of the planets, affecting human destiny as well as weather, vegetation, and the tides. But Christians cited Ptolemy: 'The soul is lord over the stars'.

10–11. *That dost . . . afflict*] The sing. form 'dost' may seem to imply that the subject is 'breath'. But the influences, not the breath, afflict man, and the sing. vb with pl. subject was a frequent usage (Abbott §333). *habitation*: residence, fig. for the body. *keep'st*: from 'keep', to dwell (*O.E.D. v.* 37).

11. *Merely*] Absolutely.

11–13. *Death's fool . . . still*] Warburton: 'In morality plays, the Fool comically tries to avoid Death and gets nearer to him thereby'. Ritson rightly objected that no such episode occurs in any morality play extant. But the theme was traditional. Douce (I. 129–30) mentions Holbein's picture in Whitehall Palace relating to Death and the Fool; also initial 'A' in Stow's *Survey* (1618 ed.), where the Fool is shown heading left but being dragged by Death to the right.

14–15. *For all . . . baseness*] 'All the delicacies of the table may be traced back to the shambles and the dunghill, all magnificence of building was hewn from the quarry, and all the pomp of ornament dug from among the damps and darkness of the mine' (Johnson). *accommodations*: 'conveniences', 'comforts'. A new word at this time, of vague application, which Jonson described as a 'perfumed term' (*Discoveries, Perspicuitas*). Shakespeare has it again in 'unaccommodated man', *Lr.,* III. iv. 109–10. *bear'st . . . nurs'd*: life's 'accommodations' are personified as its child, fed by 'baseness'. So in *Ant.,* v. ii. 7–8: 'sleepes, and neuer pallates more the dung, / The beggers Nurse, and *Caesers*' (F spelling).

16–17. *the soft and tender fork Of a poor worm*] the forked tongue of a snake. Ridley suggests that the phrase means 'the penetration of the worm into the dead body': but 'fork' applies only to a snake, and Cleopatra calls the 'worm of Nilus' 'poor venomous fool' (*Ant.,* v. ii. 307).

17–19. *Thy . . . more*] from Cicero, *Disp. Tusc.*: '*Habes somnum imaginem mortis, eamque quotidie induis, et dubitas quin sensus in morte nullus sit, cum in eius simulacro videas esse nullum sensum*' (Warburton). The analogy to sleep was a commonplace of the 'consolation', but usually Christianized by making death the sleep from which one woke to eternity. *provok'st*: 'dost invoke', 'summon'.

For thou exists on many a thousand grains   20
That issue out of dust. Happy thou art not;
For what thou hast not, still thou striv'st to get,
And what thou hast, forget'st. Thou art not certain;
For thy complexion shifts to strange effects
After the moon. If thou art rich, thou'rt poor;   25
For, like an ass whose back with ingots bows,
Thou bear'st thy heavy riches but a journey,
And Death unloads thee. Friend hast thou none;
For thine own bowels which do call thee sire,

20. exists] *F;* exist'st *Rowe 3.*   24. effects] *F;* affects *Rann, conj. Johnson.*
29. thee sire,] *F4* (thee sire?) *;* thee, fire *F.*

20. *exists*] 2nd person sing. form; a common variant to avoid such tongue-twisters as 'exist'st'. See Abbott §340, and cf. 'splits', II. ii. 117.

20–1. *many . . . dust*] 'grains' are seeds (*O.E.D. sb.*[1] 1). Cf. 'seeds', *Wint.*, IV. iv. 492: 'germens', *Mac.*, IV. i. 59, *Lr*, III. ii. 8. L. C. Martin (*R.E.S.*, XXI (1945) 177 f.) discusses the influence of Epicurean atomic theory; and William Elton (*M.L.N.*, LXV (1950), 196–7) suggests a direct source in T. Bright's *Treatise of Melancholie* (1586), p. 34: 'This earth he [God] hath endued with a fecunditie of infinite seeds of all things: . . . to bring forth, and . . . to entertaine with nourishment that which it had borne'. For 'nourishment' and 'borne', cf. 'nurs'd' and 'bear'st', lines 15, 14. See also W. C. Curry, *Shakespeare's Philosophical Patterns* (Louisiana 1937), pp. 29–48. *out of dust*: recalling Gen. ii. 7; pagan philosophy and Christian doctrine are blended in one phrase.

24. *complexion*] combination of humours. The influence of the moon upon these was a commonplace of Elizabethan psychology. Cf. lines 8–11, *Oth.*, V. ii. 107–9, etc.

effects] outward manifestations.

26–8. *For . . . thee. Friend . . . none*] Hankins points out the proximity in the *Zodiake* of the ass image—'It is an Asses parte to beare the saddle styll wee see'—and a passage on the loneliness of old age (cf. lines 29–32). The ass loaded with gold but eating only thistles was proverbial. The association of 'ass' with 'death' may have been suggested by an episode in *The Golden Asse of Apuleius* (tr. Adlington): 'Then they brake open a great chest . . . wherin was layd all the treasure of Milo . . . and laded vs . . .' Later, when the other ass was exhausted, 'they tooke his burthen, . . . and cut off his legs, and threw his body from the point of an hill downe into a great valley' (*Tudor Transl.*, IV. 78–9, 86).

29–32. *For thine . . . sooner*] Cf. *Zodiake*, p. 73: 'And when that aged hayres shal hap and sickenesse shall thee hent, / Who shall thy wearied age relieue? who shall thy hurts lament? / Thy brother or thy kinsman neere, or will doe this thy friend? / No sure, for to be heyre to thee they rather wish thyne end.' The Latin original begins: '*Cumque senex fueris, aut morbo oppressus iniquo . . .*' (lib. v). This passage in Palingenius forms part of a eulogy of marriage, whose offspring will comfort their father when all others fail him. The Duke's scepticism adds children's neglect to that of other kinsmen and friends. *own bowels*: children, from the biblical 'child of my bowels'. *mere*: absolute, unmodified. *proper*: own. *serpigo*: 'sapego' (F) or 'sarpego' were variant spellings. The

The mere effusion of thy proper loins,   30
Do curse the gout, serpigo, and the rheum
For ending thee no sooner. Thou hast nor youth, nor
    age,
But as it were an after-dinner's sleep
Dreaming on both; for all thy blessed youth
Becomes as aged, and doth beg the alms   35
Of palsied eld: and when thou art old and rich,
Thou hast neither heat, affection, limb, nor beauty
To make thy riches pleasant. What's yet in this
That bears the name of life? Yet in this life
Lie hid moe thousand deaths; yet death we fear   40
That makes these odds all even.
Cla.   I humbly thank you.
To sue to live, I find I seek to die,
And seeking death, find life. Let it come on.

---

31. serpigo] *Rowe;* Sapego *F;* Sarpego *F2.*   34. all] *F;* pall'd, *Warburton, conj.
Theobald.*   blessed] *F;* blazed *Warburton, conj. Theobald;* blasted *conj. Johnson;*
boasted *conj. Collier 2.*   34–5. youth / Becomes] *F;* Youth / [/] Becomes *conj.
N.C.S.*   35. as aged] *F;* assuaged *conj. Theobald, Johnson, Collier 2;* engaged,
abased, *and other conjs. in Hart.*   38. yet in] *F;* in *Pope.*   39. Yet] *F;* Yea
Keightley.   40. moe] *F;* more *Rowe;* some *Keightley.*

---

disease is properly herpes or ring-
worm; but its symptoms were commonly confused with those of venereal
disease. Cf. *Troil.*, II. iii. 82.

33–4. *an after-dinner's sleep Dreaming
on both*] 'Our life, of which no part is
filled with the business of the present
time, resembles our dreams after
dinner, when the events of the morning
are mingled with the designs of the
evening' (Johnson).

34–6. *for all . . . palsied eld*] Numerous
emendations to 'as aged' have been
proposed—'assuaged', 'assailed', 'a-
based', etc. The conceit is merely a
play on the homophone 'alms–arms'.
Palsied old age ('eld') begs youth for
arms: impecunious youth begs old age
for *alms*.

37.] *heat*: desire (heat of blood).
affection: passion (cf. II. i. 10, II. iv. 167).
limb: any organ of the body. 'Neither'
may be a sophistication of 'nor'.

38. *What's yet in this*] 'yet' is metrically awkward, and in three lines
appears three times in the same position. Perhaps a compositor's error.

40. *moe*] a word in its own right,
spelt 'mo' or 'moe', not merely 'more'
contracted.

41. *That makes these odds all even*] Cf.
Seneca, *Epistolae Morales,* xci. 16:
'*Impares nascimur, pares morimur*', and
De Ira, III. 43. 1: '*Venit ecce mors quae
vos pares faciat*'. 'Pares', 'inpares':
equal, unequal; also even and odd
numbers. 'Shakespeare has transferred this double usage to English. In
life we may be "odds", i.e. of unequal
fortunes; but at death we become
"evens", i.e. equal in fortune' (John E.
Hankins, *Shakespeare's Derived Imagery*
(1953), 137).

42–3. *To sue . . . life*] paraphrases
Matth., xvi. 25.

43. *Let it come on*] Let death proceed.

Isab. [*within.*] What hoa! Peace here; grace and good
      company!
Prov. Who's there? Come in; the wish deserves a welcome.
Duke. Dear sir, ere long I'll visit you again.   46
Cla. Most holy sir, I thank you.

Enter ISABELLA.

Isab. My business is a word or two with Claudio.
Prov. And very welcome. Look, signior, here's your sister.
Duke. Provost, a word with you.   50
Prov. As many as you please.
Duke. Bring me to hear them speak, where I may be conceal'd.
                                    [DUKE *and* PROVOST *retire.*]
Cla. Now, sister, what's the comfort?
Isab. Why,
      As all comforts are: most good, most good indeed.   55
      Lord Angelo, having affairs to heaven,
      Intends you for his swift ambassador,
      Where you shall be an everlasting leiger.
      Therefore your best appointment make with speed;
      Tomorrow you set on.
Cla.   Is there no remedy?   60
Isab. None, but such remedy as, to save a head,
      To cleave a heart in twain.
Cla.   But is there any?
Isab. Yes, brother, you may live;
      There is a devilish mercy in the judge,
      If you'll implore it, that will free your life,   65
      But fetter you till death.

---

44. S.D.] *Capell; Enter Isabella. F (after 43).*   47. S.D.] *as Dyce; Capell (after 45).*
52. me . . . them speak] *Malone, conj. Steevens;* them . . . me speak *F;* them to
speak *F2.*   conceal'd] *F;* conceal'd, yet heare them. *F2.*   S.D.] *N.C.S.;*
not in F; Exeunt. F2; Exeunt Duke and Provost. Rowe; Provost leads him aside | Winny.
54–5. Why, / As . . . most good, most good indeed.] *as F;* Why, as . . . most good
indeed. *Pope.*

44. S.D.] See Intro., p. xxv. The
Provost goes to one door to admit Isa-
bella, while the Duke, taking leave of
Claudio, is withdrawing to the other.
    52. S.D.] On the staging here, see
Intro., p. xxvi.

58. *leiger*] ambassador.
59. *appointment*] arrangement.
60. *set on*] go forward.
62. *To cleave*] perhaps a misreading of 'To-cleaves', the intensive prefix.

Cla.　　　　　　　　　Perpetual durance?

Isab. Ay, just, perpetual durance; a restraint,
Though all the world's vastidity you had,
To a determin'd scope.

Cla.　　　　　　　　　But in what nature?

Isab. In such a one as, you consenting to't,　　　70
Would bark your honour from that trunk you bear,
And leave you naked.

Cla.　　　　　　　　　Let me know the point.

Isab. O, I do fear thee, Claudio, and I quake
Lest thou a feverous life shouldst entertain,
And six or seven winters more respect　　　75
Than a perpetual honour. Dar'st thou die?
The sense of death is most in apprehension;
And the poor beetle that we tread upon
In corporal sufferance finds a pang as great
As when a giant dies.

Cla.　　　　　　　Why give you me this shame?　80
Think you I can a resolution fetch
From flowery tenderness? If I must die,
I will encounter darkness as a bride
And hug it in mine arms.

Isab. There spake my brother: there my father's grave　85

66. durance?] *F;* durance! *F3.*　　　68. Though] *Rowe 3;* Through *F.*

66. *durance*] confinement.

68–9. *Though . . . scope* 'Though all
the immensity of the world were yours
to wander in, your mind would be tied
to one fixed thought'. F has 'Through',
defended by Sisson, who glosses the
lines 'reducing the vastidity you once
had to a fixed limit' (*N.R.* I. 83). But
it is hyperbolical to say that Claudio
once 'had' all the world's 'vastidity',
and the sense is forced in its context.
vastidity: a Shakespeare coinage for
vastness.

71.] a play on 'trunk' as body and as
tree-trunk.

bark] strip off the bark.

74. *feverous*] feverish: a common
variant.

entertain] keep up, maintain (*O.E.D.*

3); or, admit to consideration (*O.E.D.*
14b).

75. *respect*] regard.

78–80. *And the poor beetle . . . dies*]
Douce comments: 'fear is the chief
sensation in death, which has no pain:
the giant has no more pain than the
beetle. The arrangement makes the
passage liable to an opposite construction, but which would totally destroy
the illustration of the sentiment' (*Var.
1821*).

82–4. *If I must die . . . arms*] Cf. II.
iv. 101–4, and *Ant.*, IV. xii. 99–101:
'I will be / A bridegroom in my
death, and run into't / As to a lover's
bed'.

85. *my father's grave*] Cf. II. i. 7 and
line 140 *infra.*

Did utter forth a voice. Yes, thou must die.
Thou art too noble to conserve a life
In base appliances. This outward-sainted deputy,
Whose settl'd visage and deliberate word
Nips youth i'th'head and follies doth enew   90
As falcon doth the fowl, is yet a devil:
His filth within being cast, he would appear
A pond as deep as hell.

Cla.   The precise Angelo!

Isab. O, 'tis the cunning livery of hell
The damnedst body to invest and cover   95
In precise guards! Dost thou think, Claudio,

90. enew] *Keightley;* emmew *F;* enmew *Steevens '93.*   93, 96. precise] *Knight (after Tieck);* prenzie, *F;* Princely *F2;* priestly *Hanmer;* prence (*Italian*) *conj. Collier;* proxy *conj. Bulloch (Camb.);* phrenzied *anon. conj. (Camb.).*   95. damnedst] *F2;* damnest *F;* damned *F3.*

88. *appliances*] 'compliances', 'sub-serviences' (*O.E.D.* 1, citing this).

outward-sainted deputy] 'outward saint' may have been the term intended, with 'deputy' an alternative left standing in the authorial copy.

89. *settl'd*] composed.

90–1. *Nips . . . fowl*] The figure is from hawking, nipping in the head being the usual way a bird of prey kills. *enew*: 'drive (the fowl) into the water' (*O.E.D.*). For a description see *Shakespeare's England*, II. 363 n. F 'emmew' is probably a confusion of 'ennew' with 'enmew', to coop up.

92. *cast*] a word of many meanings. Onions renders as 'vomited, thrown up', but the Shakespearean parallels are all in a context of swallowing. Hart suggested 'computed', from the medical 'casting water'. *O.E.D.* v 28, 29, 'dig up with a spade (as of a ditch etc.)' is the most fitting. 'Cast' was also 'letting hawks fly', and the word, like 'pond' below, may have been brought to mind by the previous hawking image.

93, 96. *precise Angelo! . . . precise guards*] Collier suggested *prence*, and Br. Nicholson, *N. & Q.* (1883) 464, described 'prenzie' (F) as 'an English adjective from the old Italian word used by Boccaccio and others, *prenze, alias prence,* a prince or ruler'. L. Hotson (*T.L.S.,* 22 Nov. 1947) mentions that *prenze* appears in Florio (1611) and compares the formation 'prenzie' with 'countie', from Italian *conte,* 'count'. But the word was certainly obscure, or it would not have been changed in F2. It is even less likely as an adjective with 'guards'. 'Precise' could have been misread as 'prenzie', was sometimes accented on the first syllable (with 'i' normally pronounced as in French), and makes good sense in the second instance. For another possible misreading of –*se* as –*zie,* cf. 'Dizie', IV. iii. 12 and note.

94. *the cunning livery of hell*] 'livery' is a verbal noun, 'the dispensing of clothing to retainers or servants' (*O.E.D.* 1a).

95. *damnedst*] F. 'damnest' may be an elocutionary simplification, like 'exists', line 20.

96. *guards*] ornamental borders or trimmings, fig. for a virtuous exterior. The compatibility of 'precise' with 'guards' appears from Dekker, *Seven Deadly Sins* (1607, Percy Reprints, 4, p. 17): 'O veluet-garded Theeues! O yea-and-by-nay Cheaters' (alluding to the 'precisian's' refusal to swear).

If I would yield him my virginity
Thou mightst be freed?
Cla.　　　　　　　　O heavens, it cannot be!
Isab. Yes, he would give't thee, from this rank offence,
　　So to offend him still. This night's the time　　100
　　That I should do what I abhor to name;
　　Or else thou diest tomorrow.
Cla.　　　　　　　　Thou shalt not do't.
Isab. O, were it but my life,
　　I'd throw it down for your deliverance
　　As frankly as a pin.
Cla.　　　　　　Thanks, dear Isabel.　　105
Isab. Be ready, Claudio, for your death tomorrow.
Cla. Yes.—Has he affections in him,
　　That thus can make him bite the law by th'nose
　　When he would force it?—Sure, it is no sin;
　　Or of the deadly seven it is the least.　　110
Isab. Which is the least?
Cla. If it were damnable, he being so wise,
　　Why would he for the momentary trick
　　Be perdurably fin'd?—O Isabel!
Isab. What says my brother?
Cla.　　　　　　　Death is a fearful thing.　　115
Isab. And shamed life a hateful.
Cla. Ay, but to die, and go we know not where;

99–100. *Yes . . . still*] 'He would grant you freedom to go on offending as a reward for my rank offence'. *give*: grant.

101. *what I abhor to name*] Cf. I. ii. 128 and *Per.*, IV. vi. 75–6.

105. *As . . . a pin*] Cf. II. ii. 45–6.

108. *bite the law by th'nose*] mock the law: a proverbial expression (Tilley N 241). In ironical contrast to 'most biting laws', I. iii. 19.

109. *force*] enforce. Claudio asks whether Angelo's desires can be so strong as to lead him, while seeking to enforce the law, into making a mockery of it.

109–110. *Sure . . . least*] In Lodge's *Wits Miserie* (1596), where the seven deadly sins are presented, Fornication says 'Tut . . . lechery is no sinne, find me one Philosopher that held simple fornication for offensiue' (sig. G3ᵛ).

111. *Which is the least?*] since all sins are 'deadly'. But the Christian answer to Claudio is surely that of Perkins, *Veniall Sinne* (*Works*, ed. 1617, II. 520): 'All sin, . . . is . . . deadly. . . No offence is veniall in it selfe, but onelye through Gods mercy, who will not impute all offences expressly vnto death, when as in iustice hee might'.

113. *trick*] trifle, toy.

114. *perdurably fin'd*] punished everlastingly.

117–131. *Ay, . . . death*] Claudio's speech is implicitly a reply to the

To lie in cold obstruction, and to rot;
This sensible warm motion to become
A kneaded clod; and the delighted spirit   120
To bath in fiery floods, or to reside
In thrilling region of thick-ribbed ice;
To be imprison'd in the viewless winds
And blown with restless violence round about
The pendent world: or to be worse than worst   125
Of those that lawless and incertain thought
Imagine howling,—'tis too horrible.
The weariest and most loathed worldly life

120. delighted] F; dilated Hanmer; delinquent conj. Johnson.   121. bath] F;
bathe F2.   122. region] F; Regions Rowe.   126–7. thought / Imagine] F;
thoughts / Imagine Theobald; thought / Imagines Halliwell.

Duke's discourse, and springs from the same amalgam of pagan philosophy and Christian tradition. His conception of punishment in the after-life is based upon classical descriptions of Hades tinged with a Lucretian scepticism. See Intro., pp. lxxxvii–lxxxviii.

118. To lie . . . rot] referring to the body; 'cold obstruction' in contrast to 'warm motion', line 119.

119. sensible] endowed with sensation.

motion] power of movement, particularly the movement of the blood.

120. A kneaded clod] compressed into a lump of earth.

the delighted spirit] 'delighted', though accepted by modern editors, presents problems. It may mean (i) 'attended with delight' (O.E.D. 2) as in Oth., I. iii. 291, Cym., v. iv. 102; but this applies rather to the 'sensible warm motion' than the spirit: (ii) 'beloved' (Latin dilectus, Middle Eng. 'delited'). But Hanmer's 'dilated' fits the context better than either, making effective contrast between the constriction of the body in earth and the extension of the spirit through all the other elements. Cf. Ham., I. i. 153 f.: 'Whether in sea or fire, in earth or air, / Th' extravagant and erring spirit hies / To his confine'.

121. bath] Usually the F2 spelling 'bathe' is followed, but cf. Spenser, Amoretti, LXXII. 10: 'my fraile fancy . . . doth bath in blisse'. The two words may be no more than spelling variants.

122. In thrilling region of thick-ribbed ice] Blakeway compared Jonson's Catiline, I. i. 213–14: 'W'are spirit bound, / In ribs of ice; our whole blouds are one stone'. The cold purgatory is described in Virgil, Aeneid, VI, the main locus, which influenced Dante and Milton. It was the more fitting punishment for sins of passion.

123. viewless] invisible.

124–5. And blown . . . world] Hankins, P.M.L.A., LXXI (1956), 494, cites from Somnium Scipionis: 'Nam eorum animi, qui se corporis voluptatibus dediderant, . . . corporibus elapsi circum terram ipsam volutantur'. Chaucer follows this in The Parlement of Foules, 78 ff.

125. pendent] hanging unsupported in space. Cf. Paradise Lost, II. 1052.

126–7. lawless and incertain thought Imagine howling] the dubious fantasies of poets, according to Lucretius: lawless, because unwarranted by Christian teaching: see Intro., p. lxxxvii, note. Imagine: plural form after two adjectives, cf. I. ii. 174 and note on 'move'.

That age, ache, penury and imprisonment
Can lay on nature, is a paradise   130
To what we fear of death.

Isab.   Alas, alas!

Cla. Sweet sister, let me live.
What sin you do to save a brother's life,
Nature dispenses with the deed so far
That it becomes a virtue.

Isab.   O, you beast!   135
O faithless coward! O dishonest wretch!
Wilt thou be made a man out of my vice?
Is't not a kind of incest, to take life
From thine own sister's shame? What should I think?
Heaven shield my mother play'd my father fair: 140
For such a warped slip of wilderness
Ne'er issued from his blood. Take my defiance,
Die, perish! Might but my bending down
Reprieve thee from thy fate, it should proceed.
I'll pray a thousand prayers for thy death;   145
No word to save thee.

Cla.   Nay hear me, Isabel.

Isab. O fie, fie, fie!
Thy sin's not accidental, but a trade;

---

129. penury] *F2;* periury *F.*   140. shield] *F;* shield: *F2.*

134. *dispenses with*] grants a dispensation for, condones.

137. *made a man*] given life again. Cf. 'man new made' (II. ii. 79), 'a man already made' (II. iv. 44), and see Intro., p. lxxxvi.

138–9. *a kind of incest . . . shame*] since through Isabella's shameful intercourse her own brother would be 'born' again. The hysterical conceit is in keeping with the speech as a whole.

140. *Heaven shield . . . fair*] 'Heaven forbid that my mother should have been faithful to my father when you were conceived'. F2 colon makes the lines that follow meaningless. Hart, interpreting 'shield' as 'protect', paraphrases: 'God protect my mother from such a suspicion, but it would seem almost necessary'. In the context this seems too vague and elliptical.

141. *warped*] also used in *All's W.,* v. iii. 49, and *Lr.,* III. vi. 56.

slip of wilderness] scion of wild stock. (*O.E.D.* 'slip' *sb.*², 'wilderness' 5). Cf. *Ham.,* II. i. 22: 'wanton, wild, and usual slips'.

142. *defiance*] *O.E.D.* 5, citing only this instance, glosses: 'declaration of aversion or contempt'. The more common sense, renunciation of friendship (*O.E.D.* 1), is also more dramatically relevant.

148. *not accidental, but a trade*] 'not a chance occurrence but a habitual course of life' (*O.E.D.* 'trade' *sb.* 3). 'Trade' also links Claudio's situation with Pompey's and Overdone's.

Mercy to thee would prove itself a bawd;
'Tis best that thou diest quickly.   [*Going.*]
Cla.   O hear me, Isabella.
Duke. [*Advancing.*] Vouchsafe a word, young sister, but
    one word.   151
Isab. What is your will?
Duke. Might you dispense with your leisure, I would by
    and by have some speech with you: the satisfaction
    I would require is likewise your own benefit.   155
Isab. I have no superfluous leisure; my stay must be
    stolen out of other affairs: but I will attend you a
    while.   [*Waits behind.*]
Duke. Son, I have overheard what hath passed between
    you and your sister. Angelo had never the purpose 160
    to corrupt her; only he hath made an assay of her
    virtue, to practise his judgement with the disposi-
    tion of natures. She, having the truth of honour in
    her, hath made him that gracious denial which he
    is most glad to receive. I am confessor to Angelo,   165
    and I know this to be true; therefore prepare your-
    self to death. Do not satisfy your resolution with

---

150. S.D.] *Capell.*   151. S.D.] *N.C.S. subst.; not in F; Duke steps in F2; Enter Duke and Provost | Rowe; Re-enter Duke | Capell.*   158. S.D.] *this edn; not in F; Walks apart. Capell; Duke* [*takes Claudio aside*] *N.C.S.* (at *159*).   161. assay] *F*; essay *Rowe.*   167. satisfy] *F*; falsify *Hanmer.*

149.] Claudio is thought of as an addict of lechery; mercy, in assisting his designs, becomes itself a bawd.

150. S.D.] Isabella must withdraw before the Duke intercepts her, so that while waiting for him to end his interview with Claudio, she may not seem to overhear them.

151. S.D.] F has no stage direction here; F2 'Duke steps in' may derive from theatrical practice. See Intro., p. xxvi.

153. *dispense with*] forgo.

153–4. *by and by*] in the modern sense 'soon', not, as often, 'immediately'.

154. *satisfaction*] The Duke as friar may be hinting at 'satisfaction' in the ecclesiastical sense, i.e. performance of a penance enjoined by one's confessor.

157. *attend*] await.

158. S.D.] This follows from Isabella's withdrawal at line 150. Capell's direction 'Walks apart' shows appreciation of the need for Isabella to withdraw; but she has only to remain at the back of the stage (where the Provost is still waiting) to be conventionally out of earshot.

161. *assay*] trial or test; specifically, 'the trial of metals by touch, . . . the determination . . . of the fineness of coin or bullion' (*O.E.D.* 6).

162–3. *disposition*] control, ordering.

163. *truth*] uprightness, integrity.

166–7. *prepare yourself to*] 'get ready to go to'. 'To' carries the implication of a journey ('prepare' *O.E.D. v.* 3). Cf. line 60 and IV. iii. 57.

    hopes that are fallible; tomorrow you must die; go
    to your knees, and make ready.

Cla. Let me ask my sister pardon; I am so out of love   170
    with life that I will sue to be rid of it.

Duke. Hold you there: farewell.—[*Claudio retires.*] Pro-
    vost, a word with you.

Prov. [*advancing*] What's your will, father?

Duke. That, now you are come, you will be gone. Leave   175
    me a while with the maid; my mind promises with
    my habit no loss shall touch her by my company.

Prov. In good time. *Exit* [*with Claudio. Isabella comes forward*].

Duke. The hand that hath made you fair hath made you
    good. The goodness that is cheap in beauty makes   180
    beauty brief in goodness; but grace, being the soul
    of your complexion, shall keep the body of it ever
    fair. The assault that Angelo hath made to you,
    fortune hath conveyed to my understanding; and,
    but that frailty hath examples for his falling, I   185
    should wonder at Angelo. How will you do to con-
    tent this substitute, and to save your brother?

---

172. S.D.] *this edn; not in F; Exit Claudio. Capell; Exit. F2 (after 171).*   174. S.D.] *this edn; not in F; Re-enter Provost. Capell (after 171).*   178. S.D.] *this edn; Exit. F; Exit Provost. Isabella comes forward. Camb.*

---

172. *Hold you there*] Cf. I. i. 42, II. iii. 36.

S.D.] F1 rightly gives no exit here for Claudio. He must first ask pardon of Isabella; and as a prisoner he must leave, as he entered, in custody of the Provost.

172–5. *Provost . . . gone*] This summons leaves Claudio alone with Isabella for a mimed reconciliation. The Duke's call is intentionally fatuous, and would be understood as such between the two older men.

175–6. *Leave . . . maid*] i.e. 'take Claudio away'.

176–7. *my mind . . . company*] In asking to be left alone with a maid his intentions are in keeping with his friar's habit.

178. *In good time*] 'Very well'. Cf. French *à la bonne heure* (Schmidt and O.E.D.).

S.D.] F '*Exit*' is used frequently with a plural sense.

180–1. *The goodness . . . goodness*] 'The pleasing qualities that cost little effort when you are beautiful make beauty soon cease to be good'. 'Goodness' is first used for physical appeal ('good' O.E.D. 3e, cf. *Per.*, IV. ii. 51), then in the moral sense.

181–2. *the soul of your complexion*] 'the vital principle of your disposition'; with play on 'complexion' in the modern sense.

183. *assault*] 'sexual advances'. Cf. *Ado*, II. iii. 129.

185. *frailty . . . falling*] referring either to the fall of the angels, with play on Angelo's name, or to the fall of Adam tempted by Eve, or both.

187. *substitute*] 'deputy' (in place of the Duke). So in IV. ii. 183, V. i. 136.

Isab. I am now going to resolve him. I had rather my
brother die by the law, than my son should be un-
lawfully born. But O, how much is the good Duke   190
deceived in Angelo! If ever he return, and I can
speak to him, I will open my lips in vain, or discover his government.

Duke. That shall not be much amiss. Yet, as the matter
now stands, he will avoid your accusation—he   195
made trial of you only. Therefore fasten your ear on
my advisings, to the love I have in doing good; a
remedy presents itself. I do make myself believe
that you may most uprighteously do a poor wronged
lady a merited benefit; redeem your brother from   200
the angry law; do no stain to your own gracious
person; and much please the absent Duke, if peradventure he shall ever return to have hearing of
this business.

Isab. Let me hear you speak farther. I have spirit to do   205
anything that appears not foul in the truth of my
spirit.

Duke. Virtue is bold, and goodness never fearful. Have
you not heard speak of Mariana, the sister of
Frederick, the great soldier who miscarried at sea?   210

Isab. I have heard of the lady, and good words went
with her name.

Duke. She should this Angelo have married: was affianced to her oath, and the nuptial appointed.

197. advisings, . . . good;] *as F;* advisings: . . . good, *Pope.*   205. farther] *F;* father
F4.   213. She] *F;* Her *Pope.*   213–14. was affianced] *F;* he was affianced *Col-
lier.*   214. to her oath] *F;* to her by oath *F2, Collier;* by oath *Pope;* by her oath
Bald.

188. *resolve*] make certain.
188–90. *I had rather . . . born*] Cf.
Angelo's speech, II. iv. 42–9, and
Isabella's answer.
192–3. *discover*] reveal.
193. *government*] (i) moral conduct
(*O.E.D.* 2b, cf. *Oth.,* III. iii. 256: 'Fear
not my government'); (ii) his way of
governing.
195–6. *avoid . . . trial*] 'invalidate
(saying that)', etc. 'Avoid' is used as a
legal term.

197. *advisings, . . . good;*] F punctuation is restored. The omission of the
semi-colon makes 'remedy' unneces-
sarily ambiguous.
208. *Virtue is bold*] The usual form
was 'Innocence is bold' (Tilley I 82).
213–14. *She should . . . to her oath*]
Mariana had pledged herself in betrothal (Angelo's reciprocal oath
being assumed). The meaning is clear,
but most editions emend to 'to her *by*
oath', making Angelo the subject of

Between which time of the contract and limit of the　215
solemnity, her brother Frederick was wracked at
sea, having in that perished vessel the dowry of his
sister. But mark how heavily this befell to the poor
gentlewoman. There she lost a noble and renowned brother, in his love toward her ever most　220
kind and natural; with him, the portion and sinew
of her fortune, her marriage dowry; with both, her
combinate husband, this well-seeming Angelo.

Isab. Can this be so? Did Angelo so leave her?

Duke. Left her in her tears, and dried not one of them　225
with his comfort: swallowed his vows whole, pretending in her discoveries of dishonour: in few,
bestowed her on her own lamentation, which she
yet wears for his sake; and he, a marble to her tears,
is washed with them, but relents not.　230

Isab. What a merit were it in death to take this poor
maid from the world! What corruption in this life,
that it will let this man live! But how out of this can
she avail?

Duke. It is a rupture that you may easily heal: and the　235

---

228. her on her] *F;* on her her *conj. Malone.*

---

the sentence, 'She' a disjunctive, and
'should this Angelo' an inversion.

215. *the contract*] i.e. *sponsalia de
futuro*; a marriage contract to take
effect in the future, and liable to dissolution in some circumstances up to
the time of consecration. See Intro., p.
liv.

215–16. *limit of the solemnity*] 'prescribed time for solemnizing the marriage' (*O.E.D.* 'limit' *sb.* 2 f. Cf. *R2,*
I. iii. 151).

221. *sinew*] fig. for mainstay. Cf. 'the
very nerves of state' (I. iv. 53), and
Troil., I. iii. 143.

223. *combinate*] bound by the particular kind of marriage contract mentioned in lines 213–14. Cf. 'combined'
IV. iii. 144. A Shakespearean form for
'bound by pledge', perhaps suggested
by the now obsolete verb 'to combind'
(*N.C.S.*).

226. *swallowed*] fig. for retracted.

226–7. *pretending*] alleging.

227. *dishonour*] valid ground for a
dissolution of the contract.

227. *in few*] in short.

228–9. *bestowed her on her own lamentation . . . sake*] Malone's conjecture of a
transposition here is very plausible.
The phrase 'bestowed on her her own
lamentation' has characteristic irony:
all that Angelo gave her as a husband
was the lamentation she was possessed
of already, and continued to 'wear'
as if it were a keepsake. See Intro.,
p. xxix.

229. *a marble . . . tears*] Cf. *1 Prom.,* v.
iii: '*Andrugios* Tombe with dayly
teares, *Polina* worship wyll', and see
Intro., p. xlii.

234. *avail*] profit. Elliptical, for
'avail herself'.

235. *rupture*] breach of agreement.

cure of it not only saves your brother, but keeps you
from dishonour in doing it.

Isab. Show me how, good father.

Duke. This forenamed maid hath yet in her the continuance of her first affection. His unjust unkindness,   240
that in all reason should have quenched her love,
hath, like an impediment in the current, made it
more violent and unruly. Go you to Angelo; answer his requiring with a plausible obedience;
agree with his demands to the point. Only refer   245
yourself to this advantage: first, that your stay with
him may not be long; that the place may have all
shadow and silence in it; and the time answer to
convenience. This being granted in course, and
now follows all. We shall advise this wronged maid   250
to stead up your appointment, go in your place. If
the encounter acknowledge itself hereafter, it may
compel him to her recompense; and hear, by this is
your brother saved, your honour untainted, the
poor Mariana advantaged, and the corrupt deputy   255
scaled. The maid will I frame, and make fit for his

247–8. place . . . time] *this edn; conj. Ridley;* time . . . place *F.*   253. hear,]
this edn; heere, *F;* here, *F3.*   256. scaled] *F;* foiled *White;* sealed *conj.*
Staunton.

240. *unjust*] unfaithful, false.

242–3. *like an impediment . . . unruly*] a
familiar analogy, found in Pettie,
Lyly, and Greene (Tilley S 929).

245–6. *refer yourself to this advantage*]
'entrust yourself to this favourable
condition'. Cf. *Wint.*, III. ii. 116: 'I do
refer me to the oracle'.

247–8. *that the place . . . and the
time answer*] Ridley remarks convincingly that the sense requires the F
'time' and 'place' to be transposed.
Cf. Isabella's description of the place
and time of assignation in IV. i. 28–
36.

251. *stead up*] 'serve to keep up': cf.
'stead me' (I. iv. 17). *O.E.D. v.* 3 renders 'fulfil in stead of', by analogy with
'in the stead of', but gives no other
instance.

252. *acknowledge itself*] come to be
known. Cf. *Ado,* I. ii. 14.

253. *hear*] Cf. v. i. 34. F 'heere' could
be either 'hear' or 'here': F3 having
chosen 'here', all editions follow: but
the effect is awkwardly repetitive.

256. *scaled*] weighed as in scales (his
moral worth truly estimated). So
O.E.D. v.¹ 2, citing *Cor.*, II. iii. 257.
This suits the recurrent imagery of
testing. Steevens suggested 'scattered,
dispersed', found also in Holinshed.
More fanciful suggestions are: 'climbed
up to' (as on a scaling ladder); 'stripped of scales' (as of a fish) (Johnson,
Steevens).

frame] prepare, make ready in advance. This sense survives in northern
dialects (*E.D.D.* 11) and perhaps in
the American 'frame-up'.

attempt. If you think well to carry this as you may,
the doubleness of the benefit defends the deceit
from reproof. What think you of it?

Isab. The image of it gives me content already, and I   260
trust it will grow to a most prosperous perfection.

Duke. It lies much in your holding up. Haste you speedily to Angelo; if for this night he entreat you to his
bed, give him promise of satisfaction. I will presently to Saint Luke's; there at the moated grange   265
resides this dejected Mariana; at that place call
upon me; and dispatch with Angelo, that it may be
quickly.

Isab. I thank you for this comfort. Fare you well, good
father.   *Exit.*   270

[III. ii.]

Enter ELBOW [*and*] *Officers* [*with*] POMPEY.

Elbow. Nay, if there be no remedy for it, but that you will
needs buy and sell men and women like beasts, we

270. S.D.] *F; Exeunt. Pope; Exeunt severally. Theobald.*

Scene II

[III. ii.] *as F (no scene division); The Street. Pope; Scene II. Street before the Prison.
Capell.   S.D.] Sisson; Enter Elbow, Clowne, Officers. F; Enter Duke, Elbow, Clown
and Officers. Pope; Enter on one side, Duke . . . on the other, Elbow, and Officers with
Pompey. Dyce.*

257. *attempt*] assault.

258. *the doubleness of the benefit*] Four
'benefits' are mentioned in lines 253–6.
But the benefit for both Mariana and
Isabella is what is meant.

260. *image*] idea, conception.

262. *holding up*] power of sustaining
(the scheme). 'Hold up the jest' = keep
it going; cf. *MND.*, III. ii. 239; *Wiv.*,
v. v. 111 (Hart).

262–3. *Haste you speedily*] not a
pleonasm, but a play on 'speedy' as
advantageous. Cf. 'speedy haste' (*R3*,
III. i. 59–60).

265. *grange*] usually, country house;
but in conjunction with 'Saint Luke's',

probably 'an outlying farm-house belonging to a religious establishment'
(*O.E.D.* 2b).

266. *dejected*] lowered (i) in spirits,
(ii) in estate. Both meanings were
current.

267. *dispatch with*] settle matters
with, combining the sense of 'make
haste'.

270. S.D.] On the unlocalized
Elizabethan stage the scene is continuous to the end of the act. For convenience in cross-reference the lines
are numbered for what editors have
traditionally distinguished as scene
ii.

shall have all the world drink brown and white
bastard.

Duke. O heavens, what stuff is here!   5

Pom. 'Twas never merry world since, of two usuries, the
merriest was put down, and the worser allowed by
order of law; a furred gown to keep him warm; and
furred with fox on lambskins too, to signify that craft,
being richer than innocency, stands for the facing.   10

Elbow. Come your way, sir.—Bless you, good father friar.

Duke. And you, good brother father. What offence hath
this man made you, sir?

Elbow. Marry, sir, he hath offended the law; and, sir, we
take him to be a thief too, sir: for we have found upon   15
him, sir, a strange pick-lock, which we have sent to
the deputy.

---

5. here!] *F* (heere); *here? Camb.*   8. law;] *F; law, Rowe 3; law Capell;* law [ ] *War-burton.*   9. fox on] *Rann (after Mason); Foxe and F.*   11. Bless] *Rowe;* 'blesse *F.*

3–4. *drink brown and white bastard*]
procreate bastards of all races. Bastard
was a sweet wine, originally from
Spain (cf. *1H4,* II. iv. 30). The pun is
made in Middleton and Rowley's *A
Faire Quarrell,* v. i. 123: 'has she drunk
bastard?' and in Middleton, *A Mad
World, My Masters,* II. i. 'Drink', as
Winny suggests, probably includes the
archaic sense of paying the penalty.

6. *'Twas never merry world*] 'Things
have never been right'. A common
expression, in the positive or negative
form.

two usuries] money-lending and
lechery, resulting in interest and issue.
See 'use', *O.E.D. sb.* 2b and 4. The two
concepts were traditionally associated,
the Greek word for interest, τόκος,
being literally offspring. Cf. Dekker,
Seven Deadly Sins, p. 20: 'The Vsurer
liues by the lechery of mony, and is
Bawd to his owne bags'. Conversely
procreation was often seen as a virtuous form of usury, e.g. *Sonn.,* IV. 7–8,
VI. 5–6. Related to the coin imagery.

7–8. *the worser allowed by the order of
law; a furred gown to keep him warm*]
Punctuation follows F. All editors be-

fore Ridley altered this to make the
furred gown 'allowed by order of law'.
No legal regulation ever mentioned
such a gown for usurers. Pompey
claims that usury is now 'allowed',
because the statute of 1570 limited
interest charges to 10 per cent: a view
vigorously contested by Henry Smith,
Sermons (1593), p. 183: 'our law doth
not allow ten in the hundred . . . nor
any vsurie at all: but there is a restraint
in our law, that no vsurer take aboue
ten in the hundred'. *to keep him warm:*
usury personified as the usurer, with
word-play on 'warm' as 'secure' and
'amorous'. Cf. *Lr,* IV. vi. 170. Elizabethan literature abounds in references to fox-furred usurers; instances
are given by Hart.

9–10. *fox on lambskins . . . facing*]
Mason's 'on' for F's 'and' is necessary
to make the point about 'facing', i.e.
outer covering. The lamb symbolized
innocence, the fox craftiness.

11–12. *father friar . . . brother father*]
The Duke plays on Elbow's vulgarism
('friar' from Fr. *frère*).

16. *a strange pick-lock*] a sly reference
to 'chastity belts'. The suggestion

Duke. Fie, sirrah, a bawd, a wicked bawd;
　　　 The evil that thou causest to be done,
　　　 That is thy means to live. Do thou but think　　　20
　　　 What 'tis to cram a maw or clothe a back
　　　 From such a filthy vice. Say to thyself,
　　　 From their abominable and beastly touches
　　　 I drink, I eat, array myself, and live.
　　　 Canst thou believe thy living is a life,　　　25
　　　 So stinkingly depending? Go mend, go mend.
Pom. Indeed it does stink in some sort, sir. But yet, sir, I
　　　 would prove—
Duke. Nay, if the devil have given thee proofs for sin,
　　　 Thou wilt prove his. Take him to prison, officer:　　　30
　　　 Correction and instruction must both work
　　　 Ere this rude beast will profit.
Elbow. He must before the deputy, sir; he has given him
　　　 warning. The deputy cannot abide a whoremaster.
　　　 If he be a whoremonger and comes before him, he　　　35
　　　 were as good go a mile on his errand.
Duke. That we were all, as some would seem to be,
　　　 From our faults, as faults from seeming, free!

---

24. eat, array] *Theobald (after Bishop)*; eate away *F.*　　27–8.] *as Pope*; Indeed . . . sort, Sir: / . . . proue. / *F (verse)*.　　38. From our] *F;* Free from our *F2, Sisson;* Free from all *F4, Hanmer.*　　 as faults from] *F;* or faults from *Sisson, conj. Johnson;* as his faults from *Alexander;* as from faults *Hanmer.*　　 seeming, free!] *Var. 1821;* seeming, free. *F;* seeming, free. *Alexander.*

---

shocked Hart, but cf. Jonson, *Volpone,* II. v. 57 (Steevens). The 'lock' is referred to figuratively in *Cym.,* II. ii. 41 f.: 'I think I have pick'd the lock and ta'en / The treasure of her honour'.

16–17. *which we have sent to the deputy*] unconscious irony.

23. *abominable and beastly touches*] F 'abhominable' brings out the old, popular derivation from *ab homine,* 'inhuman', which 'beastly' reinforces. *touches*: sexual contacts; also the numismatic stamp on money; indicating the kind of 'touch' that provides Pompey with his livelihood.

24. *eat, array*] Theobald's unchallenged emendation of F 'eate away'.

27. *it does stink*] Cf. Boult in *Per.,* IV. vi. 149–50: 'She makes our profession as it were to stink'. The word 'abhominable' (Q) appears in the previous line.

29–30. *Nay . . . prove his*] 'If the devil has given you arguments to defend sin, you will turn out to be his'.

31. *work*] act in co-operation. Cf. 'work', I. i. 9.

33–4. *he . . . warning*] actually the warning was given by Escalus.

36. *as good . . . errand*] proverbial (Tilley M 927): 'do anything rather than that'.

38. *From our . . . free*] 'free' governs both clauses, meaning in the first, 'not subject to', in the second, 'dissociated from'. 'Would that we were all as little

Elbow. His neck will come to your waist—a cord, sir.

Enter LUCIO.

Pom. I spy comfort, I cry bail! Here's a gentleman, and a   40
    friend of mine.
Lucio. How now, noble Pompey! What, at the wheels of
    Caesar? Art thou led in triumph? What, is there
    none of Pygmalion's images newly made woman to
    be had now, for putting the hand in the pocket and   45
    extracting clutched? What reply, ha? What say'st
    thou to this tune, matter and method? Is't not
    drowned i'th'last rain? Ha? What say'st thou, trot?
    Is the world as it was, man? Which is the way? Is it
    sad, and few words? Or how? The trick of it?   50
Duke. Still thus, and thus: still worse!

---

39. S.D.] *Alexander; F (after 38)*, *Dyce (after 41)*.   46. clutched] *F* (clutch'd); it
clutch'd *Rowe 3*.   48. rain] *F*; reign *Warburton*.   51. worse!] *Johnson;* worse? *F*.

subject to our faults, as faults are dissociated from seeming (i.e. for persons
like Angelo)'. Cf. *Oth.*, III. iii. 126–7.

  39.] 'His neck will come to be in the
same condition as your waist: it will
have a cord round it'. Referring to the
friar's habit worn by the Duke.

  42–3. *at the wheels of Caesar . . .
triumph?*] recalling Escalus' threat, II.
i. 245–6. The historical Pompey was
not led in triumph by Caesar, but his
sons were, after their defeat at Munda.
Cf. *Cæs.*, I. i. 55: 'That comes in
triumph over Pompey's blood'.
'Caesar' here, as in the Gospel, represents state authority.

  44. *Pygmalion's images*] The story of
Pygmalion was familiar through
Ovid, *Metamorph.*, X. Because the
Elizabethan statue was often painted,
Pygmalion's beloved suggested the
idea of a prostitute. Cf. Middleton,
Micro-Cynicon, VIII. 133: 'Trust not a
painted puppet, as I've done, / Who
far more doted than Pygmalion'.
Marston's *Metamorphosis of Pygma-
lion's Image* may have popularized the
expression.

  46. *extracting clutched*] taking the
hand out with money grasped therein.
'it' is usually inserted before 'clutched';
but 'extracting' may be an elocutionary simplification of 'extracting't': cf.
'exists', III. i. 20, etc.

  ha?] Cf. II. ii. 164; II. iv. 42.

  48. *drowned i'th'last rain*] probably
'now out of fashion'. Sometimes interpreted as a topical allusion to the
heavy rains of the winter 1602–3; but
the mention is too vague, and rain too
common in England, to signify much.
Warburton's substitution of 'reign' for
'rain' seems far-fetched, but there may
have been popular word-play on
'rain–reign' to make this a catch-
phrase round about 1604.

  trot] contemptuously for a midwife
or old woman. This seems to be the
only known example of its application
to a man. Perhaps, as R. G. Shedd
suggests, 'stage business' would make
the transference, as well as Pompey's
silence here, intelligible to the audience.

  50. *trick of it*] 'way (of the world)'.
Cf. v. i. 503.

Lucio. How doth my dear morsel, thy mistress? Procures
    she still, ha?

Pom. Troth, sir, she hath eaten up all her beef, and she is
    herself in the tub.   55

Lucio. Why, 'tis good: it is the right of it: it must be so.
    Ever your fresh whore, and your powdered bawd; an
    unshunned consequence; it must be so. Art going to
    prison, Pompey?

Pom. Yes, faith, sir.   60

Lucio. Why, 'tis not amiss, Pompey. Farewell: go, say I
    sent thee thither.—For debt, Pompey, or how?

Pom. For being a bawd, for being a bawd.

Lucio. Well, then, imprison him. If imprisonment be the
    due of a bawd, why, 'tis his right. Bawd is he doubt-   65
    less, and of antiquity, too: bawd born. Farewell,
    good Pompey. Commend me to the prison, Pompey;
    you will turn good husband now, Pompey; you will
    keep the house.

Pom. I hope, sir, your good worship will be my bail?   70

Lucio. No, indeed will I not, Pompey; it is not the wear. I
    will pray, Pompey, to increase your bondage; if you

72–3. bondage; . . . patiently,] *Theobald;* bondage . . . patiently: *F.*

52. *morsel*] used in a lecherous sense
for a woman; cf. *2H4*, II. iv. 401, *Ant.*,
III. xi. 116 f. Modern analogies might
be 'bit' or 'piece'.

55. *in the tub*] (i) the tub for salting
beef, then called 'powdering'; (ii) the
sweating-tub, where fumes of cinnabar
were used as a cure for venereal disease
(cf. *H5*, II. i. 79). This is a clown's
'gag', not information: cf. the 'hot-
house', II. i. 65 and note.

57. *Ever your . . . bawd*] 'the young
prostitute always grows into the old
brothel-keeper, "powdered" like beef
in the tub'.

58. *unshunned*] unshunnable. Cf.
'unsevered' for 'inseparable', *Cor.*, III.
ii. 42 (Onions).

61–2. *say I sent thee thither*] Perhaps a
catch-phrase like 'say Pompey told
you so' (II. i. 240); but it may well
confirm Overdone's accusation, line

192 *infra*, that Lucio has been acting as
an informer.

62. *For debt . . . ?*] Lucio is being dis-
ingenuous: he himself is more likely to
be arrested for debt than Pompey. Cf.
I. ii. 123 ff.

66. *of antiquity*] of long standing.

68–9. *you will turn good husband . . .
you will keep the house*] 'we call the wife
Huswife . . . to shewe that a good wife
keeps her house' (Henry Smith, *A
Preparatiue to Mariage, Sermons*, 1593. p.
50). The 'house' here is the prison.

71. *the wear*] the fashion. Cf. 'Mot-
ley's the only wear', *AYL.*, II. vii. 34.

72–3. *if you take it . . . more*] Theobald's punctuation has been univers-
ally followed. Lucio provides (i)
ironical encouragement, (ii) a pun on
'metal': if Pompey is restive in prison,
he will have more fetters put on
him.

take it not patiently, why, your mettle is the more!
Adieu, trusty Pompey.—Bless you, friar.

Duke. And you.   75

Lucio. Does Bridget paint still, Pompey? Ha?

Elbow. [*to Pompey.*] Come your ways, sir, come.

Pom. You will not bail me then, sir?

Lucio. Then, Pompey, nor now.—What news abroad,
friar? What news?   80

Elbow. [*to Pompey.*] Come your ways, sir, come.

Lucio. Go to kennel, Pompey, go.

> [*Exeunt* ELBOW *and Officers with* POMPEY.]

What news, friar, of the Duke?

Duke. I know none: can you tell me of any?

Lucio. Some say he is with the Emperor of Russia; other   85
some, he is in Rome: but where is he, think you?

Duke. I know not where: but wheresoever, I wish him
well.

Lucio. It was a mad, fantastical trick of him to steal from
the state and usurp the beggary he was never born to.   90
Lord Angelo dukes it well in his absence: he puts
transgression to't.

Duke. He does well in't.

Lucio. A little more lenity to lechery would do no harm in
him. Something too crabbed that way, friar.   95

Duke. It is too general a vice, and severity must cure it.

Lucio. Yes, in good sooth, the vice is of a great kindred;

---

82. S.D.] *Dyce; not in F; Exeunt. F2; Exeunt Elbow, Clown and Officers. Rowe.*

82. *Go to kennel, Pompey*] 'Be off to prison'. Johnson's comment that 'Pompey' was then the common name for a dog is unconfirmed: but there may well be a word-play on 'Pompey–puppy'.

85. *with the Emperor of Russia*] Cf. I. iii. 14.

90. *usurp the beggary he was never born to*] N. Coghill takes the remark as an indication that Lucio sees through the Duke's disguise as a mendicant friar, with 'an overtone reference to the Incarnation' (*S.S.* 8 (1955), 24 and note 32). It is more likely to be what

Coghill rejects, 'a stage situation contrived to raise a laugh', with a latent irony for the audience. Lucio's 'Come, sir, I know what I know', adduced as a confirmation, occurs 58 lines later, in a different context.

91. *dukes it*] acts the duke. Cf. Marston, *Malcontent*, IV. iii: 'Ha ye murthering Polititian, how dost Duke?'

91–2. *puts . . . to't*] 'drives to extremities' (Onions); approximately as in *Wint.*, I. ii. 16: 'tougher . . . Than you can put us to 't!'

95 *crabbed*] harsh. Cf. *Temp.*, III. i. 8.

it is well allied; but it is impossible to extirp it quite,
friar, till eating and drinking be put down.—They
say this Angelo was not made by man and woman,　　100
after this downright way of creation: is it true, think
you?

Duke. How should he be made, then?

Lucio. Some report, a sea-maid spawned him. Some,
that he was begot between two stockfishes. But it is　　105
certain that when he makes water, his urine is con-
gealed ice; that I know to be true. And he is a
motion ungenerative; that's infallible.

Duke. You are pleasant, sir, and speak apace.

Lucio. Why, what a ruthless thing is this in him, for the　　110
rebellion of a codpiece to take away the life of a
man! Would the Duke that is absent have done
this? Ere he would have hanged a man for the getting a hundred bastards, he would have paid for the
nursing a thousand. He had some feeling of the　　115
sport; he knew the service; and that instructed him
to mercy.

Duke. I have never heard the absent Duke much de-

---

101. this] *F*; the *Pope.*　　107–8. a motion ungenerative] *Theobald;* a motion
generatiue *F;* no motion generative *Hanmer.*

98. *extirp*] the earlier form of 'extirpate'. See Intro., p. lxxxv.

101. *this downright way*] the plain,
ordinary way. Also in an obscene
sense by analogy with 'upright'. For
use of 'this', cf. 'these black masks',
II. iv. 79, and note.

104. *sea-maid*] mermaid, as in
MND., II. i. 154.

105. *stockfishes*] cod, haddock, etc.,
slit and dried in the open air. Figuratively for a thin person (*1H4,* II. iv.
275), also for one without sexual
desire or appeal; cf. Day, *Law-tricks*
(*M.S.R.,* 750–2): 'shriueld Bawd, . . .
more irrelishable / Then ore-dried
Stock-fish'.

107–8. *a motion ungenerative*] 'a puppet without power of generation'.
Theobald's emendation for F 'generatiue' is necessary: otherwise the phrase

is pointless. Angelo has just been
associated with 'stockfishes', and is
called an 'ungenitured agent' in lines
167–8. 'Motion' carried the implication of sexlessness in Jonson, *The Silent
Woman,* III. iv. 37–8: 'did you thinke
you had married a statue? or a
motion, onely?', and in Fletcher, *Rule
A Wife,* II. i: 'If he be that motion that
you tell me of . . . I shall entertain
him' (III. 183).

109. *pleasant*] joking, facetious.

111. *codpiece*] part of the Elizabethan
male attire; here, as often, in an
obscene sense.

116. *the service*] 'the profession', seen
as a public service of the state, as in
I. ii. 102.

instructed] trained (*O.E.D.* 1c).

118–19. *detected*] accused in public.

tected for women; he was not inclined that way.

Lucio. O sir, you are deceived.   120

Duke. 'Tis not possible.

Lucio. Who, not the Duke? Yes, your beggar of fifty; and his use was to put a ducat in her clack-dish; the Duke had crotchets in him. He would be drunk too, that let me inform you.   125

Duke. You do him wrong, surely.

Lucio. Sir, I was an inward of his. A shy fellow was the Duke; and I believe I know the cause of his withdrawing.

Duke. What, I prithee, might be the cause?   130

Lucio. No, pardon: 'tis a secret must be locked within the teeth and the lips. But this I can let you understand: the greater file of the subject held the Duke to be wise.

Duke. Wise? Why, no question but he was.   135

Lucio. A very superficial, ignorant, unweighing fellow—

Duke. Either this is envy in you, folly, or mistaking. The very stream of his life, and the business he hath helmed, must upon a warranted need give him a better proclamation. Let him be but testimonied in   140 his own bringings-forth, and he shall appear to the envious a scholar, a statesman, and a soldier. Therefore you speak unskilfully: or, if your knowledge be more, it is much darkened in your malice.

Lucio. Sir, I know him and I love him.   145

---

123. *use*] custom.

a ducat in her clack-dish] 'clack-dish', or 'clap-dish', was a beggar's wooden bowl, with a lid that was clapped or 'clacked' to draw attention. The ducat (Italian *ducato*, ducal coin) would serve almost as the Duke's visiting card. The Duke's secret charities are made by Lucio into occasions for slander.

127. *inward*] intimate friend (*O.E.D.* B.3).

shy] reserved, wary. Cf. v. i. 57.

133. *the greater file*] the majority, from 'file', a body of men. Cf. 'the common file', *Cor.*, i. vi. 43.

the subject] Cf. ii. iv. 27.

136. *unweighing*] injudicious. Another figure of 'measuring'; cf. 'scaled', iii. i. 256, 'weighing', iii. ii. 259, etc.

139. *helmed*] steered in the fig. sense. Cf. Marston, *What You Will*, ii. i (ii. 253): 'Fate helmeth all'.

upon a warranted need] *N.C.S.* glosses: 'needed there a warrant'; but 'in a proven (or truly sufficient) case of necessity' seems closer to the sense. (*O.E.D. ppl. a.*1).

139–40. *a better proclamation*] a more favourable reputation.

141. *bringings-forth*] public acts.

Duke. Love talks with better knowledge, and knowledge
　　with dearer love.

Lucio. Come, sir, I know what I know.

Duke. I can hardly believe that, since you know not
　　what you speak. But if ever the Duke return—as　150
　　our prayers are he may—let me desire you to make
　　your answer before him. If it be honest you have
　　spoke, you have courage to maintain it; I am bound
　　to call upon you, and I pray you your name.

Lucio. Sir, my name is Lucio, well known to the Duke.　155

Duke. He shall know you better, sir, if I may live to
　　report you.

Lucio. I fear you not.

Duke. O, you hope the Duke will return no more; or you
　　imagine me too unhurtful an opposite. But indeed,　160
　　I can do you little harm. You'll forswear this again?

Lucio. I'll be hanged first. Thou art deceived in me,
　　friar. But no more of this.—Canst thou tell if
　　Claudio die tomorrow, or no?

Duke. Why should he die, sir?　165

Lucio. Why? For filling a bottle with a tun-dish. I would
　　the Duke we talk of were returned again: this un-
　　genitured agent will unpeople the province with
　　continency. Sparrows must not build in his house-
　　eaves, because they are lecherous.—The Duke yet　170
　　would have dark deeds darkly answered: he would
　　never bring them to light: would he were returned!
　　Marry, this Claudio is condemned for untrussing.
　　—Farewell, good friar, I prithee pray for me. The

147. dearer] *Hanmer;* deare *F.*

152. *honest*] true.
160. *opposite*] opponent.
162. *I'll be hanged first*] dramatic
irony.
166. *For . . . tun-dish*] obscene innuendo. 'Tun-dish': a kind of funnel.
Still used in some dialects and in Ire-
land: 'Is that called a funnel? Is it not
a tundish?' James Joyce, *A Portrait of
the Artist As A Young Man,* §5.
167–8. *ungenitured*] sterile, seedless;
or without genitals. (*O.E.D.* 'geniture'

4, 5). A Shakespearean formation. Cf.
107–8 and note.
168. *agent*] deputy.
169–70. *Sparrows . . . lecherous*] Sparrows were traditionally regarded as
lecherous (Tilley S 715).
171. *darkly*] secretly. Shakespeare
seems to have initiated this usage
(Onions).
173. *condemned for untrussing*] for un-
tying the 'points' attaching hose to
doublet.

Duke, I say to thee again, would eat mutton on Fri-   175
days. He's now past it; yet, and I say to thee, he
would mouth with a beggar though she smelt brown
bread and garlic, say that I said so. Farewell.   *Exit.*
Duke. No might nor greatness in mortality
     Can censure 'scape. Back-wounding calumny   180
     The whitest virtue strikes. What king so strong
     Can tie the gall up in the slanderous tongue?
     But who comes here?

Enter [severally] ESCALUS; PROVOST, *and [Officers with]*
Mistress OVERDONE.

Esc. Go, away with her to prison.
Mis. O. Good my lord, be good to me. Your honour is   185
     accounted a merciful man. Good my lord.
Esc. Double and treble admonition, and still forfeit in
     the same kind! This would make mercy swear and
     play the tyrant.

176. now past it; yet,] F (now past it, yet); not past it yet *Hanmer;* now past it:
yea *Capell.*   176–8. and ... garlic,] *this edn;* (and ... thee) ... Garlicke: F;
and, ... thee, ... garlick: *Hanmer (subst.).*   183. S.D.] *Dyce (subst.); Enter*
Escalus, Prouost, and Bawd. F; Enter Escalus, Provost, Bawd and Officers. Theobald 2.
188. kind!] *Camb.;* kind? F.

175–6. *would eat mutton on Fridays*]
'would do forbidden things', with
word-play on 'mutton', a slang term
for prostitutes.
   176–8. *He's now past it; yet, and I ...*
said so] If 'and' is read as the conditional, this sentence presents no problems. Lucio says that the Duke, although sexually 'past it', would kiss
the beggar, and he is willing to be
reported as having said so. *smelt:*
smelt of. *brown bread:* coarse rye, or rye
and wheat bread, the food of the poor,
which rapidly turned musty and
affected the breath. So Tucca calls
Horace a 'browne-bread-mouth stin-
ker' in Dekker's *Satiromastix,* I. ii. 305.
say that I said so: Cf. II. i. 240.
   179–82.] Warburton, noting that
these lines are closely connected with
the Duke's soliloquy, IV. i. 60–5, suggested that a single ten-line speech was

intended. Lascelles (p. 107) thinks
that the whole speech should come
here, commencing with the soliloquy
of IV. i and continuing with the present
lines. The composite passage would
then be 'within the convention of the
formal soliloquy ... apostrophe, the
release of pent-up bitterness, is calmed
to sententious observation, and *sen-*
tence clinched with a couplet'. See
Intro., pp. xx f. *mortality:* mortal beings. *Back-wounding:* back-biting.
   183. S.D.] Lascelles (p. 93 and note
3) reconstructs the staging. Escalus
has come to inform the Provost that
the appeal for Claudio has failed. He
enters by another door as the Officers
are delivering Mistress Overdone to
the Provost, and speaks in answer to
her attempt to obtain his favour.
   188–9. *swear and play the tyrant*] Cf.
'tyrant' in II. iv. 168. Douce links the

Prov. A bawd of eleven years' continuance, may it please   190
    your honour.

Mis. O. My lord, this is one Lucio's information against
    me, Mistress Kate Keep-down was with child by
    him in the Duke's time, he promised her marriage.
    His child is a year and a quarter old come Philip   195
    and Jacob. I have kept it myself; and see how he
    goes about to abuse me.

Esc. That fellow is a fellow of much license. Let him be
    called before us. Away with her to prison.—Go to,
    no more words.   200

           [Exeunt Officers with Mistress OVERDONE.*]*
    Provost, my brother Angelo will not be altered;
    Claudio must die tomorrow. Let him be furnished
    with divines, and have all charitable preparation.
    If my brother wrought by my pity, it should not be
    so with him.   205

Prov. So please you, this friar hath been with him, and
    advised him for th'entertainment of death.

Esc. Good even, good father.

Duke. Bliss and goodness on you!

Esc. Of whence are you?   210

Duke. Not of this country, though my chance is now
    To use it for my time. I am a brother
    Of gracious order, late come from the See
    In special business from his Holiness.

Esc. What news abroad i'th'world?   215

---

200. S.D.] *Dyce; not in F; Exeunt with the Bawd. Rowe.*   208. even] *F4;* 'euen *F.*
213. See] *Theobald;* Sea *F.*

phrase with morality performances of
the massacre of the innocents, where
Herod 'rages' and swears 'by Ma-
hound'.

  192. *one Lucio's information*] Cf. lines
61–2.

  195–6. *come Philip and Jacob*] next
1 May, when the annual festival of St
Philip and St James was held. The
style of reckoning age indicates that
Lucio's child owed its origin to a more
pagan way of celebrating May Day.

  203. *charitable preparation*] spiritual
preparation for death, as enjoined by
Christian charity.

  204. *wrought . . . pity*] 'directed
affairs with such pity as I have'.

  207. *entertainment*] reception.

  212. *time*] occasion.

  213. *the See*] the Holy See. *N.C.S.*
notes the recurrence of the spelling
'sea', a common variant, in the three
other places in F where the word
appears.

Duke. None, but that there is so great a fever on goodness that the dissolution of it must cure it. Novelty is
  only in request, and it is as dangerous to be aged in
  any kind of course as it is virtuous to be constant in
  any undertaking. There is scarce truth enough alive   220
  to make societies secure; but security enough to
  make fellowships accurst. Much upon this riddle
  runs the wisdom of the world. This news is old
  enough, yet it is every day's news. I pray you, sir, of
  what disposition was the Duke?   225
Esc. One that, above all other strifes, contended especially to know himself.
Duke. What pleasure was he given to?
Esc. Rather rejoicing to see another merry, than merry
  at anything which professed to make him rejoice.   230
  A gentleman of all temperance. But leave we him to
  his events, with a prayer they may prove prosperous, and let me desire to know how you find Claudio
  prepared. I am made to understand that you have
  lent him visitation.   235

218–19. it is as . . . constant] *F3;* as it is as . . . constant *F;* as it is, as . . . constant
Alexander; as it is . . . course; as . . . inconstant *Hudson;* as it is, as . . . inconstant
Sisson; it is as . . . inconstant *N.C.S., conj. Staunton.*   220. undertaking. There
is] *F;* undertaking; there is *Hudson.*   226–7. One . . . himself.] *as Capell;*
One . . . strifes, / Contended especially . . . himselfe. *F;* One . . . strifes / Contended
specially . . . himself. *Pope.*

216–17. *so great a fever . . . cure it*] The
fever can only be 'cured' by the death
of the patient (i.e. of goodness).

217–18. *Novelty is only in request*] Cf.
B.D., p. 52: 'But vnto one fault is
all the common people . . . subject . . .
to judge and speake rashlie of their
Prince . . . ever wearying of the present
estate, and desirous of nouelties'.

218–19. *it is as . . . constant in*] following F3 and assuming an obtrusive 'as'
in F. Alexander and Sisson restore the
first 'as', punctuating 'as it is, as'; i.e.
'as it (novelty) is only in request, (it is)
as dangerous', etc. But this elliptical
construction is rather strained. Possibly Shakespeare wrote 'as is it is as
. . .', which at some stage of transmission was 'corrected' by eliminating

one 'it is'. Similar 'correction' may
have altered 'it is virtuous to be inconstant' a few words on, to the truism 'it
is virtuous to be constant'.

221–2. *security enough to make fellowships accurst*] 'security' seems in apposition to 'truth', 'fellowships' to
'society': but the 'riddle' (222) lies in
the quibble on (i) security, as the
pledges demanded in return for advances of capital, and (ii) fellowships,
as the corporations formed for trad-
ing ventures. Such corporations are
'accurst' by the high security they
must offer to have their ventures
financed.

231–2. *to his events*] 'to the outcome
of his affairs'.

235. *lent him visitation*] 'granted him

Duke. He professes to have received no sinister measure
   from his judge, but most willingly humbles himself
   to the determination of justice. Yet had he framed
   to himself, by the instruction of his frailty, many
   deceiving promises of life, which I, by my good   240
   leisure, have discredited to him; and now is he
   resolved to die.

Esc. You have paid the heavens your function, and the
   prisoner the very debt of your calling. I have
   laboured for the poor gentleman to the extremest   245
   shore of my modesty, but my brother-justice have I
   found so severe that he hath forced me to tell him he
   is indeed Justice.

Duke. If his own life answer the straitness of his proceed-
   ing, it shall become him well: wherein if he chance   250
   to fail, he hath sentenced himself.

Esc. I am going to visit the prisoner; fare you well.

Duke. Peace be with you.   [*Exeunt* ESCALUS *and* PROVOST.]
   He who the sword of heaven will bear

249–50. If... proceeding] *as Pope; verse F* (life, / Answere).   253. S.D.] *not in F.*

---

a visit'. 'Visitation' was Shakespeare's
regular word for 'visit', a substantive
he never used.
   236. *sinister measure*] unjust treatment: the 'measure' theme again.
   238–9. *framed to himself*] formed in
his mind.
   239. *instruction*] prompting.
   240–1. *by my good leisure*] 'in my own
time'.
   243–4. *You . . . function, and the
prisoner . . . calling*] Escalus applies the
concept of function, stated by the
Duke in I. i. 29–40, to the Duke himself as Friar.
   246. *shore*] limit, boundary.
   248. *indeed Justice*] justice personified.
   249. *answer*] correspond with.
   254. ff.] Hart regarded 'this un-
Shakespearian chorus' as 'a needless
interpolation'; *N.C.S.* likens it to the
Gower choruses in *Pericles* as the work
of a reviser. Lascelles (pp. 103–4) compares the metre with that of Prospero's

epilogue to *The Tempest*. She con-
cludes that verse of this sort is only
proper for a prologue, an epilogue, or
'a formal pause midway', and marks
here the renewal of the action after an
interval, on some occasion when the
play was presented in two parts. But
the metre, with its staple seven syl-
lables and variations into dissyllabic
rhyme and octosyllables, was not uncommon. Cf. 'Harke, now every thing
is still' in Webster's *Duchess of Malfi*,
IV. ii. 180, which fulfils no such function as Miss Lascelles describes. The
Duke's rhyming speech provides a
sententious *finale* to an act full of sur-
prises, and affords a much-needed
point of rest. It falls into four parts: (i)
lines 254–9, stating the pattern for a
ruler to follow; (ii) 260–5, denouncing
Angelo for his misrule; (iii) 266–9, an
obscure passage, asking how Angelo's
abuses are to be rectified; (iv) 270–5,
declaring how the Duke intends to
proceed. Each part except (iii) con-

Should be as holy as severe: 255
Pattern in himself to know,
Grace to stand, and virtue, go:
More nor less to others paying
Than by self-offences weighing.
Shame to him whose cruel striking   260
Kills for faults of his own liking!
Twice treble shame on Angelo,
To weed my vice, and let his grow!
O, what may man within him hide,
Though angel on the outward side!   265
How may likeness made in crimes,

256. Pattern in] *F;* Patterning *conj. Johnson.*   know] *F;* show *conj. Staunton.*
257. and virtue,] *this edn;* and Vertue *F;* virtue to *Ridley, conj. Coleridge (Collier 2);*
an virtue *Hart.*   259. Than] *F4;* Then *F;* Them *conj. N.C.S.*   266. may like-
ness] *F;* may that likeness *Theobald (after Warburton);* my likeness *conj. Hart;* may
lightness *(conj. Seager) (Camb.).*   made in] *F;* shading *Theobald (after Warburton);* wade in *Halliwell, conj. Malone (withdrawn).*

sists of three couplets; (iii) has almost
certainly lost two lines.

254. *the sword of heaven*] Cf. 'the
deputed sword' (II. ii. 60), 'the demi-
god, Authority' (I. ii. 112), and see W.
Tindale, *The obedyence of a Chrysten man,
Works* (1561), fol. xxxvi: 'These hier
powers are the temporal kinges and
princes to whom god hath geuē the
swerd to punysh whosoeuer synneth'.

256. *Pattern in himself to know*] 'To
know that the precedent for his judgments lies in his own conduct'.
'Pattern' as a precedent *(O.E.D. sb.* 7)
rather than a model for imitation, is a
Shakespearean usage; cf. *Tit.,* v. iii.
44, *John,* III. iv. 16, and (as a verb)
II. i. 30 *supra.*

257. *Grace to stand, and virtue, go*]
'"Grace" to hold himself upright, and
"Virtue" upon which to go forward'
(Porter, cited by Durham). Ridley
points out 'the contrast, much more
pointed to the Elizabethans than to us,
between "stand" and "go" (i.e.
"walk") with which "Grace" and "virtue" are exactly appropriate'. The
phrase 'in grace and virtue to proceed'
is given twice by Nashe as a tag (II.

209, lines 27–8; III. 247, 439–40) and
seems to have been a familiar phrase
(Hart). See Intro., pp. lxxiii–lxxiv.

258. *More nor less*] neither more no
less.

259. *Than by self-offences weighing*]
'than the amount determined by
weighing one's own offences'. 'self-' is
adverbial, i.e. committed by oneself;
cf. Milton, *Samson Agonistes,* 514: Self-
displeas'd / For self-offence' *(O.E.D.* 3).

263. *To weed my vice, and let his grow*]
Jenkins points out that the Duke is at
this point in the monologue speaking
chorically as an 'everyman'. 'My vice'
here signifies that of other persons in
contrast to Angelo's own.

265. *angel on the outward side*] Angelo
is the spurious 'angel' in terms of the
coin imagery, and also according to
the moral symbolism of II. iv. 16–17.

266–9.] Neither the F text nor the
many emendations and conjectures
makes the passage intelligible. This
edition assumes that lines 268–9 continue the sense of a lost couplet.

266. *How may likeness made in crimes*]
Some of the editorial struggles with
this line are recorded in the collation:

Making practice on the times
[

                                          ]
To draw with idle spiders' strings
Most ponderous and substantial things!
Craft against vice I must apply.   270
With Angelo tonight shall lie
His old betrothed, but despised:
So disguise shall by th'disguised
Pay with falsehood false exacting,
And perform an old contracting.   *Exit.* 275

267. Making] *F*; Mocking, *Malone*; Masking, *conj. Collier 2.*   times, []] *this edn*; Times, *F.*   268. To draw] *F*; Draw *Theobald (after Warburton)*; To-draw *N.C.S., conj. Gow (Camb.)*; So draw *conj. Staunton.*

if a couplet is missing, little can be done to clarify it. 'likeness made' seems to iterate the theme of man 'made' (i.e. created), as in II. ii. 79 and III. i. 137. But 'may' could be 'my'—the Duke's likeness being his 'substitute' Angelo; and 'made' might even be 'wade'.

267. *practice*] trickery. Cf. v. i. 110.

268-9. *To draw . . . things*] alludes to the Renaissance commonplace, supposedly a saying of Anacharsis, that the laws were like spiders' webs which caught the small flies but let the big insects break through (*O.D. Eng.*

Prov., p. 255). No other interpretation presents itself for the figure 'idle spiders' strings', and 'to draw . . .' cannot therefore be the object-clause of 'Making practice'. In the couplet presumed missing, the Duke would have to ask how the web of the law can be made strong enough to catch such 'big flies' as Angelo.

273-4. *So disguise . . . exacting*] Mariana's physical disguise (as Isabella) will pay with 'falsehood' (illusion) the false exaction by Angelo, in his moral disguise of 'seeming'.

275. *an old contracting*] Cf. III. i. 215.

ACT IV

SCENE I [*A Grange.*]

Enter MARIANA, *and* [*a*] *Boy singing.*

Song

> *Take, o take those lips away*
> > *that so sweetly were forsworn,*
> *And those eyes, the break of day*
> > *lights that do mislead the morn:*
> *But my kisses bring again,*
> > > *bring again;*   5
> *Seals of love, but seal'd in vain,*
> > > *seal'd in vain.*

Enter DUKE [*disguised*].

Mariana. Break off thy song, and haste thee quick away;
  Here comes a man of comfort, whose advice
  Hath often still'd my brawling discontent.   [*Exit Boy.*]

ACT IV

Scene I

Act IV Scene I] *Actus Quartus, Scœna Prima. F.*   *A Grange.*] *Theobald; A Room in Mariana's House. Capell; A Room at the Moated Grange. Collier; The Garden of a moated grange: late afternoon. N.C.S.*   3. *day*] F; day, *Rowe.*   6. *vain, seal'd in vain.*] *vain. F4, Rowe.*   6. S.D.] *Enter Duke. F, Capell (after 9).*   9. S.D.] *Malone; not in F; Exit. Capell (after* comfort, *8*).

1–6.] For a discussion of the connection between this song and the version found, together with a second stanza, in Beaumont and Fletcher's *Rollo Duke of Normandy or The Bloody Brother*, v. ii, see Appendix II, by F. W. Sternfeld, which also provides John Wilson's musical setting, and MS. emendations.

3–4. *break of day . . . morn*] 'break of day' has no comma and seems adjectival with 'lights'.

6. *Seals of love*] Cf. *Sonn.*, cxlii: 'those lips of thine, / That have . . . seal'd false bonds of love', and *Ven.*, 511–12.

7. *Break off thy song*] suggesting that a second stanza was expected.

9. *brawling*] clamorous.

96

I cry you mercy, sir, and well could wish   10
  You had not found me here so musical.
  Let me excuse me, and believe me so;
  My mirth it much displeas'd, but pleas'd my woe.
Duke. 'Tis good; though music oft hath such a charm
  To make bad good, and good provoke to harm.   15
  I pray you tell me, hath anybody enquired for me
  here to-day? Much upon this time have I promised
  here to meet.
Mariana. You have not been enquired after: I have sat
  here all day.   20

Enter ISABELLA.

Duke. I do constantly believe you: the time is come even
  now. I shall crave your forbearance a little; may be
  I will call upon you anon for some advantage to
  yourself.
Mariana. I am always bound to you.   *Exit.*   25
Duke [*to Isab.*] Very well met, and well come.
  What is the news from this good deputy?
Isab. He hath a garden circummur'd with brick,
  Whose western side is with a vineyard back'd;

26. well come] *F;* welcome *Warburton.*

10. *cry you mercy*] lit. 'beg mercy from you', i.e. beg your pardon. The earliest use of 'cry' had this meaning (*O.E.D. v.* 1b).

12. *excuse me*] reflexive.

13.] 'The nature of the song did not encourage mirth but soothed my woe'. Cf. Polina's song, *2 Prom.*, I. i: 'as in my woes I sing'.

15.] 'to give sin a pleasing aspect and lead virtue into harm'.

21. *constantly*] assuredly (*O.E.D.* 1b).

26. *well come*] a common form. Warburton's 'welcome' spoils the apposition to 'well met'.

28–36.] No mention of a garden assignation appears in the sources. In *1 Prom.*, III. ii, Cassandra is told to visit the court of Promos disguised as a page; in *2 Siuqila*, sig. N2ᵛ, the Judge orders the Gentlewoman to come at night to 'a priuie dore of my house'. But 'garden houses' in the suburbs were associated with secret love-trysts. Cf. Stubbes, *Anatomy of Abuses*: 'In the Feeldes and Suburbes of the Cities thei haue Gardens, either paled, or walled round about very high, with their Harbers and Bowers fit for the purpose... Then to these Gardens thei repaire when thei list, with a basket and a boy, where thei, meeting their sweete hartes, receiue their wished desires' (p. 88). Note 'circummur'd' for 'walled round about', and the detail of the escort in lines 45–7 *infra*, who will in fact be Mariana's Boy.

28. *circummur'd*] walled round: a Shakespearean formation. Cf. Kyd's 'countermurde', *The Spanish Tragedy*, III. vii. 16.

And to that vineyard is a planched gate,   30
That makes his opening with this bigger key.
This other doth command a little door
Which from the vineyard to the garden leads;
There have I made my promise
Upon the heavy middle of the night   35
To call upon him.
Duke. But shall you on your knowledge find this way?
Isab. I have ta'en a due and wary note upon't;
With whispering and most guilty diligence,
In action all of precept, he did show me   40
The way twice o'er.
Duke.   Are there no other tokens
Between you 'greed, concerning her observance?
Isab. No; none, but only a repair i'th'dark;
And that I have possess'd him my most stay
Can be but brief: for I have made him know   45
I have a servant comes with me along,
That stays upon me; whose persuasion is
I come about my brother.
Duke.   'Tis well borne up.
I have not yet made known to Mariana
A word of this.—What hoa, within! Come forth.   50

Enter MARIANA.

34–6. There . . . him.] *as Camb.;* There . . . promise, vpon the / . . . night, . . . him. / *F; as prose, Staunton;* There . . . promise to call on him, / Upon the . . . night. *Capell.*   40. action . . . precept] *F;* precept . . . action *conj. Johnson.* 50. S.D.] *Rowe; F (after 49).*

30. *planched*] made of planks.

34–6.] The F lineation is obviously at fault. The arrangement here preserves word-order, but 'To call on him' (sophisticated to 'vpon him') probably completed line 34, with line 35 as a later addition wrongly interposed by the transcriber. See Intro., p. xxix.

35. *the heavy middle of the night*] Cf. *Ham.,* I. ii. 198: 'the dead wast (F, Q2) and middle of the night', and Marston, *Malcontent,* II. v: 'the immodest waste of night'. 'Heavy middle', like 'waist', carries an association with 'pregnant',

figurative or actual. See Intro, lxxxvi.

38. *wary*] careful.

40. *In action all of precept*] Johnson and Hart wished to transpose 'action' and 'precept'. However, Angelo showed the way not by leading Isabella to it ('action') but by detailed directions ('precept', *O.E.D.* 2b).

42. *her observance*] the instructions she must observe.

43. *repair*] act of making one's way.

44. *possess'd*] given to understand.

47. *persuasion*] belief; cf. 'persuade yourself', line 53.

48. *borne up*] upheld.

[*to Mariana.*] I pray you be acquainted with this maid;
She comes to do you good.

Isab.   I do desire the like.

Duke. Do you persuade yourself that I respect you?

Mariana. Good friar, I know you do, and so have found it.

Duke. Take, then, this your companion by the hand,   55
Who hath a story ready for your ear.
I shall attend your leisure; but make haste,
The vaporous night approaches.

Mariana. [*to Isab.*] Will't please you walk aside?

                    [MARIANA *and* ISABELLA *withdraw.*]

Duke. O place and greatness! Millions of false eyes   60
Are stuck upon thee: volumes of report
Run with these false, and most contrarious quest
Upon thy doings: thousand escapes of wit
Make thee the father of their idle dream

---

54. so have] *this edn;* haue *F;* I have *Pope;* oft have *Dyce 2.*   59. S.D. *Mariana and Isabella withdraw.*] *N.C.S.* (*subst.*)*; Exit. F; Ex. Mar. and Isab. Rowe 3.*   62. false, . . . quest] *F;* false . . . Quests *F2.*   64. dream] *F* (dreame)*; Dreams Rowe 3.*

53. *respect you*] 'have regard for your interests'.

54.] Some monosyllabic word like 'so' or 'oft' seems to have dropped out in F.

59. *Will't . . . walk aside?*] an invitation to retire from the centre of the stage, not, as F stage directions imply, to make a full exit: cf. III. i. 158, and see Intro., pp. xxi, xxvi.

60–5.] See note to III. ii. 179–82 and Intro., pp. xx f. A monologue is needed to fill the time while Isabella and Mariana confer; but the lines have, as Warburton perceived, been transferred from the Duke's earlier soliloquy in III. ii. They are irrelevant in their context and insufficient to provide for the interval.

60–2. *Millions . . . these false*] Hart cited the description of Fame in Jonson's *Poetaster*, v. ii. 85 ff.: 'Looke, how many plumes are plac't / (On her huge corps, so many waking eyes / Sticke vnderneath: and (which may stranger rise / In the report) as many tongues

shee beares'. The imagery suggests a figure from pageantry or emblem literature. Ripa's *Iconologia*, 1603, p. 182 depicts '*Gelosia*' as a woman whose robe is covered with eyes and ears. So the Induction to *2H4* is spoken by 'Rumour, painted full of tongues'.

61. *stuck*] fixed, set. Cf. *LLL.*, III. i. 207: 'two pitch balls stuck in her face for eyes'.

62. *Run . . . quest*] 'run like a hostile pack of hounds, and chase or give tongue to (*quest*) what these false eyes see'. Thiselton pointed out that 'quest', generally emended as 'quests', was a verb governed by 'volumes of report', and that 'false' related to 'eyes', line 60. To quest = (i) to search for game, (ii) to bark at the sight of it (*O.E.D.* v.[1] 1, 2). Either meaning, or both, would apply.

63. *escapes*] sallies (*O.E.D. sb.*[1] 5). The first recorded use in this sense.

64.] 'make you the subject or source of their own fantasies'.

And rack thee in their fancies.
                    [MARIANA *and* ISABELLA *return.*]
                              Welcome; how agreed?   65
Isab. She'll take the enterprise upon her, father,
     If you advise it
Duke.   It is not my consent,
     But my entreaty too.
Isab.   Little have you to say
     When you depart from him, but, soft and low,
     'Remember now my brother'.
Mariana.   Fear me not.   70
Duke. Nor, gentle daughter, fear you not at all.
     He is your husband on a pre-contract:
     To bring you thus together 'tis no sin,
     Sith that the justice of your title to him
     Doth flourish the deceit.—Come, let us go;   75
     Our corn's to reap, for yet our tithe's to sow.   *Exeunt.*

SCENE II [*The Prison.*]

Enter PROVOST *and* POMPEY.

Prov. Come hither, sirrah. Can you cut off a man's head?

65. S.D.] *N.C.S.*; *Enter Mariana and Isabella. F (after* agreed?)*; Johnson (after* fancies). 70. 'Remember ... brother.'] *as Theobald;* Remember ... brother. *F.* 76. tithe's] *Johnson;* Tithes *F;* Tilth's *Theobald.*

Scene II] *Scena Secunda. F.   The Prison.*] *Rowe; Scenes II and III | The Prison. Ridley; The prison; night | Winny.*

72. *a pre-contract*] a future contract of marriage. This signified *sponsalia de futuro,* or betrothal, and had not in itself the binding force of the marriage contract, *sponsalia de praesenti.* The union which the Duke is arranging will transform its character. Cf. III. i. 215 and see Intro., pp. liv, lv.

75. *flourish*] embellish. *O.E.D. v.* 6 cites Fleming, *Contn. Holinshed* (1587), III. 1323/1: 'Deceipt [sheweth] finest when he is cunninglie florished'. Cf. III. i. 258–9.

76. *Our corn's to reap . . . sow*] 'Our corn has still to be reaped, since our tithe is yet to be sown': i.e. the preliminary work must be done before the reward is forthcoming. 'to' signifies intention, with the infinitive used in a passive sense (cf. ' a house to let'). Johnson noted that the tithe metaphor was well suited to the Duke in his character as friar. 'Tilth' has been suggested for 'tithe', but the latter, indicating the corn sown for tithe dues, makes good sense.

Pom. If the man be a bachelor, sir, I can; but if he be a
married man, he's his wife's head; and I can never
cut off a woman's head.

Prov. Come, sir, leave me your snatches, and yield me a   5
direct answer. Tomorrow morning are to die Claudio
and Barnardine. Here is in our prison a common
executioner, who in his office lacks a helper; if you
will take it on you to assist him, it shall redeem you
from your gyves: if not, you shall have your full time   10
of imprisonment, and your deliverance with an un-
pitied whipping; for you have been a notorious
bawd.

Pom. Sir, I have been an unlawful bawd time out of
mind, but yet I will be content to be a lawful hang-   15
man. I would be glad to receive some instruction
from my fellow-partner.

Prov. What hoa, Abhorson! Where's Abhorson there?

Enter ABHORSON.

Abhor. Do you call, sir?

Prov. Sirrah, here's a fellow will help you tomorrow in   20
your execution. If you think it meet, compound with
him by the year, and let him abide here with you; if
not, use him for the present, and dismiss him. He
cannot plead his estimation with you: he hath been a
bawd.   25

Abhor. A bawd, sir? Fie upon him, he will discredit our
mystery.

Prov. Go to, sir, you weigh equally: a feather will turn the
scale.   *Exit.*

2–4. If . . . woman's head.] *as Pope;* If . . . can: / . . . wiues head, / . . . womans
head. *F (verse).*

3. *he's his wife's head*] a commonplace, originating in Eph., v. 23
(Geneva): 'For the husband is the
wiues head' (Noble).

3–4. *and . . . woman's head*] with equivocation on 'head' as in I. ii. 161 ff.,
and on 'woman' in contrast to 'maid'.

5. *snatches*] quibbles.

18. *Abhorson*] The name combines

the associations of 'abhor' and 'whore-
son'.

21. *compound*] come to terms.

24. *estimation*] reputation; for lack of
which, Pompey cannot expect courteous treatment from his colleague.

27. *mystery*] skilled trade.

28–9. *a feather . . . scale*] See note to
II. iv. 169.

Pom. Pray, sir, by your good favour—for surely, sir, a   30
    good favour you have, but that you have a hanging
    look—do you call, sir, your occupation a mystery?
Abhor. Ay, sir, a mystery.
Pom. Painting, sir, I have heard say, is a mystery; and
    your whores, sir, being members of my occupation,   35
    using painting, do prove my occupation a mystery.
    But what mystery there should be in hanging, if I
    should be hanged, I cannot imagine.
Abhor. Sir, it is a mystery.
Pom. Proof?   40
Abhor. Every true man's apparel fits your thief. If it be
    too little for your thief, your true man thinks it big
    enough. If it be too big for your thief, your thief
    thinks it little enough. So every true man's apparel
    fits your thief.   45

Enter PROVOST.

Prov. Are you agreed?
Pom. Sir, I will serve him; for I do find your hangman is
    a more penitent trade than your bawd; he doth
    oftener ask forgiveness.

43. If] *Capell; Clo.* If *F.*

30-1. *a good favour*] playing on 'favour' as face, countenance.

31-2. *a hanging look*] a downcast expression; but quibbling on Abhorson's occupation. Such quibbles were common in drama of the time.

34-6. *Painting . . . a mystery*] Painting is a skilled trade; whores, who are members of Pompey's 'company', paint; therefore Pompey's is a skilled trade or 'mystery'.

41-5.] F inexplicably distributes Abhorson's answer between the two speakers. The 'proof' that the true man's apparel 'fits' (satisfies) the thief shows the thief to be a fitter of clothes, i.e. tailor, whose occupation is a 'mystery'. Executioners and thieves are associated because the clothes of the condemned man were the hangman's perquisite. Heath comments: 'The argument of the Hangman is exactly similar to that of the Bawd . . . the former equally lays claim to the thieves, as members of his occupation, and in their right endeavours to rank his brethren, the hangmen, under the mystery of fitters of apparel, or tailors'. One stage in the syllogism, relating the executioner to the thief, is missing, and the faulty distribution may be due to a gap at some stage of transmission. *true man*: honest man; the usual antithesis to 'thief'. *too little . . . big enough*: little and big in terms of (i) size, (ii) value.

48-9. *he . . . forgiveness*] Part of the ritual of hanging was the executioner's request to be forgiven by the condemned man. Cf. *AYL.,* III. v. 3-6.

Prov. You, sirrah, provide your block and your axe to-   50
morrow four o'clock.

Abhor. Come on, bawd, I will instruct thee in my trade.
Follow.

Pom. I do desire to learn, sir; and I hope, if you have
occasion to use me for your own turn, you shall find   55
me yare. For truly, sir, for your kindness I owe you a
good turn.

Prov. Call hither Barnardine and Claudio.

> *Exeunt* [ABHORSON *and* POMPEY].

Th'one has my pity; not a jot the other,
Being a murderer, though he were my brother.   60

> *Enter* CLAUDIO.

Look, here's the warrant, Claudio, for thy death;
'Tis now dead midnight, and by eight tomorrow
Thou must be made immortal. Where's Barnardine?

Cla. As fast lock'd up in sleep as guiltless labour
When it lies starkly in the traveller's bones.   65
He will not wake.

Prov.   Who can do good on him?
Well, go; prepare yourself.   [*Knocking within.*]
But hark, what noise?

---

56. yare] *Theobald;* y'are *F;* yours *Rowe.*   58. S.D.] *Exit | F (after 57)*
67. S.D.] *Staunton; Rowe (after* noise*); not in F.*

---

56. *yare*] brisk, ready.

56–7. *I owe you a good turn*] One good
turn deserves another; but Pompey's
will be a turn of the ladder, to hang the
hangman. Cf. Dekker, *The Wonderfull
Yeare (Plague Pamphlets,* ed. F. P. Wilson, p. 61): 'praying that *Derick* [the
hangman] or his executors may liue to
do those a good turne, that haue done
so to others'.

59–60. *Th'one . . . brother*] The formal couplet bridges a pause for
Claudio's entry while calling to mind
Isabella's attitude to her brother, III. i.
143 ff.

62. *by eight tomorrow*] On the con-

flicting times for these arrangements
(cf. lines 50–1) see Intro., pp. xv–xvi.
In *2 Siuqila,* the husband is beheaded
'next morning, about 8, or 9. of the
clocke' (sig. N4).

64–5. *As fast . . . bones*] From Eccles.,
v. 12. The Geneva text has: 'The
sleepe of him that trauaileth is sweete';
the Bishops': 'A labouring man sleep-
eth sweetely'. 'Travail' and 'travel'
were interchangeable spellings, and
'traveller' here means 'labouring
man'. Cf. *H5,* IV. i. 288 ff. *starkly:*
stiffly. Transferred epithet from the
condition of the 'traveller'.

66. *do good on*] benefit.

Heaven give your spirits comfort!   [*Exit* CLAUDIO.]
                    [*Knocking*.] —By and by.—
I hope it is some pardon or reprieve
For the most gentle Claudio.

                    Enter DUKE [*disguised*].

                              Welcome, father.   70
Duke. The best and wholesom'st spirits of the night
        Envelop you, good Provost! Who call'd here of late?
Prov. None since the curfew rung.
Duke. Not Isabel?
Prov.   No.
Duke.   They will then, ere't be long.
Prov. What comfort is for Claudio?
Duke.   There's some in hope.   75
Prov. It is a bitter deputy.
Duke. Not so, not so; his life is parallel'd
        Even with the stroke and line of his great justice.
        He doth with holy abstinence subdue
        That in himself which he spurs on his power   80
        To qualify in others: were he meal'd with that
        Which he corrects, then were he tyrannous;
        But this being so, he's just.
                    [*Knocking within.* PROVOST *goes to the door.*]
                    —Now are they come.

68. S.D. *Exit Claudio*] *Capell; not in F; Theobald* (*at* yourself, 67).   S.D. *Knocking*]
Kittredge (*subst.*); *not in F.*   70. S.D.] *Rowe* (*subst.*); *Enter Duke. F.*   74.] *as
Camb.;* Not *Isabell?* | ... No. | ... long. | *F.*   75–7.] *this edn;* What ... *Claudio?* |
... hope. | ... Deputie. | ... paralel'd | *F.*   81. meal'd] *F;* moal'd *conj. N.C.S.*
83. S.D. *Knocking within.*] *Dyce; not in F; Knock again. Rowe* (*after* come).   S.D.
Provost ... door.] *this edn; not in F; Capell* (*at* come); *Provost goes out. Theobald, Dyce
subst.* (*at* come).

68. *By and by*] 'presently', 'at
once'. Addressed to the person knocking.

73. *the curfew*] the evening bell of the
prison.

78. *stroke and line*] capable of several
interpretations. Johnson has 'line
made with a pen', i.e. *au pied de la
lettre. N.C.S.* finds an ironical sense,
with 'stroke' as the blow of the executioner's axe and 'line' the hangman's

cord. The essential meaning is that
Angelo's life and his acts of justice are
exactly parallel.

81. *qualify*] Cf. i. i. 65.

meal'd] *O.E.D. v.*[3] gives 'spotted',
citing this instance. But Hart's suggestion is surely right, that 'meal'd'
means 'compounded with', 'of the
same mixture', as in Jonson, *Catiline,*
iv. 222: 'Except he were of the same
meale, and batch'.

This is a gentle provost; seldom when
The steeled gaoler is the friend of men.   [*Knocking.*]   85
How now? What noise? That spirit's possess'd with haste
That wounds th'unsisting postern with these strokes.

                                      [PROVOST *returns.*]

Prov. There must he stay until the officer
    Arise to let him in. He is call'd up.
Duke. Have you no countermand for Claudio yet,   90
    But he must die tomorrow?
Prov.   None, sir, none.
Duke. As near the dawning, Provost, as it is,
    You shall hear more ere morning.
Prov.   Happily
    You something know: yet I believe there comes
    No countermand. No such example have we.   95
    Besides, upon the very siege of justice
    Lord Angelo hath to the public ear
    Profess'd the contrary.

Enter a Messenger.

This is his lordship's man.

85. S.D.] *Craig; not in F.*   87. th'unsisting] *F*; th'insisting *F4*; th'unresisting *Rowe;* the unshifting *Capell;* the resisting *Collier 2;* the unlisting *White (after M. Mason).*   S.D.] *Theobald; not in F.*   89. up.] *F*; up. (*Speaking to one at the Door;) Capell.*   93. Happily] *F3*; Happely *F.*   98–9. This . . . / *Duke.* And] *Knight, conj. Tyrwhitt (Steevens '78); Duke.* This . . . / *Pro.* And *F.*   lordship's] *Rowe 3;* Lords *F.*

87. *unsisting*] Capell's 'unshifting' is very plausible: 's' and 'sh' were often interchangeable (see note to 'enciel'd', II. iv. 80) and the confusing of 'f' and medial 's' was a common error. Hart and *N.C.S.* conjectured 'un'sisting' (unassisting); Blackstone found a derivation in Latin *sistere*, hence 'never at rest'. Both suggestions are rather strained. Kittredge glossed 'shaken, made to vibrate', but gave no authority.

90.] The Duke's words might have recalled a contemporary parallel in James I's last-minute reprieve of the traitors at Winchester: see Intro., p. l. But no attempt is made, as in II.

iv. 27–30, to bring out an analogy, and the expectation of a countermand is implicit in the plot.

93. *Happily*] i.e. haply. F 'Happely' might be either 'happily' or 'haply', which had the same meaning, but the metre calls for a trisyllable.

98–9. *This is . . . pardon*] F gives the first remark to the Duke and the second to the Provost; yet the Provost has clearly stated his disbelief that Claudio will be pardoned. The presence of the S.D. for the Messenger's entry between the first and second halves of line 98 probably explains the error. If the second half of 98 ('This . . . man') appeared in the MS. as a new

Duke. And here comes Claudio's pardon.

Messenger. My lord hath sent you this note, and by me   100
    this further charge: that you swerve not from the
    smallest article of it, neither in time, matter, or
    other circumstance. Good-morrow; for, as I take it,
    it is almost day.

Prov. I shall obey him.   [*Exit Messenger.*]   105

Duke [*aside*] This is his pardon, purchas'd by such sin
    For which the pardoner himself is in.
    Hence hath offence his quick celerity,
    When it is borne in high authority.
    When vice makes mercy, mercy's so extended   110
    That for the fault's love is th'offender friended.
    Now, sir, what news?

Prov. I told you: Lord Angelo, belike thinking me re-
    miss in mine office, awakens me with this un-
    wonted putting-on; methinks strangely, for he hath   115
    not used it before.

Duke. Pray you, let's hear.

Prov. [*Reads*] *Whatsoever you may hear to the contrary, let*
    Claudio be executed by four of the clock, and in the after-
    noon, Barnardine. For my better satisfaction, let me have   120
    Claudio's head sent me by five. Let this be duly performed,

100–4.] *as Pope;* My . . . note, / . . . charge; / . . . it, / . . . circumstance. / . . . day. / F.
105. S.D.] *Rowe; not in F.*   113–16. I . . . before.] *as Pope;* I . . . you: / . . .
remisse / . . . mee / . . . strangely: / . . . before. / F.   118. S.D. *Prov.* (*Reads*)]
Rowe subst.; The Letter. F (*centred S.D.*).   118–24.] *italics as F.*   120. *Barnardine*] F2; Bernardine F.

line, the copyist may have assumed
that a speech-prefix had been left out,
inserted 'Duke', and altered that of line
99 from 'Duke' to 'Provost' in keeping
with the exchange of dialogue. Cf. IV.
iii. 64–5 and note. *lordship's:* F 'Lords'
was a frequent MS. abbreviation.

100–4.] printed in F as irregular
lines of verse.

108. *his quick celerity*] This seems to
be tautology; but 'quick' combines
with 'borne', line 109, and 'makes', line
110, to form a submerged image of
propagation: 'Offence is soon pardoned when it is the child of high
authority'. See Intro., p. lxxxvi.

111.] 'the offender is befriended because his fault is loved'.

113–16.] printed in F as irregular
lines of verse.

115. *putting-on*] urging, impulsion.

118–20. *Whatsoever you may hear . . .
and in the afternoon, Barnardine*] Angelo's
new instructions delay the execution
of Barnardine, and advance Claudio's
by four hours, ensuring that he be
already dead before the countermand
promised to Isabella can arrive. In
Epitia, III. i the messenger describes a
letter received by the Podestà from
Iuriste, ordering him '*senza vdir cosa,
che fusse detta, Leuar gli fesse il capo*'.

> *with a thought that more depends on it than we must yet*
> *deliver. Thus fail not to do your office, as you will answer*
> *it at your peril.*
>
> What say you to this, sir?   125

Duke. What is that Barnardine, who is to be executed in
th'afternoon?

Prov. A Bohemian born, but here nursed up and bred;
one that is a prisoner nine years old.

Duke. How came it that the absent Duke had not either   130
delivered him to his liberty, or executed him? I
have heard it was ever his manner to do so.

Prov. His friends still wrought reprieves for him; and
indeed, his fact till now in the government of Lord
Angelo came not to an undoubtful proof.   135

Duke. It is now apparent?

Prov. Most manifest, and not denied by himself.

Duke. Hath he borne himself penitently in prison? How
seems he to be touched?

Prov. A man that apprehends death no more dreadfully   140
but as a drunken sleep; careless, reckless, and fear-
less of what's past, present, or to come: insensible of
mortality, and desperately mortal.

Duke. He wants advice.

Prov. He will hear none. He hath evermore had the   145
liberty of the prison: give him leave to escape
hence, he would not. Drunk many times a day, if

---

141. reckless] *Pope* (rechless); wreaklesse *F.*

126. *What is*] 'What manner of man
is he?' cf. II. i. 61.

128. *A Bohemian born*] suggested by
2 Prom., II. ii, where Corvinus is styled
'King of *Hungarie* and *Boemia*'. Under
Matthias Corvinus, the two kingdoms
were for a time united, and Shakespeare transfers the connection to his
fictional duchy of Vienna.

129. *a prisoner nine years old*] 'nine
years a prisoner'. Cf. *Ham.*, IV. vi. 16:
'two days old at sea'; *Err.*, I. i. 44,
II. ii. 152 (Hart).

134. *fact*] crime. Cf. v. i. 432.
government] period of rule.

139. *touched*] affected.

140. *apprehends*] understands.

141. *reckless*] The F spelling 'wreaklesse' arises from the confusing of 'reck'
and 'wreak'. Cf. *AYL.*, II. iv. 81–2,
which in F reads: 'My master . . . little
wreakes to finde the way to heauen'. The
rare word 'wreakless' meant 'unaven-
ged', which would be out of context.

142–3. *insensible . . . mortal*] 'with no
sensibilities in regard to death, and no
hope of escaping it'. Perhaps 'desperately mortal' means 'without hope of
immortality'.

144. *advice*] spiritual counsel.

not many days entirely drunk. We have very oft
awaked him, as if to carry him to execution, and
showed him a seeming warrant for it; it hath not   150
moved him at all.

Duke. More of him anon. There is written in your brow,
Provost, honesty and constancy; if I read it not
truly, my ancient skill beguiles me. But in the boldness of my cunning, I will lay myself in hazard.   155
Claudio, whom here you have warrant to execute,
is no greater forfeit to the law than Angelo who
hath sentenced him. To make you understand this
in a manifested effect, I crave but four days' respite: for the which, you are to do me both a present   160
and a dangerous courtesy.

Prov. Pray sir, in what?

Duke. In the delaying death.

Prov. Alack, how may I do it? Having the hour limited,
and an express command under penalty to deliver   165
his head in the view of Angelo? I may make my
case as Claudio's to cross this in the smallest.

Duke. By the vow of mine order, I warrant you, if my
instructions may be your guide: let this Barnardine
be this morning executed, and his head borne to   170
Angelo.

Prov. Angelo hath seen them both, and will discover the
favour.

Duke. O, death's a great disguiser; and you may add to
it. Shave the head, and tie the beard, and say it was   175

168–73. By . . . favour.] *as Pope;* By . . . you, / . . . guide, / . . . executed, / . . .
Angelo. / . . . both, / . . . fauour. / *F (verse).*   175. tie] *F;* tye *F2* (tie *F4*)*; dye*
White, conj. Simpson (Steevens '73).

154–5. *in . . . cunning*] 'in the boldness
given to me by my skill'. Cf. 'in the
truth of my spirit', III. i. 206–7.

155. *I will . . . hazard*] 'I will take a
personal risk'.

157. *forfeit to the law*] Cf. II. ii. 73.

159. *in a manifested effect*] in a clear
demonstration.

159–60. *four days' respite*] Line 197
has 'within these two days', which is
sufficient. See Intro., p. xvi.

160–1. *present and . . . dangerous*]
requiring to be done immediately and
involving risk.

164. *limited*] fixed, specified.

172–3. *discover the favour*] 'distinguish the face'.

175. *tie the beard*] Various suggestions have been made to read F 'tie' as
'trim', 'tire', or 'die' (dye). F2, 3 alter
it to 'tye'; with this spelling it may
have had the meaning 'dress' or 'trim';

the desire of the penitent to be so bared before his
death: you know the course is common. If anything fall to you upon this, more than thanks and
good fortune, by the saint whom I profess, I will
plead against it with my life.　　　　　　　　　　180

Prov. Pardon me, good father; it is against my oath.

Duke. Were you sworn to the Duke, or to the Deputy?

Prov. To him, and to his substitutes.

Duke. You will think you have made no offence if the
Duke avouch the justice of your dealing?　　　185

Prov. But what likelihood is in that?

Duke. Not a resemblance, but a certainty. Yet, since I
see you fearful, that neither my coat, integrity, nor
persuasion can with ease attempt you, I will go
further than I meant, to pluck all fears out of you.　190
Look you, sir, here is the hand and seal of the Duke:
you know the character, I doubt not, and the signet
is not strange to you?

Prov. I know them both.

Duke. The contents of this is the return of the Duke: you　195
shall anon over-read it at your pleasure, where you
shall find within these two days he will be here.
This is a thing that Angelo knows not; for he this
very day receives letters of strange tenour, perchance of the Duke's death, perchance entering　200
into some monastery; but, by chance, nothing of

---

176. bared] *F* (bar'de); barb'd *F4*.　　200. entering] *F*; his entering *Keightley*;
of his entering *Hudson, conj. Dyce 2*.

---

cf. Dekker, *2 Honest Whore*, I. ii. 200 ff.:
'Say I should shaue off this Honor of an
old man, or tye it vp shorter'. Cf.
'Shoe-tie', IV. iii. 17.

　176. *bared*] stripped of hair. Cf. *All's
W.*, IV. i. 54. Referring to the head.

　177. *the course is common*] Reed cited
P. Mathieu's *Heroyke Life . . . of Henry
the Fourth of France*, trans. Grimeston,
1612, p. 181, on 'the custome in Ger-
many, Swisserland, and divers other
places, to shave off . . . all the haire . . .
of those who are convicted for any
notorious crimes'. Monck Mason
found an allusion to an old Catholic

custom of requesting the tonsure of a
monk before death, but there seems to
be no confirmation of this.

　179. *the saint . . . profess*] the patron
of the order of friars to which the Duke
supposedly belongs.

　183. *substitutes*] Cf. III. i. 187.

　185. *avouch*] acknowledge.

　187. *resemblance*] seeming.

　188. *coat*] clerical garb.

　189. *attempt*] tempt, win over.

　192. *character*] handwriting (*O.E.D.
sb.* 4c). Cf. I. i. 27.

　200. *entering*] 'of his entering'.

　201–2. *nothing of what is writ*] There

what is writ. Look, th'unfolding star calls up the
shepherd. Put not yourself into amazement how
these things should be; all difficulties are but easy
when they are known. Call your executioner, and   205
off with Barnardine's head. I will give him a present shrift, and advise him for a better place. Yet
you are amazed; but this shall absolutely resolve
you. Come away; it is almost clear dawn.   *Exeunt.*

SCENE III [*The Same.*]

Enter POMPEY.

Pom. I am as well acquainted here as I was in our house
     of profession: one would think it were Mistress
     Overdone's own house, for here be many of her old
     customers. First, here's young Master Rash; he's in

---

202. writ] *F;* here writ *Hanmer;* right *conj. Collier 2.*   209. S.D.] *Pope 2;*
Exit. F.

Scene III

Scene III] *Scena Tertia. F; no scene division Ridley.*   *The Same.*] *this edn (N.C.S.*
subst.); Another Room in the same. Capell; The Prison. Alexander; The prison; morning |
Winny.   S.D.] *Dyce; Enter Clowne. F.*

---

is a gap in the sense. Hanmer and
Warburton assumed that the Duke
points to the letter he is carrying, and
would insert 'here' before 'writ'.
Collier suggested 'right' for 'writ'.
Perhaps the original phrase was 'nothing of what is writ is right', which
was aurally mistaken for a dittography,
'is writ is writ'. Cf. note to III. ii. 218–
19.

202–3. *th'unfolding star . . . shepherd*]
'the star that by its rising tells the shepherd the time to release the sheep from
the fold' (Onions). These pastoral
associations bring relief in the claus-
trophobic prison atmosphere. Cf.
Milton's 'The Star that bids the Shepherd fold' (*Comus* 93). A similar dramatic effect is got in Horatio's mention of
'the morn in russet mantle clad' (*Ham.,*
I. i. 166 ff.).

204–5. *all difficulties . . . known*] a
commonplace (Tilley D 418).

208. *this*] the information in the
letter the Duke now delivers to the
Provost.

209. *Come away*] 'Come along',
'Come on'. Cf. *Tw.N.,* II. iv. 51: 'Come
away, death'.

Scene III

1–20.] Pompey will probably mime
the characters he mentions. They furnish some lively specimens of Jacobean
'men about town', whose activities the
government was seeking to restrain by
such measures as the Statute of Stabbing. See Intro., p. xxxiii.

1–2. *house of profession*] Cf. II. i. 64–5.

4. *Rash*] reckless, with a play on
'rash', a smooth-finished silken or
worsted cloth.

for a commodity of brown paper and old ginger,   5
nine score and seventeen pounds; of which he made
five marks ready money: marry, then, ginger was
not much in request, for the old women were all
dead. Then is there here one Master Caper, at the
suit of Master Three-pile the mercer, for some four   10
suits of peach-coloured satin, which now peaches
him a beggar. Then have we here young Dizie, and
young Master Deep-vow, and Master Copperspur,
and Master Starve-Lackey the rapier and dagger
man, and young Drop-heir that killed lusty Pud-   15
ding, and Master Forthright the tilter, and brave

5. paper] *F*; pepper *Rowe*.   6. nine score] *F*; ninescore *F2*.   12. Dizie] *F*;
Dizy *F2*; Dizzy *Pope*; Dicey *conj. Steevens '03*.   16. Forthright] *Warburton*
(Forth-right); *Forthlight F*.

5. *a commodity . . . ginger*] 'Commodities' evaded the statutory fixing of
interest at 10 per cent. Part of the
principal was lent in kind, at an arbitrary valuation; often in commodities
out of demand or otherwise hard to
sell; while interest on the whole sum
was charged for. Complaints against
this abuse were frequent: cf. Greene,
A Defence of Cony-catching (ed. Grosart,
XI. 53): 'if he borrow a hundred pound,
he shal haue fortie in siluer, and
threescore in wares, dead stuffe God
wot; as Lute strings, Hobby horses, or
(if he be greatly fauored) browne
paper or cloath' (Hart).
6. *nine . . . pounds*] presumably the
value set on the goods by the usurer.
7.] The mark was valued at 13s. 4d.
8–9. *the old . . . dead*] probably a
reference to the plague in 1603.
9. *Caper*] To 'cut a caper' was a
fashionable accomplishment for young
gallants, either in the lavolta dance or
as a general display of agile leaping.
Cf. *Tw.N.*, I. iii. 131 ff., *Wiv.*, III. ii. 71.
10. *Three-pile*] Cf. I. ii. 31 ff.
11. *peaches*] denounces, accuses (as).
12. *Dizie*] either (i) 'Dizzy', i.e.
foolish (*O.E.D. a.* 1), as in 'the dizzy
Multitude', *Paradise Regained*, II. 420;
a sense surviving in Yorks. dialect, or
(ii) 'Dice', written as 'Dise' or possibly

'Dize', and printed 'Dizie'; i.e. a
gambler; on this '-zie' ending for '-se'
cf. 'prenzie'–'precise', III. i. 93, 96, and
note.
13. *Deep-vow*] a heavy swearer,
rather than 'a lover' (*N.C.S.*).
Copperspur] 'simulating gold, like
Falstaff's grandfather's seal-ring'
(Hart). Copper carried the implication of cheap or worthless.
14–15. *the rapier and dagger man*] defending his 'honour' in the latest style.
The traditional gentleman's weapons
were sword and buckler, but rapier
and dagger duelling supplanted them
in the latter part of Elizabeth's reign.
Cf. *Ham.*, v. ii. 152. It was frequently
condemned as degenerate, e.g. Porter's
Two Angry Women of Abington (*M.S.R.*
1339 ff.): 'dearth of swoord and
buckler fight, begins to grow out, . . .
this poking fight of rapier and dagger
will come vp then; . . . a boy will be as
good as a man'.
15–16. *young Drop-heir . . . lusty Pudding*] Hart saw 'Drop-heir' as a
usurer; but young usurers are hard to
find in Elizabethan literature. 'Drop-
heir' suggests a figure like Middleton's
'Bawd-gallant'; cf. *Father Hubburds
Tales* (VIII. 78): 'a most glorious-
spangled gallant . . . that fed upon
young landlords, riotous sons and

Master Shoe-tie the great traveller, and wild Half-
can that stabbed pots, and I think forty more, all
great doers in our trade, and are now 'for the Lord's
sake'.   20

Enter ABHORSON.

Abhor. Sirrah, bring Barnardine hither.
Pom. Master Barnardine! You must rise and be hanged,
    Master Barnardine.
Abhor. What hoa, Barnardine!
Barnardine. [*within.*] A pox o' your throats! Who makes   25
    that noise there? What are you?
Pom. Your friends, sir, the hangman. You must be so
    good, sir, to rise and be put to death.
Barnardine. [*within.*] Away, you rogue, away; I am sleepy.
Abhor. Tell him he must awake, and that quickly too.   30

---

17. Shoe-tie] *Steevens '73* (Shoo-tye *Capell*); *Shootie* F; *Shooty* F2; Shooter *Warburton.*   18. pots] *Halliwell;* Pots F, *Rowe.*   19. now] F; now in *Pope.*   19–
20. 'for . . . sake'] *Rann;* for . . . sake F.   25. S.D.] *Barnardine within.* F *(centred
S.D.).*   27. friends] F; friend F3.

heirs . . . and would not stick to be a
bawd or pander to such'. This is supported by the equivocations 'heir-
hair' (cf. I. ii. 32–3) and 'Pudding' (=
sausage; cf. *Oth.*, II. i. 258–60).

16. *Forthright the tilter*] 'Forth-light'
in F has not been explained. Warburton's 'Forthright' is in accordance
with Sidney's description of tilting at
the ring, in *Arcadia,* lib. II, cap. 5: 'he
ever going so just with the horse, either
foorthright, or turning' (Hart).

17. *Shoe-tie the great traveller*] F
'Shootie'. Shoe-tie (or 'tye') was shoe
trimming, an affected foreign fashion.
Cf. Jonson *Every Man Out of his Humour,*
Ind. 112: 'A yard of shooetye, or the
Switzers knot / On his *French* garters'
and the parallels in the editors' notes
to this passage. Allusions are frequent,
usually with spelling 'ty' or 'tye'. Cf.
'tie the beard' (IV. ii. 175).

17–18. *wild Half-can . . . pots*] possibly a tapster who falsified the capacity marks on ale-pots: this was usually
called 'nicking' (*O.E.D. v.*² 12), but

'stabbed' may have been used for a
burlesque effect. Cf. Greene, *Def. of
Cony Catching* (Grosart, XI. 68): 'The
Ale-wife vnles she nicke her Pots . . .
can hardly paye her Brewer'. 'Pots' (F)
is printed in roman as a common noun,
whereas all names were in italics: cf.
'*Thomas* Tapster' (F) I. ii. 104.

19. *doers*] Cf. I. ii. 80–1, etc.

19–20. '*for . . . sake*'] the cry of poor
prisoners begging from the grating or
window of their prison. The practice
is illustrated in *The Manner of Crying
Things in London* (c. 1599) with the
caption 'Some broken Breade and
meate for yᵉ poore prisoners for the
Lords sake pittey the poore'.

22. *rise . . . hanged*] Cf. lines 28, 44–5
infra. The point is the play on 'rise',
(i) to get up from bed, (ii) to mount
the scaffold.

26. *What*] Cf. IV. ii. 126.

27. *friends . . . hangman*] Pompey and
Abhorson are both, in Pompey's
phrase, 'friends' to Barnardine, but
only Abhorson is the official hangman.

Pom. Pray, Master Barnardine, awake till you are executed, and sleep afterwards.

Abhor. Go in to him and fetch him out.

Pom. He is coming, sir, he is coming. I hear his straw
rustle.   35

Enter BARNARDINE.

Abhor. Is the axe upon the block, sirrah?

Pom. Very ready, sir.

Barnardine. How now, Abhorson? What's the news with
you?

Abhor. Truly, sir, I would desire you to clap into your   40
prayers; for look you, the warrant's come.

Barnardine. You rogue, I have been drinking all night; I
am not fitted for't.

Pom. O, the better, sir; for he that drinks all night, and
is hanged betimes in the morning, may sleep the   45
sounder all the next day.

Enter DUKE [*disguised*].

Abhor. Look you, sir, here comes your ghostly father. Do
we jest now, think you?

Duke. Sir, induced by my charity, and hearing how
hastily you are to depart, I am come to advise you,   50
comfort you, and pray with you.

Barnardine. Friar, not I. I have been drinking hard all
night, and I will have more time to prepare me, or
they shall beat out my brains with billets. I will not
consent to die this day, that's certain.   55

Duke. O sir, you must; and therefore I beseech you
Look forward on the journey you shall go.

---

35. S.D.] *F; Capell (after 38).*   46. S.D.] *Enter Duke. F; Ridley (after 48).*
56–7. O . . . go] *as F; prose, F3.*

40. *clap into*] 'enter briskly into'
(*O.E.D. v.*[1] 15b).

45–6. *hanged . . . next day*] Pompey
has adapted to Barnardine's situation
the proverbial 'He rises over soon who
is hanged ere noon' (Tilley N 208),
which is implicit in 'rise and be
hanged', line 22.

47. *ghostly*] spiritual.

54. *billets*] (i) blocks of wood
brought in on barges for sale as fire
wood. Contemporary plays describe
their use as weapons by barge-
men. (ii) sticks used for offensive purposes.

57.] Cf. III. i. 27.

Barnardine. I swear I will not die today for any man's
  persuasion.
Duke. But hear you—   60
Barnardine. Not a word. If you have anything to say to
  me, come to my ward: for thence will not I today.   *Exit.*

Enter PROVOST.

Duke. Unfit to live or die! O gravel heart.
Prov. After him, fellows, bring him to the block!
                       [*Exeunt* ABHORSON *and* POMPEY.
  Now sir, how do you find the prisoner?   65
Duke. A creature unprepar'd, unmeet for death;
  And to transport him in the mind he is
  Were damnable.
Prov.   Here in the prison, father,
  There died this morning of a cruel fever
  One Ragozine, a most notorious pirate,   70
  A man of Claudio's years; his beard and head
  Just of his colour. What if we do omit

64–5. *Prov.* After . . . block! / Now] *this edn, conj. Johnson;* After . . . blocke. / *Pro.*
Now *F.*   64. S.D.] *Capell; not in F.*

62. *ward*] one of the divisions of a
prison.
  63. *gravel*] 'hard as stone'.
  64.] In F the '*Provost*' speech-prefix
heads line 65, leaving line 64 as part of
the Duke's speech. Coghill (following
Johnson's conjecture) points out privately that it is incongruous for the
Duke as Friar to shout orders to the
executioners, while their drift ab-
surdly contradicts his comment in 63
and opinion in 66–8. Spoken by the
Provost, lines 64–5 are an ironic 'I told
you so' after his remarks at IV. ii. 59–
60 and 145–51. The 'Provost' speech-
prefix may have been indicated in
MS. by a marginal '*Enter Provost*' S.D.
at line 64. Cf. IV. ii. 98–9, and note,
and see Intro., p. xxvii.
  66. *unprepar'd*] a recurrent theme.
Cf. II. i. 35, II. ii. 85, III. i. 166.
  67. *transport*] 'i.e. to the next world'
(Durham).
  68–75.] The substitution of a pri-

soner already dead is in Whetstone,
1 Prom., IV. v: 'A dead mans head,
that suffered th' other day', also in his
Heptameron: 'the head of a yonge man
newe executed, who somewhat resembled *Andrugio*' (sig. O1). In *Epitia*,
v. vii, '*un malvagio estremamente*' is
reported to have been executed instead of Vico, '*Essendo così simile di
viso / Egli à Vico, che parea quegli istesso*'
(cf. v. i. 485–7).
  70. *Ragozine, a most notorious pirate*]
The name is suggested by 'argosy',
earlier 'ragusye', from Ital. *ragusea*, a
merchant-ship from Ragusa. The
imprisoning of pirates was topical in
view of the 1604 proclamations against
piracy and the imprisonment of
Raleigh. See Intro., pp. xxxi–xxxii.
  71–2. *his beard . . . colour*] obviating
the necessity to 'shave the head, and
tie the beard' (IV. ii. 175).
  72. *omit*] disregard, take no notice
of (*O.E.D.* v. 2c). A Shakespearean

This reprobate till he were well inclin'd,
And satisfy the deputy with the visage
Of Ragozine, more like to Claudio?   75
Duke. O, 'tis an accident that heaven provides.
Dispatch it presently; the hour draws on
Prefix'd by Angelo. See this be done,
And sent according to command, whiles I
Persuade this rude wretch willingly to die.   80
Prov. This shall be done, good father, presently.
But Barnardine must die this afternoon;
And how shall we continue Claudio,
To save me from the danger that might come
If he were known alive?   85
Duke. Let this be done: put them in secret holds,
Both Barnardine and Claudio.
Ere twice the sun hath made his journal greeting
To yonder generation, you shall find
Your safety manifested.
Prov.   I am your free dependant. 90
Duke. Quick, dispatch, and send the head to Angelo.

                                        Exit [PROVOST].
Now will I write letters to Angelo,

86–9. Let . . . find] *Dyce;* Let . . . done, / . . . *Claudio,* / . . . greeting / . . . finde *F;*
Let . . . holds, / . . . twice / . . . to / . . . find *Steevens '93;* Let . . . holds, / . . . twice /
. . . greeting / . . . find *Singer 2.*   89. yonder] *Rowe 3;* yond *F;* th'under *Hanmer.*
91. S.D.] *Pope; Exit. F (after 90).*   92. Angelo] *F;* Varrius *conj. N.C.S.*

---

usage. Cf. *2H4,* IV. iv. 27, *2H6,* III. ii.
382, *Cor.,* III. i. 145.
    78. *Prefix'd*] fixed in advance.
    83. *continue*] retain.
    86–7.] The F lineation is defective.
See Intro., p. xxviii.
    86. *holds*] cells.
    88. *journal*] diurnal. Cf. *Cym.,* IV. ii.
10; Spenser, *Faerie Queene,* I. xi. 31.
    89. *yonder*] F 'yond' is awkward.
Rowe's 'yonder' (written like 'yond'
with a back-stroke) is supported by
Sisson (*N.R.,* I. p. 87). Hart explains:
'the rest of the world outside this prison, which admitted no sunlight'. But
Greg (in *N.C.S.*) defended Hanmer's
'th' under', the word in F being taken
as a misreading of 'yᵉonder'. 'Th'

under generation' would signify 'men
under the sun', or 'men at the Antipodes', and line 88, 'Before the sun has
risen twice at the Antipodes'. Durham
cites as analogies 'this lower world'
(*Temp.,* III. iii. 54), and 'this under
globe' (*Lr.,* II. ii. 170). However,
Greg's explanation assumes a double
error, the text reading not 'yonder'
but 'yond'.
    generation] (human) race (*O.E.D.*
6).
    90. *free*] i.e. from guilt or blame
(*O.E.D.* 7). Cf. *Ham.,* III. ii. 255, V. ii.
346.
    92–end of scene.] See Intro., pp. xxii
f. on the anomalies presented. The
Provost bears no letters; he does not re-

The Provost, he shall bear them, whose contents
Shall witness to him I am near at home;
And that by great injunctions I am bound   95
To enter publicly. Him I'll desire
To meet me at the consecrated fount
A league below the city; and from thence,
By cold gradation and well-balanc'd form,
We shall proceed with Angelo.   100

Enter PROVOST.

Prov. Here is the head; I'll carry it myself.
Duke. Convenient is it. Make a swift return;
        For I would commune with you of such things
        That want no ear but yours.
Prov.   I'll make all speed.   *Exit.*
Isab. [*within.*] Peace, hoa, be here!   105
Duke. The tongue of Isabel. She's come to know
        If yet her brother's pardon be come hither;
        But I will keep her ignorant of her good,
        To make her heavenly comforts of despair
        When it is least expected.

Enter ISABELLA.

Isab.   Hoa, by your leave!   110
Duke. Good morning to you, fair and gracious daughter.
Isab. The better, given me by so holy a man.
        Hath yet the deputy sent my brother's pardon?
Duke. He hath releas'd him, Isabel,—from the world.

99. well-balanc'd] *F* (Weale-ballanc'd).   105. S.D.] *Isabell within. F (centred
S.D.).*

turn; Angelo is to be met at the city
gates, not the consecrated fount; Isabella, present after Lucio's entry, is
given no exit. A partial and hasty
revision may be inferred.

    92. *to Angelo*] On the view that 'Var-
rius' was intended, see Intro., xxiii f.

    99. *by cold gradation*] 'by cold process
of reasoning'? Cf. Baldwin on '*gra-
datio*', II. 165. The phrase has never
been satisfactorily explained.

    well-balanc'd form] 'with due ob-

servance of all forms' (Schmidt).

    102. *Convenient*] fit.

    103. *commune*] confer.

    110. *it*] i.e. 'comforts'.

    114.] In Cinthio, the keeper of the
prison brings Vico's corpse to the
house of Epitia with the words: '*il
Fratel uostro, che ui manda il sig. Gouer-
natore libero dalla prigione*'. This casuistry also appears in Iuriste's soliloquy,
Epitia, II. ii, and in the messenger's
report, *ibid.*, III. i. In substituting

His head is off, and sent to Angelo.   115

Isab. Nay, but it is not so!

Duke. It is no other. Show your wisdom, daughter,
    In your close patience.

Isab. O, I will to him and pluck out his eyes!

Duke. You shall not be admitted to his sight.   120

Isab. Unhappy Claudio! wretched Isabel!
    Injurious world! most damned Angelo!

Duke. This nor hurts him, nor profits you a jot.
    Forbear it therefore; give your cause to heaven.
    Mark what I say, which you shall find   125
    By every syllable a faithful verity.
    The Duke comes home tomorrow;—nay, dry your
      eyes—
    One of our covent, and his confessor
    Gives me this instance. Already he hath carried
    Notice to Escalus and Angelo,   130
    Who do prepare to meet him at the gates
    There to give up their power. If you can pace your
      wisdom

117–18. It . . . patience] *Camb.;* It . . . other. / . . . patience. /*F.*   132. can pace]
F; can, pace *Rowe.*

'world' for 'prison' the Duke adds an
overtone in keeping with his part as
friar.

117–18.] Lineation is defective in F:
cf. lines 86–7 and see Intro., p. xxviii.

118.   *close*]   uncommunicative
(*O.E.D. adj.* 7). The two 'yours' are
non-metrical and suggest 'sophistication'.

119.] So in *Epitia*, III. ii, Angela
says: '*Male ne hò detto à Iuriste, & poco
meno | Che non gli habbia cacciati ambiduo
gli occhi*'; which is repeated by Iuriste
in his monologue of III. v, speaking of
Angela: '*che uoleua trarmi | gli occhi del
capo, perch'io hauea mandato | A Epitia il
Fratel morto.*'

121–2.] Epitia's lady-in-waiting,
hearing the messenger's account of
Iuriste's instructions, exclaims: '*Ò
scelerato, ò traditore Iuriste, | Ò dolorosa
Epitia, ò miserella*' (*Epitia*, III. i).

127. *tomorrow*] At the end of IV. ii it

was 'almost clear dawn', and in line 69
above, Ragozine is reported to have
died 'this morning'. A full day elapses
between this scene and the Duke's
formal entry into Vienna in V. i,
during which time the events of IV. iv,
and the Duke's meeting at Mariana's
house (see lines 139–40 *infra*), take
place.

128–32.] This is deliberate mystifi-
cation, though Friar Peter is to be
taken as having carried the messages
mentioned in IV. ii. 198 ff. and to be
intended here (cf. lines 137–8 *infra*).
As the Duke's confessor he must be
identical with the 'Friar' of I. iii. See
Intro., pp. xviii–xix. *covent*: early form
of 'convent', as in 'Covent Garden'.
Cf. *H8*, IV. ii. 19.

132–3. *If you can pace . . . And*]
Editors place a comma after 'can': it
is unnecessary, since the construction
is merely an ellipsis of the regular con-

In that good path that I would wish it go,
And you shall have your bosom on this wretch,
Grace of the Duke, revenges to your heart,   135
And general honour.
Isab.   I am directed by you.
Duke. This letter then to Friar Peter give;
'Tis that he sent me of the Duke's return.
Say, by this token I desire his company
At Mariana's house tonight. Her cause and yours   140
I'll perfect him withal, and he shall bring you
Before the Duke; and to the head of Angelo
Accuse him home and home. For my poor self,
I am combined by a sacred vow,
And shall be absent. Wend you with this letter.   145
Command these fretting waters from your eyes
With a light heart; trust not my holy order,
If I pervert your course.—Who's here?

Enter Lucio.

Lucio.   Good even.
Friar, where's the Provost?
Duke.   Not within, sir.
Lucio. O pretty Isabella, I am pale at mine heart to see   150
thine eyes so red: thou must be patient.—I am fain

133. wish it go,] *F;* wish it, go, *Ridley, conj. Young.*   134. And] *F;* Then *Hudson,
conj. Keightley;* / [ ] / And *conj. Walker (Dyce).*   148. even] *Rowe;* 'euen *F.*

ditional: 'if you can pace, etc. (do so)
And . . .' *pace:* figurative, from putting
a horse through its paces.

134. *have your bosom*] 'have your
desires'. Cf. *Oth.,* III. i. 58: 'To speak
your bosom'.

138.] further dissimulation, as in
lines 128 ff.

141. *perfect*] give complete information.

143. *home and home*] 'right to the
point'. Cf. 'tax him home' (*Ham.,* III.
iii. 29). For 'home' repeated as intensive, cf. 'through and through', 'out
and out', etc.

144. *combined*] Shakespeare seems to
have used this word in the sense

'bound by oath, pledged'. Cf. *AYL.,* v
iv. 157: 'Thy faith my fancy to thee
doth combine' (Onions). See also
'combinate', III. i. 223 and note. Here
too the influence of 'bind' affects the
meaning.

145. *Wend you*] Betake yourself (reflexive).

146. *fretting*] wearing away. Cf. *Lr.,*
I. iv. 309: 'tears fret channels in her
cheeks'.

148. *pervert*] turn aside.

Good even] conflicting with the
Duke's 'Good morning', line 111. Cf.
'clear dawn', IV. ii. 209, 'this morning',
line 69 *supra,* and see Intro., pp. xxii–
xxiii.

to dine and sup with water and bran: I dare not for
my head fill my belly: one fruitful meal would set
me to't.—But they say the Duke will be here tomorrow. By my troth, Isabel, I loved thy brother;   155
if the old fantastical duke of dark corners had been
at home, he had lived.   [*Exit* ISABELLA.]

Duke. Sir, the Duke is marvellous little beholding to
your reports; but the best is, he lives not in them.

Lucio. Friar, thou knowest not the Duke so well as I do.   160
He's a better woodman than thou tak'st him for.

Duke. Well! you'll answer this one day. Fare ye well. [*going.*]

Lucio. Nay tarry, I'll go along with thee: I can tell thee
pretty tales of the Duke.

Duke. You have told me too many of him already, sir, if   165
they be true: if not true, none were enough.

Lucio. I was once before him for getting a wench with
child.

Duke. Did you such a thing?

Lucio. Yes, marry, did I; but I was fain to forswear it;   170

157. S.D.] *Theobald; not in* F.   162. S.D.] *Collier; not in* F.   163–4. Nay . . .
Duke.] *as Pope;* Nay . . . thee, / . . . Duke. F (*verse*).

151–4. *I am fain . . . to't*] Cf. Lyly,
Euphues, I. 256: 'refraine from all such
meates as shall prouoke thine appetite
to lust. . . Take cleere water for stronge
wine, browne bread for fine manchet';
and the punishment of Costard for
lechery in *LLL.,* I. i. 299: 'fast a week
with bran and water'. *bran*: bran
bread, of the coarsest kind of meal.
for my head: to save my head (from the
fate of Claudio's). *to't*: cf. 'past it',
III. ii. 176.

156. *fantastical*] Cf. III. ii. 89.

duke of dark corners] Lucio means
'keeper of secret assignations', which
he assumes to be the Duke's unofficial
occupation. But the phrase had unconscious irony; the Duke visits obscure places in order to learn the state
of his people after the manner of
Severus, who had 'visible Lightes, in
obscure Corners' (Whetstone, *A Mirour
for Magestrates of Cyties* (1584), sig.
A3ᵛ); 'in euery corner, he had

(secretly) such faythfull Explorers, as
mens proper Houses, were no Couerts
for naughtie practises' (sig. F4ᵛ). See
Intro., pp. xliv–xlv.

157. S.D.] F provides no exit, nor
can one be inferred from the dialogue.
Perhaps a suitable cue for Isabella's
departure belonged to an earlier version of this scene. See Intro., pp. xxii–
xxiv.

158. *beholding*] beholden (*O.E.D.
ppl. a.* 1: originally an error, but continuing independently into the 18th
cent.). Cf. *Wiv.,* I. i. 285.

159. *lives not*] is not to be found, is
not present.

161. *woodman*] hunter of women.
Hart cites Greene's *Philomela* (Grosart,
XI. 151): 'seeke another wood man,
for I will not play an apple-squire'. Cf.
Beaumont and Fletcher, *The Chances,*
I. ix: 'I see ye are a wood-man, and
can chuse / Your dear, tho' it be i' th'
dark' (Steevens); also *Wiv.,* V. v. 30.

they would else have married me to the rotten
medlar.

Duke. Sir, your company is fairer than honest; rest you
well.   [*going.*]

Lucio. By my troth, I'll go with thee to the lane's end. If   175
bawdy talk offend you, we'll have very little of it.
Nay, friar, I am a kind of burr, I shall stick.   *Exeunt.*

SCENE IV [*In Vienna.*]

Enter ANGELO *and* ESCALUS.

Esc. Every letter he hath writ hath disvouched other.

Ang. In most uneven and distracted manner. His actions
show much like to madness; pray heaven his wisdom
be not tainted. And why meet him at the gates and
redeliver our authorities there?   5

Esc. I guess not.

Ang. And why should we proclaim it in an hour before

171–2. they . . . medlar] *as Pope;* They . . . Medler. *F* (*? verse*).   174. S.D.] *this
edn; not in F; He opens the door | N.C.S.*

                              Scene IV
Scene IV] *Scena Quarta. F.   In Vienna.*] *this edn; The Palace. Rowe; A Room in
Angelo's House. Capell.*   5. redeliver] *Capell;* re- / liuer *F;* deliver *F2.*

171–2. *the rotten medlar*] Cf. 'rotten
orange', *Ado,* IV. i. 32, of the supposedly unchaste Hero. The medlar, 'a
fruit rotten before it is ripe', was
slang for a prostitute. So Middleton,
Women Beware Women, IV. ii: 'he that
marries a whore looks like a fellow
bound all his lifetime to a medlar
tree'.

177. *a kind of burr, I shall stick*] proverbial (Tilley B 724). Cf. *MND.,* III.
ii. 260, *Troil.,* III. ii. 119.

                    Scene IV

1. *disvouched*] disavowed: a variant
of 'disavouched'.

4. *tainted*] impaired. Cf. *Tw.N.,* III.
iv. 14.

5. *redeliver*] Capell's 'redeliver' con-

veys more exactly the requisite sense
of giving the power held back to its
deliverer, the Duke' (Sisson, *N.R.,*
I. 87: in whose edition, however,
'deliver' appears).

6. *guess not*] cannot guess.

7–9.] In *2 Prom.,* II. iii, an officer
reads the royal proclamation, calling
on all subjects with grievances 'to
repayre to Syr *Ulrico,* one of his highnesse priuie Counsell', who will investigate them before presentation to the
King. Whetstone follows English con-
stitutional procedure: Shakespeare
eliminates this for a more dramatic
effect.

7. *in an hour*] 'leaving a clear hour',
so that petitioners may not find access
obstructed.

his entering, that if any crave redress of injustice,
they should exhibit their petitions in the street?

Esc. He shows his reason for that: to have a dispatch of   10
complaints, and to deliver us from devices hereafter,
which shall then have no power to stand against us.

Ang. Well, I beseech you, let it be proclaim'd
Betimes i'th'morn: I'll call you at your house.
Give notice to such men of sort and suit   15
As are to meet him.

Esc.   I shall, sir: fare you well.

Ang. Good night.   *Exit* [ESCALUS].
This deed unshapes me quite; makes me unpregnant
And dull to all proceedings. A deflower'd maid;
And by an eminent body, that enforc'd   20
The law against it! But that her tender shame
Will not proclaim against her maiden loss,
How might she tongue me! Yet reason dares her no,
For my authority bears so credent bulk
That no particular scandal once can touch,   25

13–16.] *as Capell; prose, F.*   13–14. proclaim'd / Betimes . . . morn:] *this edn,*
conj. Malone; proclaim'd be- / times . . . morne, *F (as prose);* proclaim'd: / . . .
morn *Capell.*   23. her no,] *F;* her: no, *Hanmer;* her No. *Johnson;* her? no;
Capell; her on *White;* her not *conj. Steevens '78.*   24. so] *this edn;* of a *F;* off a *F4;*
a *Theobald;* a so *Alexander.*

---

9. *exhibit*] submit for consideration.

10. *dispatch*] prompt settlement. 'The reply of Escalus is such as arises from an undisturbed mind' (Johnson).

11. *devices*] plots, contrivances.

13–16.] F prints as prose. Most editions place a colon after 'proclaimed', making 'betimes' refer to Angelo's call on Escalus. The change from F pointing is unwarranted. Angelo's embarrassment is not at the submission of petitions, a normal practice, but at the special arrangements to ensure their direct and public presentation to the Duke.

15. *men of sort and suit*] men of rank with a retinue ('sort', *O.E.D. sb.*² 2b, 'suit', *sb.* 16). (Cf. 'suit and service'.) Steevens's interpretation of 'suit' as feudal vassals gives too specialized a sense.

20. *an eminent body*] a person of commanding importance. Cf. 'eminence', I. ii. 153.

21. *it*] defloration.

23. *tongue*] assail with words, reproach. Cf. *Oth.*, I. ii. 18 f., 'My services . . . Shall out-tongue his complaints'.

dares her no] 'no' as complement to the verb implies a prohibition; cf. Beaumont and Fletcher, *A Wife for a Month,* IV. i: 'I charg'd him no' (v. 50), (Hart).

24. *bears so credent bulk*] 'carries such great capacity to induce belief'. F 'of' seems to follow a slip of the pen in the original MS, with 'a' added to make the sense intelligible. *credent*: plausible; cf. *Wint.*, I. ii. 143–4: ' 'tis very credent / Thou mayst co-join with something'.

25. *particular*] personal.

But it confounds the breather. He should have liv'd;
Save that his riotous youth, with dangerous sense,
Might in the times to come have ta'en revenge
By so receiving a dishonour'd life
With ransom of such shame. Would yet he had lived.   30
Alack, when once our grace we have forgot,
Nothing goes right; we would, and we would not.   [*Exit.*

SCENE V [*A Friar's Cell.*]

Enter DUKE [*in his own habit*] *and* FRIAR PETER.

Duke. These letters at fit time deliver me.
The Provost knows our purpose and our plot;
The matter being afoot, keep your instruction,
And hold you ever to our special drift,
Though sometimes you do blench from this to that   5
As cause doth minister. Go call at Flavius' house,

Scene v

Scene V] Scena Quinta. F; Act V. Winny, conj. Johnson.   A Friar's Cell.] this edn;
Fields without the Town. Rowe; A consecrated fount, a league below the city. N.C.S.
6. Flavius'] Pope; Flauia's F.

27–30. *Save that . . . shame*] No such
motive appears in the sources to the
play. In *Epitia*, II. ii, Vico is to be executed because Iuriste fears that the
Podestà will otherwise make trouble
for him with the Emperor. Other
versions of the story are silent on this
point.

27. *sense*] passion, as in II. ii. 143
and elsewhere.

32.] Johnson comments: 'Here...the
Act should end ... for here is properly a
cessation of action, and a night intervenes, and the place is changed... The
next Act beginning with the following
scene, proceeds without any interruption of time or change of place'.

Scene v

S.H.] Rowe's 'Fields without the
Town', generally followed, is a literary
embellishment. The most likely place

to find a friar is at his cell, which is not
inconsistent with the site of a 'consecrated fount'. In terms of the Jacobean theatre, an entry of the Friar
would suggest a return to the location
of I. iii.

1.] 'Peter never delivers the letters,
but tells his story without any credentials. The poet forgot the plot
which he had formed' (Johnson).
N.C.S. points out that *me* signifies 'for
me', not 'to me'. The letters would be
the Friar's credentials to Flavius,
Valencius, etc.

2.] a reassurance in view of the Provost's failure to return in IV. iii (see
Intro., pp. xxii–xxiv).

3. *keep*] observe, as in the biblical
'keep my commandments'.

4. *drift*] scheme, device.

5. *blench*] turn aside.

6, 8. *Flavius . . . Valencius . . . Crassus*]

And tell him where I stay. Give the like notice
To Valencius, Rowland, and to Crassus,
And bid them bring the trumpets to the gate:
But send me Flavius first.

Friar Peter.   It shall be speeded well.   10

                                        [*Exit* FRIAR.]

                    Enter VARRIUS.

Duke. I thank thee, Varrius, thou hast made good haste.
Come, we will walk. There's other of our friends
Will greet us here anon. My gentle Varrius!   *Exeunt.*

                    SCENE VI [*In Vienna.*]

            Enter ISABELLA *and* MARIANA.

Isab. To speak so indirectly I am loth;
I would say the truth, but to accuse him so
That is your part; yet I am advis'd to do it,
He says, to veil full purpose.

8. To Valencius] *F;* Unto Valentius *Pope;* To Valentinus *Capell.*   10. first.] *F2;*
first *F.*   S.D. *Exit Friar.*] *Theobald; not in F.*   13. anon. . . .Varrius!] *Kittredge;*
anon: . . . *Varrius. F;* anon, . . . *Varrius. Rowe 3.*

                        Scene VI
Scene VI] *Scena Sexta. F.   In Vienna.*] *this edn (Winny subst.); Street near the Gate*
Capell.   4. to veil full] *F* (vaile); to vail-full *Rowe;* t'availful *Theobald.*

characters in Plutarch's *Lives.* There is
a 'Flavius' in *Cæs.,* I. i, and *Timon.* On
the use of Latin names, see Intro.,
p. xlv. Mention of these figures without speaking parts adds 'depth', suggesting a ducal court.

    9. *bid . . . gate*] Whetstone, *2 Prom.,*
I, suggests far more elaborate preparations for the arrival of Corvinus, inspired by the royal progresses of the
time. They include pageants of 'the
nyne worthyes' and 'the fowre vertues', Hercules fighting giants and
wild beasts, 'greene men' with
'clubbes of fyreworke', and a mixed
choir. In Shakespeare's more con-
centrated action, the Duke's sudden

return allows no time for such devices.
trumpets: perhaps trumpeters (*O.E.D.
sb.* 4); but 'trumpets' may mean the
instruments, to be sounded by the
Duke's four courtiers.

    10. *speeded*] accomplished, expedi-
ted.

    Enter Varrius] On this name see
Intro., pp. xviii, xlv. There is a messenger called Varrius in *Ant.,* II. i. The
chief function of Varrius here is to
escort the Duke, now in his proper
person, off and on the stage.

    11. *I thank thee, Varrius*] This looks
like the acknowledgement of a greeting which has dropped out of the
text.

Mariana.   Be rul'd by him.
Isab. Besides, he tells me that, if peradventure   5
      He speak against me on the adverse side,
      I should not think it strange, for 'tis a physic
      That's bitter to sweet end.

                Enter FRIAR PETER.

Mariana.   I would Friar Peter—
Isab. O peace, the friar is come.
Friar Peter. Come, I have found you out a stand most fit,   10
      Where you may have such vantage on the Duke
      He shall not pass you. Twice have the trumpets sounded.
      The generous and gravest citizens
      Have hent the gates, and very near upon
      The Duke is ent'ring: therefore hence, away.   *Exeunt.* 15

8. S.D.] *Capell; Enter Peter. F; Rowe 3 (after 9); Alexander (after Peter 8).*   12.]
as Rowe 3; He . . . you: / . . . sounded. *F (verse).*   15.] *as Rowe 3;* The . . .
entring: / . . . away. *F (verse).*

10. *a stand most fit*] In *2 Prom.,* I. iv, v, Phallax orders stands to be erected at 'saynt *Annes* crosse', 'Jesus gate', and 'Ducke Alley'. No fixture is necessarily implied here.

11. *have such vantage on*] be so advantageously placed (for intercepting).

12. *Twice . . . sounded*] Fanfares should probably be sounded off-stage at the beginning of the scene, and here again.

13. *generous and gravest*] The superlative governs both adjectives. *generous*: noble, high-born (Lat. *generosus*).

14. *hent*] lit. 'taken hold of' (cf. *Wint.,* IV. ii. 134): here, 'occupied (places) at' (*O.E.D. v.* 3b).

ACT V

SCENE I [*A public place near the city gate.*]

Enter at several doors DUKE [*in his own habit*], VARRIUS, *Lords*
[*and Attendants*] ; ANGELO, ESCALUS, LUCIO, [*and*] *Citizens.*

Duke. My very worthy cousin, fairly met.
    Our old and faithful friend, we are glad to see you.
Ang. and Esc. Happy return be to your royal grace!
Duke. Many and hearty thankings to you both.
    We have made enquiry of you, and we hear   5
    Such goodness of your justice that our soul
    Cannot but yield you forth to public thanks,
    Forerunning more requital.
Ang. You make my bonds still greater.
Duke. O, but your desert speaks loud, and I should wrong it
    To lock it in the wards of covert bosom,   11
    When it deserves with characters of brass

ACT V

Scene I

Act V Scene I] *Actus Quintus. Scœna Prima. F.*   *A public place near the city gate.*]
Malone; The city gate. Capell.   S.D.] *F* (*subst.*) *; A state . . . Provost, Officers, etc.*
attending : Mariana veil'd, Isabell, and Friar Peter at their stand. Enter, at opposite doors,
Duke, Varrius; Angelo, Escalus; and their Trains. Capell.

S.D.] All edd. follow Capell in providing an entry here for the Provost
and his officers; but see note to lines
251–2.

1.] spoken as the Duke meets
Angelo. *cousin*: 'used by a sovereign in
addressing . . . a nobleman of the same
country' (*O.E.D.* 5a).

2. *Our . . . friend*] Escalus.

4. *thankings*] words of thanks.

5–7.] Cf. Corvinus in *2 Prom.*, I. ix:
'*Promos*, the good report, of your good
gouernment I heare, / . . . To in-

courage you the more, in Iustice to
perseauer / Is the cheefe cause, I dyd
addresse, my Progresse heather'.

6. *soul*] Cf. I. i. 17 and note.

11. *in . . . bosom*] figurative, from the
wards of a prison; cf. IV. iii. 62, and
'sure wards of trust', *Sonn.*, xlviii. 4.
covert bosom: undisclosed affection.

12–14. *When . . . oblivion*] The inspiration is Horace, *Odes*, III. xxx:
'*Exegi monumentum aere perennius*', and
Ovid, *Metam.*, xv. 871 ff.; a Renaissance commonplace for eternal fame.

A forted residence 'gainst the tooth of time
And razure of oblivion. Give we our hand,
And let the subject see, to make them know   15
That outward courtesies would fain proclaim
Favours that keep within. Come, Escalus,
You must walk by us on our other hand;
And good supporters are you.

Enter Friar PETER *and* ISABELLA.

Friar Peter. Now is your time: speak loud, and kneel before
     him.   20
Isab. Justice, O royal Duke! Vail your regard
Upon a wrong'd—I would fain have said, a maid.
O worthy prince, dishonour not your eye
By throwing it on any other object,
Till you have heard me in my true complaint,   25
And given me justice! Justice! Justice! Justice!
Duke. Relate your wrongs. In what? By whom? Be brief.

---

14. we our] *this edn;* we your *F;* me your *F3.*   15. subject] *F;* subjects *Theobald.*
19. S.D.] *Enter Peter and Isabella. F; Peter and Isabella come forward. Capell.*
20. Now . . . him.] *as Pope;* Now . . . time / . . . him. *F.*   22. I . . . maid.] *as Rowe;*
(I . . . Maid) *F.*   I would] *F;* I'd *Pope.*   27. Relate . . . brief.] *as Pope;*
Relate . . . wrongs; / briefe: / *F.*

Cf. *LLL.,* I. i. 1–7; *Sonn.,* lv. 1–4, cvii.
13–14.

13. *forted*] fortified. Cf. *Sonn.,* xvi. 3.
the tooth of time] Cf. 'Devouring
Time. . . Pluck the keen teeth from the
fierce tiger's jaws', *Sonn.,* xix. 1–3.
From Ovid's '*tempus edax rerum*'.

14. *razure of oblivion*] Cf. *Sonn.,*
cxxii. 7: 'raz'd oblivion'. *razure:*
obliteration, effacement. *we our:* All
editors have taken F's *we* as *me,* due to
a turned 'm'. But the context suggests
rather a misreading as 'your' of a contracted 'our' in manuscript.

15. *the subject*] Cf. II. iv. 27.

16–17. *That outward . . . within*]
ironical reversal of the iterative 'seeming and being' theme.

19. *supporters*] like the heraldic 'supporters' on each side of a shield.

S.D.] The entry would have begun

while Angelo and Escalus re-grouped
themselves, but Peter and Isabella
reach their stand at this point. Their
deferred arrival, which is dramatically
effective here, has been implied in IV.
vi. 12–15, coinciding in time with the
opening of V. i.

21, 26. *Justice, . . . Justice!*] So Kyd's
Hieronimo seeks to intercept the king
in *The Spanish Tragedy,* III. xii: 'Iustice,
O, iustice to *Hieronimo* . . . Iustice, O,
iustice, iustice, gentle King . . . Iustice,
O iustice'. Angelo's imputation that
Isabella's 'wits . . . are not firm' (line
35) may also have been suggested by
Lorenzo's comments in this scene.

21. *Vail your regard*] 'Look down'.
Cf. Corvinus in *2 Prom.,* I. viii: 'it
tends to great behove / That Prynces
oft doo vayle their eares to heare, /
The Misers playnt'.

Here is Lord Angelo shall give you justice,
Reveal yourself to him.

Isab.   O worthy Duke,
You bid me seek redemption of the devil.   30
Hear me yourself: for that which I must speak
Must either punish me, not being believ'd,
Or wring redress from you.
Hear me! O hear me, hear!

Ang. My lord, her wits I fear me are not firm.   35
She hath been a suitor to me for her brother,
Cut off by course of justice.

Isab.   By course of justice!

Ang. And she will speak most bitterly and strange.

Isab. Most strange: but yet most truly will I speak.
That Angelo's forsworn, is it not strange?   40
That Angelo's a murderer, is't not strange?
That Angelo is an adulterous thief,
An hypocrite, a virgin-violator,
Is it not strange, and strange?

Duke. Nay, it is ten times strange!   45

Isab. It is not truer he is Angelo,
Than this is all as true as it is strange;
Nay, it is ten times true, for truth is truth
To th'end of reck'ning.

33–4. you. / Hear . . . me,] *as F;* you: hear me, oh hear me, *Johnson;* you: oh hear me *Pope;* you: oh, hear me, hear me. *Theobald.*   hear!] *Neilson and Hill, conj. Keightley (Camb.);* heere *F;* here *F2;* om. *Theobald.*   45. strange!] *N.C.S.;* strange? *F;* strange. *F4.*

29. *Reveal yourself*] 'disclose your complaint'.

34. *hear!*] F spells 'heere', F3 'here', leading to the weak conclusion 'hear me here' adopted by all editors except Kittredge. See note to III. i. 253.

38. *strange*] The word is played on down to line 47. In *2 Prom.*, II. v, Ulrico, investigating the charges against Promos, comments: 'Tys more then straunge, to see with honest show, / What fowle deceytes, lewde officers can hyde'.

44. *strange, and strange*] intensive; cf. IV. iii. 143.

47. *as . . . strange*] proverbial as 'No more strange than true' (Tilley S 914). Hart notes that the play on 'true', 'truer', 'truth' is a trope from Sidney's *Arcadia*, described by Puttenham under the title '*Traductio* or The Tranlacer'.

48–9. *Nay . . . reck'ning*] 'Truth is truth' was proverbial (Tilley T 581); cf. *LLL.*, IV. i. 48, *John*, I. i. 105, etc. Noble cites 1 Esdras, IV. 38: 'As for the trueth it endureth, . . . for euermore without end'. In *Epitia*, IV. iii, the Emperor interrupts Epitia's denunciation of Iuriste with: '*E questo è uero?*',

Duke.   Away with her. Poor soul,
   She speaks this in th'infirmity of sense.   50

Isab. O Prince, I conjure thee, as thou believ'st
   There is another comfort than this world,
   That thou neglect me not with that opinion
   That I am touch'd with madness. Make not impossible
   That which but seems unlike. 'Tis not impossible   55
   But one, the wicked'st caitiff on the ground,
   May seem as shy, as grave, as just, as absolute,
   As Angelo; even so may Angelo,
   In all his dressings, caracts, titles, forms,
   Be an arch-villain. Believe it, royal Prince,   60
   If he be less, he's nothing; but he's more,
   Had I more name for badness.

Duke.   By mine honesty,
   If she be mad, as I believe no other,
   Her madness hath the oddest frame of sense,
   Such a dependency of thing on thing,   65
   As e'er I heard in madness.

Isab.   O gracious Duke,
   Harp not on that; nor do not banish reason
   For inequality; but let your reason serve
   To make the truth appear where it seems hid,
   And hide the false seems true.

Duke.   Many that are not mad 70

---

66. e'er] *F* (ere), *F4* (e're) *;* ne'er *Dyce, conj. Capell.*   70. And ... false seems true]
F; And ... false-seems-true *Singer 2;* Not ... false, seems true *Theobald.*

---

to which she replies: '*Più uer, che il
uero*'.

   51. *conjure*] call upon, adjure.

   52. *comfort*] source of consolation.

   55. *unlike*] unlikely.

   56. *caitiff*] villain.

   57. *shy*] reserved, cautious.

   absolute] free from limitations.

   59. *dressings*] decorations (of office).

   caracts] distinctive marks, badges
(cognate with 'characters').

   forms] ceremonies.

   60. *arch-villain*] also used in *Tim.*,
v. i. 113.

   64. *frame of sense*] structure or form

of rationality. 'sense' as in II. ii. 142.

   65. *dependency*] dependence, logical
sequence.

   67. *on that*] on the 'string' of her supposed madness.

   68. *inequality*] Johnson's 'inequality
of rank' (*O.E.D.* 1b) suits the context.
Because Isabella is a commoner, her
charges against Angelo are dismissed
as unreasonable. But Schmidt interprets 'inequality' as 'incongruity', i.e.
lack of accord with the general
opinion; and Hart and Onions gloss as
'injustice'.

   70. *hide*] put out of sight.

Have, sure, more lack of reason. What would you say?

Isab. I am the sister of one Claudio,
　　Condemn'd upon the act of fornication
　　To lose his head; condemn'd by Angelo.
　　I—in probation of a sisterhood—　　　　　　75
　　Was sent to by my brother; one Lucio
　　As then the messenger.

Lucio.　　　　　　　　　That's I, and't like your Grace.
　　I came to her from Claudio, and desir'd her
　　To try her gracious fortune with Lord Angelo
　　For her poor brother's pardon.

Isab.　　　　　　　　　That's he indeed.　　80

Duke. [*to Lucio.*] You were not bid to speak.

Lucio.　　　　　　　　　No, my good lord,
　　Nor wish'd to hold my peace.

Duke.　　　　　　　I wish you now, then;
　　Pray you take note of it;
　　And when you have a business for yourself,
　　Pray heaven you then be perfect.

Lucio.　　　　　　　I warrant your honour.

Duke. The warrant's for yourself: take heed to't.　　86

Isab. This gentleman told somewhat of my tale.

Lucio. Right.

Duke. It may be right, but you are i'the wrong
　　To speak before your time.—Proceed.

Isab.　　　　　　　　　I went　　　90
　　To this pernicious caitiff Deputy.

Duke. That's somewhat madly spoken.

Isab.　　　　　　　　　Pardon it;
　　The phrase is to the matter.

---

71. Have ... say?] *as Hanmer;* Haue ... reason: / ... say? *F.*　　81. S.D.] *Rowe.*
83–5.] *as Capell;* Pray ... haue / ... then / ... perfect. / *F.*

the false seems true] elliptical: 'the falsehood which seems true'.

73. *upon*] consequent on. Cf. 'upon a true contract', I. ii. 134.

fornication] See note to II. ii. 23.

74. *by Angelo*] with ironical stress.

77. *As then*] being at that time ('as' with adv. of time, *O.E.D.* 34a). Ridley's suggested 'Was' for 'As' seems unnecessary.

82. *wish'd*] past participle: 'was I wished'.

84. *a business for yourself*] 'a matter which concerns you'.

85. *perfect*] 'correct (in stating your case)'. Cf. *Mac.*, I. v. 2: 'the perfectest report'.

86. *The warrant's for yourself*] quibbles on 'warrant': 'The warrant is against you'. Cf. line 105.

Duke. Mended again. The matter: proceed.

Isab. In brief, to set the needless process by—   95
  How I persuaded, how I pray'd and kneel'd,
  How he refell'd me, and how I replied
  (For this was of much length)—the vile conclusion
  I now begin with grief and shame to utter.
  He would not, but by gift of my chaste body   100
  To his concupiscible intemperate lust,
  Release my brother; and after much debatement,
  My sisterly remorse confutes mine honour,
  And I did yield to him. But the next morn betimes,
  His purpose surfeiting, he sends a warrant   105
  For my poor brother's head.

Duke.   This is most likely!

Isab. O, that it were as like as it is true.

Duke. By heaven, fond wretch, thou know'st not what thou
      speak'st,
  Or else thou art suborn'd against his honour
  In hateful practice. First, his integrity   110
  Stands without blemish; next, it imports no reason
  That with such vehemency he should pursue
  Faults proper to himself. If he had so offended,

---

105. surfeiting] *F*; forfeiting *F4*.   106. likely!] *Rowe 2*; likely. *F*.   108. thou know'st] *F3*; yᵘ knowst *F*.

---

94. *Mended again*] 'The apparent madness of speech has been amended again'.

The matter :] 'come to the point' (cf. II. ii. 33). A word may be missing to the line: perhaps 'the matter, *then*' or '*pray*, proceed'.

95. *to set . . . by*] 'to cut a long story short'. 'process' = narration (*O.E.D. sb.* 4).

97. *refell'd me*] 'rejected my request'.

101. *concupiscible*] vehemently desirous (*O.E.D.* 2). A term from psychology, which Shakespeare employs only here. Cf. Wright, *Passions of the Minde*, chap. v, where the 'appetite of the senses' is classed as both 'concupiscible' ('Coveting, Desiring, Wishing') and 'irascible'.

intemperate] a more forceful term than now. Cf. *Ado*, IV. i. 59 ff.

103. *remorse*] compassion (cf. II. ii. 54).

confutes] confounds, brings to nought.

107.] 'O that it had as much of the likeness or appearance, as it has of the reality, of truth!' (Malone). Another variation on 'being' and 'seeming'.

110. *practice*] machination, conspiracy.

111. *it imports no reason*] 'it (that he should pursue, etc.) has no implicit reason'. Cf. *Lr.*, IV. iii. 5: 'which imports to the kingdom so much fear and danger.'

112. *pursue*] persecute.

113. *proper to*] belonging to. Cf. I. i. 30.

He would have weigh'd thy brother by himself,
And not have cut him off. Someone hath set you on: 115
Confess the truth, and say by whose advice
Thou cam'st here to complain.

Isab.   And is this all?
Then, O you blessed ministers above,
Keep me in patience, and with ripen'd time
Unfold the evil which is here wrapt up   120
In countenance! Heaven shield your Grace from woe,
As I, thus wrong'd, hence unbelieved go.

Duke. I know you'd fain be gone. An officer!
To prison with her!   [*Isabella is placed under guard.*]
                              Shall we thus permit
A blasting and a scandalous breath to fall   125
On him so near us? This needs must be a practice.
Who knew of your intent and coming hither?

Isab. One that I would were here, Friar Lodowick.

                                        [*Exit guarded.*]

Duke. A ghostly father, belike.—Who knows that
          Lodowick?

Lucio. My lord, I know him. 'Tis a meddling friar;   130
I do not like the man; had he been lay, my lord,
For certain words he spake against your Grace

---

124. S.D.] *this edn; Isabella is taken aside, guarded. Sisson.*   128. S.D.] *this edn; not in F; At a motion of the Duke, the Officer and Isabella withdraw to a distance. N.C.S.*
129. A . . . Lodowick?] *as Johnson; A . . . belike: / . . . Lodowicke? / F.*

114.] Follows the 'measure' theme: cf. III. ii. 259 and note. In 2 *Prom.*, III. iii, the king quotes to Promos: '*Hoc facias alteri, quod tibi vis fieri*'.

118. *ministers above*] messengers of God; angels (Schmidt). Cf. 'ministers of grace', *Ham.*, I. iv. 39.

120–1. *wrapt up In countenance*] a disputed phrase, for which 'concealed by royal privilege' seems the best rendering. Cf. *1H4*, I. ii. 33: 'under whose countenance we steal' and *Sonn.*, lxxxvi. 13. Hart cites *Menechmus*, IV. i (1595): 'a poore man . . . is . . . outfaste and overlaide with countenance'. But Onions interprets 'countenance' as 'show, pretence' (*O.E.D.* 2), and

N.C.S. finds in 'wrapt up' a complex of meanings.

124, 128. S.D.] suggested by *N.C.S.* F provides no exit, but in line 241 Isabella is said to have gone; and she re-enters at line 276. Most editors follow Capell in placing her exit at line 164, but she has no further part in the action from here until her return, and 'it is absurd to take her off immediately after Friar Peter's declaration that she shall be "disproved to her eyes"' (*N.C.S.*). Possibly a withdrawal conventionally out of earshot is intended; cf. the Duke and Provost, III. i. 52; Isabella, *ibid.*, 158; Claudio, *ibid.*, 172; and Isabella and Mariana, IV. i. 59.

In your retirement, I had swing'd him soundly.
Duke. Words against me! This' a good friar belike.
    And to set on this wretched woman here   135
    Against our substitute! Let this friar be found.
Lucio. But yesternight, my lord, she and that friar,
    I saw them at the prison: a saucy friar,
    A very scurvy fellow.
Friar Peter.   Bless'd be your royal Grace!
    I have stood by, my lord, and I have heard   140
    Your royal ear abus'd. First hath this woman
    Most wrongfully accus'd your substitute,
    Who is as free from touch or soil with her
    As she from one ungot.
Duke.   We did believe no less.
    Know you that Friar Lodowick that she speaks of?   145
Friar Peter. I know him for a man divine and holy,
    Nor scurvy, not a temporary meddler,
    As he's reported by this gentleman;
    And, on my trust, a man that never yet
    Did, as he vouches, misreport your Grace.   150
Lucio. My lord, most villainously; believe it.
Friar Peter. Well, he in time may come to clear himself;
    But at this instant he is sick, my lord:
    Of a strange fever. Upon his mere request,
    Being come to knowledge that there was complaint   155
    Intended 'gainst Lord Angelo, came I hither,
    To speak, as from his mouth, what he doth know
    Is true and false; and what he with his oath
    And all probation will make up full clear

---

134. This' a] *F* (this 'a); this a *F4;* This is a *Rowe;* this's a *Camb.*   153. lord:] *F;*
Lord, *Rowe.*

133. *swing'd*] thrashed. The irony of this appears in Lucio's own later predicament; confirming Whetstone's '*Hoc facias alteri*'.

134. *This' a*] for F 'this 'a'. Shakespeare's own spelling omitted the apostrophe, as in *More, M.S.R.*, Add. II (D), 212: 'nay this a sound fellowe'.
belike] 'it would seem' (ironically).

138. *saucy*] (i) impudent, or (ii) lascivious (cf. II. iv. 45).

139. *scurvy*] loathsome. Derived from the condition of this skin disease.

141. *abus'd*] imposed upon.

147. *temporary*] temporal or secular (*O.E.D.* 2, citing this as the first instance).

153. *lord:*] The colon in F brings out the tone of improvised excuse.

154. *mere*] personal (*O.E.D. a.* 2).

159. *probation*] proof.

Whensoever he's convented. First, for this woman,   160
To justify this worthy nobleman
So vulgarly and personally accus'd,
Her shall you hear disproved to her eyes,
Till she herself confess it.

Duke.   Good friar, let's hear it.
Do you not smile at this, Lord Angelo?   165
O heaven, the vanity of wretched fools!
Give us some seats.—Come, cousin Angelo,
In this I'll be impartial: be you judge
Of your own cause.

Enter MARIANA [*veiled*].

Is this the witness, friar?
First, let her show her face, and after, speak.   170
Mariana. Pardon, my lord; I will not show my face
Until my husband bid me.
Duke.   What, are you married?
Mariana. No, my lord.
Duke. Are you a maid?
Mariana. No, my lord.   175
Duke. A widow, then?
Mariana. Neither, my lord.

164. hear it.] *F;* hear it. *Officers bear off Isabella; and Mariana comes forward. Capell; Isabella is taken to one side guarded; and Mariana comes forward | Ridley; Exit Isabella guarded. Alexander.*   168. I'll be impartial] *F;* I will be partial *Theobald.*
169. S.D.] *Alexander; Enter Mariana. F (after* friar*); Isabella is carried off, guarded. Enter Mariana veil'd. Theobald (after* friar*); Mariana stands forth. N.C.S.*   170. her face] *F2;* your face *F.*   173–9.] *as F;* No ... lord. *Duke.* Are ... *Mari.* No ... lord. | *Duke.* A ... *Mari.* Neither ... lord. *Duke* ... you | ... wife? | *Steevens '93, conj. Capell.*

160. *convented*] summoned.
161. *justify*] vindicate. Cf. *Wint.*, I. i. 10, *2H6*, II. iii. 16.
162. *vulgarly*] publicly.
167. *Give ... seats*] The re-grouping on the stage allows time for Mariana to make her entry. Cf. Isabella's and Peter's entry during lines 14–19.
168. *impartial*] 'surely this Duke had odd notions of impartiality' (Theobald, emending to 'partial'). But 'impartial' here means 'taking no part

in the action' (Schmidt). Cf. *Ven* 748: 'Whereat the impartial gazer late did wonder'.
168–9. *be ... cause*] a free hand for Angelo to exact his revenge. Cf. *Tw.N.*, v. i. 366–7, where Malvolio is told: 'Thou shalt be both the plaintiff and the judge / Of thine own cause'.
170. *her face*] F has 'your face': a literal error perhaps due to a confusion of *h* and *y* in the contraction 'h^r'.

Duke. Why, you are nothing then: neither maid,
    widow, nor wife!
Lucio. My lord, she may be a punk; for many of them   180
    are neither maid, widow nor wife.
Duke. Silence that fellow! I would he had some cause
    to prattle for himself.
Lucio. Well, my lord.
Mariana. My lord, I do confess I ne'er was married;   185
    And I confess besides, I am no maid.
    I have known my husband; yet my husband
    Knows not that ever he knew me.
Lucio. He was drunk then, my lord; it can be no better.
Duke. For the benefit of silence, would thou wert so too.   190
Lucio. Well, my lord.
Duke. This is no witness for Lord Angelo.
Mariana. Now I come to't, my lord.
    She that accuses him of fornication
    In self-same manner doth accuse my husband,   195
    And charges him, my lord, with such a time
    When I'll depose I had him in mine arms
    With all th'effect of love.
Ang. Charges she moe than me?
Mariana.   Not that I know.
Duke. No? You say your husband.   200
Mariana. Why just, my lord, and that is Angelo,
    Who thinks he knows that he ne'er knew my body,
    But knows, he thinks, that he knows Isabel's.
Ang. This is a strange abuse. Let's see thy face.

178–9. Why, you are . . . wife!] *Bald;* Why you are . . . Wife? *F;* Why are you
. . . Wife? *F2;* Why, . . . wife. *Alexander.*   187–8.] *as F;* I . . . not / . . . me. /
Capell; I've known . . . not / . . . me. *Pope.*

178–9. *neither . . . wife!*] so Cassandra, in *1 Prom.*, IV. iii: 'I monster now,
no mayde nor wife, haue stoupte to
Promos lust'. The phrase was traditional (Tilley M 26, citing Ray: 'She is
neither wife, widow, nor maid; A
whore'). F's question-mark after 'wife'
signified an exclamation.
    180. *punk*] prostitute.

186–8. *I am . . . knew me*] See Intro.,
p. liv. *known, knew*: had sexual relations with. A biblical usage, from
Hebrew.
    190. *For the benefit of*] For the sake of.
    198. *th'effect of*] Cf. III. i. 24 and note.
    202–3.] For the word-play on
'know', cf. lines 187–8 and 212–15.
    204. *abuse*] deception.

Mariana. [*unveiling.*] My husband bids me; now I will
    unmask.   205
    This is that face, thou cruel Angelo,
    Which once thou swor'st was worth the looking on:
    This is the hand which, with a vow'd contract,
    Was fast belock'd in thine: this is the body
    That took away the match from Isabel   210
    And did supply thee at thy garden-house,
    In her imagin'd person.
Duke.   Know you this woman?
Lucio. Carnally, she says.
Duke.   Sirrah, no more!
Lucio. Enough, my lord.
Angelo. My lord, I must confess I know this woman;   215
    And five years since, there was some speech of marriage
    Betwixt myself and her; which was broke off,
    Partly for that her promised proportions
    Came short of composition; but in chief
    For that her reputation was disvalu'd   220
    In levity: since which time of five years
    I never spake with her, saw her, nor heard from her,
    Upon my faith and honour.
Mariana.   Noble Prince,
    As there comes light from heaven, and words from
        breath,
    As there is sense in truth, and truth in virtue,   225
    I am affianc'd this man's wife, as strongly
    As words could make up vows. And, my good lord,

205. S.D.] *Rowe.*   218. promised] *Rowe;* promis'd *F.*

205. *unmask*] unveil.

208–9. *the hand . . . thine*] referring to
the 'handfasting' ceremony of spousals.
Cf. III. i. 213 ff., IV. i. 72, and see
Intro., pp. liii–lv.

210. *match*] assignation.

211. *supply*] satisfy.

218–21. *Partly . . . levity*] Both
reasons would provide valid grounds
in law for dissolving a *de futuro* contract.

218. *proportions*] marriage portion.
Cf. 'proportion', *Per.*, IV. ii. 29.

219. *Came short of composition*] proved
insufficient for the agreement to be
confirmed. Cf. III. i. 215–18, and 'composition', I. ii. 2.

220. *disvalu'd*] depreciated.

221. *In levity*] In consideration, in
the case of, (moral) levity. For this use
of 'in', see Abbott §162.

225. *sense*] meaning, significance.

But Tuesday night last gone, in's garden house,
He knew me as a wife. As this is true
Let me in safety raise me from my knees,   230
Or else for ever be confixed here,
A marble monument.

Ang.   I did but smile till now:
Now, good my lord, give me the scope of justice.
My patience here is touch'd: I do perceive
These poor informal women are no more   235
But instruments of some more mightier member
That sets them on. Let me have way, my lord,
To find this practice out.

Duke.   Ay, with my heart;
And punish them to your height of pleasure.
Thou foolish friar, and thou pernicious woman,   240
Compact with her that's gone: think'st thou thy oaths,
Though they would swear down each particular saint,
Were testimonies against his worth and credit,
That's seal'd in approbation? You, Lord Escalus,
Sit with my cousin; lend him your kind pains   245
To find out this abuse, whence 'tis deriv'd.
There is another friar that set them on;
Let him be sent for.

Friar Peter. Would he were here, my lord; for he indeed
Hath set the women on to this complaint.   250
Your Provost knows the place where he abides,
And he may fetch him.

---

239. to] *F;* unto *Pope;* even to *Capell.*

231. *confixed*] firmly fixed. A Shakespearean formation.

232. *A marble monument*] Cf. 'a
marble to her tears', III. i. 229 and note.

233. *scope*] Cf. I. ii. 119.

234. *touch'd*] injured, hurt. Cf.
Troil., II. ii. 194.

235. *informal*] mentally disordered.
Only here in this sense (*O.E.D.* 2).
Similarly, Shakespeare uses 'formal'
for mentally normal in *Err.,* v. i. 105.

236. *member*] participant in a cause:
cf. *2H4,* IV. i. 171. Angelo claims to
suspect a political intrigue. Cf. lines
109–10.

239.] metrically defective: perhaps
'to' should be 'unto' or 'up to'.

241. *Compact*] joined in compact,
leagued.

242. *particular*] 'one among many
considered in itself' (Schmidt; *O.E.D.*
6).

244. *seal'd in approbation*] ratified by
proof.

251–2 and S.D.] Capell and later
editors take Friar Peter's remarks to
signify that the Provost is sent out;
supply an exit for him; and to make
this possible, give him an entry at the
beginning of Act v. But there is no

Duke.   Go, do it instantly.

                                              [*Exit an Attendant.*]
And you, my noble and well-warranted cousin,
Whom it concerns to hear this matter forth,
Do with your injuries as seems you best   255
In any chastisement. I for a while will leave you;
But stir not you till you have well determin'd
Upon these slanderers.

Esc.   My lord, we'll do it throughly.

                                              Exit [DUKE].
Signior Lucio, did not you say you knew that Friar
Lodowick to be a dishonest person?   260

Lucio. Cucullus non facit monachum: honest in nothing but
   in his clothes, and one that hath spoke most vil-
   lainous speeches of the Duke.

Esc. We shall entreat you to abide here till he come, and
   enforce them against him. We shall find this friar a   265
   notable fellow.

Lucio. As any in Vienna, on my word!

Esc. Call that same Isabel here once again; I would
   speak with her.   [*Exit an Attendant.*]
   Pray you, my lord, give me leave to question; you   270
   shall see how I'll handle her.

Lucio. Not better than he, by her own report.

Esc. Say you?

252. S.D.] *this edn; not in F; Exit Provost. Capell.*   256–8.] *as Cambridge (after
Spedding);* In . . . while / . . . haue / . . . Slanderers. / *F;* In . . . while / . . . well /
Determined . . . Slanderers / *Theobald.*   258. S.D.] *Capell. Exit. F (after* Slander-
ers).   269. S.D.] *Dyce; not in F; (To an Attendant.) Capell (after* again).

reason to have the Provost present
before line 276: the Duke's command
is to some unspecified attendant. Cf.
I. i. 15 and 269 *infra.*

   253. *well-warranted*] approved by
good warrant.

   255. *with*] in the matter of.

   256–8.] There is mislineation in F,
perhaps due to rearrangement of the
verse lines on the assumption that
Escalus' 'My Lord . . . throughly' is
part of the prose which follows. The
words should complete the Duke's
final half-line. *determin'd*: reached a

judicial decision. *throughly*: thoroughly.

   260. *dishonest*] dishonourable.

   261. *Cucullus . . . monachum*] 'A holie
Hood, makes not a Frier deuoute',
I Prom., III. vi. The proverb was
familiar (Tilley H 586); cf. *H8,* III.
i. 23. Shakespeare also gives the Latin
form in *Tw.N.,* I. v. 61–2. There is
irony, for the hood of the Duke's disguise does not make him the friar
Lucio takes him to be.

   265. *enforce*] put forward strongly,
emphasize.

   269. S.D.] Cf. S.D. to line 252.

Lucio. Marry, sir, I think if you handled her privately
    she would sooner confess; perchance publicly she'll   275
    be ashamed.

    Enter [at several doors] PROVOST *[with]* DUKE *[in disguise and*
    hooded], [and] ISABELLA *[under guard].*

Esc. I will go darkly to work with her.
Lucio. That's the way; for women are light at midnight.
Esc. Come on, mistress, here's a gentlewoman denies all
    that you have said.   280
Lucio. My lord, here comes the rascal I spoke of, here
    with the Provost.
Esc. In very good time. Speak not you to him till we call
    upon you.
Lucio. Mum.   285
Esc. Come, sir: did you set these women on to slander
    Lord Angelo? They have confess'd you did.
Duke. 'Tis false.
Esc. How! Know you where you are?
Duke. Respect to your great place; and let the devil   290
    Be sometime honour'd for his burning throne.
    Where is the Duke? 'Tis he should hear me speak.
Esc. The Duke's in us; and we will hear you speak;
    Look you speak justly.
Duke. Boldly, at least. But O, poor souls,   295
    Come you to seek the lamb here of the fox?

---

276. S.D.] *this edn; Enter Duke, Prouost, Isabella. F ; Enter Duke in the Friar's habit, and
Prouost; Isabella is brought in. Theobald; Re-enter Officers with Isabella. Dyce (after 278,
and) Re-enter Duke disguised as a Friar, and Provost. Dyce (after 285).*   279–80.] *as
F4;* Come . . . gentlewoman, / . . . said. / F *(verse).*   281–2.] *as Pope;* My . . . of, /
. . . *Prouost.* / F *(verse).*   296. fox?] *F2;* Fox; *F.*

277. *darkly*] secretly. Cf. III. ii. 171.
Lucio quibbles on 'darkly' for 'in the
dark' (cf. 'darkling').

278. *women . . . midnight*] apparently
a stock adage, though not in Tilley;
e.g. Marston, *Antonio and Mellida*, II;
Middleton, *A Mad World My Masters*,
v. i; Webster, *Appius and Virginia*, III.
i. 12. Cf. Guilpin, *Skialetheia*, Epigram
61: 'light wenches care not for the
light'.

283. *In . . . time*] 'a good thing, too'.
Cf. III. i. 178, and *Lr*, II. iv. 253.

290–1. *let the devil . . . throne*] 'all
authority calls for some respect'. The
phrase sounds proverbial, but has not
been traced.

293. *The Duke's in us*] Cf. I. i. 64 ff.

296. *to seek . . . fox*] proverbial, from
Erasmus' adage '*ovem lupo commisisti*'
(Tilley W 602). Shakespeare substi-
tutes 'fox' for the usual 'wolf'

Good-night to your redress! Is the Duke gone?
Then is your cause gone too. The Duke's unjust
Thus to retort your manifest appeal,
And put your trial in the villain's mouth   300
Which here you come to accuse.
Lucio. This is the rascal: this is he I spoke of.
Esc. Why, thou unreverend and unhallow'd friar!
Is't not enough thou hast suborn'd these women
To accuse this worthy man, but in foul mouth,   305
And in the witness of his proper ear,
To call him villain? And then to glance from him
To th'Duke himself, to tax him with injustice?
Take him hence! To th'rack with him!—We'll touse you
Joint by joint, but we will know his purpose.   310
What! Unjust!
Duke.   Be not so hot: the Duke
Dare no more stretch this finger of mine than he
Dare rack his own. His subject am I not,
Nor here provincial. My business in this state
Made me a looker-on here in Vienna,   315
Where I have seen corruption boil and bubble
Till it o'errun the stew: laws for all faults,

307–11.] *as* F; To ... villain; / ... himself, / ... hence; / ... joint, / ... unjust? /
Johnson.   309. touse you] F; touse him *Yale, conj. Malone.*   310. his] F; this
Hanmer; your *Johnson.*   311. Unjust!] *Hart;* vniust? F.   311–12. Duke /
Dare no] *as Hanmer;* Duke dare / No F.

(cf. *2H6*, III. i. 253, *Gent.*, IV. iv. 99).
299. *retort*] reject (*O.E.D. v.* 7a, citing only this instance).

manifest] obvious (in its justice).

300. *put . . . mouth*] 'give the villain the right to pronounce judgment'.

305–6. *in foul . . . ear*] 'with foul words and in his own hearing'.

307. *glance*] combines (i) pass quickly over a subject in discussion and (ii) glide (like an arrow or bullet) from one object to another. Cf. *Shr.*, v. ii. 61–2: 'as the jest did glance away from me, / 'Tis ten to one it maim'd you two outright'.

309. *touse*] pull roughly about, rack. Only here in Shakespeare.

310. *his*] Hanmer and others emended 'his' to 'this' or 'your', to keep the pronouns consistent. But Boswell notes that elsewhere in his speech Escalus alternately addresses the Duke and the bystanders (e.g. 'him'—'you' in line 309).

311–13. *the Duke . . . his own*] dramatic double-entendre.

314. *provincial*] subject to the jurisdiction of the local ecclesiastical province.

316–17. *boil and bubble . . . stew*] Cf. 'Like a hell-broth boil and bubble', *Mac.*, IV. i. 19. There is also word-play on 'stew' = brothel; corruption has spread to all quarters of the city, Perhaps echoing Bilson's coronation sermon: see Intro., p. lxv.

But faults so countenanc'd that the strong statutes
Stand like the forfeits in a barber's shop,
As much in mock as mark.

Esc.   Slander to th'state!   320
Away with him to prison!

Ang. What can you vouch against him, Signior Lucio?
Is this the man that you did tell us of?

Lucio. 'Tis he, my lord.—Come hither, goodman Baldpate, do you know me?   325

Duke. I remember you, sir, by the sound of your voice;
I met you at the prison, in the absence of the Duke.

Lucio. O, did you so? And do you remember what you
said of the Duke?

Duke. Most notedly, sir.   330

Lucio. Do you so, sir? And was the Duke a fleshmonger,
a fool, and a coward, as you then reported him to
be?

Duke. You must, sir, change persons with me, ere you
make that my report. You indeed spoke so of him,   335
and much more, much worse.

Lucio. O, thou damnable fellow! Did not I pluck thee by
the nose for thy speeches?

Duke. I protest, I love the Duke as I love myself.

Ang. Hark how the villain would close now, after his   340
treasonable abuses!

Esc. Such a fellow is not to be talked withal. Away with

---

340. close] *F;* glose *Singer 2 (sc.* gloze).

319–20. *like . . . mark*] It was customary for barber-surgeons to hang up
jocular lists of graded penalties (blood-
letting, extraction of teeth, etc.) for
bad manners on their customers' part;
thereby alluding to their parallel occupation as surgeons. Steevens and Hen-
ley mentioned having seen such lists.
Hart, after rejecting this explanation
in his edition, recanted in *N. & Q.*
(July 1908, p. 64), citing from *Plaine
Percevall* (1842 reprint, p. 19): 'Speake
a blooddy word in a Barbors shop, you
make a forfet'.

324–5. *goodman Baldpate*] 'goodman'
was a prefix, often ironical, for persons

below the rank of gentleman. 'Baldpate' alludes to the Duke's supposed
tonsure as friar (cf. line 350).

326. *I remember . . . voice*] The Duke is
heavily hooded and cannot see or be
seen clearly. The remark serves to
avoid overstraining the disguise convention in a scene of quick changes (cf.
lines 350–1).

331. *fleshmonger*] fornicator. Cf.
'fishmonger', *Ham.*, II. ii. 174.

337–8. *pluck . . . nose*] Cf. III. i. 108.

340. *close*] come to terms (*O.E.D. v.*
14: the first instance given of this use).

342. *withal*] For 'with', as preposi-
tion ending a sentence. (Abbott §196.)

him to prison! Where is the Provost? Away with
him to prison! Lay bolts enough upon him: let him
speak no more. Away with those giglets too, and   345
with the other confederate companion!

> [*The Provost lays hands on the Duke.*]

Duke. Stay, sir, stay a while.

Ang. What, resists he? Help him, Lucio.

Lucio. Come, sir! Come, sir! Come, sir! Foh, sir! Why,
you bald-pated, lying rascal!—You must be hood-   350
ed, must you? Show your knave's visage, with a
pox to you! Show your sheep-biting face, and be
hanged an hour! Will't not off?

> [*Pulls off the friar's hood and discovers the Duke.*]

Duke. Thou art the first knave that e'er mad'st a duke.
First, Provost, let me bail these gentle three.   355
[*to Lucio.*] Sneak not away, sir, for the friar and you
Must have a word anon.—Lay hold on him.

Lucio. [*aside.*] This may prove worse than hanging.

Duke. [*to Escalus.*] What you have spoke, I pardon: sit you
down.   360
We'll borrow place of him. [*To Angelo.*] Sir, by your
leave.

---

346. S.D.] *Johnson; not in F.*   353. S.D.] *Rowe; not in F.*   354. e'er] *F* (ere),
Rowe (e're *F4*).   356. S.D.] *Johnson.*   359. S.D.] *Rowe.*   360. S.D.]
Hanmer; thrusts Angelo from his Chair, and seats himself in it. Capell.

---

345. *giglets*] 'connected with gig . . .
a giddy girl, a wanton . . . The radical
sense of gig is "anything which whirls
or is whirled"' (Partridge, *Shakespeare's Bawdy*).

352. *sheep-biting face*] 'sheep-biter',
i.e. a dog or wolf that attacked sheep,
was a common epithet for a dangerous
rogue, especially a sanctimonious one.
See J. R. Brown's note on 'a wolf who
hang'd for human slaughter', *Mer.V.*,
IV. i. 134, in the 'Arden' edition. Hart,
N. & Q. (July 1908, p. 64), points out
that 'sheep-biter' was used by the Mar-
tinists for Puritans, who attacked the
'fold', and cites Sir Toby's description
of Malvolio, *Tw.N.*, II. v. 6. Cf.
Vaughan, *The Golden-groue*: 'The inward Atheist . . . slyly carieth the

countenaunce of a sheepe, and yet is
. . . a sheep-biter . . . notwithstanding
hauing Scripture in his mouth' (sig.
C3ᵛ).

352–3. *be hanged an hour*] Dogs were
hanged for sheep-biting: the specified
period of an hour, however, implies
the identical execution of human
malefactors. See Intro., p. xv.

353. *Will't not off?*] i.e. the hood.

354. *mad'st a Duke*] invested with a
ducal title (only to be done by one of
superior rank).

355. *bail*] the 'security' given being
the Duke's own authority.

these gentle three] Isabella, Mariana,
and Friar Peter.

361. *We'll . . . him*] The Duke takes
Angelo's seat, employing the regal 'we'.

Hast thou or word, or wit, or impudence,
That yet can do thee office? If thou hast,
Rely upon it till my tale be heard,
And hold no longer out.
Ang.   O my dread lord,
    I should be guiltier than my guiltiness   365
    To think I can be undiscernible,
    When I perceive your Grace, like power divine,
    Hath looked upon my passes. Then, good prince,
    No longer session hold upon my shame,
    But let my trial be mine own confession.   370
    Immediate sentence, then, and sequent death
    Is all the grace I beg.
Duke.   Come hither, Mariana.—
    Say: wast thou e'er contracted to this woman?
Ang. I was, my lord.
Duke. Go, take her hence, and marry her instantly.   375
    Do you the office, friar; which consummate,
    Return him here again. Go with him, Provost.
        Exeunt [ANGELO, MARIANA, *Friar* PETER *and* PROVOST].
Esc. My lord, I am more amaz'd at his dishonour
    Than at the strangeness of it.
Duke.   Come hither, Isabel.
    Your friar is now your prince. As I was then,   380
    Advertising and holy to your business,
    Not changing heart with habit, I am still

---

373. e'er] *F* (ere), *Pope;* ever *F2.*   377. S.D.] *Pope; Exit. F; Exeunt Angelo,*
Mariana and Provost. Rowe.

368. *passes*] *O.E.D.* (*sb.*[2] 2) doubt-
fully suggests 'course of action'.
Schmidt cites *Sonn.*, ciii. 11: 'to no
other pass my verses tend', but this is
rather 'event, issue'. H. D. Sykes (in
Lucas) compared Webster, *Duchess of
Malfi*, v. iii. 42: 'Make scrutiny
throughout the passes / Of your owne
life'; but the word, emended to 'passages' in Qto D, is possibly a misprint.
Harold Jenkins privately suggests
'proceedings', 'doings', 'course of
action', as close to the primary meaning of 'pass' as 'step'. Cf. *Tw.N.*, v. i.
364: 'This practice hath most shrewd-
ly pass'd [i.e. acted] upon thee'.

373. *e'er*] F 'ere' was a common
variant spelling.

375.] In all the sources, the marriage ordered was between the counterparts to Angelo and Isabella; the
latter subsequently pleaded for her
new husband's life.

381. *Advertising*] a late instance of
the intransitive use (*O.E.D.* 1):
'taking note, giving heed'. The stress
is on the second syllable.

holy] 'wholly' gives better sense:
this may be an error, influenced by
'friar 'in the previous line.

Attorney'd at your service.

Isab.   O, give me pardon,
That I, your vassal, have employ'd and pain'd
Your unknown sovereignty.

Duke.   You are pardon'd, Isabel.
And now, dear maid, be you as free to us.   386
Your brother's death, I know, sits at your heart:
And you may marvel why I obscur'd myself,
Labouring to save his life, and would not rather
Make rash remonstrance of my hidden power   390
Than let him so be lost. O most kind maid,
It was the swift celerity of his death,
Which I did think with slower foot came on,
That brain'd my purpose. But peace be with him.
That life is better life, past fearing death,   395
Than that which lives to fear. Make it your comfort,
So happy is your brother.

Isab.   I do, my lord.

Enter ANGELO, MARIANA, *Friar* PETER, [*and*] PROVOST.

Duke. For this new-married man approaching here,
Whose salt imagination yet hath wrong'd
Your well defended honour, you must pardon   400

390. remonstrance] *F;* demonstrance *Staunton, conj. Malone (Var. 1821).*   397.
S.D. *Mariana*] *Rowe; Maria F.*

383. *Attorney'd*] taking the part of an
agent. A Shakespearean formation; cf.
Wint., I. i. 30: 'attorneyed with interchange of gifts'.

386–97. *And now ... brother*] This
prolix speech is deliberately made unconvincing. It is meant to satisfy
Isabella on the stage, without misleading an audience already in the
Duke's secret.

386. *free*] generous.

390. *remonstrance*] manifestation
(*O.E.D.* 2). Only here in Shakespeare.

392–4. *the swift celerity ... brain'd my
purpose*] perhaps a diffuse recurrence
of the image in *Sonn.*, lxv. 11, 'Or what
strong hand can hold his swift foot
back?' echoing 'swift' and 'foot' at the

cost of tautology in 'swift celerity' (cf.
'quick celerity', IV. ii. 108). The figurative use of 'brain'd' ('dashed the
brains out') is apparently unique.
Both figures may be unconscious
recollections of 'Death and The Fool':
cf. III. i. 11–13 and note.

395–6. *That life ... fear*] 'The life to
come, beyond fear of death, is better
than earthly life that is coupled with
this fear'. Alluding to Claudio's fears,
III. i. 117 ff.

397. *So happy*] 'happy in this way'.
The Duke's conclusion accords with
the attitude expressed in III. i. 5–41, in
contrast to Claudio's dread of punishment after death.

399. *salt*] salacious, lecherous.

For Mariana's sake: but as he adjudg'd your brother,
Being criminal in double violation
Of sacred chastity and of promise-breach
Thereon dependent, for your brother's life,
The very mercy of the law cries out   405
Most audible, even from his proper tongue:
'An Angelo for Claudio; death for death.
Haste still pays haste, and leisure answers leisure;
Like doth quit like, and Measure still for Measure.'
Then, Angelo, thy fault's thus manifested,   410
Which, though thou would'st deny, denies thee vantage.
We do condemn thee to the very block
Where Claudio stoop'd to death, and with like haste.
Away with him.
Mariana.   O my most gracious lord,
I hope you will not mock me with a husband.   415
Duke. It is your husband mock'd you with a husband.
Consenting to the safeguard of your honour,
I thought your marriage fit: else imputation,
For that he knew you, might reproach your life,
And choke your good to come. For his possessions,   420
Although by confiscation they are ours,
We do instate and widow you with all,

---

409. Measure . . . Measure] *F* (*Measure . . . Measure*), *Johnson.*   421. confiscation]
F2; confutation *F.*   422. with all] *F;* withall *F2;* withal *F4.*

401. *adjudg'd*] condemned.

402–4. *in double violation . . . life*]
Angelo has violated (i) the principle of
'sacred chastity', (ii) his promise to
spare Claudio's life in return for the
first violation. But the rhetorical
structure conceals an anomalous
double negative, 'violation . . . of
promise-breach'.

405. *The very mercy of the law*] Cf.
Angelo's words, II. ii. 101 ff. and note.

407–9.] These parallelisms may be
compared with 'Blood cries for bloode,
and murder murder craves' (Marston,
Antonio's Revenge, III. iii); 'Measure for
measure, and lost bloud for bloud' (*A
Warning For Fair Women* (1599), sig.
G1 (Malone)). The structure is ulti-

mately derived from the Bible; see
Gen., ix. 6, Lev., xxiv. 17–20, and cf.
note on *Measure for Measure* as the
play's title. Whetstone, *1 Prom.,* II. vii,
has 'Blood axeth blood' (Tilley B458).

411.] 'Though you were to deny
this, your fault is such as denies you the
right to claim superior treatment'.
Angelo has already confessed his
'fault' (lines 364–72): what he might
still hypothetically 'deny' is that he
deserves the identical treatment de-
creed for Claudio.

418. *imputation*] 'the imputation that
he knew you', personified.

422. *widow*] endow with a widow's
right (*O.E.D.* 3, but giving this as the
only instance).

    To buy you a better husband.

Mariana.   O my dear lord,

    I crave no other, nor no better man.

Duke. Never crave him; we are definitive.   425

Mariana. Gentle my liege—

Duke.   You do but lose your labour.

    Away with him to death. [*to Lucio.*] Now, sir, to you.

Mariana. [*kneeling.*] O my good lord—sweet Isabel, take my
        part;

    Lend me your knees, and all my life to come

    I'll lend you all my life to do you service.   430

Duke. Against all sense you do importune her.

    Should she kneel down in mercy of this fact,

    Her brother's ghost his paved bed would break,

    And take her hence in horror.

Mariana.   Isabel!

    Sweet Isabel, do yet but kneel by me;   435

    Hold up your hands, say nothing: I'll speak all.

    They say best men are moulded out of faults,

    And, for the most, become much more the better

    For being a little bad. So may my husband.

    O Isabel! Will you not lend a knee?   440

Duke. He dies for Claudio's death.

Isab. [*kneeling.*]   Most bounteous sir:

    Look, if it please you, on this man condemn'd

    As if my brother liv'd. I partly think

    A due sincerity govern'd his deeds

    Till he did look on me. Since it is so,   445

    Let him not die. My brother had but justice,

---

427. S.D.] *Johnson.*   428. S.D.] *this edn; Johnson (after* liege *426).*   430. lend
you] *F;* lend you, *Rowe.*   441. S.D. *Rowe.*

431. *sense*] 'reason and natural affection . . . a single word that implies
both' (Johnson). One of the many connotations of 'sense' in this play.

432. *in mercy of*] in the exercise of
mercy for.

fact] Cf. iv. ii. 134.

441–52.] In *Epitia* the heroine remains obdurate until the Captain
reveals that her brother is not dead;

whereupon she asks the Emperor to
show mercy: '*Prego, da poi che la crudel
cagione / È leuata per cui dannato à morte /
Egli era, in uita per clemenza uostra / Hora
rimanga*' (v. vii, Bullough, 442). Whetstone's Cassandra pleads for Promos
out of wifely concern for her new husband (*2 Prom.*, v. v). But even when she
thought her brother dead, she had
wished the king to save Promos (v. iii).

In that he did the thing for which he died:
For Angelo,
His act did not o'ertake his bad intent,
And must be buried but as an intent   450
That perish'd by the way. Thoughts are no subjects;
Intents, but merely thoughts.
Mariana.   Merely, my lord.
Duke. Your suit's unprofitable. Stand up, I say.
    I have bethought me of another fault.
    Provost, how came it Claudio was beheaded   455
    At an unusual hour?
Prov.   It was commanded so.
Duke. Had you a special warrant for the deed?
Prov. No, my good lord: it was by private message.
Duke. For which I do discharge you of your office.
    Give up your keys.
Prov.   Pardon me, noble lord;   460
    I thought it was a fault, but knew it not;
    Yet did repent me after more advice.
    For testimony whereof, one in the prison
    That should by private order else have died,
    I have reserv'd alive.
Duke.   What's he?
Prov.   His name is Barnardine.
Duke. I would thou hadst done so by Claudio.   466
    Go, fetch him hither, let me look upon him.
                                    [*Exit* PROVOST.]
Esc. I am sorry one so learned and so wise
    As you, Lord Angelo, have still appear'd,
    Should slip so grossly, both in the heat of blood   470
    And lack of temper'd judgement afterward.
Ang. I am sorry that such sorrow I procure,
    And so deep sticks it in my penitent heart

448-9. Angelo, / His] *as Johnson; Angelo,* his *F.*   467. S.D.] *Hanmer; not in F.*

451. *Thoughts are no subjects*] 'subjects' may mean 'whatever owes alle-
giance or is amenable to law'; alter-
natively, in the personal sense,
'thoughts are not like the Duke's
subjects, who are liable to be punished or controlled' (Durham).
    462. *advice*] deliberation.
    471. *temper'd judgement*] judgement
restored to the right 'temper', or temperament, after the excess of passion
implied in 'heat of blood', line 470.

That I crave death more willingly than mercy;
'Tis my deserving, and I do entreat it.   475

Enter PROVOST *with* BARNARDINE, CLAUDIO, [*muffled, and*]
JULIET.

Duke. Which is that Barnardine?
Prov.   This, my lord.
Duke. There was a friar told me of this man.
    Sirrah, thou art said to have a stubborn soul
    That apprehends no further than this world,
    And squar'st thy life according. Thou'rt condemn'd;
    But, for those earthly faults, I quit them all,   481
    And pray thee take this mercy to provide
    For better times to come. Friar, advise him;
    I leave him to your hand.—What muffl'd fellow's that?
Prov. This is another prisoner that I sav'd,   485
    Who should have died when Claudio lost his head;
    As like almost to Claudio as himself. [*Unmuffles Claudio.*]
Duke [*to Isab.*] If he be like your brother, for his sake
    Is he pardon'd; and for your lovely sake
    Give me your hand and say you will be mine.   490
    He is my brother too: but fitter time for that.
    By this Lord Angelo perceives he's safe;
    Methinks I see a quickening in his eye.
    Well, Angelo, your evil quits you well.
    Look that you love your wife: her worth, worth yours.
    I find an apt remission in myself.   496

---

475. S.D.] *Dyce (subst.); Enter Barnardine and Prouost, Claudio, Iulietta. F; Re-enter Provost, with Barnardine; Claudio behind, and Julietta, both muffled up. Capell.*
487. S.D.] *Malone; unmuffles, and discovers him. Capell; not in F.*   488. S.D.] *Theobald 2.*   489. Is he] *F; He's Hanmer; Is he too Capell.*   495. worth, worth] *F; worth works Hanmer; worth work Hudson, conj. Walker (Dyce); worth's worth Keightley, conj. Heath (Dyce).*

---

480. *squar'st*] 'square': to regulate, direct (*O.E.D. v.* 4).

481. *quit*] absolve, acquit.

484. *muffl'd*] blindfold (*O.E.D.* 2). Cf. *Rom.*, I. i. 176: 'love, whose view is muffled still'. Claudio, led in with his eyes covered, does not see Isabella until line 487. It is possible to take his appearance as an emblem of 'blind love'.

493. *quickening*] return of life.

494. *quits*] requites.

495. *Look . . . wife*] In 2 *Prom.*, v. v, the king says to Promos: 'Be louing to good *Cassandra*, thy Wife'. *her worth, worth yours*: '(look that) to her worth yours be equal'.

496. *remission*] 'pardon for political or legal offence'. Here, an inclina-

And yet here's one in place I cannot pardon.
[*To Lucio.*] You, sirrah, that knew me for a fool, a
    coward,
One all of luxury, an ass, a madman:
Wherein have I so deserv'd of you   500
That you extol me thus?

Lucio. Faith, my lord, I spoke it but according to the
    trick: if you will hang me for it, you may: but I had
    rather it would please you I might be whipped.

Duke. Whipp'd first, sir, and hang'd after.   505
Proclaim it, Provost, round about the city,
If any woman wrong'd by this lewd fellow,
—As I have heard him swear himself there's one
Whom he begot with child—let her appear,
And he shall marry her. The nuptial finish'd,   510
Let him be whipp'd and hang'd.

Lucio. I beseech your Highness, do not marry me to a
    whore. Your Highness said even now, I made you
    a duke; good my lord, do not recompense me in
    making me a cuckold.   515

Duke. Upon mine honour, thou shalt marry her.
Thy slanders I forgive, and therewithal
Remit thy other forfeits.—Take him to prison,
And see our pleasure herein executed.

Lucio. Marrying a punk, my lord, is pressing to death,   520
Whipping, and hanging.

---

498. S.D.] *Rowe.*   500. so deserv'd] *F;* deserved so *Pope;* so well deserv'd
Collier 2; so undeserv'd *conj. Walker (Dyce);* sir, so deserv'd *conj. Cartwright
(Camb.).*   507. If ... woman] *F;* If ... woman's *Hanmer;* Is ... woman *Camb.*
520–1. Marrying ... hanging] *as F;* prose, *Pope.*

---

tion to exercise such pardon (*O.E.D.*
2d).

497. *in place*] at hand.

499. *luxury*] lasciviousness.

500.] Emendations have been proposed on the assumption that the line
is unmetrical. But the speech stress
makes a trochaic pentameter.

503. *trick*] custom. Cf. 'the trick of
it', III. ii. 50.

507–9. *If any woman wrong'd ... let her
appear*] All edd. except Durham's

either change 'If' to 'Is', or 'woman' to
'woman's'. But the sentence may be
elliptical, due the intrusion of the
parenthesis 'As . . . child'. Such con-
structions were common.

513. *even now*] at line 354.

517. *therewithal*] therewith; cf. 'withal', line 342.

520. *pressing to death*] the penalty of
peine forte et dure, imposed on those who
refused to give incriminating evidence.
Hart lists several contemporary allu-

Duke.   Slandering a prince deserves it.
She, Claudio, that you wrong'd, look you restore.
Joy to you, Mariana; love her, Angelo:
I have confess'd her, and I know her virtue.
Thanks, good friend Escalus, for thy much goodness;
There's more behind that is more gratulate.   526
Thanks, Provost, for thy care and secrecy;
We shall employ thee in a worthier place.
Forgive him, Angelo, that brought you home
The head of Ragozine for Claudio's: 530
Th'offence pardons itself. Dear Isabel,
I have a motion much imports your good;
Whereto if you'll a willing ear incline,
What's mine is yours, and what is yours is mine.
So bring us to our palace, where we'll show   535
What's yet behind that's meet you all should know.
                                        [*Exeunt omnes.*]

---

521. it] *F;* it. *Exeunt Officers with Lucio. Dyce.*   536. that's] *F2* (thats), *F3;* that *F.*
S.D.] *Rowe; not in F; They pass through the gates | N.C.S.*

sions. Shakespeare uses the term figuratively in *Ado,* III. i. 76, *R2,* III. iv. 72,
and *Troil.,* III. ii. 217–18.

521. *Slandering . . . it*] See Intro.,
p. xlix. Dyce and most later editors
provide an exit for Lucio after this
line. It distracts attention from the
Duke's speech and sacrifices a welcome touch of humour in the final
exit. See note to S.D. line 536.

523.] Cf. line 495.

526.] For Escalus there will follow a
more tangible reward than thanks

alone. *gratulate*: gratifying (Schmidt).
A Shakespearean nonce-usage.

528. *place*] office, position.

532. *motion*] proposal.

536. *behind*] to follow (cf. line 526).
S.D. *Exeunt omnes*] Not marked in F.
A processional exit in pairs seems to be
indicated by the dialogue; led by the
Duke and Isabella; then Claudio and
Juliet; Angelo and Mariana; Escalus
and the Provost; Friar Peter and Barnardine; with Lucio under guard
bringing up the rear.

APPENDIX I

1. LETTER OF JOSEPH MACARIUS TO GEORGE PERNEZITH

From the Nádasdy family archive, *Magyar Országos Levéltar*, Budapest

1 . . . Nova quaedam historiola sed memorabilis apud nos talis circumfertur, duo quidam cives oppidi non procul a mediolano siti, dum forte vehemens inter eos contentio oborta esset, eo furoris ac insaniae progrediuntur ut alter alterum enchiridio transverberaret. Capitur mox flagranti crimine cruentatus homicida, et in publicum carcerem coniicitur: sed eius uxor iuven-

2 cula, forma venustissima, / magno erga maritum amore affecta conatur modis omnibus reum

generalem (ut vocant) comitem Hispanum liberare et redimere, accedit iudicem supplex, et procidens ad pedes eius, orat ne extremo mortis supplicio illum a se animae dimidium suae separet, sed alia poena seu potius mulcta puniat superstitem, promittitque ingentem pecuniae summam, quae ex omnibus bonis ipsorum divenditis conflari possit. Qui cum absque uxori esset, captus pulchritudine mulieris, nullum aliud redemptionis pretium postulat, quam eius copiam. Tum vero haec et pudicitiae periculo et amore mariti anxie sollicitatur, petit brevissimi temporis deliberationem quam impetrat. Interim clam ad cognatos et affines suffugit, pravam iudicis iniqui cupiditatem aperit, consilium quid faciat in tam dubia re implorans. Verum isti concedendum suadent, et eius animum, qui non voluntarie peccet, inviolatum fore, ratiocinantur. Quare et fratrum consensu et caeco (ut sic dicam)

mariti amore impulsa obsequium iudici praestat,
sed vultu maesto ac lachrymantibus oculis, ut
violentus adulter ingratam [ac *deleted*] et extor-
tam sentiret voluptatem. Ecce autem sequenti die
insperato maritum decollari videt, Exacerbata

3   itaque iterum adit iudicem, / et miserabili querela
expostulat, quia et charissimo marito [et *deleted*]
spoliata, et pudicitiae dampno irrecuperabili esset
affecta honestae etiam famae dispendium fecisset.

Don ferdinandum
de Gonzaga
fratrem ducis
Mantuae

Sed surdo narrari fabulam et petulanter se deri-
deri ut vidit, ad cesareae maiestatis in ea provincia
locum tenentem, mediolanum proficiscitur, de
illata sibi iniuria et dolo acerrime conqueritur
perque superos omnes ad ulciscendum obtesta-
tur. Ceterum iste [bonus vir *deleted*] supremus ca-
pitaneus indicto mulieri silentio, post duos men-
ses, quasi nihil de illius morte sciret, iudicem cum
aliquot civibus ad convivium invitat, viduam
etiam ipso inscio advocari iubet. Post ibi ac potus
satietatem in secretum conclave causa colloquii
ducit iudicem, ibique flagitium commissum illi
exprobrat, [et si eam in uxorem legittimam
ducere nollet, *deleted*] obstupefacto mox ait, Tu
hoc inhoneste et cum magna contumelia fecisti,
volo ergo, ut numeres statim illi in dotem 3000
ducatos. Quibus in praesenti adductis, iterum ait,
restituas iam illam, cum ita constupraveris, pris-
tinae dignitati, hoc pacto scilicet, ut eam in legittimam uxorem ducas. Mox itaque advocato
sacerdote, fides compromissa est, et annuli (ut
solet) commutati. Postremo ad mulierem inquit,
Tibi quidem optima mulier dos et prior honesta
fama restituta est, Tibi (ad comitem Hispanum
iudicem generalem conversus ait) caput tuum
pro capite illius cras auferetur, quod et factum
est. Iustum iudicium fuisse, ipsa caesarea mai-

4   estas censuit. / Varie narratur iam haec historia,
si scirem domino magnifico nondum esse audi-
tum, melius et certius iterum describerem.
Quaeso Eandem dominationem tuam ut quam
primum suam mittat nobis responsoriam. Eandem christus salvator conservet. Datum Viennae

1 octobris, anno domini 1547. Eiusdem Dominationis vestrae
servator ac filius obsequentissimus
Ioseph Macarius.

[*superscription:*]
Egregio domino Georgio
Pernezith, domino
patrono et tanquam
patri suo semper
observans

[Scribal contractions expanded]

[A new but quite memorable story is going the rounds amongst us.
There were two citizens of a town situated not far from Milan, who,
in the course of a heated quarrel that had sprung up between them,
went so far in their mad fury that one stabbed the other through
with his dagger. The bloody killer was taken in the very act and
thrown into the town gaol; but his young wife, a woman of great
beauty, so loved her guilty husband that she tried all means to
redeem him and have him freed. She went as a humble petitioner
to the judge [general, the Spanish Count, as they call him, *added in
margin*] and, falling at his feet, begged him not to part from her by
the extreme penalty of death this man who was the half of her very
soul, but asked that some other punishment be imposed that would
allow him to survive; or, better still, that a fine be levied; promising
a huge sum of money to be raised by selling off all their goods. The
judge, who had no wife of his own, was so taken with the woman's
beauty that he required no other price of ransom than to have
access to her. Greatly distressed and torn between the threat to her
chastity and her love of her husband, she asked for a very brief
respite in which to consider what she should do. Meanwhile she
made off in secret to her own and her husband's kinsmen, dis-
closed to them the vicious desire of that wicked judge, and en-
treated them for advice on how to act in so doubtful a case. They
recommended her to submit to him, declaring that in their opinion
the spirit of a person who was made to sin against her own will
remained inviolate. So, urged on by the brothers' consent and her
own blind love of her husband (as I would say), she complied with
the judge's demand; but with woeful looks and weeping eyes, that
the adulterer by violence might be well aware that his pleasure was
unwelcome and compelled. But mark you, on the next day, against
her expectation, she saw her husband beheaded. In great bitterness she went again to the judge, and with pitiful lament sought to
know why she had been deprived of her most dear husband, as well
as made to suffer the irrecoverable loss of her chastity and the

squandering of her good name. But when she saw that her story was told to deaf ears and that she was being wantonly mocked, she set out for Milan, to the representative of his imperial majesty in that province, [Don Ferdinando de Gonzaga, brother of the Duke of Mantua *added in margin*] and complained with the utmost bitterness of the injury and grief inflicted upon her, beseeching him by all the powers above to avenge her wrongs.

This [good man *deleted*] supreme governor enjoined the woman to keep silence; then, two months later, just as if he knew nothing about the husband's death, he invited the judge with a number of citizens to a party, and had the widow summoned, all unknown to his guest. When the judge was there and had drunk his fill, he led him into a private room, saying he wished to have a talk with him, and there accused him of the crime he had committed [and if he refused to take her as his lawful wife *deleted*]. Then he said to the astonished man: 'You have behaved dishonourably and to your great disgrace: I desire you, therefore, immediately to pay out three thousand ducats to that woman for a dowry.' When the ducats had been brought into his presence, he said again: 'You will now restore the woman you have so debauched to her former dignity by entering into this contract, that you take her as your lawful wife.' Accordingly a priest was summoned, marriage vows were made, and rings exchanged (as is the custom). Finally he said: 'You, who are so excellent a woman, have now had your dowry and your former good name restored; as for you,' (he said, turning to the Spanish Count) 'your head will be taken off tomorrow in return for the other man's head.' This was done, too, and his imperial majesty himself held it to be a just judgment.

This story is now being told in various versions; if I knew that my noble lord had not yet heard it, I would tell it again better and more specifically. I beg your lordship to send us his reply as soon as possible. May Christ the Saviour preserve him. Given at Vienna, 1st October 1547.

Your lordship's most obedient servant and son,

Joseph Macarius.

To his excellent lord Georgius Pernezith,
his master, patron and virtual father,
ever respectful.]

[Editor's translation]

2. EXTRACT FROM THE *HECATOMMITHI* OF GIRALDI CINTHIO

DÉCADA 8, NOVELLA V (1565)

. . . When everyone was silent, Fulvia said: Those lords who are appointed by God to govern the world should punish ingratitude, whenever it comes to their notice, no less severely than they punish murders, adulteries and thefts; which, although they are grave sins, deserve perhaps a lighter penalty than ingratitude. To this end Maximian the Great, a most worthy Emperor, sought at the same time to punish the ingratitude and injustice of one of his ministers; and the effects would have followed, but for the lady towards whom this ingrate had shown himself so unjust, who in her goodness and courtesy freed him from the penalty, as I am about to show you.

While this great Lord, who was a rare example of courtesy, magnanimity and singular justice, ruled most happily over the Roman Empire, he sent out his ministers to govern the states which flourished under his sway. And amongst others, he sent to govern Innsbruck one of his intimate friends, a man very dear to him, named Iuriste. Before dispatching him there, he said: 'Iuriste, the good opinion I have conceived of you while you have been in my service leads me to send you as Governor of so noble a city as Innsbruck; concerning the rule of which I could command you many things. However, I would compress all these into one; which is, that you keep justice inviolate, even if you have to give judgment against me in person, who am your lord. And I would inform you that I can forgive you all other failings, due either to ignorance or to negligence (though I would have you guard against them so far as possible), but any deed which is contrary to justice shall receive no pardon from me. If perhaps you do not feel obliged to show yourself the kind of person I want—since no man is fit for all things —do not take this post, but remain here at court, where I hold you dear, in your accustomed duties; rather than lead me, when you are governor of that city, to act against you in such a way as, to my great displeasure, I should have to do for the sake of justice, should you not maintain justice.' And with this he was silent.

Iuriste was more glad of the office to which the Emperor had called him than sound in the knowledge of himself. He thanked his master for this token of affection, and said that he was himself of a mind to uphold justice, but that now he would uphold it the more earnestly; the Emperor's words being as it were a torch which had fired him to greater efforts, and made him desirous of thus far succeeding in this post, that his majesty would have some cause to praise him. The Emperor was pleased with Iuriste's speech and said to him: 'I shall indeed have some cause to praise you, if your deeds are as good as your words.' And, having had the letters patent, already prepared, given to him, he sent him to that place.

Iuriste commenced to rule the city with a great deal of prudence and diligence, showing much care and concern that the balance of justice be kept true, not only in judgements but also in the allocation of offices, the rewarding of virtue and the punishment of vice. Thus for a long time ruling with such temperance, he gained great favour with his master, and earned the good will of the whole people. He might have acquired a happier reputation than others, if he had continued to govern in this manner.

It happened that a young man of that territory named Vico had forced a young woman, a citizen of Innsbruck, concerning which a complaint was made to Iuriste. He at once had the young man apprehended, who confessed that he had done violence to a virgin, and condemned him according to the law of that city, which required that such as he should be punished by beheading, even if they were prepared to marry those whom they had wronged.

This young man had a sister, a virgin who was not more than eighteen years old. Besides being adorned with extraordinary beauty, she had a most pleasant manner of speaking, and an amiable presence and bearing, accompanied by such honesty as befits a lady. This maiden, Epitia by name, perceiving that her brother was sentenced to death, was overcome with intense grief, and resolved to go and see if she could either have her brother set free or at least obtain some mitigation of his sentence; for she had been, together with her brother, under the tutelage of an old man whom her father had kept in the house to teach them both their philosophy, albeit that the brother had made no good use of his learning. She went to Iuriste, and begged him to have compassion on her brother, on account of his youth—for he was not more than sixteen years old—which made him deserving of pardon, as well as his inexperience, and the goading of love in his side; pointing out to him that, in the opinion of the wisest, adultery committed through the force of love and not in order to wrong a lady's husband deserved a less severe punishment than if it were done in order to cause injury; and that the same was to be said in the case of her brother, who had done the deed for which he had been condemned not injuriously, but spurred on by ardent love; that by way of amend for the error he had committed, he would take the young lady as his wife, and do whatever else the law required; that even if the analogy did not hold good for those who had forced virgins, yet might Iuriste, prudent as he was, mitigate such severity, which was more offensive than just; for he was in that place, through the authority he had received from the Emperor, the living law; and such authority, she would like to believe, had been given to him by his majesty that he might show himself in equity more inclined to be clement than harsh. If such temperance was to be used in any case, surely it should be in cases of love, especially when the honour of the forced lady remained safe, as it would in the case of her brother, who was most willing to take her as his wife. And she believed that the law had been framed in this fashion rather to induce terror than to be strictly observed; for it seemed to her sheer cruelty to seek to punish with death a crime which could be atoned for honourably and in holy fashion by giving satisfaction to the injured party. So, with the addition of other arguments besides these, she sought to induce Iuriste to pardon that young man.

Iuriste, whose ears were no less delighted by Epitia's eloquence than his eyes had been by her great beauty, longed to see and hear her. He urged her to repeat what she had said; and the lady, taking this as a good augury, spoke again, with even greater persuasiveness than formerly. Overcome now by Epitia's graceful speech and rare beauty, and stricken by lustful desire, his thoughts turned to committing against her the same wrong for which he had condemned Vico to death. He said to her, 'Epitia, your pleas on your brother's behalf have helped so far that whereas he should have been beheaded tomorrow, the execution will be deferred until I have considered the arguments you have put to me, and if I find that they allow me to set your brother free, I shall give him to you all the more willingly because it would grieve me to have seen him led to his death through the rigour of the hard law which required it.'

Epitia took good hope from these words, and thanked him much for having shown himself so courteous, and told him that she would be eternally obliged to him; thinking to find him no less courteous in the matter of freeing her brother than he had been in prolonging the limit of his life. And, she added, she firmly hoped that, if he considered what had been said, he would thoroughly content her by setting her brother free. Iuriste replied that he would consider it, and if he could possibly do so without offending justice, he would not fail to grant her desire.

Full of hope, Epitia departed, and went to her brother. She told him all she had done for him with Iuriste, and how much hope she had conceived from this first interview. In his extreme plight the report was most welcome to Vico, who begged her not to desist from pleading for his freedom; and his sister promised to aid him in every way. Iuriste, who had impressed the form of this lady upon his mind, turned all his thoughts, lascivious as they were, towards seeking the enjoyment of Epitia, and waited for her to come again and speak to him. After three days she returned, and asked him courteously what he had decided. As soon as he saw her, Iuriste felt inflamed with desire. He said: 'You are welcome, fair maid. I have not failed to look diligently into what your pleading might do on your brother's behalf, and have also sought further arguments that you might remain content. But I find that everything points conclusively to his death: for it is a universal law that when one sins not out of ignorance but ignoring the consequences, nothing can excuse his sin. He must know, as all men know everywhere, how to live well, and anyone who sins in disregard of this deserves neither pardon nor compassion. Your brother was in this position, and must have known quite well that according to the law he who forces a virgin deserves death; he ought to die, and I cannot with reason exercise pity. Yet in truth, in as much as it concerns you, whom I greatly desire to please, should you out of your great love for your brother allow me to take pleasure from you, I am disposed to grant him his life and change the death sentence into a less severe penalty.'

At these words Epitia's face burnt with shame, and she said: 'My brother's life is very dear to me, but dearer still is my honour; and I would rather seek to save him by losing my life than by losing my honour. But abandon this dishonest thought: if by any other mode of pleasing you I can regain my brother, I shall most willingly adopt it.' 'There is no other way', said Iuriste, 'than that which I have said. Nor should you show yourself so fastidious, for it may easily happen that as a result of our first union you may become my wife.' 'I refuse,' said Epitia, 'to put my honour in danger.' 'And why in danger?' said Iuriste. 'Perhaps you will become what you now think cannot possibly be. Think well upon it, and I shall expect your answer tomorrow at latest.' 'I give you my answer now,' said she. 'Unless you take me as your wife, since you wish my brother's freedom to depend on that, you may throw your words to the wind.' Iuriste replied that she should think it over and return him an answer after considering carefully who he was, what power he held in that territory, and how useful he could be, not only to her, but to anyone who was her friend, since in that place both right and might were in his keeping.

Epitia departed from him greatly disturbed, and went to her brother, to whom she told all that had passed between her and Iuriste, saying in conclusion that she would not lose her honour to save his life. And in tears she begged him to be ready to bear patiently that fate, which either the necessity of fate, or his own ill fortune, had brought upon him. At this point Vico fell to weeping and to begging his sister not to consent to his death, since she could, in the manner Iuriste proposed, have him set free. 'Do you wish, Epitia,' said he, 'to see me with the axe upon my neck, and with my head cut off, I who was born of the same womb as you and begotten of the same father, who grew up with you to my present age and was educated together with you? Would you see me thrown to the ground by the executioner? Ah, sister, may the pleadings of nature, of blood, of the affection there has always been between us, have such power over you as to make you free me, as you can, from so shameful and miserable an end. I have erred, I confess; and you, sister, who can atone for my error, do not be miserly in your aid. Iuriste has said that he may marry you, and why should you not think that this must be so? You are very beautiful, adorned with all the graces that nature can bestow upon a noble lady; you are indeed noble and attractive; you have marvellous eloquence; so that not only all these qualities together, but each one separately, would endear you, not to Iuriste only, but to the emperor of the world. You have no reason to doubt that Iuriste will take you as his wife, and thus your honour, and at the same time your brother's life, will be saved.'

Vico wept as he spoke these words, and Epitia wept with him; embracing him and not leaving him before she was constrained— overcome as she was by her brother's laments—to promise that she would give herself to Iuriste, should he agree to save Vico's life and support her hope of marriage.

So the matter was concluded between them. Next day the maiden went to Iuriste and told him that the hope he had given her of taking her as his wife after their first union, and her desire to free her brother, not only from the death sentence, but from any other penalty which he might have incurred for the fault he had committed, had induced her to put herself wholly at his disposal. That, for one reason or the other, she was content to submit to him; but above all else she wished him to promise the safety and liberty of her brother. Iuriste thought himself the happiest of men, in that he was to enjoy so fair and delightful a maiden, and told her that he confirmed the hope he had previously given her, and would, on the morning after he had been with her, restore to her her brother freed from prison. So, having dined together, Iuriste and Epitia went afterwards to bed, and this villain took his full pleasure of the lady. But before going to lie down with that virgin, instead of freeing Vico, he gave orders for his head to be struck off at once. The lady, longing to see her brother free, looked only for the hour when day would break, and it seemed to her that never had the sun taken so long to bring in the day as on that night. When morning came, Epitia separated herself from Iuriste's embrace, and asked him in gentle fashion to be so good as to fulfil the hope of marriage that he had given her, and meanwhile send her back her brother free. He answered that her stay with him had been most enjoyable, that he was pleased that she entertained the hope he had given her, and would send her brother back to her at home. Whereupon he called for the gaoler, and said to him: 'Go to the prison, bring out this lady's brother, and conduct him to her house.'

Epitia, hearing this, went home most joyfully, expecting to see her brother free. The gaoler had had the body of Vico laid upon a bier, with the head placed at the feet and the body covered with a black pall; going before it himself, he had it carried to Epitia. Entering the house, he called the young lady, and said: 'Here is your brother, whom my lord the governor sends you freed from prison.' So saying, he caused the bier to be uncovered, and presented her brother in such fashion as you have heard.

I do not think that tongue could tell, or human mind conceive, the nature and degree of Epitia's woe and affliction, as she saw her brother presented to her dead in this fashion, whom she was so joyfully expecting to see alive and quit of all penalties. I am sure you will believe, ladies, that this poor lady's grief was such as to surpass all other forms of distress. Yet she shut it up within her heart; and whereas any other lady would have fallen to weeping and cries of lament, she, whom philosophy had taught how the human soul should endure any kind of fortune, bore herself calmly. To the gaoler she said, 'You will tell your lord and mine that I accept my brother in the manner in which he is pleased to send him to me; and that, although he has not wished to fulfil my desire, I remain content that he has fulfilled his own, that I might make his will mine; with the thought that what he has done he must have done justly. So I commend myself to him, offering myself as ever ready to do his pleasure.'

The gaoler reported to Iuriste what Epitia had said, telling him that she had shown no sign of discomfiture at so dreadful a sight.

Iuriste was pleased with himself on hearing this, and thought of how he had the young lady as much in his power as if she had been his wife and he had given her back Vico alive.

As for Epitia, once the gaoler had gone, she wept torrents over her dead brother and made long and pitiful lament, cursing Iuriste's cruelty and her own simplicity at having given herself to him before she had gained freedom for her brother. Then, having shed many a tear, she caused Vico's body to receive burial. With-drawing afterwards all alone to her room, and prompted by just anger, she began to say to herself: 'Will you, Epitia, suffer it that this scoundrel should rob you of your honour by promising to give you back your brother free and alive, and should then present him to you dead in so pitiful a state? Will you suffer it that he should be able to boast of practising upon your simplicity two such decep-tions, without you yourself giving him the punishment he de-serves?' Kindling herself to vengeance with these words, she said: 'My simplicity has opened the way for this sinner to consummate his dishonest desire. I resolve that his lust shall give me the means of taking my revenge; and though vengeance will not give me back my brother alive, it will at least remove my vexation.' In such per-turbation of mind she came to this decision. Expecting that Iuriste would again send for her to demand that she lie with him, she intended to go, carrying a knife in concealment, and at the first opportunity to stab him, sleeping or awake. If she saw her chance, she would cut off his head, carry it to her brother's grave, and make it a sacrifice to his shade. But on maturer thought she saw that even if she succeeded in killing the deceiver, it might well be supposed that she, as a woman dishonoured and roused therefore to any evil deed, had done this in anger and scorn rather than because he had been faithless. Accordingly, bearing in mind the great justice of the Emperor, who was then at Villaco, she determined to go and find him, and complain to his majesty of Iuriste's ingratitude and the injustice done to her; for she was firmly of the opinion that that best and most just of emperors would cause a most suitable punishment to be inflicted on the villain for his injustice and ingratitude.

So, dressed in mourning, she set out alone and in secret on the journey. She came to Maximian, asked for an audience with him, and obtained it; she threw herself at his feet, and matching her sad voice to her woeful attire, said: 'Most holy Emperor, I have been driven to appear before your majesty by the savage ingratitude and unbelievable injustice with which I have been treated by Iuriste, your imperial majesty's governor in Innsbruck; hoping that your justice will so operate that no other wretch will ever suffer such infinite grief as has come to me from Iuriste through the wrong he has done me, so great that no greater has ever been heard of, and no proud man will do as he has done, who has miserably assassin-ated me (if I am permitted to use that word in your majesty's pre-sence) ; so that, though he suffer heavily, his punishment would not match the cruel and unheard-of shame done to me by this evil man, who has given me cause to know at one and the same time that he is most unjust and ungrateful.' Whereupon, with copious weeping and sighs, she told his majesty how Iuriste, offering hope that he would marry her and free her brother, had taken her virginity and afterwards sent her brother back dead upon a bier with his head at his feet. At this point she gave so great a cry, and her eyes were so filled with tears, that the Emperor and the lords who were about his majesty were deeply moved and stood, for pity, like the mere shadows of men.

But although Maximian was full of compassion, yet having given one ear to Epitia (whom at the end of her speech he made rise to her feet), he kept the other ear for Iuriste. Sending the lady away to take some repose, he at once had Iuriste summoned, charging both the messenger and all those who had been present, as much as they desired to be in his good grace, to speak no word to Iuriste concerning this matter.

Iuriste, who would have thought anything possible rather than that Epitia should go to the Emperor, came cheerfully enough. Arrived in his majesty's presence, he made reverence to him, and asked what were his wishes. 'You will know immediately,' said Maximian, and straight away he had Epitia summoned. Seeing her there, Iuriste, who knew how gravely he had offended, was conscience-stricken and so overcome that his vital spirits aban-doned him and he began to tremble all over. When Maximian saw this, he was sure that the lady had told nothing less than the truth, and turning towards him, speaking with the severity that fitted so terrible a case, said: 'I have heard this young lady's com-plaint against you.' Then he called on Epitia to declare the nature of her complaint; and she recounted the whole story in due order, at the end lamenting as formerly and asking for justice at the hands of the Emperor.

Hearing the accusation, Iuriste sought to appease the lady with flattery, and said: 'I would never have believed that you, whom I love so dearly, would have come to accuse me in this way before his majesty.' But Maximian would not allow Iuriste to escape with soothing words. 'This is no time,' said he, 'to play the lover. Answer the accusation she has made against you.' Thereupon

Iuriste abandoned a form of defence which could only harm him. 'It is true,' he said, 'that I have had this woman's brother beheaded, for having raped and forced a virgin; and this I did to keep the sanctity of the law inviolate and to preserve justice, as your majesty so strongly recommended me to do: for he could not have remained alive without my doing offence to that principle.'

Here spoke Epitia: 'If you believed that this was what justice required, why did you promise to restore him to me alive, and why, under that promise, and with the hope of marriage that you gave me, did you deprive me of my virginity? If my brother deserved for his one sin to bear the full severity of justice, you for your two sins are more deserving of his punishment.' Iuriste stood as if he were mute. Then the Emperor said, 'Does it seem to you, Iuriste, that this deed served justice, or that it injured the lady so gravely as almost to kill her? Have you not treated this gentle young lady with worse ingratitude than any criminal? But you will not get off lightly, believe me.'

Now Iuriste began to plead for mercy, and Epitia, in contrast, to demand justice. Maximian, knowing the innocence of the young lady and the wickedness of Iuriste, thought suddenly of a means by which her honour might be served and justice equally upheld. Having decided what he should do, he required Iuriste to marry Epitia. The lady refused to consent, saying that she could not think that she would ever receive from him anything but crimes and betrayals. But Maximian required her to content herself with what he had resolved.

So the lady was wedded, and Iuriste believed that his troubles were at an end; but it turned out otherwise. While the lady was permitted to retire to a hostelry, Maximian now turned to Iuriste, who remained behind, and said: 'You have committed two crimes, both exceedingly grave: one in having abused that young lady with such deception as may be said to constitute a rape; the other in having killed her brother contrary to the pledge you gave, which no less merited death. While you were bent on violating justice, you might at least have kept your faith to his sister, since your dissolute lust reduced you to promising him to her, rather than, after shaming her, to send him to her dead, as you have done. Now, since I have provided for your first sin by making you marry the forced lady, to make amends for the second I require that your head be taken from you, even as you had her brother's head taken from him.'

How great was Iuriste's woe on hearing the Emperor's sentence can be more readily imagined than fully described. He was handed over to the serjeants of the law for execution next morning, in accordance with the sentence passed. Thenceforward Iuriste was fully prepared to die and expected nothing else but destruction at the hands of the executioner. Meanwhile Epitia, who had been so ardently against him, when she heard of the Emperor's decision, showed her natural kindness. She judged that it was unworthy of her, after the Emperor had required Iuriste to become her husband and she had accepted him as such, to consent to his undergoing death on her account. It seemed to her that such a penalty might be attributed to a lust for revenge and cruelty rather than to a desire for justice. Accordingly, turning all her thoughts to the task of saving the poor wretch, she went to the Emperor, and, obtaining permission to speak, said as follows:

'Most holy Emperor, the injustice and ingratitude with which Iuriste treated me led me to ask your majesty for justice against him. Most just as you are, you suitably provided for the two crimes which he committed: for the one, in robbing my virginity by deceit, by making him take me as his wife; and for the other, in his killing of my brother contrary to the pledge he gave me, by condemning him to death. But just as, before I was his wife, it was desirable that your majesty should condemn him to death, as your majesty has very justly done, now, since you have been pleased to bind me to Iuriste by the sacred bond of marriage, I should, if I consented to his death, deserve the name of a pitiless and cruel lady, with perpetual infamy. Such would be quite contrary to your majesty's intention in seeking my honour as well as justice. But, most holy Emperor, in order that your majesty's good will should achieve its end, and my honour remain unstained, I would beg you, in all humility and reverence, not to require that through your majesty's sentence the sword of justice should miserably cut the knot with which you have been pleased to bind me to Iuriste. Whereas your majesty's sentence has given clear proof of your justice, I earnestly beg you now to show your clemency by giving him back to me alive. It is no less praise, most holy Emperor who holds the government of the world, as your majesty now most worthily holds it, to practise clemency than to practise justice. For whereas justice shows that vices are hated, and gives them their due punishment, clemency makes a ruler most like to the immortal gods. As for me, if I obtain this singular grace through your kindness exercised towards me, who am your majesty's most humble servant, I shall always devoutly pray God to preserve your majesty through long and happy years, that you may long practise your justice and clemency for the good of mortal men and your own honour and immortal glory.' Here Epitia brought her speech to an end.

It seemed wonderful to Maximian that she should cast into oblivion the grave injury she had received of Iuriste, and plead for him so warmly; and he thought that such goodness as he saw in that lady deserved as an act of grace the granting of life to a man who had been condemned by justice to die. So, causing Iuriste to be summoned before him at the very hour when he was waiting to be led to death, he said: 'Guilty man, the goodness of Epitia has so worked upon me, that whereas your crime deserves to be punished with a double death, not with one death only, she has moved me to pardon your life; which life, I would have you know, is from her; and since she agrees to live with you, bound in the bond into which I required you both to enter, I agree that you should live with her. But if I ever perceive that you treat her as less than a most loving and noble wife, I shall give you cause to learn what great displeasure that will cause me.'

With these words the Emperor took Epitia by the hand and gave her to Iuriste. She and Iuriste together gave their thanks to his majesty for the grace and favour granted to them. And Iuriste, bearing in mind how nobly Epitia had behaved towards him, held her ever most dear; so that she lived with him in great happiness for the rest of her life.

Novella VI

It would be hard to say whether the ladies were more pleased with Maximian's justice or his clemency. At first it seemed that they would have been content if the grave outrage done with such ingratitude to the virtuous young lady had been suitably punished. But they thought it no less praiseworthy that, since it had pleased his majesty for her to marry Iuriste, and since the lady whose honour Iuriste had stained had become his wife, he should have so far acceded to her pleading as to turn justice into clemency. Concerning this, the more mature said that clemency is a very worthy companion to the justice of kings, since it tempers penalties, and for that reason we read that it is most fitting for princes: for it induces a certain temperance in their minds, which causes them to be kind towards their subjects. They concluded that Maximian had shown himself, both in his justice and his clemency, truly worthy of empire. 'And so he is indeed,' said Lucrezia. Then, following the agreed order of narration, she began the next story.

[Translated by the Editor from the edition of 1565]

3. EXTRACT FROM *THE HISTORIE OF PROMOS AND CASSANDRA*

by George Whetstone (1578)

THE ARGUMENT OF THE WHOLE HISTORYE

In the Cyttie of *Iulio* (sometimes under the domination of *Coruinus* Kinge of *Hungarie*, and *Boemia*) there was a law, that what man so euer commited Adultery, should lose his head, & the woman offender, should weare some disguised apparrel, during her life, to make her infamouslye noted. This seuere lawe, by the fauour of some mercifull magistrate, became little regarded, vntill the time of Lord *Promos* auctority: who conuicting, a yong Gentleman named *Andrugio* of incontinency, condemned, both him, and his minion to the execution of this statute. *Andrugio* had a very vertuous, and beawtiful Gentlewoman to his Sister, named *Cassandra*: *Cassandra* to enlarge her brothers life, submitted an humble petition to the Lord *Promos*: *Promos* regarding her good behauiours, and fantasyng her great beawtie, was much delighted with the sweete order of her talke: and doyng good, that euill might come thereof: for a time, he repryu'd her brother: but wicked man, tourning his liking vnto vnlawfull lust, he set downe the spoile of her honour, raunsome for her Brothers life: Chaste *Cassandra*, abhorring both him and his sute, by no perswasion would yeald to this raunsome. But in fine, wonne with the importunitye of hir brother (pleading for life:) vpon these conditions, she agreede to *Promos*. First that he should pardon her brother, and after marry her. *Promos* as feareles in promisse, as carelesse in performance, with sollemne vowe sygned her conditions: but worse then any Infydel, his will satisfyed, he performed neither the one nor the other: for to keepe his aucthoritye, vnspotted with fauour, and to preuent *Cassandraes* clamors, he commaunded the Gayler secretly, to present *Cassandra* with her brothers head. The Gayler, with the outcryes of *Andrugio*, abhorryng *Promos* lewdenes, by the prouidence of God, prouided thus for his safety. He presented *Cassandra* with a Felons head newlie executed, who (being mangled, knew it not from her brothers, by the Gayler, who was set at libertie) was so agreeued at this trecherye, that at the pointe to kyl her selfe, she spared that stroke, to be auenged of *Promos*. And deuisyng a way, she concluded, to make her fortunes knowne vnto the kinge. She (executinge this resolution) was so highly fauoured of the King, that forthwith he hasted to do Iustice on *Promos*: whose iudgement was, to marrye

Cassandra, to repaire her crased Honour: which donne, for his hainous offence he should lose his head. This maryage solempnised, *Cassandra* tyed in the greatest bondes of affection to her husband, became an earnest suter for his life: the Kinge (tendringe the generall benefit of the comon weale, before her special ease, although he fauoured her much) would not graunt her sute. *Andrugio* (disguised amonge the company) sorrowing the griefe of his sister, bewrayde his safetye, and craued pardon. The Kinge, to renowne the vertues of *Cassandra*, pardoned both him and *Promos*. The circumstances of this rare Historye, in action lyuelye foloweth.

THE HISTORIE, OF *PROMOS* AND *CASSANDRA*.

Actus I. *Scena*. I.

Promos, Mayor, Shirife, Swordebearer: One with a bunche
of keyes: Phallax, *Promos man*.

You Officers which now in *Iulio* staye,
Know you our leadge, the King of *Hungarie*;
Sent me *Promos*, to ioyne with you in sway:
That styll we may to *Iustice* have an eye.
And now to show, my rule & power at lardge,
Attentiuelie, his Letters Pattents heare:
Phallax, reade out my Soueraines chardge.
   PHAL. As you commaunde, I wyll: giue heedefull eare.
*Phallax readeth the Kinges Letters Patents, which must be fayre written in
parchment, with some great counterfeat zeale.**
   PRO. Loe, here you see what is our Soueraignes wyl,
Loe, heare his wish, that right, not might, beare swaye:
Loe, heare his care, to weede from good the yll,
To scoorge the wights, good Lawes that disobay.
Such zeale he beares, vnto the Common weale,
(How so he byds, the ignoraunt to saue)
As he commaundes, the lewde doo rigor feele.
Such is his wish, such is my wyll to haue:
And such a Iudge, here *Promos* vowes to be.
No wylfull wrong, sharpe punishment shall mysse,
The simple thrall, shalbe iudgde with mercie,
Each shall be doombde, euen as his merite is:
Loue shall not staye, nor hate reuenge procure,
Ne yet shall Coyne, corrupt or foster wrong:
I doo protest, whylste that my charge indure,

* *seal.*

For friende nor foe, to singe a partiall song.
Thus have you heard, howe my Commission goes,
He absent, I present our Soueraigne styll:
It aunsweres then, each one his dutie showes,
To mee, as him, what I commaunde and wyll.

MA. Worthy Deputie, at thy chardge we ioye,
We doe submitte our selues, to worke thy heast:
Receyue the sword of *Iustice* to destroy,
The wicked impes, and to defend the rest.

SHRI. Our Citty keyes take wisht Liftenaunt heare;
We doe committe our safetie to thy head:
Thy wyse foresight, will keepe us voyde of feare,
Yet wyll we be assistant still at neede.

PRO. Both Swoorde and Keies, unto my Princes vse,
I doo receyue and gladlie take my chardge.
It resteth nowe, for to reforme abuse,
We poynt a tyme, of Councell more at lardge,
To treate of which a whyle we wyll depart.

AL SPEAKE. To worke your wyll, we yeelde a wylling hart.
[*Exeunt.*

Actus. I. Scena. 2.

Lamie, a Curtizane, entreth synging.

The Song. Al aflaunt now vaunt it, braue wenche cast away care,
With Layes of Loue chaunt it, for no cost see thou spare:
Sith Nature hath made thee, with bewty most braue,
Sith Fortune doth lade thee, with what thou wouldst haue.
Ere Pleasure doth vade thee, thy selfe set to sale:
All wantons wyll trade thee, and stowpe to thy stale.
All aflaunt, *Vt Supra.*
Yong Ruflers maintaines thee, defends thee and thine,
Old Dottrels retaines thee, thy Beuties so shine:
Though many disdaynes thee, yet none maye thee tuch:
Thus Enuie refraynes thee, thy countenaunce is such.
All aflaunt, *Vt Supra:*
Triumphe fayre *Lamie* now, thy wanton flag aduaunce,
Set foorth thy selfe to brauest show, bost thou of happy chaunce:
Shee speaketh.
Gyrle, accompt thou thy selfe the cheefe, of Lady Pleasures traine,
Thy face is faire, thy forme cōtent, thy Fortunes both doth staine.
Euen as thou wouldst thy house doth stande, thy furniture is gay,

Thy weedes are braue, thy face is fine, & who for this doth paye?
Thou thy selfe? no, the rushing Youthes, yᵗ bathe in wanton blisse,
Yea, olde and doting fooles sometimes, doo helpe to pay for this.
Free cost betweene them both I haue, all this for my behoue,
I am the sterne, yᵗ gides their thoughts, looke what I like, they loue:
Few of them sturre, that I byd staie, if I bid go, they flye:
If I on foe pursue reuenge, *Alarme* a hundred crye.
The brauest I their harts, their handes, their purses holde at wyl,
Ioynde with the credite of the best, to bowlster mee in yll.
But see wher as my trustie man, doth run, what newes brings he?

Actus. I. Scena. 3.

Rosko (Lamias man) *Lamia.*

ROS. Good people, did none of you, my mistresse *Lamia* see?

LA. *Rosko*, what newes, that in such haste you come blowing?

ROS. Mistresse, you must shut vp your shops, & leaue your occupying.

LA. What so they be, foolish knaue, tell mee true?

ROS. Oh, yll, for thirtie? besydes you.

LA. For mee good fellowe, I praye thee why so?

ROS. Be patient Mistresse, and you shall knowe.

LA. Go too, saye on:

ROS. Marrie, right nowe at the Sessions I was,
And thirtie must to *Trussum corde* go.
Among the which (I weepe to showe) alas:

LA. Why, what's the matter man?

ROS. O *Andrugio,*
For louing too kindlie, must loose his heade,
And his sweete hart, must weare the shamefull weedes:
Ordainde for Dames, that fall through fleshly deedes.

LA. Is this offence, in question come againe?
Tell, tell, no more, 'tys tyme this tale were done:
See, see, howe soone, my triumphe turnes to paine.

ROS. Mistresse, you promised to be quiet,
For Gods sake, for your owne sake, be so

LA. Alas poore *Rosko*, our dayntie dyet,
Our brauerie and all we must forgo.

ROS. I am sorie.

LA. Yea, but out alas, sorrowe wyll not serue:
Rosko, thou must needes prouide thee else where,

My gaynes are past, yea, I my selfe might starue:
Saue that, I did prouide for a deare yeare.

ROS. They rewarde fayre (their haruest in the stacke,)
When winter coms, that byd their seruaunts packe.
Alas Mistresse, if you turne mee off now,
Better then a Roge none wyll me allowe.

LA. Thou shalt have a Pasporte,

ROS. Yea, but after what sorte?

LA. Why, that thou wart my man.

ROS. O the Iudge, sylde showes the fauour,
To let one theefe, bayle another:
Tush I know, ere long you so wyll slyp awaye,
As you, for your selfe, must seeke some testimony
Of your good lyfe.

LA. Never feare: honestly
Lamia nowe meanes to lyue, euen tyll she dye.

ROS. As iumpe as Apes, in vewe of Nuttes to daunce,
Kytte wyll to kinde, of custome, or by chaunce:
Well, howe so you stande vpon this holy poynt,
For the thing you knowe, you wyll ieobarde a ioynt.

[Rosko suggests that Lamia should ingratiate herself with Phallax, Promos' officer, 'a paltrie petyfogger' who will protect her.

1. 4. Lamia's maid Dalia calls her home to meet a customer who awaits her. She departs with a song, 'Gallants adue'.]

Actus. 2. Scena. 1.

Cassandra, a mayde.

CASS. Aye, mee, vnhappy wenche, that I must liue the day,
To see *Andrugio* tymeless dye, my brother and my stay.
The onely meane, God wot, that should our house aduaunce,
Who in the hope of his good hap, must dy through wanton
   chance:
O blynde affectes in loue, whose tormentes none can tell,
Yet wantons wyll byde fyre, and frost, yea hassard death, nay
   hell:
To taste thy sowre sweete frutes, digested styll with care,
Fowle fall thee loue, thy lightning ioyes, hath blasted my welfare
Thou fyerst affection fyrst, within my brothers brest.
Thou mad'st *Polina* graūt him (earst) euen what he would
   request:
Thou mad'st him craue, and haue, a proofe of *Venus* meede,

For which foule act he is adiudgd, eare long to lose his heade.
The lawe is so seuere, in scourging fleshly sinne,
As marriage to worke after mends doth seldome fauor win.
A law first made of zeale, but wrested much amis.
Faults should be measured by desart, but all is one in this, *A good*
The lecher fyerd with lust, is punished no more *lawe yll*
Then he which fel through force of loue, whose mariage *executed,*
    salues his sore:
So that poore I dispayre, of my *Andrugios* lyfe,
O would my dayes myght end with his, for to appease my stryfe.

Actus. 2. Scena. 2.

Andrugio in prison, *Cassandra.*

AN. My good Syster *Cassandra?*

CAS. Who calleth *Cassandra?*

AN. Thy wofull brother *Andrugio.*

CAS. *Andrugio,* O dismall day, what greefes doe mee assayle?
Condempned wretch to see thee here, fast fettered now in Iayle,
How haps thy wits were witched so, yᵗ knowing death was meede
Thou wouldest commit (to slay vs both) this vile laciuious deede.

AN. O good *Cassandra,* leaue to check, and chide me thraule
    therfore
If late repentaunce, wrought me helpe I would doe so no more.
But out alas, I wretch, too late, doe sorrowe my amys,
Vnles Lord *Promos* graunt me grace: in vayne is had ywist,
Wherfore sweete sister, whylst in hope, my dāpned lyfe yet were,
Assaulte his hart, in my behalf, with battering tyre of teares.
If thou by sute doest saue my lyfe, it both our ioyes will be,
If not it may suffice thou soughst, to set thy brother free:
Wherefore speede to proroge my dayes, to morrowe else I dye.

CAS. I wyll not fayle to pleade and praye, to purchase the
    mercye,
Farewell a whyle, God graunte mee well to speede.

AN. Syster adew, tyl thy returne, I lyue, twene, hope, and
    dreede.

CAS. O happy tyme, see where Lord *Promos* coms:
Now tongue addresse thy selfe, my minde to wray.
And yet least haste worke waste, I hold it best,
In couert, for some aduauntage, to stay.

Actus. 2. Scena. 3.

Promos with the *Shriefe* and their Officers.

PRO. Tis strange to thinke, what swarms of vnthrifts liue,
Within this towne, by rapine spoyle and theft:
That were it not, that *Iustice* ofte them greeue,
The iust mans goods, by Ruflers should be reft.
At this our Syse, are thirty iudgde to dye,
Whose falles I see, their fellowes smally feare:
So that the way is by seuerity
Such wicked weedes, euen by the rootes to teare:
Wherefore *Shriefe*, execute with speedy pace,
The dampned wightes, to cutte of hope of Grace.
     SHRIEFE. It shalbe done.

Cassandra   CAS. O cruell words they make my hart to bleede,
to hir selfe, Now, now, I must, this dome seeke to reuoke,
Lest grace come short when starued is the steede:
She kneeling   Most mighty Lord, & worthy Iudge, thy iudgemēt sharpe
speakes to   abate,
Promos
Vaile thou thine eares, to heare the plaint, that wretched I relate,
Behold the wofull Syster here, of poore *Andrugio*,
Whom though that lawe awardeth death, yet mercy do him
     show:
Weigh his yong yeares, the force of loue, which forced his amis,
Way, Way, that Mariage, works amends, for what committed is,
He hath defilde no nuptial bed, nor forced rape hath mou'd,
He fel through loue, who never ment, but wiue yᵉ wight he lou'd.
And wātons sure, to keepe in awe, these statutes first were made,
Or none but lustfull leachers, should, with rygrous law be payd.
And yet to adde intent thereto, is farre from my pretence,
I sue with teares, to wyn him grace, that sorrows his offence.
Wherefore herein, renowned Lorde, Iustice with pitie payse:
Which two in equal ballance waide, to heavē your fame will raise.
     PRO. *Cassandra*, leave of thy bootlesse sute, by law he hath
          bene tride,
Lawe founde his faulte, Lawe judgde him death:
     CAS. Yet this maye be replide,
That law a mischiefe oft permits, to keepe due forme of lawe,
That lawe small faultes, with greatest doomes, to keepe men styl
     in awe:
Yet Kings, or such as execute, regall authoritie:
If mends be made, may ouer rule, the force of lawe with mercie.
Here is no wylful murder wrought, which axeth blood againe,

Andrugios faulte may valued be, Mariage wipes out his stayne.

PRO. Faire Dame, I see yᵉ naturall zeale, thou bearest to
   Andrugio,
And for thy sake (not his desart) this fauour wyll I showe:
I wyll reprive him yet a whyle, and on the matter pawse,
To morrowe you shall lycence haue, a fresh to pleade his cause:
Shriefe execute my chardge, but staye *Andrugio,*
Vntill that you in this behalfe, more of my pleasure knowe.

SHRI. I wyll performe your wyll:

CAS. O most worthy Magistrate, my selfe thy thrall I finde,
Euen for this lytle lightning hope, which at thy handes I finde.
Now wyl I go and comfort him, which hangs twixt death & life.
                                                          [*Exit.*

PRO. Happie is the man, that inioyes the loue of such a wife,
I do protest, hir modest wordes, hath wrought in me a maze.
Though she be faire, she is not deackt, with garish shewes for
   gaze,
Hir bewtie lures, hir lookes cut off, fond sutes with chast disdain,
O God I feele a sodaine change, that doth my freedome chayne.
What didst thou say? fie *Promos* fie: of hir auoide the thought,
And so I will, my other cares wyll cure what loue hath wrought.
Come awaye.   [*Exeunt.*

[2. 4. Phallax bids his henchmen, Gripax and Rapax, seek out all
law-breakers and report them to him. He boasts of his power to
extort bribes. 5. Promos tells Phallax of his unrequited love for
Cassandra. Phallax suggests that he should bargain with her over
Andrugio. 6. The Hangman rejoices at acquiring twenty-nine
suits of apparel from Promos' victims. 7. A procession of prisoners
on their way to execution.]

                      Actus. 3. Scena. 1.

                      Promos, alone.

PRO. Do what I can, no reason cooles desire,
The more I striue, my fonde affectes to tame:
The hotter (oh) I feele, a burning fire
Within my breast, vaine thoughts to forge and frame.
O straying effectes, of blinde affected Loue,
From wisdomes pathes, which doth astraye our wittes:
Which makes vs haunt, that which our harmes doth moue,
A sicknesse lyke, the Feuer Etticke fittes:
Which shakes with colde, when we do burne like fire.
Euen so in Loue, we freese, through chilling feare,

When as our hartes, doth frye with hote desire:
What saide I? lyke to Etticke fittes, nothing neare:
In sowrest Loue, some sweete is euer suckt.
The Louer findeth peace, in wrangling strife,
So that if paine, were from his pleasure pluckt,
There were no Heauen, like to the Louers life.
But why stande I to pleade, their ioye or woe?
And rest vnsure, of hir I wish to haue.
I knowe not if *Cassandra* loue, or no?
But yet admytte, she graunt not what I craue,
If I be nyce, to hir brother lyfe to giue:

Might masters right. Hir brothers life, too much wyll make hir yeelde,
A promise then, to let hir brother lyue:
Hath force inough, to make hir flie the fielde,
Thus though sute fayle, necessitie shall wyn,
Of Lordlie rule, the conquering power is such:
But (oh sweete sight) see where she enters in,
Both hope and dreade, at once my harte doth tuch.

Actus. 3. Scena. 2.

Cassandra, Promos.

Cassandra speakes to her selfe. CASS. I see two thralles, sweete seemes a lytle ioye,
For fancies free, *Andrugios* breast hath scope:
But lest detract, doth rayse a new annoye,
I nowe will seeke to turne, to happe his hope.
See, as I wisht, Lord *Promos* is in place,
Nowe in my sute, God graunt I maye finde grace.

Shee knee-ling speaks to Promos. Renowned Lorde, whylst life in me doth last,
In homage bondes, I binde my selfe to thee:
And though I did thy goodnesse latelie taste,
Yet once againe, on knees I mercie seeke:
In his behalfe, that hanges twene death and life,
Who styll is preast, if you the mendes do leeke:
His lawles loue, to make his lawfull wife.

PRO. Faire Dame, I wel haue wayd thy sute, & wish to do
thee good,
But all in vaine, al things conclude, to haue thy brothers blood:
The stricknes of the lawe condempnes, an ignoraunt abuse,
Then wylfull faultes are hardlie helpt, or cloked with excuse:
And what maye be more wylfull, then a Maide to violate.

CAS. The force was smal, when with hir wyl, he wretch ye
conquest gate.

PRO. Lawe euer at the worst, doth conster euyl intent.

CAS. And lawe euen with the worst, awardes them
punishment:

And sith that rigorous lawe adiudgd him to dye,

Your glorie will be much the more, in showing him mercie.

The world will think, how y^t you do, but graūt him grace on
cause,

And where cause is, there mercy should abate the force of lawes.

PRO. *Cassandra* in thy brothers halfe, thou hast sayde what
may be

And for thy sake, it is, if I doe set *Andrugio* free:

Short tale to make, thy beauty hath, surprysed mee with loue,

That maugre wit, I turne my thoughts, as blynd affections
moue.

And quite subdude by *Cupids* might, neede makes mee sue for
grace

To thee *Cassandra*, which doest holde, my freedome in a lace.

Yeelde to my will, and then commaund, euen what thou wilt of
mee,

Thy brothers life, and all that else, may with thy liking gree.

CAS. And may it be, a Iudge himself, the selfe same   Cassādra
fault should use: *to hir self.*

For which he domes, an others death, O crime without excuse.

Renowned Lorde, you vse this speach (I hope) your thrall to
trye,

If otherwise, my brothers life, so deare I will not bye.

PRO. Faire Dame my outward looks, my inward thoughts
bewray,

If you mistrust, to search my harte, would God you had a kaye.

CAS. If that you loue (as so you saye) the force of loue you
know,

Which fealt, in conscience you should, my brother fauour show.

PRO. In doubtfull warre, one prisoner still, doth set another
free.

CAS. What so warre seekes, loue vnto warre, contrary is, you
see.

Hate fostreth warre, loue cannot hate, then maye it couet force?

PRO. The Louer ofte sues to his foe, and findeth no remorse:

Then if he hap to haue a helpe, to wyn his frowarde foe,

Too kinde a foole, I will him holde, that lets such vantage goe.

CAS. Well, to be short, my selfe wyll dye, ere I my honor
staine,

You know my minde, leaue off to tempt, your offers are in vaine.

PRO. Bethink your self, at price inough I purchase sweet your loue,

Andrugios life suffis'd alone, your straungenes to remoue:

The which I graunt, with any wealth that else you wyll require.

Who buyeth loue at such a rate, payes well for his desire.

CAS. No *Promos*, no, honor neuer at value maye be solde,

Honor farre dearer is then life, which passeth price of golde:

PRO. To buie this Iuell at the full, my wife I may thee make:

CAS. For vnsure hope, that peereles pearle, I neuer will forsake:

PRO. These sutes seemes strange at first I see, wher modesty beares sway,   *To himself.*

I therfore wil set down my wyll, & for hir answer staye.

Fayre *Cassandra*, the iuell of my ioye,

Howe so in showe, my tale, seemes straunge to thee:

The same well waide, thou need'st not be so coye,

Yet for to giue thee respite to agree,

I wyll two daies hope styll of thy consent,

Which if thou graunt (to cleare my clowdes of care)

Cloth'd like a Page (suspect for to preuent,)

Vnto my Court, some night, sweet wenche repaire.

Tyl then adue; thou these my words, in works perform'd shalt find.

CAS. Farewel my Lord, but in this sute, you bootles wast your wind:

Cassandra, O most vnhappy, subiect to euerie woe,

What tōgue can tel, what thought cōceiue, what pen thy griefe can show?

Whom to scurge, Nature, heavē & earth, do heapes of thral ordain,

Whose words in waste, whose works are lost, whose wishes are in vain.

That which to others cōfort yeelds, doth cause my heuy cheer,

I meane my beautie breedes my bale, which many hold so deere.

I woulde to God that kinde else where, bestowed had this blase,

My vertues then had wrought regard, my shape now gives yᵉ gaze;

This forme so *Promos* fiers with Loue, as wisdom can not quench,

His hote desire, tyll he lust, in *Venus* seas hath drencht.

[3. 3. Cassandra tells Ganio, Andrugio's boy, that her mission has failed. Ganio bids her go and comfort his master.]

Actus. 3. Scena. 4.

Andrugio *out of prison,* Cassandra *on the stage.*

AN. My *Cassandra* what newes, good sister, showe?
CAS. All thinges conclude thy death *Andrugio*:
Prepare thy selfe, to hope it ware in vaine.
AN. My death, alas what raysed this new disdayne?
CAS. Not Iustice zeale, in wicked *Promos* sure:
AN. Sweete, show the cause, I must this doome indure?
CAS. If thou dost liue I must my honor lose,
Thy raunsome is, to *Promos* fleshly wyll
That I do yelde: then which I rather chose,
With torments sharpe, my selfe he first should kyll:
Thus am I bent, thou seest thy death at hand,
O would my life, would satisfie his yre,
Cassandra then, would cancell soone thy band.

AN. And may it be a Iudge of his account,
Can spot his minde, with lawles loue or lust?
But more, may he doome any fault with death?
When in such faute, he findes himselfe iniust.
Syster, that wise men loue we often see,
And where loue rules, gainst thornes doth reason spurne.
But who so loues, if he reiected be,
His passing loue, to peeuish hate will turne.
Deare sister then, note how my fortune stands,
That *Promos* loue, the like is oft in vse:
And sith he craue, this kindnesse, at your hands,
Thinke this, if you he pleasure do refuse,
I in his rage (poore wretch) shall sing *Peccaui.*
Here are two euyls, the best harde to digest,
But where as things are driuen vnto necessity,
There are we byd, of both euyles choose the least:

CAS. And of these euils, the least, I hold is death,
To shun whose dart, we can no meane deuise,
Yet honor lyues, when death hath done his worst,
Thus fame then lyfe is of farre more emprise:

AN. Nay *Cassandra,* if thou thy selfe submyt,
To saue my life, to *Promos* fleashly wyll,
Iustice wyll say, thou dost no cryme commit:
For in forst faultes is no intent of yll.

CASS. How so th' intent, is construed in offence,
The Prouerbe saies, that tenne good turnes lye dead,
And one yll deede, tenne tymes beyonde pretence,

By enuious tongues, report abrode doth spread
Andrugio so, my fame, shall vallewed bee,
Dispite wyll blase my crime, but not the cause:
And thus although I fayne would set thee free,
Poore wench I feare, the grype of slaunders pawes.

AN. Nay sweete sister more slaunder would infame,
Your spotles lyfe, to reaue your brothers breath:
When you have powre, for to enlarge the same,
Once in your handes, doth lye my lyfe, and death.
Way that I am, the selfe same flesh you are,
Thinke I once gone, our house will goe to wrack:
Knowe forced faultes, for slaunder neede not care:
Looke you for blame, if I quaile through your lack.
Consider well, my great extremitie,
If other wise, this doome I could reuoke:
I would not spare, for any ieberdye,
To free thee wench, from this same heauy yoke.
But ah I see, else, no way saues my life.
And yet his hope, may further thy consent,
He sayde, he maye percase make thee his wife,
And t'is likelie, he can not be content
With one nights ioye: if loue he after seekes,
And I dischargd, if thou aloofe then be,
Before he lose thy selfe, that so he leekes,
No dought but he, to marryage, wyll agree.

CAS. And shall I sticke to stoupe, to *Promos* wyll,
Since my brother inioyeth lyfe thereby?
No, although it doth my credit kyll,
Ere that he should, my selfe would chuse to dye.
My *Andrugio*, take comfort in distresse,
Cassandra is wonne, thy raunsome great to paye,
Such care she hath, thy thraldome to releace:
As she consentes, her honor for to slay.
Farewell, I must, my virgins weedes forsake:
And lyke a page, to *Promos* lewde repayre.   *Exit.*

AN. My good sister, to God I thee betake,
To whome I pray, that comforte change thy care.

[3. 5. Phallax describes Promos' wild infatuation, from which he
hopes to profit.]

Actus. 3. Scena. 6.

Phallax, Gripax, Rapax, a *Bedell,* and one with a browne Byll, bring in *Lamia,* and *Rosko* hir man.

LA. Teare not my clothes my friends, they cost more thē you are aware.

BE. Tush, soon you shal have a blew gown, for these take you no care

RO. If she tooke thy offer poore knaue, thy wife would starue wᵗ cold:

GRI. Well syr, whipping shall keepe you warme.

[Lamia is brought before Phallax, who declares that he will investigate the case himself. He offers to pardon her in return for her favours. Urged by Rosko to 'dally, but do not', she puts on a show of mock-modesty, pretends not to understand him, and finally invites him to her house.]

Actus. 3. Scena. 7.

Cassandra, apparelled like a Page.

CAS. Vnhappy wretche, I blush my selfe to see,
Apparelled thus monstrous to my kinde:
But oh, my weedes, wyll with my fault agree,
When I haue pleasde, lewde *Promos* fleshlie minde.
What shall I doo, go proffer what he sought?
Or on more sute, shall I giue my consent?
The best is sure, since this must needes be wrought:
I go, and showe, neede makes me to his bent.
My fluddes of teares, from true intent which floe,
Maye quench his lust, or ope his mufled eyen,
To see that I deserue to be his wife;
Though now constrainde to be his Concubine.
But so, or no, I must the venter giue,
No daunger feares the wight, prickt foorth by neede:
And thus lyke one more glad to dye, then lyue,
I forewarde set, God graunt me well to speede.   *Exit.*

[4. 1. Dalia comments on Lamia's good fortune in having Phallax as her protector. 2. Soliloquy of Promos: 'no reason cooles desire'. Having enjoyed Cassandra, he decides to break his oath. It was made through 'rage of Loue', but reason bids him look to his credit. He will order the Gaoler to behead Andrugio and take his head to

Cassandra with the words: 'To *Cassandra*, as *Promos* promist thee, /
From prison, loe, he sendes thy Brother free.']

Actus. 4. Scena. 3.

Cassandra.

CAS. Fayne would I wretch conceale, the spoyle of my
    virginity,
But O my gilt doth make mee blush, chast virgins here to see:
I monster now, no mayde nor wife, haue stoupte to *Promos* lust,
The cause was nether sute nor teares, could quench his wātō
    thurst
What cloke wyl scuse my crime? my selfe, my conscience doth
    accuse
And shall *Cassandra* now be termed, in common speeche, a
    stewes?
Shall she, whose vertues bare the bell, be calld a vicious dame?
O cruell death, nay hell to her, that was constraynd to shame:
Alas few wyll giue foorth I synd, to saue my brothers lyfe:
And fayntly I through *Promos* othes, doo hope to be his wife.
For louers feare not how they sweare, to wyn a Lady fayre,
And hauing wonne what they did wish, for othes nor Lady care.
But be he iust or no, I ioy *Andrugio* yet shall lyue.
But ah, I see a sight, that doth my hart asunder ryue.

Actus. 4. Scena. 4.

Gaylar, *with a dead mans head in a charger*. Cassandra.

GAY. This present wilbe Galle I know, to fayre *Cassandra*,
Yet if she knewe as much as I, most swete I dare well say,
In good tyme, see where she doth come, to whome my arrand is:
    CAS. Alas, his hasty pace to me, showes some what is amys.
    GAY. Fayre *Cassandra* my Lord *Promos*, commends him unto
    thee,
To keepe his word, who sayes from prison he sends thy brother
    free.
    CAS. Is my *Andrugio* done to death? fye, fye O faythles trust,
    GAY. Be quiet Lady, law found his fault, thē was his
    iudgemēt iust
    CAS. Wel my good friend, show *Promos* this, since law hath
    don this deed
I thank him yet* he would vouchsafe on me my brothers head,

    * *that*

Loe this is all now geue me leaue to rew his losse alone.

   G AY. I wyll performe your will, and wish you cease your mone.

   CASS. Farewell.

   G AY. I sure had showen what I had done, her teares I pittied so,

But that I wayde, that women syld, do dye with greefe and woe,

And it behoues me to be secret or else my neck verse cun,

Well now to pack my dead man hence, it is hye tyme I run.

   CAS. Is he past sight, then haue I time to wayle my woes alone,

Andrugio, let mee kis thy lippes, yet ere I fall to mone.

O would that I could wast to teares, to wash this bloddy face,

Which fortune farre beyond desart hath followed with disgrace.

O *Promos* falce, and most vnkinde, both spoyld of loue and ruth,

O *Promos* thou dost wound my hart, to thinke on thy vntruth,

Whose plyghted fayth, is tournd to frawd, & words to works vniust

Why doe I lyue vnhappy wench, syth treason quites my trust,

O death deuorse me wretch at once, from this same worldly lyfe,

But why do I not slay my selfe, for to appease thys stryfe?

Perhaps within this wombe of myne, an other *Promos* is:

I so by death shalbe auengd of him in murthring his,

And ere I am assured that, I have reuengd this deede,

Shall I dispatch my lothed life? that hast, weare more then speede.

So *Promos* would triumphe that none his Tiranny should know,

No, no this wicked fact of his so slightly shall not goe:

The king is iust and mercyfull, he doth both heare and see:

See mens desarts, heare their complaynts, to Iudge with equity.

My wofull case with speede, I wyll vnto his grace addresse,

And from the first, vnto the last, the truth I wyll confesse.

So *Promos* thou, by that same lawe shalt lose thy bated breth,

Through breach wherof, thou didst condemne *Andrugio* vnto death

So doing yet, the world will say I broke *Dianas* lawes,

But what of that? no shame is myne, when truth hath showne my cause:

I am resolued, the king shall knowe of *Promos* iniury,

Yet ere I goe, my brothers head, I wyll ingraued see.   *Exit*

Actus. 4. Scena. 5.

Gayler, Andrugio.

GAY. *Andrugio*, as you loue our liues, forthwith post you away.
For Gods sake to no lyuing friend, your safety yet bewraye:
The prouerbe sayth, two may keepe counsell if that one be gone.
  AN. Assure thy selfe, most faithful friend, I wylbe knowne to
    none:
To none alas, I see my scape yeeldes mee but smal releefe,
Cassandra, and *Polina* wyll destroye themselues, with greefe:
Through thought y^t I am dead: they dead, to liue what helpeth
    me?
  GAY. Leaue of these plaints of smal auaile, thank God y^t you
    are free,
For God it was, within my mind, that did your safety moue,
And that same God, no doubt wyl worke for your and their
    behoue:
  AN. Most faithful friend, I hope that God, wyl worke as you
    do saye,
And therfore, to some place vnknowne, I wyl my self conuaye.
Gayler, fare wel: for thy good deede I must remayne thy debter,
In meane whyle yet receyue this gyft, tyll fortune sends a better:
  GAY. God bwy syr, but kepe your mony, your need you do
    not know.
  AN. I pas not now for fortuns threats, yea though hir force
    she show
And therefore styck not to receyue this smale reward in part.
  GAY. I wyll not sure, such proffers leaue, tys time you doe
    depart.
  AN. Since so thou wilt, I wylbe gone adue tyl fortune smile.
                                                        Exit.
  GAY. Syr, fare you wel, I wyl not fayle to pray for you the
    while.
Well, I am glad, that I haue sent him gone,
For by my fayth, I lyu'd in perlous feare:
And yet God wot, to see his bytter mone,
When he should dye, would force a man forbeare,
From harming him, if pitty might beare sway:
But see how God hath wrought for his safety?
A dead mans head, that suffered th'other day,
Makes him thou'ht dead, through out the citie.
Such a iust, good and righteous God is he:
Although awhyle he let the wicked raygne.

Yet he releeues, the wretch in misery,
And in his pryde, he throwes the tyraunt downe.
I vse these wordes, vpon this onely thought,
That *Promos* long his rod cannot escape:
Who hath in thought, a wylfull murder wrought,
Who hath in act performd a wicked rape,
Gods wyll be done, who well *Andrugio* speede,
Once well, I hope to heare of his good lucke,
For God thou knowest my conscience dyd this deede,
And no desire of any worldly muck.   *Exit.*

[4. 6. Dalia returns from market, where she has bought expensive
provisions for Lamia. 7. She meets Grimbal, who offers her a white
pudding in return for a kiss. They sing together. Grimbal will continue his courtship at Lamia's house.

5. 1. Phallax comments on Promos' guilty and conscience-stricken
demeanour. 2. Phallax meets Rosko, who offers him his good
services.]

Actus. 5. Scena. 3.

Polina, (the mayde, that Andrugio lou'd) in a blew gowne.

P O . *Polina* curst, what dame alyue hath cause of griefe lyke
        thee?
Who (wonne by loue) hast yeeld the spoyle of thy virginity?
And he for to repayre thy fame, to marry thee, that vowde,
Is done to death for first offence, the second mends not lowde.
Great shame redounds to thee, O *Loue*, in leauing vs in thrall:
Andrugio and *Polina* both, in honoryng thee did falle.
Thou so dydst witch our wits, as we from reason strayed quight,
Prouockt by thee, we dyd refuse, no vauntage of delight:
Delight, what did I say? nay death, by rash and fowle abuse,
Alas I shame to tell thus much, though loue doe worke excuse.
So that (fayre dames) from such consent, my accydents of
        harme,
Forewarneth you, to keepe aloofe though loue your harts do
        arme,
But ah *Polina*, whether runnes thy words into aduise,
When others harmes, inforst by loue, could neuer make the*
        wise?
The cause is plaine, for that in loue, no reason stands in stade,
And reason is the onely meane, that others harmes we dreade.
Then, that the world hereafter may, to loue inferre my yll,

* *thee*

Andrugios Tombe with dayly teares, *Polina* worship wyll.
And further more I vowde, whylst life in mee doth foster breth,
No one shall vaunt of conquered loue, by my *Andrugios* death.
These shameful weedes, which forst I were* that men my fault
 may know:
Whilst that I liue, shall show I morne for my *Andrugio*,
I wyll not byde the sharpe assaultes, from sugred words I sent,
I wyll not trust to careles othes, which often wyn consent:
I wyll cut off occasions all, which hope of myrth may moue,
With ceaseles teares yle quench each cause, that kindleth coles
 of loue:
And thus tyl death *Polina* wyll estraunge her selfe from ioy,
Andrugio, to reward thy loue which dyd thy life destroy.   *Exit.*

[5. 4. Rosko describes Lamia's prosperous state: Phallax defends
her reputation, and no one may speak against her. Rosko plans to
fleece Grimbal before Dalia can profit from him. 5. Rosko poses
as a barber; while shaving Grimbal, he cuts his purse and blames
the theft on an accomplice who has meanwhile slipped away.
6. Cassandra, wearing black, laments for Andrugio. She would like
to die, but decides first to go to the King and relate Promos' misdeeds. Afterwards she will kill herself with her knife.]

THE SECONDE PARTE OF THE HISTORIE OF
PROMOS AND *CASSANDRA:*

Actus. 1. Scena. 1.

Polina in a blewe Gowne, shadowed with a blacke
Sarcenet, going to the Temple to praye, vpon
Andrugios Tombe.

Promise is debt, and I vowe haue past,
Andrugios Tombe, to washe with daylie teares:
Which Sacrifice (although God wot in waste)
I wyll performe, my Alter is of cares.
Of fuming sighes, my offring incense is,
My pittious playntes, in steede of Prayers are:

[She wishes she could die: death comes too slowly to the wretched.
Yet her suffering must be the will of God, whose correction is for
our good.]

* *wear*

Polinas Song.

Amyd my bale, the lightning ioy, that pyning care doth bring,
With patience cheares my heauy hart, as in my woes I sing,
I know my Gilt, I feele my scurge: my ease is death I see:
And care (I fynde) by peecemeale weares, my hart to set mee
  free.
O care, my comfort and refuge, feare not to worke thy wyll,
With patience I, thy corsiues byde, feede on my life thy fyll.
Thy appetyte with syghes and teares, I dayly wyl procure,
And wretched I, wil vaile to death, throw when thou wilt thy
  Lure.   *Exit. Polina.*

[1. 2. A Messenger from the King arrives to tell Promos that the
King will see him straight away. 3. Rosko declares that Lamia and
Phallax are in love with one another. They 'byll together', kiss and
sigh, like true lovers. 4. Phallax makes arrangements for the King's
entry into Julio. The 'Nyne Worthyes' will be installed on a stage,
the 'fowre Vertues' on 'Jesus Gate', and the Waits will be at 'saynt
Annes crosse'. 5. The merchant tailors will present a pageant at the
end of Duck Alley, with Hercules fighting giants and wild beasts.
6. Two men, 'apparrelled lyke greene men at the Mayors feast,
with clubbes of fyre worke', will keep a passage free in 'Jesus
streete.' 7. Phallax bids Rosko tell Lamia to prepare for the entertainment of guests from the King's retinue.]

Actus. 1. Scena. 8.

Coruinus the King, *Cassandra*, two counsellors. And *Vdislao*,*
a young noble man.

KYNG. *Cassandra*, we draw neare vnto the Towne,
So that I wyll that you from vs depart:
Tyll further of our pleasure you doe heare.
Yet rest assur'd, that wycked *Promos*,
Shall abide such punishment, as the world,
Shall houlde mee iust, and cleare thee of offence.
  CAS. Dread soueraigne, as you wyl, *Cassandra* goeth hence.
                Exit.

[The King reflects on the need 'That Prynces oft doo vayle their
eares to heare, / The Misers playnt'. Judges and men in authority
may be corrupt, and subjects are afraid to tell the King their
wrongs. Had Cassandra set goods or life before her desire for
revenge, he would not have known of Promos' misdeeds.]

---

* subsequently *Ulrico*

Actus. 1. Scena. 9.

Promos, Maior, three *Aldermen*, in red Gownes, with a
Sworde bearer, awayghtes the *Kinges* comming.

Promos, his briefe Oration:

PRO. Renowned *King*, lo here your faithful subiects preast
to show
The loyall duetie, which (in ryght) they to your highnesse owe.
Your presence, cheares all sorts of vs: yet ten times more we
ioye,
You thinke vs stoarde, our warning short, for to receyue a Roye.
Our wyll, is such, as shall supplie, I trust in vs all want,
And where good wyll the welcome geues, prouision syld is scant.
Loe, this is all: yea, for vs all, that I in wordes bestowe,
Your Maiestie, our further zeale, in ready deedes shall knowe.
And first, dreade King, I render you, the swoorde of Iustice
heare,
Which as your Liuetenant I trust, vprightlie I dyd beare.

The *King* delyuers the Swordе, to one of his Counsell.

KING. *Promos*, the good report, of your good gouernment
I heare,
Or at the least, the good conceyte, that towards you I beare:
To incourage you the more, in Iustice to perseauer,
Is the cheefe cause I dyd addresse, my Progresse heather.
PRO. I thanke your Highnesse.

[The Mayor offers 'a fayre Purse', which the King graciously
declines.

2. 1. Lamia prepares to welcome the guests. 2. Two 'gentlemen
straungers' listen to a choir of women seated in Lamia's window
singing 'If pleasure be treasure, The golden world is here'. [3.]
The King's proclamation is read, calling on any subject wronged
by the authorities to present his grievances to Ulrico; the King will
judge major offences in open court. 4. Rosko reports consternation
among the King's officers. 5. Complaints are made against
Phallax. 6. Pimos, a young claimant, enquires about his suit.

3. 1. Phallax anticipates trouble. 2. John Adroynes, a 'clowne', is
arrested by Gripax and Rapax for kissing a maid. Phallax bids
them take all Adroynes' money as a bribe for his release. 3. The
King speaks of a ruler's duty to enforce equality under the law.
Ulrico presents a petition against Phallax, who confesses. His goods
are confiscated and he is dismissed from office.]

[3. 3.] *Cassandra* in a blewe gowne, shadowed with black.

    C A S . O would y^t teares myght tel my tale, I shame so much
       my fall,
Or else, Lord *Promos* lewdnes showen, would death would ende
      my thrall.
    P R O . Welcome my sweete *Cassandra*.
    C A S . Murdrous varlet, away.
Renowmed King, I pardon craue, for this my bould attempt,
In preasing thus so neare your grace, my sorrow to present;
And least my foe, false *Promos* heare, doe interrupt my tale,
Graunt gratious King, that vncontrould, I may report my bale.
    K I N G . How now *Promos*? how lyke you, of this song?
Say on fayre dame, I long to heare thy wrong.
    C A S . Then knowe dread souerayne, that he this doome did
      geue,
That my Brother, for wantonnesse should lose his head:
And that the mayde, which sind, should euer after lyue
In some religious house, to sorrowe her misdeede:
To saue my brother iug'd to dye, with teares I sought to moue
Lord *Promos* hart, to showe him grace: but he with lawles loue,
Was fyred by and by: and knowing necessity,
To saue my brothers lyfe, would make me yeeld to much,
He crau'd this raunsome, to haue my virginitie:
No teares could worke restraynt, his wicked lust was such,
Two euils here were, one must I chuse, though bad were very
      best,
To see my brother put to death, or graunt his lewde request:
In fyne, subdude with naturall loue, I did agree,
Vpon these two poyntes: that marry mee he should,
And that from prison vyle, he should my brother free.
All this with monstrous othes, he promised he would.
But O this periurd *Promos*, when he had wrought his wyll,
Fyrst cast mee of: and after causd the Gailer for to kill
My brother, raunsomde, with the spoyle of my good name:
So that for companing, with such a hellish feende,
I haue condemnde my selfe to weare these weedes of shame;
Whose cognisance doth showe, that I haue (fleshly) sind.
Loe thus, hie and renowned king, *Cassandra* endes her tale,
And this is wicked *Promos* that hath wrought her endles bale.
    K I N G . If this be true, so fowle a deede, shall not vnpunisht
      goe,
How sayst thou *Promos*, to her playnte? arte giltye? yea, or noe?

Why speakst thou not? a faulty harte, thy silence sure doth
    showe.
   PRO. My gilty hart commaunds my tongue, O king, to tell
    a troth,
I doe confesse this tale is true, and I deserue thy wrath.
   KING. And is it so? this wicked deede, thou shalt ere long
    buy deare,
Cassandra, take comfort in care, be of good cheere:
Thy forced fault, was free from euill intent,
So long, no shame, can blot thee any way.
And though at ful, I hardly can content thee,
Yet as I may, assure thy selfe I wyl.
Thou wycked man, might it not thee suffice,
By worse then force, to spoyle her chastitie,
But heaping sinne on sinne against thy oth,
Hast cruelly, her brother done to death.
This ouer proofe, ne can but make me thinke,
That many waies thou hast my subiectes wrongd:
For how canst thou with Iustice vse thy swaie?
When thou thy selfe dost make thy will a lawe?
Thy tyranny made mee, this progresse make,
How so, for sport tyll nowe I colloured it
Vnto this ende, that I might learne at large,
What other wronges by power, thou hast wrought,
And heere, I heare: the Ritche suppresse the poore;
So that it seemes, the best and thou art friendes:
I plaste thee not, to be a partiall Iudge.
Thy Offycers are couetous I finde,
By whose reportes, thou ouerrulest sutes:
Then who that geues an Item in the hande,
In ryght, and wrong, is sure of good successe.
Well, Varlet, well: too slowe I hether came,
To scourge, thy faultes, and salue the sores thou mad'st:
On thee vyle wretche, this sentence I pronounce.
That foorthwith, thou shalt marrie *Cassandra*,
For to repayre hir honour, thou dydst waste:
The next daye thou shalt lose thy hated lyfe,
In penaunce, that thou mad'st hir Brother dye.
   PRO. My faultes were great, O King, yet graunt me mercie,
That nowe with bloody sighes, lament my sinnes too late.
   KING. *Hoc facias alteri, quod tibi vis fieri*:
Pittie was no plea Syr, when you in iudgement sate,
Prepare your selfe to dye, in vaine you hope for lyfe.

My Lordes, bring him with mee: *Cassandra* come you in like case:
My selfe wyll see, thy honour salu'd, in making thee his Wife,
The sooner to shorten his dayes.

[The Clown comments on how the poor can expect true justice
from the King and the great lords about him.

4. 1. Gresco, 'a good substantiall Offycer', sends two beadles to
search for vagabonds, while he himself goes to arrest Lamia.
2. Andrugio, living in hiding in the woods, meets Adroynes seeking
his mare, who tells him of the King's sentence upon Promos. He
decides to go back to Julio in disguise.]

[4. 2.]
>   *Gresco*, with three other, with bylles, bringing in
>   *Lamia* prisoner.

GRES. Come on faire Dame, since faire words, works no heede,
Now fowle meanes shall: in you repentaunce breede.
   LA. Maister *Gresco*, where you maye helpe, hurt not.
   GRES. And nothing but chastment, wyll helpe you to amende.
Well, I wyll not hurt you, your lewdnes to defende.
   LA. My lewdnes Syr: what is the difference,
Betwixt wantons, and hoorders of pence?
   GRES. Thou hast winde at wyll, but in thy eyes no water:
Tho' arte full of Grace, howe she blusheth at the matter.
   LA. Howe sample I, your wyfe and daughter Syr?
   GRES. Axe mee, when whypping hath chaung'd thy Nature.
   LA. What whypping? why? am I a Horse or a Mare?
   GRES. No, but a beast, that meetelie well wyll bare.
   LA. In deede (as) nowe, perforce, I heare this flowt:
But vse me well, else I fayth, gette I out,
Looke for quittance.
   BYL. Binde hir to the Peace Syr.
So maye your Worship be out of daunger.   *First Bilm*
   GRES. Bring hir awaye, I knowe howe to tame hir.
   LA. Perhaps Syr, no: the worst is but shame hir.
   BYL. Come ye drab.   *Secōd Bilm*
   LA. Howe nowe scab? handes of my Gowne.
   BYL. Care not for this, yuse haue a blew one soone. *Third Bil.*
>   *Exeunt.*

>   *Cassandra.*

CAS. Vnhappy Wench, the more I seeke, for to abandon
      griefe,
The furder off, I wretched finde, both comfort and reliefe.

My Brother first, for wanton faultes, condempned was to dye:
To saue whose life, my sute, wrought hope of Grace, but haples I,
By such request, my honor spoyld, and gayned not his breath:
For which deceyte, I haue pursude, Lorde *Promos* vnto death.
Who is my Husbande nowe become, it pleasd our Soueraigne so,
For to repayre, my crased Fame: but that nowe workes my wo.
This day he must (oh) leese his head my Brothers death to quite,
And therein Fortune hath alas, showne me hir greatest spyte.
Nature wyld mee, my Brother loue, now dutie commaunds mee,
To preferre before kyn, or friend, my Husbands safetie.
But O, aye mee, by Fortune, I am made his chiefest foe:
T'was I al[a]s, euen onely I, that wrought his ouerthroe.
What shall I doo, to worke amends, for this my haynous deede?
The tyme is short, my power small, his succors axeth speede.
And shall I seeke to saue his blood, that lately sought his lyfe?
O, yea I then was sworne his foe: but nowe as faithfull Wife,
I must and wyll, preferre his health, God sende me good successe:
For nowe vnto the King I wyll, my chaunged minde to expresse.
                                                          Exit.

[Phallax reports the whipping of rogues, the public carting of
Lamia, and the general purging of the city.

5. 1. Andrugio, disguised, now wishes to free Promos. 2. He hears
Ulrico describing Cassandra's tearful pleas for Promos' life. 3. He
sees Cassandra begging Ulrico to intercede with the King on
Promos' behalf.]

[5. 3.]   Enter *Andrugio.*

   AN. Lord God, how am I tormented in thought?
My sisters woe, such rueth in me doth graue:
As fayne I would (if ought saue death I caught)
Bewray my selfe, Lord *Promos* life to saue.
But lyfe is sweete, and naught but death I eye,
If that I should, my safety now disclose:
So that I chuse, of both the euels, he dye:
Time will appease, no dought, *Cassandras* woes,
And shal, I thus acquite *Cassandras* loue?
To worke her ioy? and shall I feare to dye?
Whylst, that she lyue, no comforte may remoue
Care from her harte, if that hir husband dye?
Then shall I stycke, to hasard lym? nay life?
To salue hir greefe, since in my cure it rests.
Nay fyrst, I wilbe spoyld, with blooddy knife,

Before, I fayle, her, plunged in distres.
Death, is but death, and all in fyne shall dye
Thus (being dead) my fame, shall liue alway:
Well, to the king, *Andrugio* now wyll hye,
Hap lyfe, hap death, his safety, to bewray.   *Exit.*

[5. 4. Promos, led to execution, confesses the wickedness of his life.
He has for long 'wrested euery case', showing excessive cruelty and
growing worse daily. He hopes his fate will prove a warning to
others.]

Actus. 5. Scena. 5.

Enter *Cassandra, Polina*, and one mayde.

CAS. Aye me, alas: my hope is vntimely.
Whether goes my good Lord?
   PRO. Sweete wife, to dye.

[He takes a tender leave of Cassandra and his friends, asks for and
receives Polina's forgiveness. At Polina's bidding, Cassandra sings
a lament.]

Enter *Ganio* sometime *Andrugios* Boye.

GA. O sweete newes for *Polina* and *Cassandra.*
Andrugio lyues:
   PO. What doth poore *Ganio* saye?
   GA. *Andrugio* lyues; and *Promos* is repriu'd.
   CAS. Vaine is thy hope, I sawe *Andrugio* dead.
   GA. Well, then from death, he is againe reuyu'd.
Euen nowe, I sawe him, in the market stead.
   PO. His wordes are straunge.
   CAS. Too sweete, God wot, for true.
   GA. I praye you, who are these here in your view?
   CAS. The King.
   GA. Who more?
   PO. O, I see *Andrugio.*
   CAS. And I my Lorde *Promos*, adue sorrowe.

Enter the *King, Andrugio, Promos, Vlrico*, the *Marshall.*

PO. My good *Andrugio?*
AN. My sweete *Polina:*
CAS. Lyues *Andrugio*, welcome sweete brother.
AN. *Cassandra?*
CAS. I.

AN. Howe fare, my deare Syster?

KING. *Andrugio*, you shall haue more leysure,
To greete one another: it is our pleasure,
That you forthwith, your Fortunes here declare,
And by what meanes, you thus preserued weare.

[Andrugio tells the King that the Gaoler had substituted for his head that of one of the prisoners executed two days previously. Andrugio has since lived in hiding: now he offers his life in return for the freeing of Promos.]

KING. A strange discourse, as straungely come to light,
Gods pleasure is, that thou should'st pardoned be:
To salue the fault, thou with *Polina* mad'st,
But marry her, and heare I set thee free.

AN. Most gratious Prince, thereto I gladly gree:

POLI. *Polina*, the happiest newes of all for thee.

CAS. Most gratious King, with these my ioye to match,
Vouchsafe, to geue my dampned husbande lyfe.

KING. If I doo so, let him thanke thee his Wife:
Cassandra, I haue noted thy distresse,
Thy vertues eke, from first, vnto the last:
And glad I am, without offence it lyes,
In me to ease, thy griefe, and heauines.
Andrugio sau'd, the iuell of thy ioye,
And for thy sake, I pardon *Promos* faulte.
Yea let them both, thy vertues rare commende:
In that their woes, with this delyght both ende.

COMPANY. God preserue your Maiestie.

PRO. *Cassandra*, howe shall I discharge thy due?

CAS. I dyd, but what a Wife, shoulde do for you.

KING. Well, since all partes are pleased, as they woulde,
Before I parte, yet *Promos*, this to thee:
Henceforth, forethinke, of thy forepassed faultes,
And measure Grace, with Iustice euermore.
Vnto the poore, haue euermore an eye,
And let not might, out countenaunce their right:
Thy Officers, trust not in euery tale,
In chiefe, when they are meanes, in strifes and sutes.
Though thou be iust, yet coyne maye them corrupt.
And if by them, thou dost vniustice showe,
Tys thou shalt beare, the burden of their faultes.
Be louing to good *Cassandra*, thy Wife:

And friendlie to thy brother *Andrugio*,
Whome I commaund, as faythfull for to be
To thee, as beseemes the duety of a brother.
And now agayne, thy gouernment receyue,
Inioye it so, as thou in Iustice ioye.
If thou be wyse, thy fall maye make thee ryse.
The lost sheepe founde, for ioye, the feast was made.
Well, here an ende, of my aduise I make,
As I haue sayde, be good vnto the poore,
And Iustice ioyne, with mercie euermore.

    PRO. Most gratious King, I wyll not fayle my best,
In these preceptes, to followe your beheast.

FINIS.

4. EXTRACT from The Second part and Knitting up of
the Boke entituled *Too good to be true*. Wherin is continued
the discourse of the wonderful Lawes, commendable cus-
tomes, & strange manners of the people of Mauqsun.
Newely penned and published, by Thomas Lypton.*
(1581)

SIUQILA. There was a very yong man, not very far from the
Countrie where I was borne, who for his great learning, rare wisedom, commendable condition, and modest maners, was, by the
Magistrates and Rulers of that Countrie, chosen to be a Iudge, who
vsed him selfe for a while in his office, so vprightly and so godlie, to
the iudgement of euery one, that none but were glad that they had
suche a Iudge.

[The story is told of a quarrel between two erstwhile friends. When
both were bachelors, one had wooed a certain gentlewoman. He
had confided his troubles to his friend, who offered to act as an
intermediary. The friend, however, himself fell in love with the
lady and made advances to her, which were rejected. In time the
original suitor married the gentlewoman, who told her husband of
the deception practised upon him. He promised her to take no
revenge, but on chancing to meet the treacherous friend, he drew
his sword, fought with him, and slew him. For this he was put into
prison.]

SIUQILA. Truly when she heard that hir husbande was in prison,
and what was the cause, she swouned presently: and they that

  * Lupton.

were about hir had much ado to get any life in hir. Was not here
a goodlie gaine that he got by his fighting? As she said, neither
pacience nor reason was with him, when he gave the other his
Deathes wounde. Here we may see that all wisedom lies not in men,
and al folly and mischief is not in women. But after, like a wise
woman, she brydled hir sorrowe as wel as she could, and went
about to mend the mischief aswel as she might. . . . And so with as
N much conuenient / speed as she might, she got hir to the saide yong
Iudge before mentioned, in whome (for his wisedom, godlinesse,
and pietie,) she had suche a good opinion, that she thought through
hir humble sute and pittiful mone, he would finde some one meane
or other to saue hir husbandes life. And when she came before him
she kneeled vnto him, and with weeping teares saide: O worthie
Iudge, as you are counted a moste wise and mercifull Iudge, now
shew that in effect, which is bruted of you in talke: and saue an
Innocents life that lieth in your hands to destroy. To whom the
Iudge said: stand up Gentlewomā, it will greeue me to see you
stand, much more to kneele: therfore without any more bidding sit
downe by me, and I will not onely heare you, but also helpe you if
I be able: So that equitie do allowe, and iustice do bid, hoping that
your matter is such, that both these wil agree vnto it, for that mee
thought your request was to haue me to saue an Innocents life: and
to saue an Innocents life a smal sute shal serue. And therewith he
toke hir gently by the hande, and caused hir to sit downe by him:
who said to the Iudge then: In deed sir I saide so, for I am that
Innocent touching any law of Death, that lieth in your handes to
saue or to kill: not that any matter is laid against me worthie of
Death, but my life (being an Innocent) in this case, hangeth on
another mannes life that is not innocent: whose life to saue lieth
only in your hands. I pray you, sayde the Iudge, tell me your matter and cause as briefly and plainely as you can, and what I may do
lawfully, I will perfourme it willingly. The truth is so, saide the
Gentlewoman, I am the wife of suche a Gentleman that killed a
man of late: whose cause I come not to defend, but for whom I
come to craue mercy. I nowe knowe your matter, sayd the Iudge,
I lament his missehap, and I pittie your case. You know Gentlewoman, it hardly lies in me to saue whom the law doth condemne,
especially him, whose facte is so manifest, and which by no meanes
can be denied. O sir, saide she, it were very straite, that you being
a Iudge so well thought of, and of such great authoritie, that you
can not shewe iustice with mercie, and lawe with fauour. You
Nᵛ knowe, sayde hee againe, I am sworne to / doe equitie and iustice
according. And you are not ignorante, that both Gods law and our

law willeth, without any redemtion to kill him that killeth, and to shead his bloude that shead it. And should I doe iustice if I should saue your husband, who willingly killed a Gentleman of late, that was not determined to fight with him? who vnwares set vpon him, and so hee was slaine, whom the law would have fauoured in defending himselfe? Therefore Gentlewoman cease your sute, for it lieth not in my handes to helpe you: but if I coulde I would not. For if I shoulde saue your husbande in this case, I shoulde gette more shame and slaunder by this one thing, than I haue gotten good reporte by all the iustice and equitie that I haue done since I came in Office. I blame not you, for suing for your husbande in so euill a cause, whiche you doe for loue: but eyery one would blame mee, for graunting your request in so euill a cause, which they would say I did for monie. O sir, said the Gentlewoman, (and began againe to kneele, but he would not suffer hir,) the Gentleman is deade, and the death of my husbande will not make him liue againe: which if it might doe so, I woulde not be so importunate herein: therefore I beseech you, as euer you came of a woman, or as you will haue Christ to be mercifull to you that was borne of a woman, kill not two moe for one that is deade alreadie. . . What so euer you ask me, you shall haue: and what so euer you will have mee to doe, I will doe it. . .

[N2] Then the Iudge took the Gentlewoman by the hand, and said: I will aduise my selfe this nighte what I maye doe, and what way I may beste pleasure you: bee you of good comforte therefore in the meane space. But as I will not promise you, so I will not denay you. And come to morrowe hither to my house, about this time, and I will be heere readie to speake with you, when you shall knowe of mee, whether I can, or will pleasure you, yea or no. At which time, the Gentlewoman tooke hir leaue of him, something better heartened than when she came to him.

OMEN. I haue not hearde a more earneste suter for hir husbande than she: I pray you how sped shee after?

SIUQILA. The nexte day, I warrante you, shee brake not hir houre, but wente vnto the Iudge, as hee had appointed hir: and when shee was come before him, hee made hir to sitte downe beside him, and caused all the rest that were there, but they two, to goe awaye: and then hee carried hir into an inner Chamber with him, bicause no bodie shoulde heare what hee saide vnto hir, and then thus hee beganne to say: Gentlewoman, the more I haue considered your case, the more I have busied my selfe to helpe you, I assure you, (throughe your pittifull moane and most earnest sute,) I am determined to doe more for you and **graunt you** more fauour, than

euer was in my thought to doe for anie: I must hazarde that for you, (if I satisfie your desire) that I woulde not haue ieoperded for mine
N2ᵛ owne self. / And for as much as you saide (to pleasure you, and to saue your husbandes life) you would giue me what I would aske, and also doe whatsoeuer I would wil you, I will be briefe and make fewe wordes with you: If you will haue me to saue your husbandes life, then you shall doe thus: You shal giue me six thousande Crownes (for I knowe you are able well to spare it, considering your husbande is of such a great liuing as he is) which you shal bring me hither to morrowe at nighte. The time is very short, saide shee, and the summe is very great: but if there bee no remedie, I truste to make shifte for it. You know, said the Iudge, that if I bee not good vnto him, and finde some meanes for him, hee muste be executed within these three or foure dayes: and there fore you muste make greate speede therein, for I will haue it, before I doe deliuer him or saue him. Well sir, saide the Gentlewoman, you shall haue it: Yea but, sayde the Iudge, there is another matter behinde, whiche if you doe not, your husbande is like to die, for I will not receyue the monie without it: What is it sir, saide shee, and according to my promise, I will doe it if I can or may? I knowe, sayde hee, you will be loath to doe it: this it is, to morrowe at night you shal bring your monie vnto me your selfe alone, at whiche time, at such a priuie dore of my house I will receyue you my selfe, (for I trust none other with this matter) and then when you have deliuered me so many Crownes, you shall tarie with mee still, and lie with mee all nighte: for I assure you, that if I desired the companie of your body no more than I esteeme your Crownes, I woulde not have promised to saue your husbande. The Gentlewoman was so sodainely grypte with such a grief, that she was ready to sinke downe, but the Iudge tooke hir vp in his armes and comforted hir, saying: Gentlewoman, nowe is no time for you to fall in a traunce, nor for mee to tryfle: if you had not earnestely of your owne free will offered me, that you woulde doe whatsoeuer I willed you, I would neuer have required this at your handes, neyther put you in any comforte: therefore eyther performe your promise, and saue your husbāds life: or else
N3 be false of your promise, & therby procure his death: / for I assure you, there is none other waye to saue his life, but this. You know your lying with me shal be so secret, yᵗ none in the world shal know of it but you and I: and as I wil keepe it most secrete, so I trust you wil not vtter it: which words when she hearde, she sodainely clapt hir downe on hir knees: but hee woulde not suffer hir to kneele, but toke hir vp by the hande: to whom she saide: a sir, in what a straite haue you me now? eyther I must lose my husband to whom I have

giuen my faith, or else lose my faith that I haue giuen my husband:
my husbād I can neuer get againe if he dye, and my faith I can
neuer recouer againe if I once breake it. Therefore I most humbly
beseech you, aske me what you wil (this thing only excepted) and
if I performe it not, if I be able, moste willingly and quickely, then
let my husband die without all redemption. I am borne to some
inheritance, all which, both I and my husbande will most willingly
release vnto you: and all my Iewels, Rings and other ornaments,
I wil fetch with speede and deliuer them to you, whiche will doe
you more pleasure, stande you in more steade, & comfort you
longer, than one nights lying with a woful wretch that had rather
be buried than to go to your bedde: and besides all this that I offer
you, take freelye to your selfe those sixe thousand Crownes you
request of me. Make no more adoe, Gentlewoman, saide the Iudge:
either get you hence with your gold, or tarrie here & performe my
desire: for I am determined none other waye to saue your husbands
life but thus. Oh good God, said the Gentlewoman, how am I
wrapt in wo, on euery side: if I deny this, my husband shall die:
and if I performe it, I betray my husbande. How can I loue my
husbande, that so treacherously vse my husbande? Then saide the
Iudge, and how can you loue your husbande, that rather than you
wil lye with me one night, that neuer shal be knowne, will see the
death of your husbande? Oh sir saide she, if my husbande should
knowe it, woulde he not kil me? yes, and thereof I were wel worthy:
nay, saide the Iudge, he would the more loue you, that did that, for
the sauing of his life, whiche you preferde before your owne life:
N3ᵛ therfore, saide the Iudge, tel me what you will / do, for I wil be
quickly at a point. Well sir, saide she, wil nothing content you but
this? No, saide the Iudge: and I will tell you moreouer, if you performe this my demaunde nowe, I wil saue his life: but if you refuse
it, then, though you wold, I will not: wherfore, now you may saue
your husbandes life, or within these two or three dayes, be moste
sure of his death. To whom the Gentlewoman saide, (preferring hir
husbandes life before all other things in the worlde) well sir, seeing
there is no remedie, I doe yeelde vnto you, beseeching you (for that
I buy my husbandes life with suche a price, that all the treasure on
the earth is not able againe to redeeme) to be sure, that my husbande be not onely saued from death for this facte, but also, that all
our lands and goods may be ours, in such order as they were before
the offence was committed: and also, haue a great respecte, that
this my promise thus secretly performed, be not openly vttered.
To whome the Iudge saide, assure your selfe Gentlewoman, al this
shal be done, fear you not: which way it shal be, I have deuised

alredy. Then said she, I will be here at your priuie dore to morrow at night, when I will, not only brĩg you all your Gold, but also (though sore against my minde) will performe the rest of my promise. And so yᵉ Gentlewoman tooke hir leaue of the Iudge, as one that was lifted vp with ioy on yᵉ one side, and pulled downe with sorrow on the other side.

OMEN. Surely, that cruell harted and wicked Iudge, droue that louing Gentlewoman to a maruelous mischief. But proceede, I woulde faine heare what followed.

SIUQILA. You shal, & that willingly: yᵉ Gentlewoman brought yᵉ gold at hir houre, by such priuie means as she thought conuenient, & the Iudge receiued both it & hir, being then something darke, & so she did lie there al yᵉ night with yᵉ Iudge: to whom he said in yᵉ morning before she went frõ him: now Gentlewomã, I thank you. And thogh you haue performed your promise very vnwillingly, yet you shal wel vnderstand, yᵗ I wil performe mine most willingly. And for yᵗ I would as wel haue you to be of good cheere, & to be quiet in mind, as also not to trouble your selfe wᵗ any pains N₄ or trauel: my wil is, yᵗ you stay at home & go / not abroad: & whereas your husband should haue bin executed to morrow in yᵉ morning, I wil dispatch him, & send him home to morrow vnto you before noone at the furthest, if it be not before: & therfore play the wise womans part, & be secret: & thogh your husband shall be deliuered so quickly, shew not your selfe to ioy therfore too sodainely. Wherefore keepe your self close in your own house, & be mery in mind, thogh for a shew you seeme to be sad. Wel sir, said yᵉ Gentlewomã, as I haue satisfied your desire in an vnreasonable demaund, so I wil obey you in this reasonable request. And for yᵗ I am most sure, that my husband shal now haue his life: I wish most earnestly, yᵗ the time were come, that he were deliuered. Then saide the Iudge, yᵗ time is not long, to morrow you shal haue him safe and sounde wᵗ you. And thus she departed from yᵉ Iudge, very merie for yᵉ sauing of hir husbands life: but yet something sorrowful for the breaking of hir faith to hir husband.

OMEN. The ioy of yᵉ one did mitigate the griefe of the other, she thought long I am sure for yᵉ time appointed by the Iudge: and was the time for his execution the nexte day after?

SIUQILA. Yea, & the day of his execution too: for the next morning about 8, or 9. of the clocke, this sorrowful Gentlewomãs husband was put to death: which, after it was done, was ryfe in euery mans mouthe. And then the saide Gentlewoman standing at hir dore, saw one come running in all the haste, who seing him comming toward hir so fast, was very glad, thinking that he came to tel

hir of hir husbands life: but it fell out otherwayes, for he came to tel
hir of hir husbands death. And when he came somthing nigh hir,
she said: I pray thee what newes? is my husbande deliuered? deliuered, said he, no, he is executed. Executed? said ye Gentlewoman, I am sure y^u dost but iest. Thē he said, you may take it now
for iest, but shortly you wil find it in earnest. . . .

[She meets neighbours, who confirm the report.]

Oh, saide shee, may I credite you? is this true that you tel me?
Yea, saide they, it is too true: we had rather haue tolde you otherwayes, for we see him bothe quicke and dead, and there was great
hast made in the executing of him.

[She swoons, and on recovering determines to be revenged. This
was not how the Judge had expected her to behave. He had
thought to win her over gradually, and supposed that she would be
too ashamed to disclose what had taken place between them.]

SIUQILA. Well, he was cleane deceiued, in that she was otherwayes bent and fully determined: for she weighing with hirselfe,
howe treacherously he had serued hir, not only in defrauding hir
of sixe thousande crownes, but also bereaued hir of two of the
greatest Iewels she hadde in the worlde, that was hir husbande and
hir honestie, whiche by no meanes againe coulde be recouered,
that thereby such a detesting and abhorring of him did enter into
hir hart, that nothing was so pleasant to hir, as to procure his mischief: and had rather work his death by opening hir own shame,
than to hide her infamie by sauing his life, as the sequele doth
plainely shewe: for as speedily as she coulde, she gote hir decent
mourning attyre, and with conuenient men to waite on hir, rode in
all the haste where the Magistrates & the chiefe Rulers of the
Countrey did sit: who knocking at the Counsel Chamber dore,
within a while after was lette in, when they knewe who she was.
And when she came before them, she kneeled downe: and lament-
ably and pitifully desired them that she might haue Iustice, for that
was the onely thing she craued: and as all my sute of late (saide she)
O was chiefly for Mercie, now al my request is onely for / Iustice.

[She tells the whole story, offering as corroboration a description
of the whereabouts of the gold she had brought and a detailed
account of the furnishings of the Judge's bedroom. The Judge is
imprisoned. The Counsellors order him to marry the gentlewoman,
and also deliver a secret command to the Commissioner.]

And so to conclude, they were both married togither, wherof he was as glad as she was sorrowful. And when they were marryed, and as he was aboute to go home with his newe wofull wife, the saide Commissioner saide: Sir you muste stay a little, this Gentlewoman youre wife hathe performed all the iudgements that on hir parte are to be done: but thoughe you haue done some, yet you have not done al, there is one piece yet behinde for you to performe. What is that? said the Iudge, for I wil do it willingly: then said the Commissioner, not so willingly I belieue as you were marryed, vnlesse you are willing to goe to youre death: whereat the Iudge was astonied: and then the Commissioner saide to him: nay, there is no remedy, the Counsels iudgemente is, that immediately after you are married, you muste be executed: therefore prepare youre selfe, for I muste see it don presently. And as for you Gentlewoman, saide he, you were beste goe to dinner, and not tarry for youre husbande, for he hath another parte to play. O, saide the Gentlewoman, blessed be God that hathe giuen us suche wise and godlye Counsellours, that haue gyuen suche a worthy iudgement: the death of my firste husband did not make mee so wofull a Widowe, but the death of my seconde husbande dothe make me as ioyful a Widow. Here was a sodaine change, for whereas before the Bridegroome was mery and the Bride sad: nowe the Bride was moste merry, and the Bridegroome sorrowfull, and so shee wente to hir dinner, and hee to hys death. Whose execution was not verye long in hande, for shee was a Widowe agayne that day beefore shee 40 hadde dyned. / And to comfort hir the better, she had not only all hir golde againe, but also all the Iudges hir seconde husbands goods: for the Counsell commaunded that he shoulde lose none of hys goodes, whereby this Gentlewoman his wife enioyed them all. OMEN. Truely they were godly and wise Counsellers: ther iudgement was with greate equitie, iustice and reason. I am sure she was gladder that he shoulde goe to hys death, than with hir to dinner.

APPENDIX II

By F. W. Sternfeld

Take, o take those lips away

Shakespeare's famous stanza and its musical setting by John Wilson have been the subject of much investigation. The four studies named at the end of this note deal in considerable detail with the genealogies of the verbal and musical text. The purpose of the present note is to summarize previous research and to offer a serviceable edition of the music.

The ancestor of Shakespeare's verse was probably the popular Latin poem, 'Ad Lydiam', much admired in the sixteenth century. The earliest publication occurs in an appendix to a Latin paraphrase of the *Iliad*, beautifully printed by the famous Soncino at Fano in 1505. Modern scholars are understandably puzzled when they find the work ascribed to Pindar: *Pyndari bellum Troianum*, a misunderstanding elucidated in Vollmer's article listed below. Among many later printings of the Latin lyric one might single out two: the appendix to the handsome edition of Petronius, published by Patisson at Paris in 1587, and the convenient reprint in S. Gaselee's *Anthology of Mediaeval Latin* (London, 1925, p. 68). Such lines as *porrige labra* and *da columbatim mitia basia* were likely points of departure for Shakespeare's muse.

In Fletcher's *Rollo*, which may be dated tentatively around 1624/5, there occurs a second stanza:

> Hide, o hide those hills of snow
> that thy frozen bosom wears,
> On whose tops the pinks that grow,
> are yet of those that April wears;
> But first set my poor heart free,
> Bound in those icy chains by thee.

I can see no reason to ascribe this additional stanza to Shakespeare, and agree with Hart that here we have a subdivision of that popular category, the answer-poem that 'may perhaps be called extension poems'. In view of its pronounced popularity it seems likely that Fletcher would have re-read the Latin model, whose vocabulary includes *sinus, deliciae, luxus nivei pectoris*.

Precisely when John Wilson composed the two stanzas from Fletcher's play we do not know. In 1625 he was thirty years old, and that date seems reasonable. In any event, Wilson's setting was printed in 1652 in John Playford's *Select musicall ayres* (Wing, *Short*

Title Catalogue, P2502). It was reprinted in 1653 and 1659. There survive also five MS copies of the music, scattered in London, Oxford and New York. Of these, the Bodleian MS (Mus b.1, f. 19v) is of particular textual relevance, since it was carefully prepared under the composer's own supervision. (Wilson was professor of music at Oxford from 1656 to 1661.) The following music example derives largely from Playford's printed text, with a few emendations based on the Bodleian MS.

Shakespeare's Folio text repeats the last words in the last two lines: 'bring again', 'sealed in vain'. Wilson, on the other hand, repeats the entire two lines. This does not prove much one way or another. Still, the presence of the second stanza in Wilson makes it reasonable to assume that Wilson's setting was intended for Fletcher rather than for Shakespeare. It seems to fit Shakespeare's verse well, however, both metrically and stylistically and, as the earliest music extant for the poem, it is of considerable interest to students of literature and to theatrical directors.

The following music example has been transposed from g minor down to e minor, thus producing a range of e′ to e″. For purposes of a stage production a boy-treble (or a female singer disguised as a boy) is recommended. The accompaniment is apt either for a lute or a keyboard instrument. In accordance with seventeenth-century custom, Wilson provides merely a vocal line and a bass, and it remains the task of modern editors to expand the bass into a full-fledged accompaniment.

The only three emendations of any consequence, based on the Bodleian MS, may be assessed by a comparison with Playford's originals, printed below. In bar 2, Playford employs an extended vocal melisma. In the Bodleian MS and also in those at Christ Church (Oxford) and New York, the vocal line is simpler and shorter by two crotchets (quarter-notes). A competent singer may wish to re-instate the more ornate version, but for most purposes the accompanying edition will be found the more serviceable.

Hart, E. F. 'The Answer-Poem of the Early 17th Century', *Review of English Studies*, VII (1956), 19–29.

Jump, J. D., ed., *Fletcher: Rollo . . . or The Bloody Brother*, Liverpool, 1948, pp. 67 and 106.

Sternfeld, F. W., *Music in Shakespearean Tragedy*, London, 1963, pp. 89f., 93ff.

Vollmer, F. K., 'Zum Homerus Latinus', *Bayrische Akademie*, Sitz.-Ber., Philosoph.-Hist. Cl., 1913, 3. Abh.

Take, o take those lips a—way that so sweet—ly were for—sworn, and those eyes, the break of day, lights that do mis—lead the morn, but my kis—ses bring a—gain, seals of love but sealed in vain.

Playford, bars 2-3

o take those lips a— way

Playford, bass, bar 3; bass, bar 7